Springer Series in Supply Chain Management

Volume 17

Series Editor
Christopher S. Tang, University of California, Los Angeles, CA, USA

Supply Chain Management (SCM), long an integral part of Operations Management, focuses on all elements of creating a product or service, and delivering that product or service, at the optimal cost and within an optimal timeframe. It spans the movement and storage of raw materials, work-in-process inventory, and finished goods from point of origin to point of consumption. To facilitate physical flows in a time-efficient and cost-effective manner, the scope of SCM includes technology-enabled information flows and financial flows.

The Springer Series in Supply Chain Management, under the guidance of founding Series Editor Christopher S. Tang, covers research of either theoretical or empirical nature, in both authored and edited volumes from leading scholars and practitioners in the field – with a specific focus on topics within the scope of SCM.

This series has been accepted by Scopus.

Springer and the Series Editor welcome book ideas from authors. Potential authors who wish to submit a book proposal should contact Ms. Jialin Yan, Associate Editor, Springer (Germany), e-mail: jialin.yan@springernature.com

Sebastian Kummer • Tina Wakolbinger •
Lydia Novoszel • Alexander M. Geske
Editors

Supply Chain Resilience

Insights from Theory and Practice

Springer

Editors
Sebastian Kummer
Institute for Transport and Logistics Management, WU (Vienna University of Economics and Business)
Vienna, Austria

Tina Wakolbinger
Institute for Transport and Logistics Management, WU (Vienna University of Economics and Business)
Vienna, Austria

Lydia Novoszel
Institute for Transport and Logistics Management, WU (Vienna University of Economics and Business)
Vienna, Austria

Alexander M. Geske
Institute for Transport and Logistics Management, WU (Vienna University of Economics and Business)
Vienna, Austria

ISSN 2365-6395 ISSN 2365-6409 (electronic)
Springer Series in Supply Chain Management
ISBN 978-3-030-95400-0 ISBN 978-3-030-95401-7 (eBook)
https://doi.org/10.1007/978-3-030-95401-7

This Springer imprint is published by the registered company Springer Nature Switzerland AG
The registered company address is: Gewerbestrasse 11, 6330 Cham, Switzerland

Preface

The early 2020s were characterized by a number of high-level challenges that negatively affected global supply chains and showed their vulnerabilities. First and foremost, COVID-19 led to major changes in consumer behavior resulting in changed demand patterns as well as reduced capacities along the supply chain. Additional disruptions like the accident of the Evergreen container ship in the Suez Channel and BREXIT tested the capabilities of global supply chains to deal with unexpected disturbances.

Amid these crises, the awareness of the relevance of supply chain concepts, especially supply chain resilience, in companies, non-profit organizations, and the public increased. To cope with unforeseen and unpredictable events, supply chain resilience enables parties and networks involved to be successful during and after the disruption. Furthermore, a resilient supply chain contributes to the sustainable competitive advantage of the entire value chain.

While this term is now widely discussed, it is still not clear to many stakeholders how to implement resilient supply chains in practice. Technology is seen as a core enabler of resilient supply chains but its possible application areas and limits are not sufficiently understood. Besides an increased awareness of the importance of resilience, also sustainability is gaining in importance. The relationship between these two concepts is still not sufficiently addressed in theory and practice.

In this book, we want to lay the foundation for a better understanding of supply chain resilience. This should help students studying the area of supply chain management to get a better grasp of the associated terms and concepts. Also, it should provide insights into how different industries were affected by recent supply chain disruptions and how different companies used these disruptions as an opportunity to strengthen their supply chains. In this regard, it should also be a valuable resource for practitioners interested in this topic.

Part I starts with a definition of the term supply chain resilience and shows how it developed over time. Furthermore, it highlights the challenges that transport, logistics, and supply chain management were facing during the COVID-19 pandemic.

Part II highlights how information technologies can be applied to measure the resilience capabilities of a supply chain. The possible contribution of blockchain technologies and artificial intelligence are explored. The important role of business continuity management is shown. Insights from business as well as the non-profit sector are presented.

Part III addresses how resilience can be addressed on a national as well as a company level. It shows the potential of optimization models to contribute to the development of more resilient supply chains. Furthermore, it highlights the links to other highly relevant concepts like sustainability and accessibility.

In Part IV, resilience in theory and practice is explored. On the one hand, this part shows how research can provide guidelines for practitioners; on the other hand, it highlights insights that can be drawn from practice. A Delphi Study collects state-of-the-art insights from supply chain leaders.

Parts V and VI explore the topic of supply chain resilience from practitioners' perspectives. Essays contributed by experts from academia and practice highlight approaches, best practice use cases, methods, and tools for current and future managers in the public and private sector. Part V focuses on different functional areas, including procurement, production, warehousing, distribution, transportation, and human resource management. Part VI applies an industry perspective and highlights the importance of resilience in the parcel shipping industry, the aviation industry, the semiconductor industry, automotive industry, humanitarian supply chains, and the military.

The concluding remarks summarize the lessons learned of the book. We hope that the book helps to better prepare for future supply chain disruptions.

Vienna, Austria

Sebastian Kummer
Tina Wakolbinger
Lydia Novoszel
Alexander M. Geske

Contents

About the Editors

Sebastian Kummer is the Head of the Institute for Transport and Logistics Management at WU (Vienna University of Economics and Business) as well as an Endowed Chair Professor at the Jilin University in Changchun, China. Previously he was Professor at the TU Dresden and worked at the WHU, Vallendar, where he received his Ph.D. Prof. Kummer is responsible for program development and teaching in the fields of transportation, logistics, and supply chain management. He carries out numerous successful research and practice projects for industrial and commercial companies and for transport and logistics service providers. He supports numerous transport and logistic tenders. His publication list includes more than 180 publications, including leading textbooks.

Tina Wakolbinger, Ph.D. is Professor for Supply Chain Services and Networks. She serves as Head of the Research Institute for Supply Chain Management and Deputy Head of the Institute for Transport and Logistics Management at WU (Vienna University of Economics and Business). Her research interests lie in the modeling and analysis of complex decision-making on network systems with a focus on global issues. She serves in editorial positions in Production and Operations Management and Central European Journal of Operations Research. Her work on supply chain management and humanitarian logistics is published in renown journals.

Lydia Novoszel is Research Associate at the Institute for Transport and Logistics Management at WU (Vienna University of Economics and Business). With an international professional career in supply chain management, she incorporates practical relevance and perspectives in supply chain disruption research. Lydia has earned a master's degree in Mechanical Engineering and a master's degree in Business Administration.

Alexander Maximilian Geske is Research Associate at the Institute for Transport and Logistics Management at WU (Vienna University of Economics and Business). He has earned a bachelor's degree in International Business Administration and a master's degree in Supply Chain Management. With a professional career in the transportation industry, Alexander combines the practical and academic perspective.

Part I
Supply Chain Disruptions and Resilience

Chapter 1
Definition and Development of Supply Chain Resilience

Alexander M. Geske and Lydia Novoszel

Abstract Supply chain activities are exposed to risk and disruptions, due to their globally connected design with a high degree of connectivity between stakeholders. Recent events like the blockage of the Suez Cannel or the COVID-19 crisis have stressed the relevance of the concept of supply chain resilience. This chapter provides an overview of the term resilience in a range of selected scientific disciplines. Additionally it illustrates the definition and evolution of that term in those disciplines over time. Thereafter, the authors elaborate the development of the multidimensional and multidisciplinary concept of resilience in the field of supply chain management. Different capabilities, such as flexibility or robustness, enable resilient supply chains. This chapter summarizes the most relevant supply chain capabilities to foster supply chain resilience. The authors present common categorizations from literature first and then apply the results to develop their own definition of supply chain capabilities, which are being used for the Delphi Study.

1.1 Introduction

Each supply chain activity has an immanent risk of unforeseen disruptions. Since supply chain operations stretch globally, product life cycles become shorter and customers impose increasing requirements, organizations must become aware that any (unexpected) disruption to the value chain may lead to operational and financial impacts. To minimize risk exposure, supply chains must be prepared to respond to unexpected events, be capable of responding effectively and efficiently, and aim to return to their original or even to a better state after the disruption (Ponomarov & Holcomb, 2009).

A. M. Geske (✉) · L. Novoszel
Institute for Transport and Logistics Management, WU (Vienna University of Economics and Business), Vienna, Austria
e-mail: alexander.maximilian.geske@wu.ac.at; lydia.novoszel@wu.ac.at

S. Kummer et al. (eds.), *Supply Chain Resilience*, Springer Series in Supply Chain Management 17, https://doi.org/10.1007/978-3-030-95401-7_1

The concept of resilience was first researched in disciplines like developmental psychology or ecosystems and only recently became the subject of scientific research in supply chain management. Since there is no agreed uniform definition of the multidimensional and multidisciplinary concept of resilience (Ponomarov & Holcomb, 2009), this sections aims to provide an overview of the development of the term resilience and its most relevant definitions. Therefore, this chapter first gives an overview of the application of the term resilience in selected disciplines. Next, it presents resilience in the context of enterprises, before the scope is extended to entire supply chains. This chapter concludes with a discussion of different supply chain resilience capabilities.

1.2 The Term "Resilience" in Selected Disciplines

The term resilience has a broad perspective of definitions. It might be linked to terms like vulnerability or elasticity, the earlier one does not describe it sufficiently. Elasticity "is defined in the OED [Oxford English Dictionary] as "the art of rebounding, or springing back" from the Latin resilio, jump back" (Timmermann, 1981, p. 19) Bruneau et al. (2003) list, among others, the following two definitions for resilience:

- "the capacity to cope with unanticipated dangers after they have become manifest, learning to bounce back" (Wildavsky, 1988, p. 77)
- "the ability of a system to withstand stresses of 'environmental loading' ... a fundamental quality found in individuals, groups, organizations, and systems as a whole" (Horne and Orr (1998, p. 31) in Bruneau et al. (2003, p. 735))

Consequently, supply chains must learn to deal with a series of unexpected risks and disruptions, threatening smooth supply chain operations. Following Horne and Orr (1998), supply chains must develop the capacity to withstand negative external as well as internal stresses on an organizational and on a system level.

The research of resilience originated in the development theory of social psychology. It became an independent theory there. The theory of resilience also links to ecological and social vulnerability, politics, and psychology and relates to disaster recovery and risk management as well as to material science, engineering, sociology, and economics (Bruneau et al., 2003; Ponomarov & Holcomb, 2009). Even though there are broadly used definitions, most of them are used within one specific discipline only (Ponomarov & Holcomb, 2009). Holling (1973) was the first academic to note the characteristics of a resilient ecosystem (Melnyk et al., 2014). He describes that resilience and stability are two distinct features of a system. While resilience describes the capacity of absorbing changes, stability refers to the attribute of a system to return to an equilibrium after a disruptive event, which is contradictory to previous descriptions (Holling, 1973). Both features are essential to enable smooth supply chain processes under disruptive conditions. The initial concept of Holling (1973) has since been enhanced (Ponomarov & Holcomb, 2009).

Table 1.1 Definitions of resilience and its components from an ecological perspective.

	Definitions
Resilience	Degree, manner, and pace of restoration of initial structure and function in an ecosystem after disturbance (Clapham, 1971; Westman, 1978)
Elasticity	Rapidity of restoration of a stable state following disturbance (Orians, 1975; Westman, 1978)
Amplitude	The zone of deformation from which the system will return to its initial state (Orians, 1975; Westman, 1978)
Hysteresis	The extent to which the path of degradation under chronic disturbance and a recovery when disturbance ceases are not mirror-images of each other (Westman, 1978, 1986)
Malleability	Degree to which the steady state established after disturbance differs from the original steady state (Westman, 1978)
Damping	The degree and manner by which the path of restoration is altered by any forces that change the normal restoring force (Clapham, 1971)

Source: Ponomarov and Holcomb (2009, p. 126).

Ponomarov and Holcomb (2009) present the following definition and characteristics of resilience from the ecological perspective, based on publications from Westman (1978), Westman (1986), Clapham (1971) and Orians (1975) (Table 1.1):

Holling and Gunderson (2002) describe ecosystem resilience "[. . .] by the magnitude of disturbance that can be absorbed before the systems changes its structure by changing the variables and processes that control behavior" (p. 28). Based on Gunderson (2000), Carpenter et al. (2001) mention three properties of resilience:

1. "[. . .] the amount of change the system can undergo [. . .] and [. . .] retain the same controls on structure and function [. . .]" (p. 766)
2. "[. . .] the degree to which the system is capable of self-organization [. . .]" (p. 766)
3. "[. . .] the degree to which the system can build the capacity to learn and adapt. Adaptive capacity is a component of resilience that reflects the learning aspect of system behavior in response to disturbance" (p. 766).

According to Ponomarov and Holcomb (2009), Dovers and Handmer (1992) also focus on the adaptive capacity for proactive resilience, which acknowledges that changes are inevitable and aim at constructing a system that has the capacity to adjust to new requirements. This also applies to supply chain management. A resilient supply chain must be capable of withstanding (short-term) stresses and disruptions while maintaining its structure and processes. Nevertheless, resilient supply chains should facilitate adaptations in case of more permanent disruptions.

Resilience has been investigated from three primary perspectives: psychological, social, and economic (Ponomarov & Holcomb, 2009). According to Ponomarov and Holcomb (2009), Timmermann (1981) was one of the first authors to define resilience of societies. Here it represents "[. . .] the measure of a system's, or part of a system's capacity to absorb and recover from the occurrence of a hazardous event" (Timmermann, 1981, p. 21). The secretariat of the International Strategy for Disaster

Reduction (ISDR) further specifies the definition by referring to the capacity to adapt, resist, or change to achieve an appropriate level of functioning and structure. This is determined by the degree of self-organizing in a social system as well as by the capacity of learning from previous disasters to be able to develop a better protection and risk reduction measure for future occurrences (ISDR Secretariat, 2004, p. 6). As a result, supply chains should be able to withstand disruptions and proactively customize the system, as well as be capable of learning from past occurrences to prepare and protect for future events.

The psychological perspective of resilience, which is rooted in developmental theory and investigates people's behavior over the life span, is well researched [Conrad, 1999 in Ponomarov & Holcomb, 2009]. It focuses on developmental differences in the response to stress and adversity. Reich (2006) looked at the three Cs: control, coherence, and connectedness, which represent central principals of human resilience. The author concludes that these three human needs do not only strengthen human resilience but also increase the effectiveness and comprehensiveness of responses in disaster planning (Reich, 2006; Ponomarov & Holcomb, 2009). Grotberg (1995) mentions that "[. . .] resilience is a universal capacity which allows a person, group or community to prevent, minimize or overcome the damaging effects of adversity" (p. 3).

Dovers and Handmer (1992) identified three types of resilience in their topology of societal resilience:

- Type 1—resistance and maintenance: the unwillingness and resistance to change characterize this type. Management systems will make great efforts to avoid change and uncertainty and will invest a lot of resources to preserve the status quo.
- Type 2—change at the margins: changes that do not question the foundations of our societies but which can lead to marginal shifts in emphasis characterize this type. It usually does not serve the interest of public and its environment but usually is in favor of elites.
- Type 3—openness and adaptability: flexibility serves as an approach to reduce vulnerability. It is marked by the capability to alter operating assumptions, institutional structures, and the ability to adopt to new ones. According to Dovers and Handmer (1992), an adaptable society is open to quickly change to new and different directions (Dovers & Handmer, 1992).

The authors describe the approach to resilience of societies in Type 1 as follows:

> "Threats will be identified and anticipatory mechanisms put in place. Where proper reaction would threaten the status quo, appeals to ignorance are common: these are often expressed through calls for more information, and an insistence upon inaction because of uncertainty. A society totally reliant on Type 1 responses may be poorly equipped to deal with unexpected shocks or thresholds of change." (Dovers & Handmer, 1992, p. 270)

In order to take full advantage of supply chain resilience capabilities, the organization and most importantly every individual of that organization must be—what Dovers and Handmer (1992) define as Type 3—open and adaptable to new environments, structures or processes.

Based on Holling (1973) and Perrings (1994), static economic stability describes "the ability or capacity of a system to absorb or cushion against damage or loss [. . .]" (Ponomarov & Holcomb, 2009, p. 128). According to Rose (2006, p. 229), resilience can be targeted at three levels:

- Microeconomic: individuals (e.g., firms, households, organizations)
- Mesoeconomic: sectors, specific markets, cooperative groups
- Macroeconomic: markets and individuals combined with all interactive effects of an economy

Expanding the horizon to engineering and construction, Bruneau et al. (2003) define resilience "as the ability of the system to reduce the chances of a shock, to absorb a shock if it occurs (abrupt reduction of performance) and to recover quickly after a shock (re-establish normal performance)" (p. 736). Therefore, a resilient system has a reduced likelihood for failure, reduced consequences (lost lives, damage, negative economic impact or social consequences) and a reduced time to recover (Bruneau et al., 2003). In engineering, Merriam-Webster (2007) in Pettit et al. (2010, p. 3) defined resilience as "[. . .] the tendency of a material to return to its original shape after the removal of a stress that has produced elastic strain." Timmermann (1981) mentions that resilience is also a technical term in mechanical engineering where it describes the ability "[. . .] to store strain energy and deflect elastically under a load without breaking [. . .]" (p. 19). Besides this, it serves as a characteristic in structures which is defined as "the amount of strain energy which can be stored in a structure without causing permanent damage to it" (Gordon, 1978 in Timmermann (1981, p. 19)).

From an organizational perspective, Ponomarov and Holcomb (2009) list the following definitions:

- "[. . .] the capacity to adjust and maintain desirable functions under challenging or straining conditions (Edmondson, 1999; Weick et al., 1999; Bunderson & Sutcliffe, 2002);
- a dynamic capacity of organizational adaptability that grows and develops over time (Wildavsky, 1988); and
- the ability to bounce back from disruptive events or hardship (Sutcliffe & Vogus, 2003)" (pp. 128–129).

Hamel and Välikangas (2003) define business resilience as

> "the ability to dynamically reinvent business models and strategies as circumstances change. Strategic resilience is not about responding to a onetime crisis. It's not about rebounding from a setback. It's about continuously anticipating and adjusting to deep, secular trends that can permanently impair the earning power of a core business. It's about having the capacity to change before the case for change becomes desperately obvious." (pp. 53–54)

Thereby various researchers stress the importance of proactive mitigation actions instead of just reacting to circumstances. Therefore, organizations should focus on continuous reinvention, anticipation, adaptation, and "being ahead of the curve" (Hamel & Välikangas, 2003).

1.3 The Term "Resilience" in Supply Chain Management

Resilience as a multidimensional and multidisciplinary concept appeared around 2000 in publications targeting supply chain management (Christopher & Peck, 2004a; Hohenstein et al., 2015). Events like the fuel protests, foot and mouth disease in the United Kingdom or the terrorist attracts in the United States in the early 2000s showed the relevance for research on supply chain resilience (Rice & Caniato, 2003; Christopher & Peck, 2004a). According to Kamalahmadi and Parast (2016), the number of publications on supply chain resilience increased around 2003. This is in line with studies by Tang and Nurmaya Musa (2011) and Ghadge et al. (2012) who examined supply chain risk management. These authors explain the increased research interest by challenges and opportunities arising from outsourcing to low cost countries (Kamalahmadi & Parast, 2016). Hohenstein et al. (2015) add that disruptive events such as the hurricanes Katrina and Sandy, the volcano eruption in Iceland, or the nuclear disaster in Fukushima led to a greater attention in supply chain management literature. After varying numbers of publications until 2010, academic publications increased in 2011 and especially from 2014 onward (Kamalahmadi & Parast, 2016; Pettit et al., 2019; Zavala-Alcívar et al., 2020). Hofman et al. (2011) also list resilience as one of the four themes in the Gartner's Supply Chain Top 25 report.

Following the approach of Kamalahmadi and Parast (2016), this chapter first considers resilience from the perspective of a single organization or enterprise, before extending the scope to the entire supply chain. According to the exhaustive source of enterprise resilience definitions gathered by Kamalahmadi and Parast (2016), early definitions date back to the late 1980s and 1990s. In this context, resilience is a dynamic capability that stresses the ability of enterprises to accept and respond to change. Moreover, it depends on individuals, groups, and subsystems that resemble a system. Consequently, to achieve a resilient system, resilient components (individuals, groups, and subsystems) are required first. Next, the organization's management must fully understand the environment and its paths of change. Executives can establish tailored and effective strategies to reduce risk, when knowing the range of risks to their supply chain and their interconnectedness (Chopra & Sodhi, 2004). In addition, the organization must develop capabilities to be able to survive, adapt, and respond to changes in its environment (Kamalahmadi & Parast, 2016). Developing and sustaining resilience is not a single event but a process (Pettit et al., 2013). Organizations must understand their own risk exposure, their decision-making, as well as the changed environment and must adapt to changes (Madni & Jackson, 2009). Starr et al. (2003) suggest an integrated approach to risk management that links corporate strategy to enterprise resilience as well as to business continuity planning. As a result, Kamalahmadi and Parast (2016) developed the following definition for enterprise resilience:

> "[. . .] the dynamic capability of an enterprise, which is highly dependent on its individuals, groups, and subsystems, to face immediate and unexpected changes in the environment with proactive attitude and thought, and adapt and respond to these changes by developing flexible and innovative solutions." (p. 121)

After major disruptions to the global economy, studies investigated how supply chains could better adapt to changing environments. With the emergence of the term resilience in supply chain management, academics focused their research on attributes of enterprises that contributed to the disruption of their supply chains and on attributes that supported enterprises in preventing and coping with such disturbances (Pettit et al., 2013). Since increasing complexity of organizations reduces their resilience (Fiksel et al., 2015), it is vital to understand vulnerabilities as well as interconnectedness of mitigation actions, such as back-up suppliers. More frequent adoption of lean principles, by solely focusing on efficiency and productivity, further increases the vulnerability of firms to disruption (Wilding, 2013). "Supply chain resilience deals with multiple types of risks at multiple stages of the risk management process at the supply chain unit of analysis" (Ponomarov & Holcomb, 2009, p. 130). Craighead et al. (2007) argue that a shift in the business environment from competition between enterprises to competition among supply chains has fostered academic and practical publications on issues like supply chain resilience. Early studies by Rice and Caniato (2003) or Sheffi (2005a, 2008) stress redundancy and flexibility, in contrast to Flynn (2008), who uses robustness, resourcefulness, recovery, and review to define resilience (Pettit et al., 2013). Pires Ribeiro and Barbosa-Povoa (2018) state that definitions lack to clarify the focus events for supply chain resilience, while Kochan and Nowicki (2018) mention that the terminology for capabilities is inconsistent.

Kamalahmadi and Parast (2016) reviewed a variety of definitions of supply chain resilience. All of them "[. . .] consider SC resilience as the capability of supply chains to respond to disturbances and disruptions" (Kamalahmadi & Parast, 2016, p. 121). Here the authors refer to disturbances as "[. . .] a foreseeable or unforeseeable event which affects the usual operation and stability of an organisation or a supply chain" (Barroso et al., 2011, p. 163, based on Barroso et al. (2008)). While Fiksel (2003) introduces only four main characteristics for the resilience of systems: diversity, efficiency, adaptability, and cohesion, Christopher and Peck (2004a) present the first precise definition of supply chain resilience. It describes resilience as a system's ability to either return to the initial state or to a more desirable in the aftermath of a disruption.

A year later, Sheffi (2005b) stated that resilient enterprises are not only capable of withstanding disruptions but may also seek an advantage over competitors as they are able to react to demand changes prior to competitors. Datta et al. (2007) used a similar definition by referring to supply chain resilience

> "[. . .] as not only the ability to maintain control over performance variability in the face of disturbance, but also a property of being adaptive and capable of sustained response to sudden and significant shifts in the environment in the form of uncertain demands." (p. 189)

Falasca et al. (2008) amended the definition, as supply chain resilience is the ability to reduce the probability of disruptions, the impact when a disruption occurs, and the time to recover to normal operations.

Elkins et al. (2008) in Machowiak (2012) are among the first to mention the end customer and to focus on recovery costs in their definition:

> "building responsive and resilient supply chains that can withstand the impact of major supply chain disruptions and catastrophes, without impacting the end customer and without incurring excessive recovery costs." (pp. 280–281)

Ponomarov and Holcomb (2009) set up a more detailed definition by using key elements from other disciplines. They refer to resilience as

> "The adaptive capability of the supply chain to prepare for unexpected events, respond to disruptions, and recover from them by maintaining continuity of operations at the desired level of connectedness and control over structure and function." (p. 131)

The adaptive capacity and the retention of control over structure and function during disruptions stem from the resilience term used for ecosystems and organizations, while responding and recovering to the same or a better state are a common theme in different disciplines like ecological, social, economic, or emergency management (Ponomarov & Holcomb, 2009). The definition by Kamalahmadi and Parast (2016) implies supply chain resilience at three different stages:

- During the anticipation stage, the supply chain is prepared for any expected and unexpected disruptions. Therefore, it is crucial to fully understand the impacts of disturbances and their likelihood to proactively develop contingency plans.
- In the resistance stage, a detected disturbance must be contained before it spreads to ensure the continuity of operations.
- Finally, during the recovery and response phase, negative impacts for other stakeholders in the chain must be minimized, and the firm should have the ability to either restore the original status or even restore the firm's position at a higher level to leverage competitive advantage.

Referring back to the resilience definitions in engineering of Merriam-Webster (2007), Pettit et al. (2010) note that for supply chains not returning to the original state, but learning from the disruption to adapt and return to a reconfigured state may be more beneficial.

Ponis and Koronis (2012) incorporate the element of proactive planning and designing to be able to anticipate unexpected negative disruptions in the definition of resilience. The authors define resilience as

> "the ability to proactively plan and design the Supply Chain network for anticipating unexpected disruptive (negative) events, respond adaptively to disruptions while maintaining control over structure and function and transcending to a post-event robust state of operations, if possible, more favorable than the one prior to the event, thus gaining competitive advantage." (pp. 925–926)

Melnyk et al. (2014) emphasize that systems consist of two important complementary system capacities:

- Resistance capacity: is either the complete avoidance of the impact of a disruption on the system (avoidance) or having a minimal time span between the start of the disruption and the start of the recovery (containment).
- Recovery capacity: refers to the capability of a system to return to a fully functional state upon a disruption. The recovery is characterized by a stabilization phase in which the performance reaches a stable level. Depending on the disruption and the competition, this level may resemble the original performance level (Melnyk et al., 2014).

Wang et al. (2014) propose a definition of resilience which is applicable for various supply chain setups. It is based on these four building blocks:

- Objective: surviving refers to making profit, while maintaining function means to meet demand with supply.
- Anticipation: monitor changes in the environment and learn from past events.
- Estimation: estimate and prioritize damages that could result from anticipated disruptions.
- Preparation: adopt a resilient strategy to defeat disruptions (Wang et al., 2014).

This definition follows the ideas of classical supply chain risk management. Ho et al. (2015), for instance, define supply chain risk management as

> "[. . .] an inter-organisational collaborative endeavour utilising quantitative and qualitative risk management methodologies to identify, evaluate, mitigate and monitor unexpected macro and micro level events or conditions, which might adversely impact any part of a supply chain." (p. 5036)

Wilding (2013) builds the connection between supply chain resilience and supply chain risk management by stating that risk management must be part of the supply chain design in order to maximize supply chain resilience.

Based on the four building blocks, Wang et al. (2014) suggest that resilience is

> "[. . .] a system with an objective to survive and maintain function even during the course of disruptions, provided with a capability to predict and assess the damage of possible disruptions, and enhanced by the strong awareness of its ever-changing environment and knowledge of the past events, thereby utilizing resilient strategies for defense against the disruptions." Wang et al. (2014, p. 3)

Hohenstein et al. (2015) note that definitions of supply chain resilience may encompass four phases: readiness, response, recovery, and growth. While many existing definitions cover the response and recovery phase, only few studies include the readiness and growth phase. This trend may result from a lack of empirical testing of the elements identified, as most definitions refer to previous ones, only slightly altered (Hohenstein et al., 2015). Hohenstein et al. (2015) categorized two strategies: proactive and reactive, while Wang et al. (2014) also added the anticipation and awareness dimension (Pires Ribeiro & Barbosa-Povoa, 2018). Since response and recovery represent the reactive and basic part of resilience, these phases are stressed more frequently. In contrast, readiness and growth both require proactive interventions like safety stocks or multisourcing. Hohenstein et al. (2015) found that three of those four stages were already used by Rice and Caniato (2003). Even though the phases response, recovery, and growth were common parts in definitions over the next few years, only few publications like Christopher and Peck (2004a) or Ponomarov and Holcomb (2009) used all three phases together in their definitions. The readiness phase was first introduced by Datta et al. (2007) (Hohenstein et al., 2015). However, the proactive notion of anticipating steps for prevention and response was already mentioned by Closs et al. (2004), who defined supply chain resilience as

> "[. . .] the supply chain's ability to withstand and recover from an incident. A resilient supply chain is proactive—anticipating and establishing planned steps to prevent and respond to incidents. Such supply chains quickly rebuild or re-establish alternative means of operations when the subject of an incident." (p. 10)

Many definitions include a time component. While some refer to the term "quick," others like Falasca et al. (2008) or Ponomarov (2012) address "speed" by either minimizing the "time to recover" or "in a timely manner" (Pires Ribeiro & Barbosa-Povoa, 2018).

1.4 Capabilities for Supply Chain Resilience

Pettit et al. (2010) state that the design of global supply chains leads to high degrees of connectivity among stakeholders and partners. In order to manage the great number of interrelated operations between suppliers of different tiers and customers, organizations need to create strong capabilities in the field of collaborations, visibility and flexibility. This will strength the resilience of the entire supply chain (Pettit et al., 2010).

In their dynamic capability approach, Teece et al. (1997) explain that firm-specific capabilities can be defined as "sources of advantage, and to explain how combinations of competences and resources can be developed, deployed, and protected" (Teece et al., 1997, p. 510). The authors emphasize the use of existing internal and external competences in response to changing environments. Consequently, dynamic capabilities describe the "ability to achieve new forms of competitive advantage" (Teece et al., 1997, p. 515) and support the understanding of sources of competitive advantage (Teece et al., 1997). "Dynamic" in this context means the capacity to renew competences or to adapt to changing environments. The term "capability" takes an essential role in strategic management to "appropriately adapting, integrating, and reconfiguring internal and external organizational skills, resources, and functional competences to match the requirements of a changing environment" (Teece et al., 1997, p. 515). According to Teece (2007), dynamic capabilities can be split into the ability

> "(1) to sense and shape opportunities and threats, (2) to seize opportunities, and (3) to maintain competitiveness through enhancing, combining, protecting, and, when necessary, reconfiguring the business enterprise's intangible and tangible assets." (Teece, 2007, p. 1319)

A review by Hohenstein et al. (2015) shows that there is some inconsistency in the terminology of elements to achieve resilience. Some authors use the term elements, while others name them antecedents, resilience enhancers, competencies, or capabilities. This chapter follows the terminology of Pettit et al. (2010) and therefore refers to capabilities. Many articles take the capabilities developed by Christopher and Peck (2004b) as the basis for their refinement or for amending them. Pettit et al. (2010) list these

> "four key principles: (1) resilience can be built into a system in advance of a disruption (i.e., re-engineering), (2) a high level of collaboration is required to identify and manage risks, (3) agility is essential to react quickly to unforeseen events, and (4) the culture of risk management is a necessity." (p. 4)

that were suggested by Christopher and Peck (2004b). Besides this, they mention capabilities like agility, availability, efficiency, flexibility, redundancy, velocity, or visibility, which were treated secondarily (Pettit et al., 2010). Hohenstein et al. (2015) identified 36 different capabilities in their review. Among them capabilities like flexibility, redundancy, collaboration and visibility, and agility and multiple sourcing are most commonly used (Hohenstein et al., 2015).

A supply chain strategy is based on the corporate strategy, which determines the supply chain network design and subsequent procedures. Thereby it deduces certain supply chain capabilities. Wilding (2013) compares "the resilient supply chain" with a temple. He states that an effective supply chain strategy serves as the basis for supply chain resilience, followed by the product design. Consequently, resilience must be integrated into the supply chain design, which often involves reengineering supply chains (Scholten et al., 2014; Wilding, 2013). Comparable to the resilience capabilities of Christopher and Peck (2004b), the author suggests four pillars of capabilities:

- Supply chain collaboration: effective and mutually rewarding collaboration; requires initial investment in resources to manage these relationships.
- Supply chain design and engineering: conscious application of network design principles, which create a balance between efficiency and redundancy; understanding of the network from the organization to the end customer.
- Supply chain risk management culture: internal business culture influences risk mitigation and deals with disruptions; requires leadership encouragement and top-down reviews of the impact of company policies and practices on risk profiles; assignment of formal responsibility for resilience and establishment of business continuity teams may also help.
- Agility: "Agile supply chains not only need to be network based, but they also need to be market sensitive, with highly integrated virtual and critical processes" (Wilding, 2013, p. 58). Respond in short time periods to volume variations,

synchronize supply and demand, and adapt output to market requirements (Wilding, 2013).

Supply chain transparency spans across the four pillars, since it is a critical feature for risk mitigation. Transparency leads to confidence and trust, which will positively influence costly and unnecessary protection. Continuous monitoring and intelligence resemble the final overarching item (Wilding, 2013).

A different approach was chosen by Hohenstein et al. (2015), who distinguish supply chain resilience elements suitable prior to and after a disruption. The capability collaboration (share knowledge and information to make joint efforts), human resource management (train employees to deal with/accommodate risks and form cross-functional teams), and redundancies (absorb shocks and respond to changes) are universally applicable before and after a disruptive event. Additionally, the authors suggest inventory management to create buffers for unexpected occurrences, contingency plans, and communication protocols to reduce response time and avoid mistakes as well as visibility to sense early warning signals and achieve real-time monitoring as proactive strategies before a disruption.

After the disruption, further reactive capabilities should be applied during the response, recovery, and growth phases. These are agility and flexibility (created by backup suppliers, flexible production systems, and distribution channels) (Hohenstein et al., 2015).

In contrast, Bruneau et al. (2003) list robustness, redundancy, resourcefulness, and rapidity as properties for resilience. Robustness in this context means the ability to withstand given levels of stress without degrading or losing functionality. Redundancy describes the extend of substitutability of elements or systems, while resourcefulness refers to

> "[. . .] the capacity to identify problems, establish priorities, and mobilize resources when conditions exist that threaten to disrupt some element, system, or other unit of analysis; resourcefulness can be further conceptualized as consisting of the ability to apply material (i.e., monetary, physical, technological, and informational) and human resources to meet established priorities and achieve goals [. . .]." (Bruneau et al., 2003, pp. 737–738)

Lastly, rapidity is "[. . .]the capacity to meet priorities and achieve goals in a timely manner in order to contain losses and avoid future disruption [. . .]" (Bruneau et al., 2003, p. 738).

Jüttner and Maklan (2011) define four formative elements for supply chain resilience: flexibility, visibility, collaboration, and velocity. Based on their investigation, risk-sharing impacts flexibility, visibility, and collaboration, while redundant resources primarily address flexibility and velocity (Jüttner & Maklan, 2011). Similarly, Ponis and Koronis (2012) grouped these formative principles into four first-level elements (direct impact on resilience): agility (based on flexibility and velocity), redundancy, collaboration (including information-sharing, collaborative work, and joint decision-making) and "[. . .] knowledge of supply chain network physical and informational structure [. . .]" (Ponis & Koronis, 2012, p. 926).

For the purpose of this book and the Delphi Study in Chap. 17, we consider four main capabilities as the most relevant enablers for supply chain resilience:

- Agility
- Flexibility
- Collaboration
- Visibility

The following section describes these capabilities from various supply chain perspectives. Since different concepts are closely linked to each other, it is difficult to distinguish and allocate certain activities to one specific capability. Therefore, selected most relevant views on these four capabilities are briefly outlined, before the editors' definitions are presented.

1.4.1 Supply Chain Agility

Supply chain literature discusses the term "agility" in the context of supply chain characteristics (i.e., agile supply chains) and as a resilience capability (Kamalahmadi & Parast, 2016). Agility in view of resilience means a quick response to changes by returning to the original state or by reconfiguring the system (Bakshi & Kleindorfer, 2009; Wieland & Wallenburg, 2013). Agility does not only involve a single organization but requires the entire supply chain to be agile (Christopher & Peck, 2004a). Christopher and Peck (2004a) define visibility and velocity as two key elements of agility. Visibility thus means to be able to see to the upstream and downstream end of the supply chain. This involves inventories, supply, and demand information or production and purchasing schedules. A close collaboration sets the base for visibility. Velocity in contrast describes the time required for a product or material to move from one end of the supply chain to the other. To improve velocity, streamlining processes, reducing (in-bound) lead times, and reducing non-value-added time helps (Christopher & Peck, 2004a). Kochan and Nowicki (2018) even suggest not only viewing visibility and velocity as dimensions of agility but also flexibility. Kamalahmadi and Parast (2016) remark that other authors like Datta et al. (2007) or Wieland and Wallenburg (2013) also consider visibility as a driver for agility, while publications by Jüttner and Maklan (2011) or Ponis and Koronis (2012) have defined visibility as a separate driver of resilience. Similarly, velocity can also be seen as part of flexibility (Kamalahmadi & Parast, 2016).

In order to stress the importance of visibility in achieving supply chain resilience, we follow authors like Jüttner and Maklan (2011) and treat agility and visibility as separate capabilities. In the context of supply chain resilience, agility describes the ability on a strategic level to respond to unpredictable (and sometimes erratic) changes or disruptions in the supply chain in a quick, smooth, and cost-efficient manner. It is the ability to transform a turbulent business environment into a business opportunity on a strategic level.

1.4.2 Supply Chain Flexibility

Commonly associated with resilience are flexibility and redundancy. According to Kamalahmadi and Parast (2016), "[. . .] flexibility is defined as the ability to take different positions to better respond to abnormal situations and rapidly adapt to significant changes [. . .]" (p. 122). Redundancy can support flexibility because, e.g., multiple options (such as different sourcing options or additional stock) enhance the wiggle room to choose. Redundancy can be described as "[. . .] an additional capacity that can be used to replace the loss of capacity caused by a disturbance" (Carvalho et al., 2012, p. 331). There is an ongoing debate on the importance of redundancy and flexibility. Sheffi and Rice (2005) argue that investments into redundancy increase costs, while flexibility helps to achieve resilience. They emphasize that flexibility does not only support organizations during disruptive events but also helps in daily operations (Sheffi & Rice, 2005). According to Datta et al. (2007), flexibility is needed in all parts of the supply chain. Zsidisin and Wagner (2010) distinguish flexibility and redundancy as important characteristics depending on the controllability of risks. However, it is more appropriate to use flexibility when risk comes from the extended supply chain, while redundancy—especially in the short term—helps when dealing with risks which are beyond the control of the supply chain participants (e.g., supply market risk). "The constant monitoring of suppliers to create flexibility and organizational knowledge of external threats risk can uncover problems that may exist when sourcing from far-off locations" (Zsidisin & Wagner, 2010, p. 15). Jüttner and Maklan (2011) in contrast consider redundant resources as a means that influences flexibility and velocity. In a simulation, Carvalho et al. (2012) showed that flexibility and redundancy reduce negative effects of disruptions. However, flexibility (e.g., restructuring existing transport) has lower total costs, while redundancy (e.g., additional stock as buffer) has a better lead time ratio (ratio of actual versus promised lead time) (Carvalho et al., 2012). Flexibility can be incorporated at different stages of the supply chain: sourcing, product, process, and/or transportation (Roberta Pereira et al., 2014).

We define flexibility as the ability of a supply chain to quickly adjust to changing requirements of partners and external factors. It allows reallocating resources or changing processes when needed.

1.4.3 Supply Chain Collaboration

The relevance and importance of collaboration within supply chains have been agreed on by academia and implemented by organizations. For example, the bullwhip effect researched by Lee et al., (1997) emphasizes the relevance of information-sharing to reduce misinterpretation of varying order sizes. High levels of collaboration, for example, network-wide management of risks, aligned performance targets, communication standards, etc. ensure a common understanding as well as target vision and thus reduce exposure to supply chain vulnerabilities (or unforeseen internal and external disruptions). For cooperative relations, organizations must develop interfirm trust and information-sharing (Kamalahmadi & Parast, 2016). In a buyer-supplier relationship, Ponomarov and Holcomb (2009) found that a high degree of mutual trust increases relational resilience. Building on that, Wicher and Lenort (2012) identified trusted networks, in which organizations address challenges and problems openly, as a key component for cooperative relationships to enhance resilience. Moreover, the authors emphasize working together with common efforts to reach mutual goals. By data and information-sharing, collaborative planning, as well as performance target alignment and monitoring, collaboration can be improved and problems can be identified (Melnyk et al., 2014; Wicher & Lenort, 2012). The process of using knowledge that was generated and shared by partners was named "supply chain intelligence" by Christopher and Peck (2004a). Other authors like Datta et al. (2007) or Soni et al. (2014) consider information-sharing as a separate element directly influencing supply chain resilience.

For the remainder of this book, collaboration describes the ability of different entities to work on a common goal when planning and executing their operations to obtain a mutual benefit. Information-sharing and synchronized decisions are essential for collaboration.

1.4.4 Supply Chain Visibility

The capability of supply chain visibility should allow viewing the entire supply chain (Christopher & Peck, 2004a). Christopher and Lee (2004) state that an improved visibility from one end to the other is a key factor for risk mitigation strategies. In addition, the quality of information increases confidence proportionally. The authors state that the confidence becomes weaker when the lead time within the supply chain increases. Consequently, increased globalization due to subcontracting, offshoring, etc. decreases confidence levels because of a decrease in visibility. The main lever for increasing visibility is information-sharing among stakeholders of a supply chain (Christopher & Lee, 2004).

> "If information between supply chain members is shared, its power increases significantly. This is because shared information reduces uncertainty and thus reduces the need for safety stock. As a result, the system becomes more responsive and, ultimately, could become demand driven rather than forecast driven." (Christopher & Lee, 2004, p. 391)

In addition, it allows to properly respond to disruptions and supports the recovery since it supports the identification of vulnerable suppliers (Jüttner & Maklan, 2011). Visibility also provides knowledge about the operating assets as well as about the environment (Pettit et al., 2010). As visibility provides a clear overview of the supply chain, it supports the detection of early warning signal of disruptions (Tukamuhabwa et al., 2015).

To emphasize the relevancy of visibility in a supply chain, we consider it a separate capability. In this context, visibility describes the capability of having a transparent view of the supply chain structure and processes both upstream and downstream. It allows detecting variations from plans in a timely manner and reacting effectively and appropriately to these variations.

1.5 Summary and Outlook

This chapter outlines the development of the term resilience in various disciplines, such as ecology or psychology. The definition of supply chain resilience has developed since 2003 and accelerated amid the COVID-19 pandemic. There seems to be a general understanding of the concept to enable supply chains to inherently react to internal and external disruptions beyond risk management procedures. However, the details of the definitions vary and so do the different elements. We show how multiple authors identify and describe capabilities that contribute to supply chain resilience, which seems more holistic than identifying individual mitigating factors (such as supplier portfolio management). The detailed descriptions of capabilities and their interplay vary. We propose a concise usage of four capabilities, which were derived from literature and (empirically) applied in the Delphi Study in Chap. 17. The framework in Chap. 3 can serve as a structure to allocate activities and processes to capabilities and to understand how they influence supply chain resilience as well as their implications. Over the course of the global pandemic, further academic and practical discourses on the terms and understanding of capabilities might evolve.

Bhamra et al. (2011) conclude that research has focused on developing theories and definitions of resilience but lacks empirical evidence of theories. The authors recommend concentrating on empirical research with an emphasis on organizations to validate constructs and theories. Additionally, they found that ecological resilience has had a stronger research focus compared to socio-ecological systems. It is recommended to emphasize resilience on the organizational level as well as on extended enterprise and supply chains.

For the purpose of the Delphi Study in this book and as guideline for the authors, we used the resilience definition by the NRC (National Research Council 2012): "the ability to prepare and plan for, absorb, recover from, and more successfully adapt to adverse events" in the supply chain context. In the course of the chapters, different terms and definition are introduced, which reflects the diverse usage of the supply chain resilience term from a practitioner's perspective.

References

Bakshi, N., & Kleindorfer, P. (2009). Co-opetition and investment for supply-chain resilience. *Production and Operations Management, 18*(6), 583–603. https://doi.org/10.1111/j.1937-5956.2009.01031.x

Barroso, A. P., Machado, V. H., & Cruz Machado, V. (2008). A supply chain disturbances classification. Paper presented at the *2008 IEEE International Conference on Industrial Engineering and Engineering Management.*

Barroso, A. P., Machado, V. H., & Cruz Machado, V. (2011). Supply chain resilience using the mapping approach. In P. Li (Ed.), *Supply chain management* (pp. 161–184). InTech.

Bhamra, R., Dani, S., & Burnard, K. (2011). Resilience: The concept, a literature review and future directions. *International Journal of Production Research, 49*(18), 5375–5393. https://doi.org/10.1080/00207543.2011.563826

Bruneau, M., Chang, S. E., Eguchi, R. T., Lee, G. C., O'Rourke, T. D., Reinhorn, A. M., Shinozuka, M., Tierney, K., Wallace, W. A., & von Winterfeldt, D. (2003). A framework to quantitatively assess and enhance the seismic resilience of communities. *Earthquake Spectra, 19*(4), 733–752. https://doi.org/10.1193/1.1623497

Bunderson, J. S., & Sutcliffe, K. M. (2002). Comparing alternative conceptualizations of functional diversity in management teams: Process and performance effects. *The Academy of Management Journal, 45*(5), 875–893. https://doi.org/10.2307/3069319

Carpenter, S., Walker, B., Anderies, J. M., & Abel, N. (2001). From metaphor to measurement: Resilience of what to what? *Ecosystems, 4*(8), 765–781. https://doi.org/10.1007/s10021-001-0045-9

Carvalho, H., Barroso, A. P., Machado, V. H., Azevedo, S., & Cruz-Machado, V. (2012). Supply chain redesign for resilience using simulation. *Computers and Industrial Engineering, 62*(1), 329–341. https://doi.org/10.1016/j.cie.2011.10.003

Chopra, S., & Sodhi, M. S. (2004). Managing risk to avoid supply-chain breakdown. *MIT Sloan Management Review, 46*, 53–61.

Christopher, M., & Lee, H. (2004). Mitigating supply chain risk through improved confidence. *International Journal of Physical Distribution and Logistics Management, 34*(5), 388–396. https://doi.org/10.1108/09600030410545436

Christopher, M., & Peck, H. (2004a). Building the resilient supply chain. *The International Journal of Logistics Management, 15*(2), 1–14. https://doi.org/10.1108/09574090410700275

Christopher, M., & Peck, H. (2004b). The five principles of supply chain resilience. *Logistics Europe, 12*(1), 16–21.

Clapham, W. B. J. (1971). *Natural ecosystems*. Macmillan.

Closs, D. J., McConnell, J. H., & McGarrell, E. F. (2004). *Enhancing security throughout the supply chain*. IBM Center for the Business of Government.

Conrad, A. P. (1999). Professional tools for religiously and spiritually sensitive social work practice. In R. R. Greene (Ed.), *Human behavior theory and social work practice* (2nd ed., pp. 63–72). Aldine Transaction.

Craighead, C. W., Blackhurst, J., Rungtusanatham, M. J., & Handfield, R. B. (2007). The severity of supply chain disruptions: Design characteristics and mitigation capabilities. *Decision Sciences, 38*(1), 131–156. https://doi.org/10.1111/j.1540-5915.2007.00151.x

Datta, P. P., Christopher, M., & Allen, P. (2007). Agent-based modelling of complex production/distribution systems to improve resilience. *International Journal of Logistics Research and Applications, 10*(3), 187–203. https://doi.org/10.1080/13675560701467144

Dovers, S. R., & Handmer, J. W. (1992). Uncertainty, sustainability and change. *Global Environmental Change, 2*(4), 262–276. https://doi.org/10.1016/0959-3780(92)90044-8

Edmondson, A. (1999). Psychological safety and learning behavior in work teams. *Administrative Science Quarterly, 44*(2), 350–383. https://doi.org/10.2307/2666999

Elkins, D., Handfield, R. B., Blackhurst, J., & Craighead, C. W. (2008). A "To-Do" list to improve supply chain risk management capabilities. In R. B. Handfield & K. McCormack (Eds.), *Supply*

chain risk management. Minimizing disruptions in global sourcing (pp. 57–63). Auerbach Publications.
Falasca, M., Zobel, C., & Cook, D. (2008). A decision support framework to assess supply chain resilience. Paper presented at the *5th International ISCRAM Conference*, Washington, DC.
Fiksel, J. (2003). Designing resilient, sustainable systems. *Environmental Science and Technology, 37*(23), 5330–5339. https://doi.org/10.1021/es0344819
Fiksel, J., Polyviou, M., Croxton, K., & Pettit, T. (2015). From risk to resilience: Learning to deal with disruption. *MIT Sloan Management Review, 56*, 78–86.
Flynn, S. K. (2008). *Building a resilient nation: Enhancing security, ensuring a strong economy*. Reform Institute.
Ghadge, A., Dani, S., & Kalawsky, R. (2012). Supply chain risk management: Present and future scope. *The International Journal of Logistics Management, 23*(3), 313–339. https://doi.org/10.1108/09574091211289200
Gordon, J. E. (1978). *Structures*. Penguin Books.
Grotberg, E. H. (1995). *A guide to promoting resilience in children: Strengthening the human spirit* (p. 8). Bernard van Leer Foundation.
Gunderson, L. H. (2000). Ecological resilience—In theory and application. *Annual Review of Ecology and Systematics, 31*(1), 425–439. https://doi.org/10.1146/annurev.ecolsys.31.1.425
Hamel, G., & Välikangas, L. (2003). The quest for resilience. *Harvard Business Review, 81*(9), 52–63.
Ho, W., Zheng, T., Yildiz, H., & Talluri, S. (2015). Supply chain risk management: A literature review. *International Journal of Production Research, 53*(16), 5031–5069. https://doi.org/10.1080/00207543.2015.1030467
Hofman, D., O'Marah, K., & Elvy, C. (2011). The gartner supply chain top 25 for 2011. *World Trade, 24*(9), 22–24.
Hohenstein, N.-O., Feisel, E., Hartmann, E., & Giunipero, L. (2015). Research on the phenomenon of supply chain resilience. *International Journal of Physical Distribution and Logistics Management, 45*(1/2), 90–117. https://doi.org/10.1108/IJPDLM-05-2013-0128
Holling, C. S. (1973). Resilience and stability of ecological systems. *Annual Review of Ecology and Systematics, 4*(1), 1–23. https://doi.org/10.1146/annurev.es.04.110173.000245
Holling, C. S., & Gunderson, L. (2002). Resilience and adaptive cycles. In L. Gunderson & C. S. Holling (Eds.), *Panarchy: Understanding transformation in human and natural systems* (pp. 25–63). Island Press.
Horne, J. F. I., & Orr, J. E. (1998). Assessing behaviors that create resilient organizations. *Employment Relations Today, 24*(4), 29–39. https://doi.org/10.1002/ert.3910240405
ISDR Secretariat. (2004). *Terminology: Basic terms of disaster risk reduction*. Retrieved August 26, 2021, from https://www.unisdr.org/files/7817_7819isdrterminology11.pdf.
Jüttner, U., & Maklan, S. (2011). Supply chain resilience in the global financial crisis: An empirical study. *Supply Chain Management: An International Journal, 16*(4), 246–259. https://doi.org/10.1108/13598541111139062
Kamalahmadi, M., & Parast, M. M. (2016). A review of the literature on the principles of enterprise and supply chain resilience: Major findings and directions for future research. *International Journal of Production Economics, 171*, 116–133. https://doi.org/10.1016/j.ijpe.2015.10.023
Kochan, C. G., & Nowicki, D. R. (2018). Supply chain resilience: A systematic literature review and typological framework. *International Journal of Physical Distribution and Logistics Management, 48*(8), 842–865. https://doi.org/10.1108/IJPDLM-02-2017-0099
Lee, H. L., Padmanabhan, V., & Whang, S. (1997). The bullwhip effect in supply chains. *Sloan Management Review, 38*, 93–102.
Machowiak, W. (2012). Risk management – Unappreciated instrument of supply chain management strategy. *Log Forum, 8*(4), 277–285.
Madni, A. M., & Jackson, S. (2009). Towards a conceptual framework for resilience engineering. *IEEE Systems Journal, 3*(2), 181–191. https://doi.org/10.1109/JSYST.2009.2017397

Melnyk, S. A., Closs, D. J., Griffis, S. E., Zobel, C. W., & Macdonald, J. R. (2014). Understanding supply chain resilience. *Supply Chain Management Review, 18*(1), 40–41.

Merriam-Webster. (2007). *Merriam-Webster dictionary*. Merriam-Webster, Inc.

National Research Council. (2012). *Disaster resilience: A national imperative*. The National Academies Press. https://doi.org/10.17226/13457

Orians, G. H. (1975). Diversity, stability and maturity in natural ecosystems. In W. H. van Dobben & R. H. Lowe-McConnell (Eds.), *Unifying concepts in ecology: Report of the plenary sessions of the First international congress of ecology*, The Hague, September 8–14, 1974 (pp. 139–150). Springer Netherlands.

Perrings, C. (1994). Ecological resilience in the sustainability of economic development. Paper presented at the *International Symposium on Models of Sustainable Development*, Paris.

Pettit, T. J., Fiksel, J., & Croxton, K. L. (2010). Ensuring supply chain resilience: Development of a conceptual framework. *Journal of Business Logistics, 31*(1), 1–21. https://doi.org/10.1002/j.2158-1592.2010.tb00125.x

Pettit, T. J., Croxton, K. L., & Fiksel, J. (2013). Ensuring supply chain resilience: Development and implementation of an assessment tool. *Journal of Business Logistics, 34*(1), 46–76. https://doi.org/10.1111/jbl.12009

Pettit, T. J., Croxton, K. L., & Fiksel, J. (2019). The evolution of resilience in supply chain management: A retrospective on ensuring supply chain resilience. *Journal of Business Logistics, 40*(1), 56–65. https://doi.org/10.1111/jbl.12202

Pires Ribeiro, J., & Barbosa-Povoa, A. (2018). Supply chain resilience: Definitions and quantitative modelling approaches – A literature review. *Computers and Industrial Engineering, 115*, 109–122. https://doi.org/10.1016/j.cie.2017.11.006

Ponis, S. T., & Koronis, E. (2012). Supply chain resilience: Definition of concept and its formative elements. *The Journal of Applied Business Research, 28*, 921–930. https://doi.org/10.19030/jabr.v28i5.7234

Ponomarov, S. Y. (2012). *Antecedents and consequences of supply chain resilience: A dynamic capabilities perspective*, PhD diss., University of Tennessee. https://trace.tennessee.edu/utk_graddiss/1338

Ponomarov, S. Y., & Holcomb, M. C. (2009). Understanding the concept of supply chain resilience. *The International Journal of Logistics Management, 20*(1), 124–143. https://doi.org/10.1108/09574090910954873

Reich, J. W. (2006). Three psychological principles of resilience in natural disasters. *Disaster Prevention and Management: An International Journal, 15*(5), 793–798. https://doi.org/10.1108/09653560610712739

Rice, J., & Caniato, F. (2003). Building a secure and resilient supply network. *Supply Chain Management Review, 7*(5), 22–30.

Roberta Pereira, C., Christopher, M., & Lago Da Silva, A. (2014). Achieving supply chain resilience: The role of procurement. *Supply Chain Management: An International Journal, 19*(5/6), 626–642. https://doi.org/10.1108/SCM-09-2013-0346

Rose, A. (2006). Economic resilience to disasters: Toward a consistent and comprehensive formulation. In D. Paton & D. Johnston (Eds.), *Disaster resilience. An integrated approach* (pp. 226–248). Charles C Thomas Publisher, Ltd.

Scholten, K., Sharkey Scott, P., & Fynes, B. (2014). Mitigation processes – antecedents for building supply chain resilience. *Supply Chain Management: An International Journal, 19*(2), 211–228. https://doi.org/10.1108/SCM-06-2013-0191

Sheffi, Y. (2005a). Building a resilient supply chain. *Harvard Business Review, 1*(5), 1–4.

Sheffi, Y. (2005b). *The resilient enterprise. Overcoming vulnerability for competitive advantage*. The MIT Press.

Sheffi, Y. (2008). Logistics transformation and the resilient enterprise. Paper presented at the *43 rd Annual International Logistics Conference and Exhibition, International Society for Logistics (SOLE)*, Orlando, FL.

Sheffi, Y., & Rice, J. B. J. (2005). A supply chain view of the resilient enterprise. *MIT Sloan Management Review, 47*(1), 41–48.

Soni, U., Jain, V., & Kumar, S. (2014). Measuring supply chain resilience using a deterministic modeling approach. *Computers and Industrial Engineering, 74*, 11–25. https://doi.org/10.1016/j.cie.2014.04.019

Starr, R., Newfrock, J., & Delurey, M. (2003). Enterprise resilience: Managing risk in the networked economy. *Strategy+business Magazine*, 30.

Sutcliffe, K. M., & Vogus, T. (2003). Organizing for resilience. In K. S. Cameron, J. E. Dutton, & R. E. Quinn (Eds.), *Positive organizational scholarship: Foundations of a new discipline* (pp. 94–110). Berrett-Koehler.

Tang, O., & Nurmaya Musa, S. (2011). Identifying risk issues and research advancements in supply chain risk management. *International Journal of Production Economics, 133*(1), 25–34. https://doi.org/10.1016/j.ijpe.2010.06.013

Teece, D. J. (2007). Explicating dynamic capabilities: The nature and microfoundations of (sustainable) enterprise performance. *Strategic Management Journal, 28*(13), 1319–1350. https://doi.org/10.1002/smj.640

Teece, D. J., Pisano, G., & Shuen, A. (1997). Dynamic capabilities and strategic management. *Strategic Management Journal, 18*(7), 509–533. https://doi.org/10.1002/(SICI)1097-0266(199708)18:7<509::AID-SMJ882>3.0.CO;2-Z

Timmermann, P. (1981). *Vulnerability, resilience and the collapse of society. A review if models and possible climatic applications*. Environmental Monograph No. 1. Toronto.

Tukamuhabwa, B. R., Stevenson, M., Busby, J., & Zorzini, M. (2015). Supply chain resilience: Definition, review and theoretical foundations for further study. *International Journal of Production Research, 53*(18), 5592–5623. https://doi.org/10.1080/00207543.2015.1037934

Wang, J., Muddada, R. R., Wang, H., Ding, J., Lin, Y., Liu, C., & Zhang, W. (2014). Toward a resilient holistic supply chain network system: Concept, review and future direction. *IEEE Systems Journal, 10*(2), 410–421. https://doi.org/10.1109/JSYST.2014.2363161

Weick, K. E., Sutcliffe, K. M., & Obstfeld, D. (1999). Organizing for high reliability: Processes of collective mindfulness. In *Research in organizational behavior* (Vol. 21, pp. 81–123). Elsevier Science/JAI Press.

Westman, W. E. (1978). Measuring the inertia and resilience of ecosystems. *BioScience, 28*(11), 705–710. https://doi.org/10.2307/1307321

Westman, W. E. (1986). Resilience: Concepts and measures. In B. Dell, A. J. M. Hopkins, & B. B. Lamont (Eds.), *Resilience in mediterranean-type ecosystems* (pp. 5–19). Springer Netherlands.

Wicher, P., & Lenort, R. (2012). The ways of creating resilient supply chains. Paper presented at the *Carpathian Logistics Congress*.

Wieland, A., & Wallenburg, C. M. (2013). The influence of relational competencies on supply chain resilience: A relational view. *International Journal of Physical Distribution and Logistics Management, 43*(4), 300–320. https://doi.org/10.1108/IJPDLM-08-2012-0243

Wildavsky, A. B. (1988). *Searching for safety*. Transaction Publishers.

Wilding, R. D. (2013). Supply chain temple of resilience. *Logistics and Transport focus, 15*, 54–58.

Zavala-Alcívar, A., Verdecho, M.-J., & Alfaro-Saiz, J.-J. (2020). A conceptual framework to manage resilience and increase sustainability in the supply chain. *Sustainability, 12*(16), 6300.

Zsidisin, G. A., & Wagner, S. M. (2010). Do perceptions become reality? The moderating role of supply chain resiliency on disruption occurrence. *Journal of Business Logistics, 31*(2), 1–20. https://doi.org/10.1002/j.2158-1592.2010.tb00140.x

Alexander M. Geske is Research Associate at the Institute for Transport and Logistics Management at WU (Vienna University of Economics and Business). He has earned a bachelor's degree in International Business Administration and a master's degree in Supply Chain Management. With a professional career in the transportation industry, Alexander combines the practical and academic perspective.

Lydia Novoszel is Research Associate at the Institute for Transport and Logistics management at WU (Vienna University of Economics and Business). With an international professional career in supply chain management, she incorporates practical relevance and perspectives in supply chain disruption research. Lydia has earned a master's degree in Mechanical Engineering and a master's degree in Business Administration.

Chapter 2
Supply Chain Resilience: A Decade of Evolvement

Alexandra Anderluh and Michael Herburger

Abstract Supply chain resilience is a topic that has been gaining increasing importance over the last decade. During these few years, resilience in the field of supply chains has already undergone a change of understanding reaching from the ability of a supply chain to get back in the original state after a disruption via the ability to provide system functions in the face of shocks and stresses to the ability to persist, adapt or transform when facing a significant change. In addition, despite the short research period, numerous scientific publications tackling the resilience of supply chains can already be found. Therefore, we provide a classification of relevant papers found by a systematic literature review. The classification focuses on the type of disruption, the research methods used, and the sectors addressed. Furthermore, we point out research gaps that can serve as a basis for further research in supply chain resilience.

2.1 Introduction

The topic of supply chain resilience (SCRES) has been evolving since the 2000s, and, in the last few years, SCRES has become increasingly important. Especially the COVID-19 pandemic had—and still has—a significant impact on this field of research as it pointed out the vulnerability of our complex global supply chains in a drastic way.

In the last few years, SCRES has undergone a change of understanding which can be seen in the different definitions of this topic. While Mensah et al. (2014) state that resilience in general is "the ability of a substance to get back to its original state after

A. Anderluh (✉)
Carl Ritter von Ghega Institute for Integrated Mobility Research, St. Pölten University of Applied Sciences, St. Pölten, Austria
e-mail: alexandra.anderluh@fhstp.ac.at

M. Herburger
Logistikum Steyr, University of Applied Sciences Upper Austria, Steyr, Austria

Department of Operations Management, Copenhagen Business School, Copenhagen, Denmark

S. Kummer et al. (eds.), *Supply Chain Resilience*, Springer Series in Supply Chain Management 17, https://doi.org/10.1007/978-3-030-95401-7_2

deformation, [but] there is still no concrete definition of a 'resilient supply chain' or 'supply chain resilience'," Meuwissen et al. (2019) defined it as "its ability to ensure the provision of the system functions in the face of increasingly complex and accumulating economic, social, environmental and institutional shocks and stresses, through capacities of robustness, adaptability, and transformability." A similar definition can be found in Gölgeci and Kuivalainen (2020) and Behzadi et al. (2020), who see SCRES as the ability to recover quickly from disruptive events, while Caputo et al. (2019) describe this ability also as a kind of performance measure. Currently, Wieland and Durach (2021) combine engineering resilience with social-ecological resilience which results in defining SCRES as "the capacity of a supply chain to persist, adapt, or transform in the face of change."

2.2 Problem Framing

Although SCRES is a topic dealt with for less than two decades, there exist already several literature reviews, each with a specific focus, for example:

- Klibi et al. (2010) dealing with supply chain networks
- Ivanov et al. (2015) reviewing research on the ripple effect in supply chains
- Heckmann et al. (2015) dealing with quantitative management approaches
- Kamalahmadi and Parast (2016) analyzing SCRES principles and strategies
- Elleuch et al. (2016), Graça and Camarinha-Matos (2017), Behzadi et al. (2020) dealing with performance measurement, indicators, and metrics
- Thomé et al. (2016) reviewing research papers for multi-organization projects
- Parkouhi and Ghadikolaei (2017) focusing on supplier selection issues
- Behzadi et al. (2018), Hosseini et al. (2019), Emenike and Falcone (2020) dealing with quantitative models and methods with a focus on Bayesian networks in Hosseini and Ivanov (2020) and on simulation optimization methods in Tordecilla et al. (2021)
- Higashi et al. (2020) dealing with organizational failures
- Shashi et al. (2020) dealing with the potential of agile supply chains
- Meyer (2020), Barbosa (2021), Ali et al. (2021) giving an overview of resilience in food supply chains with a special focus on COVID-19 in the latter one
- Aldrighetti et al. (2021) dealing with costs of SCRES
- Chowdhury et al. (2021) dealing with COVID-19-related supply chain studies
- Bui et al. (2021) analyzing trends in the field of sustainable supply chains

In contrast to that, in this paper, we conducted a meta-review on existing SCRES literature to give an overview of the evolvement of this field of research. With the combined search term "supply chain" *and (resilient or resilience)* in the category "title, abstract, keywords" we searched www.sciencedirect.com, which yielded 395 English papers (review and research articles). After searching the abstracts in more detail, 353 papers were left, starting in the year 2008 till the end of the first quarter of 2021.

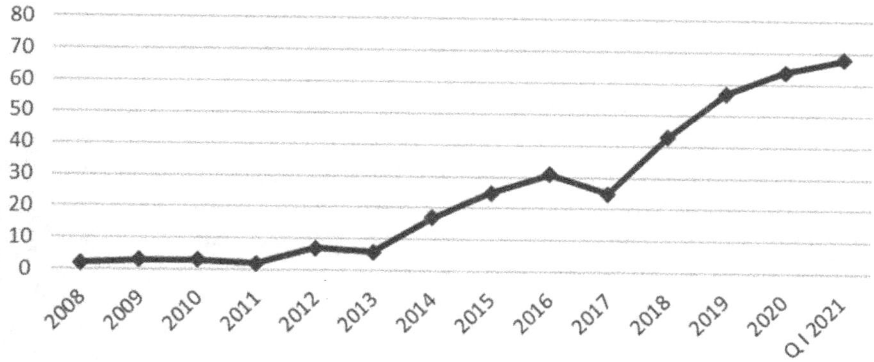

Fig. 2.1 SCRES publications per year

Figure 2.1 shows that, starting in the year 2008 at a low level and staying there for several years, the number of papers published per year has been increasing significantly since 2014 with many publications in the first quarter of 2021 (Q I 2021), which already exceeds that of the year 2020. This trend underlines the growing importance of SCRES.

2.3 Meta-analysis of Selected Literature

In this chapter, the selected literature is analyzed concerning types of disruption, research methods used, and sectors tackled.

2.3.1 Types of Disruption

Figure 2.2 depicts the changes over time of the main disruptions tackled in the literature. The focus on pandemic impact due to the COVID-19 outbreak in 2020 is clearly reflected in the SCRES literature. Before 2020 a pandemic disruption was rarely dealt with in the literature. There is only one paper from 2018 (Aviso et al., 2018) that focuses on the impact of a pandemic, but, otherwise, only natural disasters like droughts, earthquakes, and floods, man-made disasters like terror attacks or heavy accidents as well as disasters in general are typically addressed in literature. Other risks that get increasing attention in the latest literature are financial risks and cyberattacks.

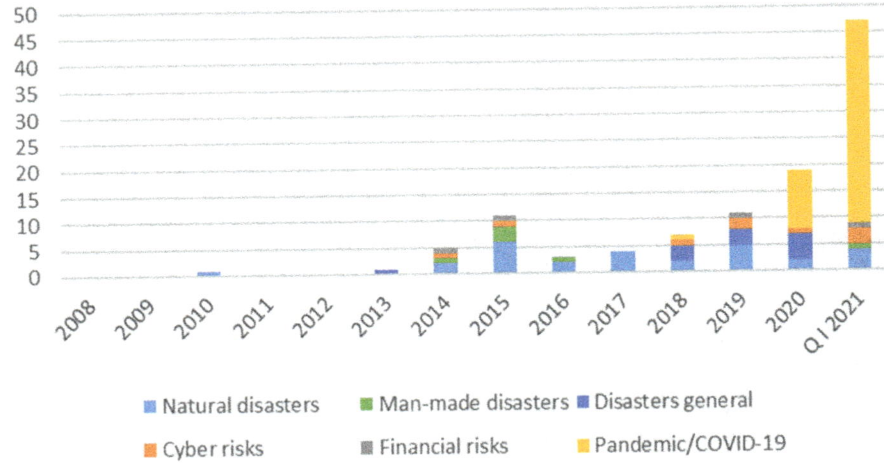

Fig. 2.2 Types of disruption

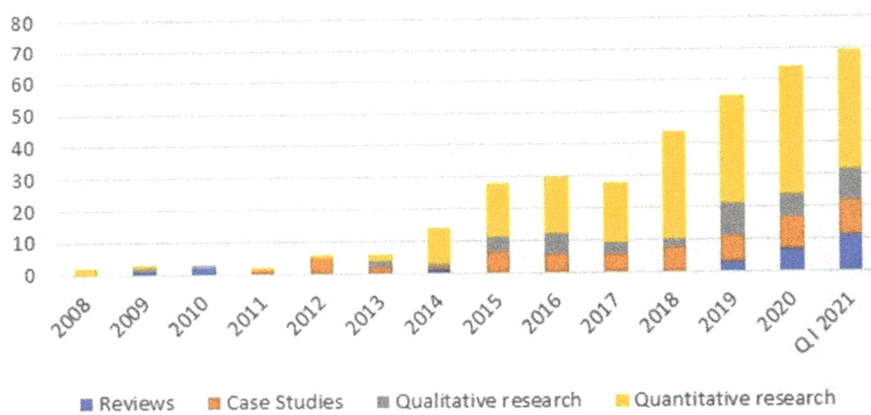

Fig. 2.3 Research methods used

2.3.2 *Research Methods Used*

The focus of this analysis is laid on the main research method used in the SCRES papers. Figure 2.3 shows that the majority of papers since 2014 deals with quantitative research approaches (e.g., optimization models, simulation models), and this number is still increasing. Case studies and qualitative research approaches (e.g., expert interviews, Delphi method) are rather stable over the last few years, while the number of reviews published shows a significant increase over this period.

2.3.3 Sectors Addressed

We identified six main sectors—energy/water, food/agriculture, raw materials/mining, health/pharmaceuticals, manufacturing/construction, and transportation/logistics—in the selected papers. Figure 2.4 summarizes the distribution of these sectors over time. Remarkable is the significant increase in food-related papers in the first quarter of 2021 that deal to a large extent with food security and the situation in low- and middle-income countries due to COVID-19. The sectors energy/water and health/pharmaceuticals are also increasing slightly, while the sectors raw material/mining and transportation/logistics are stagnating. The sector manufacturing/construction is rather stable over the years.

2.4 Relevance of the Review

The meta-review on SCRES points out trends and research gaps in this field of research. What can be seen in the previous section is the major impact of the COVID-19 pandemic since 2020. Remarkable is the fact that especially food supply chains and food security have gained increasing importance, while a similar trend for other critical materials/products (e.g., medical equipment) cannot be recognized.

Financial and cyber risks are disruptions rarely addressed in literature. Especially the latter should get increased attention because today's supply chains are increasingly digitalized and hence more and more vulnerable to cyberattacks.

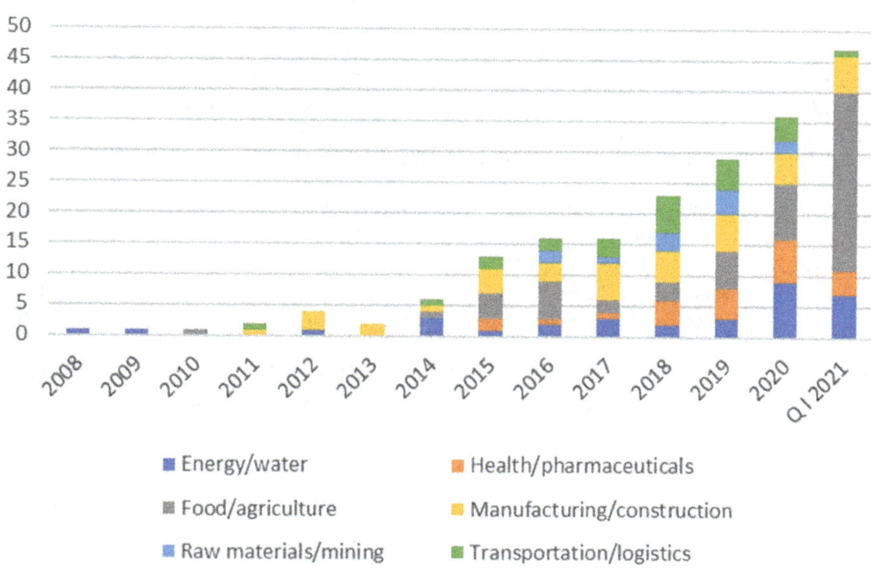

Fig. 2.4 Sectors addressed

The research methods used show the focus on quantitative approaches to support decision-making. Especially the coverage of uncertainties/stochastic aspects has gained increasing attention in the last few years, and a growing application of a combination of simulation and optimization can be seen in the SCRES literature.

2.5 Conclusion

In this paper we give insights into the increasing importance of SCRES over the last decade based on a meta-review of literature. This review points out the evolvement of the topic with respect to the types of disruptions addressed, to the research methods used, and to the sectors focused on.

On the other hand, we identified research gaps, for example, the impact of specific risks (financial risks, cyber risks) on supply chains that have hardly been covered yet. Hence, in the field of supply chain resilience, there are still huge gaps in the literature that can be addressed by future research activities in the years to come.

References

Aldrighetti, R., Battini, D., Ivanov, D., & Zennaro, I. (2021). Costs of resilience and disruptions in supply chain network design models: A review and future research directions. *International Journal of Production Economics, 235*, 108103. https://doi.org/10.1016/j.ijpe.2021.108103

Ali, M. H., Suleiman, N., Khalid, N., Tan, K. H., Tseng, M.-L., & Kumar, M. (2021). Supply chain resilience reactive strategies for food SMEs in coping to COVID-19 crisis. *Trends in Food Science and Technology, 109*, 94–102. https://doi.org/10.1016/j.tifs.2021.01.021

Aviso, K. B., et al. (2018). Allocating human resources in organizations operating under crisis conditions: A fuzzy input-output optimization modeling framework. *Resources, Conservation and Recycling, 128*, 250–258. https://doi.org/10.1016/j.resconrec.2016.07.009

Barbosa, M. W. (2021). Uncovering research streams on agri-food supply chain management: A bibliometric study. *Global Food Security, 28*, 100517. https://doi.org/10.1016/j.gfs.2021.100517

Behzadi, G., O'Sullivan, M. J., Olsen, T. L., & Zhang, A. (2018). Agribusiness supply chain risk management: A review of quantitative decision models. *Omega, 79*, 21–42. https://doi.org/10.1016/j.omega.2017.07.005

Behzadi, G., O'Sullivan, M. J., & Olsen, T. L. (2020). On metrics for supply chain resilience. *European Journal of Operational Research, 287*(1), 145–158. https://doi.org/10.1016/j.ejor.2020.04.040

Bui, T.-D., Tsai, F. M., Tseng, M.-L., Tan, R. R., Yu, K. D. S., & Lim, M. K. (2021). Sustainable supply chain management towards disruption and organizational ambidexterity: A data driven analysis. *Sustainable Production and Consumption, 26*, 373–410. https://doi.org/10.1016/j.spc.2020.09.017

Caputo, A. C., Pelagagge, P. M., & Salini, P. (2019). A methodology to estimate resilience of manufacturing plants. *IFAC-Papers OnLine, 52*(13), 808–813. https://doi.org/10.1016/j.ifacol.2019.11.229

Chowdhury, P., Paul, S. K., Kaisar, S., & Moktadir, M. A. (2021). COVID-19 pandemic related supply chain studies: A systematic review. *Transportation Research Part E: Logistics and Transportation Review, 148*, 102271. https://doi.org/10.1016/j.tre.2021.102271

Elleuch, H., Dafaoui, E., Elmhamedi, A., & Chabchoub, H. (2016). Resilience and vulnerability in supply chain: Literature review. *IFAC-PapersOnLine, 49*(12), 1448–1453. https://doi.org/10.1016/j.ifacol.2016.07.775

Emenike, S. N., & Falcone, G. (2020). A review on energy supply chain resilience through optimization. *Renewable and Sustainable Energy Reviews, 134*, 110088. https://doi.org/10.1016/j.rser.2020.110088

Gölgeci, I., & Kuivalainen, O. (2020). Does social capital matter for supply chain resilience? The role of absorptive capacity and marketing-supply chain management alignment. *Industrial Marketing Management, 84*, 63–74. https://doi.org/10.1016/j.indmarman.2019.05.006

Graça, P., & Camarinha-Matos, L. M. (2017). Performance indicators for collaborative business ecosystems—Literature review and trends. *Technological Forecasting and Social Change, 116*, 237–255. https://doi.org/10.1016/j.techfore.2016.10.012

Heckmann, I., Comes, T., & Nickel, S. (2015). A critical review on supply chain risk – Definition, measure and modeling. *Omega, 52*, 119–132. https://doi.org/10.1016/j.omega.2014.10.004

Higashi, S. Y., de Caleman, Q., de Aguiar, L. K., & Manning, L. (2020). What causes organizations to fail? A review of literature to inform future food sector (management) research. *Trends in Food Science & Technology, 101*, 223–233. https://doi.org/10.1016/j.tifs.2020.05.011

Hosseini, S., & Ivanov, D. (2020). Bayesian networks for supply chain risk, resilience and ripple effect analysis: A literature review. *Expert Systems with Applications, 161*, 113649. https://doi.org/10.1016/j.eswa.2020.113649

Hosseini, S., Ivanov, D., & Dolgui, A. (2019). Review of quantitative methods for supply chain resilience analysis. *Transportation Research Part E: Logistics and Transportation Review, 125*, 285–307. https://doi.org/10.1016/j.tre.2019.03.001

Ivanov, D., Dolgui, A., & Sokolov, B. (2015). Supply chain design with disruption considerations: Review of research streams on the ripple effect in the supply chain. *IFAC-PapersOnLine, 48*(3), 1700–1707. https://doi.org/10.1016/j.ifacol.2015.06.331

Kamalahmadi, M., & Parast, M. M. (2016). A review of the literature on the principles of enterprise and supply chain resilience: Major findings and directions for future research. *International Journal of Production Economics, 171*, 116–133. https://doi.org/10.1016/j.ijpe.2015.10.023

Klibi, W., Martel, A., & Guitouni, A. (2010). The design of robust value-creating supply chain networks: A critical review. *European Journal of Operational Research, 203*(2), 283–293. https://doi.org/10.1016/j.ejor.2009.06.011

Mensah, P., Merkuryev, Y., & Manak, S. (2014). Developing a resilient supply chain strategy by exploiting ICT. *Procedia Computer Science, 77*, 65–71. https://doi.org/10.1016/j.procs.2015.12.360

Meuwissen, M. P. M., et al. (2019). A framework to assess the resilience of farming systems. *Agricultural Systems, 176*, 102656. https://doi.org/10.1016/j.agsy.2019.102656

Meyer, M. A. (2020). The role of resilience in food system studies in low- and middle-income countries. *Global Food Security, 24*, 100356. https://doi.org/10.1016/j.gfs.2020.100356

Parkouhi, S. V., & Ghadikolaei, A. S. (2017). A resilience approach for supplier selection: Using Fuzzy Analytic Network Process and grey VIKOR techniques. *Journal of Cleaner Production, 161*, 431–451. https://doi.org/10.1016/j.jclepro.2017.04.175

Shashi, P., Centobelli, R. C., & Ertz, M. (2020). Agile supply chain management: where did it come from and where will it go in the era of digital transformation? *Industrial Marketing Management, 90*, 324–345. https://doi.org/10.1016/j.indmarman.2020.07.011

Thomé, A. M. T., Scavarda, L. F., Scavarda, A., & de Thom, S. (2016). Similarities and contrasts of complexity, uncertainty, risks, and resilience in supply chains and temporary multi-organization projects. *International Journal of Project Management, 34*(7), 1328–1346. https://doi.org/10.1016/j.ijproman.2015.10.012

Tordecilla, R. D., Juan, A. A., Montoya-Torres, J. R., Quintero-Araujo, C. L., & Panadero, J. (2021). Simulation-optimization methods for designing and assessing resilient supply chain networks under uncertainty scenarios: A review. *Simulation Modelling Practice and Theory, 106*, 102166. https://doi.org/10.1016/j.simpat.2020.102166

Wieland, A., & Durach, C. F. (2021). Two perspectives on supply chain resilience. *Journal of Business Logistics, n/a*, 1–8. https://doi.org/10.1111/jbl.12271

Alexandra Anderluh is Senior Researcher at the Carl Ritter von Ghega Institute for Integrated Mobility Research at the St. Pölten University of Applied Sciences, Department Rail Technology & Mobility. She has earned a doctoral degree in Supply Chain Management at WU (Vienna University of Economics and Business). Within the institute she is in charge of numerous research projects in the field of sustainability and resilience in logistics and she authored various publications in high-ranked journals with special focus on sustainable logistics and operations research.

Michael Herburger is Research Project Manager in the department of Supply Chain Management at the University of Applied Sciences Upper Austria, Logistikum Steyr. Within the department he is head of the research team Supply Chain Risk Management, Resilience and Security with a focus on cyber risks/security in supply chains. He earned university degrees in law, logistics management and supply chain management, is currently a PhD student at Copenhagen Business School and author of numerous publications.

Chapter 3
Supply Chain Resilience Framework

Lydia Novoszel

Abstract This framework is based on Kochan and Nowicki (International Journal of Physical Distribution and Logistics Management 48(8), 842–865, 2018) and serves as overarching structure to link the various book contributions and theoretical concepts. Enhanced by additional elements derived from literature and industry feedback, this new framework links to the respective book chapters and outlines a structure for further supply chain resilience research and practical supply chain resilience investigations.

3.1 Introduction

Various definitions of resilience and supply chain resilience constructs exist (see Chap. 1). This chapter aims to introduce an overarching supply chain resilience typology based on the literature review from Chap. 2, industry feedback, and Kochan and Nowicki (2018). Kochan and Nowicki (2018) established a framework based on a structured literature review. The context-intervention-mechanism-outcome (CIMO) approach from Denyer and Tranfield (2009) is used to investigate how supply chain capabilities and vulnerabilities create specific outcomes within the context of supply chain resilience. This chapter is structured as follows: first the framework and elements of Kochan and Nowicki (2018) are described. Next, the typology is enhanced by additional elements derived from literature and industry feedback. Finally, the new framework links to the respective book chapters and outlines a structure for further supply chain resilience research and practical supply chain resilience investigations.

L. Novoszel (✉)
Institute for Transport and Logistics Management, WU (Vienna University of Economics and Business), Vienna, Austria
e-mail: lydia.novoszel@wu.ac.at

S. Kummer et al. (eds.), *Supply Chain Resilience*, Springer Series in Supply Chain Management 17, https://doi.org/10.1007/978-3-030-95401-7_3

3.2 Supply Chain Resilience Typological Framework from Kochan and Nowicki (2018)

Amid the COVID-19 pandemic, multiple publications have been conceptualizing supply chain resilience from different perspectives and methodological approaches; see, for example, Zavala-Alcívar et al. (2020) and Ribeiro and Barbosa-Póvoa (2019). We selected the Kochan and Nowicki (2018) typology due to the closeness of search criteria and method of Chap. 2. The basis is formed by 228 peer-reviewed journal articles (from 2000 to 2017) with similar search strings "supply chain* *and* resilient*" as in Chap. 2. This indicates a similar study design as was used in Chap. 2, with 353 papers within the period of 2008 until the first quarter of 2021.

Based on a structured literature review and applying the CIMO logic from Denyer and Tranfield (2009), the typology in Fig. 3.1 is derived. Different industry sectors build the context (C), where supply chain disruptions and supply chain risks determine communalities across industries. Disruptions can have (supply chain) internal and external causes. Supply chain risks are closely related to supply chain vulnerabilities. Risk assessment and risk management are critical elements of supply chain resilience, yet not sufficient to address unexpected disruptions. Interventions (I) are addressed through supply chain vulnerabilities and supply chain capabilities. For more details of supply chain capabilities, refer to Pettit et al. (2010), Chaps. 1 (Definitions) and 17 (Delphi Study Outcome). Vulnerabilities, such as financial, resource, and design constraints, drive a supply chain's exposure to risks and disturbances and thus determine interventions for supply chain resilience. Achieving a specific outcome requires certain mechanisms (M) (Denyer & Tranfield, 2009). Kochan and Nowicki (2018) identified 20 theories (e.g., resource-based view, dynamic capability theory, or contingency theory) to investigate supply chain resilience research. Supply chain resilience outcomes (O) are based on Pettit et al. (2010), where performance is a function of balancing capabilities and vulnerabilities.

This typological framework highlights the need to understand vulnerabilities and capabilities of the respective supply chain in order to develop mitigation strategies and understand influencing factors for supply chain resilience (Kochan & Nowicki, 2018).

3.3 Enhanced Supply Chain Resilience Framework

In order to establish a holistic state-of-the-art view on supply chain resilience, the framework is enhanced. We take multiple scientific views, industry feedback, and recent academic trends into consideration. The proposed new framework can serve as a tool for supply chain practitioners, scholars, and academics to understand their supply chain resilience circumstances. It also structures the elements of this book. Figure 3.2 introduces the new framework and highlights the added elements.

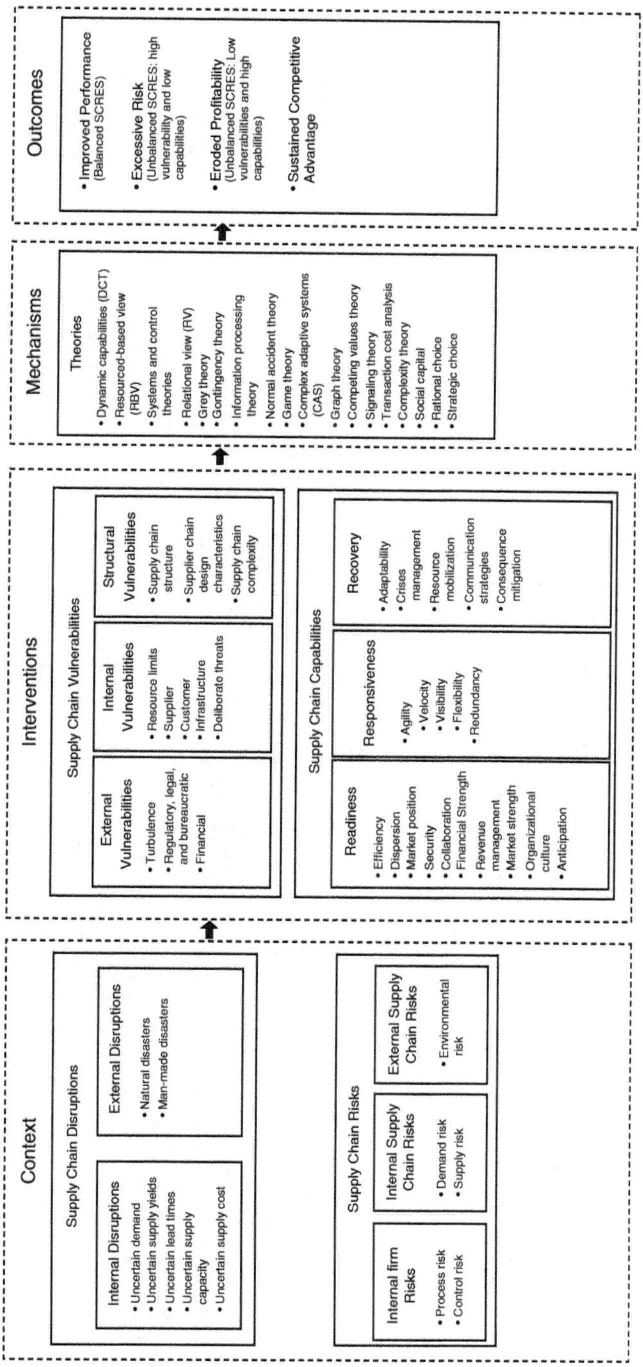

Fig. 3.1 Typology of SCRES (supply chain resilience) based on the CIMO logic; source (Kochan & Nowicki, 2018)

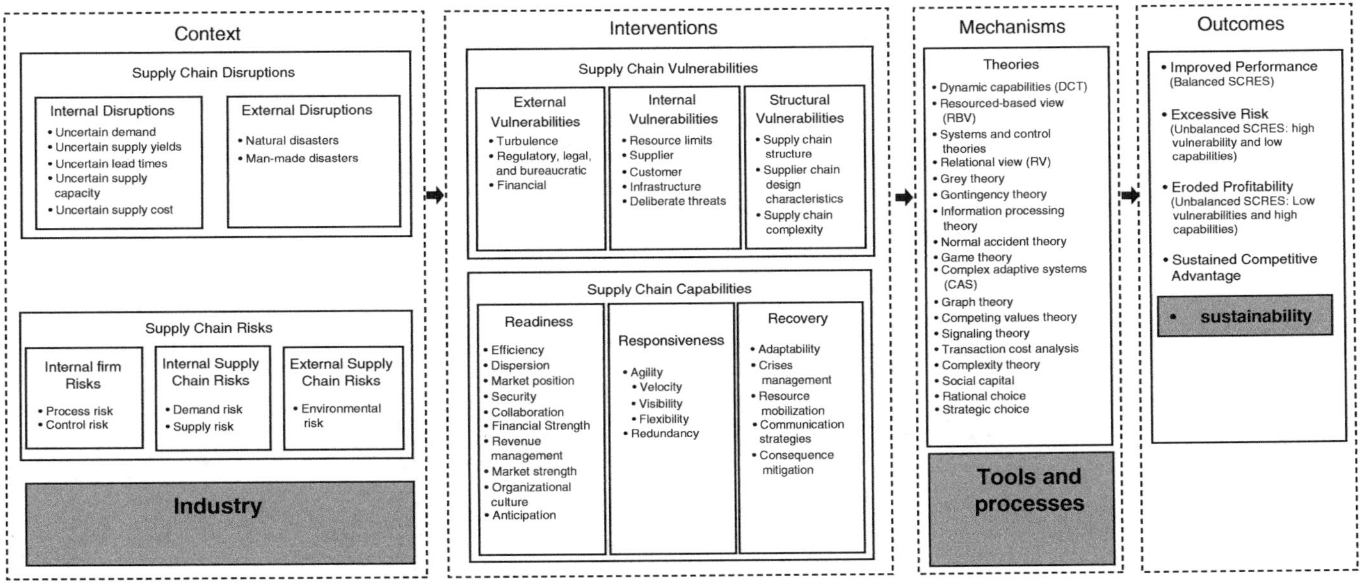

Fig. 3.2 Enhanced supply chain resilience framework based on Kochan and Nowicki (2018)

Various chapters of the book as well as the literature review from Chap. 2 highlight details on different supply chain disruptions (man-made disaster, natural disasters) and vulnerabilities. Within the context dimension, we add industry as a factor. Kochan and Nowicki (2018) investigated different industries, such as energy, military, retail, automotive, and humanitarian. The literature review from Chap. 2 identifies six main sections: energy/water, food/agriculture, raw materials/mining, health/pharmaceuticals, manufacturing/construction, and transportation/logistics, which were used to research supply chain resilience. The respective industry highlights supply chain design and network characteristics which determine the value chain's strategy (Porter, 1985). In Parts 5 and 6 use cases from different industries show exemplarily how supply chain resilience is applied. For further analysis, it might be useful to understand the supply chain function and role in the company as well as the company's position in the network. The alignment of various business objectives and the business model is relevant for maximizing the supply chain surplus (Chopra, 2019) and thus can be considered when investigating supply chain resilience. These elements find also consideration as part of the structural supply chain vulnerabilities within the interventions dimension.

Research theories serve as mechanisms for researchers to investigate supply chain resilience. The literature review in Chap. 2 highlights the methods used from a scientific perspective. Tools and processes help practitioners to drive interventions that lead to outcomes. Tools support the execution of the steps, whereas processes determine the steps for the three flows in the value chain: goods or services, funds, and information. Information serves as a key supply chain driver, because it provides visibility for decision-making. Information technology consists of the tools used in the supply chain to gain awareness, analyze and execute processes as well as communication, which serves as the basis for collaboration (Chopra, 2019). Therefore, the tools and processes used in the supply chain (e.g., risk detection and classification, supply and operations planning) and technological trends (such as artificial intelligence and blockchain) are relevant for supply chain resilience.

Kochan and Nowicki (2018) based the outcome dimension on performance as a function of balancing capabilities and vulnerabilities as introduced by Pettit et al. (2010). As ecological and social sustainability become key priorities in designing and operating supply chains (Chopra, 2019), we propose to explicitly add it into the framework as an objective.

In summary, the enhanced supply chain resilience framework is based on the work of Kochan and Nowicki (2018), the recent systematic literature review from Chap. 2, and insights from practitioners via their use cases and the Delphi Study from Chap. 17. The context dimension describes the risks, disruptions and respective industries of a supply chain. Interventions are triggered by and from supply chain vulnerabilities and capabilities. Theories (e.g., resource-based view and graph theory) are mechanisms within the scientific approach to transform interventions into outcomes, whereas tools and processes can serve as practical mechanisms. The outcomes for supply chain resilience can be improved performance, excessive risk, eroded profitability, sustained competitive advantage, and supply chain sustainability.

Table 3.1 Enhanced supply chain resilience framework linked to book chapters

Context	Interventions	Mechanisms	Outcomes
Supply chain disruptions	Supply chain vulnerabilities	Theories	• Improved performance
4	8	1	•7
5	29	2	• Excessive risk
		3	• 11, 18
Supply chain risks		Tools and processes	• Eroded profitability
6		7	• 18
11		8	• Sustained competitive advantage
Industry/sector	Supply chain capabilities	9	• 7, 9
18, 19, 20, 21, 22, 23	1	10	• Ecological and social sustainability
24, 25, 26, 27, 28, 29	16	14	• 8, 12, 28
		16	

3.4 Relevance and Limitations

This enhanced framework can serve as a possible perspective to understand different elements of supply chain resilience research and how it manifests in commercial and not-for-profit supply chains. It is based on an exploratory view of previous literature and most recent trends amid the COVID-19 pandemic. Additional methods and studies may lead to different perspectives, which are not considered at this point. This supply chain resilience framework links to different chapters of the book (see Table 3.1): Chap. 1 addresses supply chain resilience definitions and capabilities. Parts 2 and 3 cover tools and processes from academic and practical perspectives by sharing use cases and theoretical contributions. The Delphi Study documented in Chap. 17 adds to the framework with additional information on best practices, relevance of processes and capabilities, as well as future research opportunities.

References

Chopra, S. (2019). *Supply chain management: Strategy, planning, and operation*. 7th edn, Global edition. Pearson.

Denyer, D., & Tranfield, D. (2009). Chapter 39: Producing a systematic review. In D. Buchanan & A. Bryman (Eds.), *The Sage handbook of organizational research methods* (pp. 671–689). Editors Sage Publications Ltd.

Kochan, C., & Nowicki, D. R. (2018). Supply chain resilience: A systematic literature review and typological framework. *International Journal of Physical Distribution and Logistics Management, 48*(8), 842–865. https://doi.org/10.1108/IJPDLM-02-2017-0099

Pettit, T. J., Fiksel, J., & Croxton, K. L. (2010). Ensuring supply chain resilience: Development of a conceptual framework. *Journal of Business Logistics, 31*(1), 1–21. https://doi.org/10.1002/j.2158-1592.2010.tb00125.x

Porter, M. E., & Kramer, M. R. (1985). *Advantage. Creating and sustaining superior performance* (pp. 56–68). Simons.

Ribeiro, J. P., & Barbosa-Póvoa, A. (2019). Supply chain resilience: An optimisation model to identify the relative importance of SC disturbances. In M. J. Alves, J. P. Almeida, J. F. Oliveira, & A. A. Pinto (Eds.), *Operational research* (pp. 189–198). Springer International Publishing.

Zavala-Alcívar, A., Verdecho, M.-J., & Alfaro-Saiz, J.-J. (2020). A conceptual framework to manage resilience and increase sustainability in the supply chain. *Sustainability, 12*(16), 6300. https://doi.org/10.3390/su12166300

Lydia Novoszel is Research Associate at the Institute for Transport and Logistics Management at WU (Vienna University of Economics and Business). With an international professional career in supply chain management, she incorporates practical relevance and perspectives in supply chain disruption research. Lydia has earned a master's degree in Mechanical Engineering and a master's degree in Business Administration.

Chapter 4
Supply Chain Challenges During the COVID-19 Pandemic

Lydia Novoszel and Tina Wakolbinger

Abstract The COVID-19 pandemic is triggering multiple disruptions on supply, distribution and demand side as well as the propagation between supply chain nodes. Many companies are dealing with challenges due to these disruptions while others are seizing opportunities. This chapter provides examples of affected supply chains and how they cope with the situation and outlines future open supply chain issues.

4.1 Introduction

The spread of the corona virus has been affecting supply chains on multiple levels. While the crisis impacted many companies in a negative way, it also provided new opportunities for others. This chapter provides examples of affected supply chains and how they coped with the situation. Finally, the chapter links to other sections of the book and summarizes open topics.

4.2 Supply Chain Disruptions Due to COVID-19

Supply chain disruptions are unanticipated and unplanned events and occurrences that disrupt the regular flow of goods and materials within supply chain processes (Svensson, 2000; Hendricks & Singhal, 2005; Kleindorfer & Saad, 2005). During the COVID-19 pandemic, various disruptions to supply, demand, distribution, and infrastructure nodes have been happening in supply chains (Rodrigue, 2020; Ivanov, 2021).

Corporate organizations were impacted by supply disruptions, increased and shifted demands, and constraints with respect to distribution. Moreover, increased

L. Novoszel (✉) · T. Wakolbinger
Institute for Transport and Logistics Management, WU (Vienna University of Economics and Business), Vienna, Austria
e-mail: lydia.novoszel@wu.ac.at

S. Kummer et al. (eds.), *Supply Chain Resilience*, Springer Series in Supply Chain Management 17, https://doi.org/10.1007/978-3-030-95401-7_4

health and safety compliance needs put a strain on operational procedures and employee availability. Below, we indicate how the individual elements of supply chains were affected by the corona crisis.

A supply disruption occurs when the supply of parts necessary to perform a downstream task is not available when needed (this includes less quantities, delays in delivery, or poor quality) (Dudley, 2020; Rodrigue, 2020; Souza, 2020). Suppliers during the COVID-19 pandemic might struggle with limited raw material availability due to reduced mining activities, export bans, or interruptions in the transport routes. The suppliers' production capacity and quality might be reduced due to lack of trained labor and less efficient production processes due to novel health and safety regulations. Additionally limited financial resources might put a strain on a supplier's performance. Examples of supply disruptions during the crisis are availability of parts for bicycles, construction materials, and computer chips (Souza, 2020; Attinasi et al., 2021; Keshner, 2021).

Distribution activities and processes ensure the material flow from providers to users. Changes in supply and demand influenced transportation capacities for goods. Additionally, reduced passenger air travel led to limited air cargo space, since belly capacity in the aircrafts was not available. People were less mobile, due to stay-at-home orders, which impacted road transport and increased delivery service needs. The details of their role, disruptions, and implications during the pandemic are discussed in Chap. 5.

On the demand side, disruptions occur due to changed customer needs (Gupta & Maranas, 2003). Shifts in market requirements arise amid changing behavior (e.g., home office, closed restaurants, and travel restrictions) as well as increased demand because of additional applications (e.g., facemasks, ventilators, hand sanitizers, vaccines). Additionally psychological phenomena such as hoarding trigger demand spikes or damps (e.g., toilet paper or essential groceries such as rice or pasta). These changes of demand patterns might also spark additional (and potentially underexplored) market opportunities for cooperation. In this case, disruptions trigger (product) innovations (Gaimon & Ramachandran, 2021) while companies are using their capabilities (Cohen & Levinthal, 1990) to repurpose their resources (processes, technologies, people, machinery/facilities) (Liu et al., 2021; Omezzine et al., 2022). The concepts how demand disruptions trigger innovation and the role of supply chains have been investigated previously by Lee (see for example Triple A supply chain Lee (2004) and Lee and Schmidt (2017)).

Supply chains and supply networks are interdependent and collaborative constructs of multiple stakeholders within an environment. The activities (and output of goods or information) of one supply chain node may affect the subsequent levels. The disturbances occurring in one node (or section) of the supply chain do not stay isolated within the confined boundaries of the company but spread across the supply chain and its actors. The propagation of the risk, and thus of the disruption, is described by the bullwhip and ripple effects. The bullwhip effect (Lee et al., 1997, 2004) is the phenomenon that occurs with limited information flow up the supply chain in case of a sudden demand change. The changes in order quantities (on the operational level) across the supply chain trigger increased changes to the outputs of the previous stage, leading to increased stock levels or stock-outs and changes in lead times. Examples in the COVID-19 crisis are the toilet paper stock-outs on super market shelves. The ripple effect considers the structural dynamics of the supply chain network and describes the phenomenon when a severe disturbance in one node of the supply chain propagates through other nodes. In extreme cases, the ripple effect can lead to unavailability of a supply chain node (e.g., of a supplier) and has major supply chain network performance implications (Ivanov et al., 2014, 2019)

4.3 Supply Chain Disruptions in Various Industries

In the following section, three examples show how supply chains got impacted end-to-end by COVID-19.

The construction industry was exposed to multiple disruptions due to the COVID-19 pandemic. Negative effects include, for example, material availability challenges, material price increases, and productivity decline because of operational changes for construction workers and significant delays on projects due to various reasons. New opportunities occurred linked to fast-track construction of medical facilities, construction of residential buildings, and transportation infrastructure related work (Alsharef et al., 2021; Hatoum et al., 2021). Innovative technologies, such as increased usage of BIM (building information modelling) and RFID tags, are implemented to cope with the recent challenges (Bousquin, 2021; Thibault, 2021). While the industry has established coping mechanisms and best practices (Bou Hatoum et al., 2021) and overcame high infection rates (Bui et al., 2020; Bousquin, 2021; Thibault, 2021), material shortages remain high. Due to supply constraints and demand spikes, material availability and prices for, e.g., lumber and steel, are still critical (Brandt & Hoffower, 2021; Capitol Technology University, 2021; Conerly, 2021; Construction News, 2021; Schwartz, 2021; World Construction Today, 2021).

Another example of implications of supply chain disruptions and the need for supply chain resilience is the global chip shortage. The demand for chips increased because of more electronic equipment required for home office and schools, communications infrastructure investments, and other semiconductor industry applications (Burkacky et al., 2021; Wu et al., 2021). The constraints and concentration for critical raw materials for the semiconductor industry have been previously addressed by the European Commission (European Commission, 2014). Additionally, production capacities are not sufficient (due to lowered forecasts as a result of perceived COVID-19 uncertainty (Moore, 2021) to keep up with current demand). Moreover, local adverse events such as fires and droughts influence manufacturing. Trade frictions and shipping disruptions call for more resilient chip supply chains (Wu et al., 2021; Moore, 2021; Attinasi et al., 2021). The shortage of chips, as a relevant part for automotive assembly, is creating a bottleneck and is thus a root cause for reduced production (Tribe, 2021). Further details are provided in Chap. 26.

For the retail industry, the pandemic exposed multiple disruptions along the value chain (Goddard, 2020; Souza, 2020). Fulfilling grocery needs for the community is an essential task, and thus the system relevance of the sector and its employees became evident amid the crisis. Retail stores have an essential role in balancing supply shortages and demand increases. Hoarding of essential products, such as toilet paper (Esper, 2021; Paul & Chowdhury, 2020; Harvard Business School, 2021) and pasta, lead to short-term empty shelves, displaying the bullwhip effect to the general public. From an operational perspective, processes were adapted for employees to account for distancing, hygiene, and safety measures (Goddard, 2020).

4.4 New Opportunities Provided by the COVID-19 Pandemic

Opportunities might occur in disruptive situations as well. The global need and awareness of ventilators, to help COVID-19 patients, triggered a repurposing (Omezzine et al., 2022; Liu et al., 2021) initiative in the manufacturing industry. Various (for example) car manufacturers (Volkswagen AG News, 2020) adopted their production and assembly lines to build ventilators. Rapid product design, development, government authorization (Canada, 2021), and global collaboration accelerated the activities (Netland, 2020; Albergotti & Siddiqui, 2020).

The global demand for COVID-19 vaccines (and complementary products) provided opportunities for companies that responded quickly to this need. First, the know how (Hopkins, 2021), new technologies and the accelerated approval processes ensured the development of a new vaccine. Second, the ramp-up of production capacities and the raw material accessibility made the product available. The development of new packaging requirements was necessary to deal with temperature and transportation constraints. Distribution capacity was created to deliver the goods to the vaccination centers. The local administration of the vaccines and ramp-up of the infrastructure to administer the jabs for the people needed to be established (DHL, 2021). This example shows how supply chains can react fast to increased demand, develop and implement new solutions, build new cooperation, and adjust supply networks.

The crisis is leading to an acceleration of the digitalization trend. Due to changed consumer demand and especially physical distancing needs, online retail and related delivery services increased amid the pandemic (Dannenberg et al., 2020; Esper, 2021; Loske, 2020). This puts companies at an advantage which have online and delivery capabilities in place and where the business model and processes support this value chain (Dannenberg et al., 2020; Dudley, 2020). These changes in consumer demand (Goddard, 2020) open up opportunities for new digital platforms, processes, and revenue streams for companies who are reacting to this trend. Additional elements related to digitalization, such as 3D-printing and blockchain technology (Rogetzer et al., 2019) have gained relevance and applications during the COVID-19 pandemic as well.

4.5 Summary and Conclusion

This chapter describes challenges and opportunities for supply chains occurring amid the COVID-19 pandemic. Arising opportunities and challenges trigger adjustments in operational procedures and might increase stakeholder cooperation along the supply chain. With the focus on keeping value chains flowing to deliver goods and services, the understanding of supply chain networks, critical bottlenecks, and (inherent) risks got more attention. For example, the awareness of critical parts and their sourcing location might lead to adaptations of regionalization strategies for companies and countries. Previous trends, like digitalization and online processes, are getting accelerated and might gain additional leverage in the future. The changes in various processes might influence future standards, and it remains to be seen how supply chain paradigms such as cost and productivity and resilience focus will sustain, evolve, or disappear. Moreover, additional capacities (like for vaccines) and knowledge were created, and it will be seen how and for what those are going to be used in the future.

The global COVID-19 pandemic puts a strain on various elements of supply chains globally. Disruptions occur (and propagate) on supply, on demand, and across multiple supply chain nodes and their interlinks. Understanding the implications of these events and their importance for supply chains triggers mitigation actions. The preparation of response strategies form a supply chain's resilience to react to adverse events. How these apply to the pandemic situation will be covered by a separate section with an interdisciplinary Delphi Study (see Chap. 17). Multiple references on the COVID-19 pandemic will be found across the book in theoretical and use case contributions. The literature review in Chap. 2 highlights the relevance of the pandemic within academic publications since its outbreak in early 2020. An adapted resilience framework in Chap. 3 describes different considerations for supply chain resilience, which can also be applied to the current COVID-19 pandemic. The understanding of the available capabilities and mechanisms (tools and processes) applied will lead to the respective outcome.

The global pandemic situation displays the relevance of supply chain resilience in multiple manners and helps further refine its understanding and research needs. Chapter 17 of the Delphi Study outlines future research perspectives from the practitioners' view to develop more resilient supply chains. Such a crisis triggers change and opportunities for new processes, technologies, and business models (Attinasi et al., 2021).

References

Albergotti, R., & Siddiqui, F. (2020). Ford and GM are undertaking a warlike effort to produce ventilators. It may fall short and come too late. In *The Washington Post*, 4/4/2020. Retrieved August 13, 2021, from https://www.washingtonpost.com/business/2020/04/04/ventilators-coronavirus-ford-gm/

Alsharef, A., Banerjee, S., Uddin, S. M., Albert, A., & Jaselskis, E. (2021). Early impacts of the COVID-19 pandemic on the United States construction industry. *IJERPH, 18*(4), 1559. https://doi.org/10.3390/ijerph18041559

Attinasi, M. G., de Stefani, R., Frohm, E., Gunnella, V., Koester, G., Tóth, M., & Melemenidis, A. (2021). *The semiconductor shortage and its implication for euro area trade, production and prices*. Retrieved from https://www.ecb.europa.eu//pub/economic-bulletin/focus/2021/html/ecb.ebbox202104_06~780de2a8fb.en.html

Hatoum, B., Faisal, A., Nassereddine, H., & Sarvari, H. (2021). Analysis of COVID-19 concerns raised by the construction workforce and development of mitigation practices. *Frontiers in Built Environment, 7*, 66. https://doi.org/10.3389/fbuil.2021.688495

Bousquin, J. (2021). *Amid delays and rising prices, contractors turn to tech to mitigate supply disruptions*. Retrieved August 13, 2021, from https://www.constructiondive.com/news/amid-delays-and-rising-prices-contractors-turn-to-tech-to-mitigate-supply/598913/

Brandt, L., & Hoffower, H. (2021). The price of lumber is wild right now and it's a disaster for the already disastrous housing market. In *Business Insider*, 5/17/2021. Retrieved August 13, 2021, from https://www.businessinsider.com/why-is-lumber-so-expensive-prices-disaster-for-housing-market-2021-5

Bui, D. P., McCaffrey, K., Friedrichs, M., LaCross, N., Lewis, N. M., Sage, K., et al. (2020). Racial and ethnic disparities among COVID-19 cases in Workplace Outbreaks by Industry Sector - Utah, March 6-June 5, 2020. *MMWR Morbidity and Mortality Weekly Reports, 69*(33), 1133–1138. https://doi.org/10.15585/mmwr.mm6933e3

Burkacky, O., Lingemann, S., & Pototzky, K. (2021). Coping with the auto-semiconductor shortage: Strategies for success. In *McKinsey & Company*, 5/27/2021. Retrieved September 7, 2021, from https://www.mckinsey.com/industries/automotive-and-assembly/our-insights/coping-with-the-auto-semiconductor-shortage-strategies-for-success

Canada, Health (2021). *Ventilators for patients with COVID-19 - Canada.ca*. Retrieved August 13, 2021, from https://www.canada.ca/en/health-canada/services/drugs-health-products/covid19-industry/medical-devices/ventilator-access.html

Capitol Technology University. (2021). *Industry News: Construction materials shortages will continue into 2021*. Retrieved August 13, 2021, from https://www.captechu.edu/blog/managing-construction-materials-shortages-in-2021

Cohen, W. M., & Levinthal, D. A. (1990). Absorptive capacity: A new perspective on learning and innovation. *Administrative Science Quarterly, 35*, 128–152.

Conerly, B. (2021). Why lumber and plywood prices are so high—and when they will come down. In *Forbes*, 5/22/2021. Retrieved August 13, 2021, from https://www.forbes.com/sites/billconerly/2021/05/22/why-lumber-and-plywood-prices-are-so-high-and-when-they-will-come-down/

Construction News. (2021). *Materials shortage: Updates on 6 key materials | Construction News*. Retrieved June 18, 2021, from https://www.constructionnews.co.uk/supply-chain/materials-shortage-updates-on-6-key-materials-18-06-2021/

Dannenberg, P., Fuchs, M., Riedler, T., & Wiedemann, C. (2020). Digital transition by COVID-19 pandemic? The German Food Online Retail. *Tijdschrift voor economische en sociale geografie = Journal of economic and social geography = Revue de geographie economique et humaine = Zeitschrift fur okonomische und soziale Geographie = Revista de geografia economica y social, 111*(3), 543–560. https://doi.org/10.1111/tesg.12453

DHL. (2021). *Revisiting Pandemic Resilience. The race against the virus; what we've learned one year into COVID-19 and how the world's healthcare supply chains will be ready for the next public health emergency*. Retrieved June 1, 2021, from https://www.dhl.com/content/dam/dhl/global/csi/documents/pdf/Revisiting-Pandemic-Resilience-White-Paper-(English).pdf

Dudley, R. (2020). The Amazon lockdown: How an unforgiving algorithm drives suppliers to favor the e-commerce giant over other retailers. In *ProPublica*, 4/27/2020. Retrieved August 3, 2021, from https://www.nextgov.com/emerging-tech/2020/04/amazon-lockdown-how-unforgiving-algorithm-drives-suppliers-favor-e-commerce-giant-over-other-retailers/164926/

Esper, T. L. (2021). Supply chain management amid the coronavirus pandemic. *Journal of Public Policy and Marketing, 40*(1), 101–102. https://doi.org/10.1177/0743915620932150

European Commission. (2014). *Report on critical raw materials for the EU. Report of the Ad hoc Working Group on defining critical raw materials*. Retrieved November 11, 2021, from http://litio.ipg.pt/wp-content/uploads/2018/07/EC_crm-report-on-critical-raw-materials_2014.pdf

Gaimon, C., & Ramachandran, K. (2021). The knowledge value chain: An operational perspective. *Production and Operations Management, 30*(3), 715–724. https://doi.org/10.1111/poms.13312

Goddard, E. (2020). The impact of COVID-19 on food retail and food service in Canada: Preliminary assessment. *Canadian Journal of Agricultural Economics/Revue canadienne d'agroeconomie, 68*(2), 157–161. https://doi.org/10.1111/cjag.12243

Gupta, A., & Maranas, C. D. (2003). Managing demand uncertainty in supply chain planning. *Computers and Chemical Engineering, 27*(8-9), 1219–1227. https://doi.org/10.1016/S0098-1354(03)00048-6

Harvard Business School. (2021). *Managing through crisis: What toilet paper can teach us about supply chains - YouTube*. Retrieved January 20, 2021, from https://www.youtube.com/watch?v=KAm-7F2cLQQ

Hendricks, K. B., & Singhal, V. R. (2005). An empirical analysis of the effect of supply chain disruptions on long-run stock price performance and equity risk of the firm. *Production and Operations Management, 14*(1), 35–52. https://doi.org/10.1111/j.1937-5956.2005.tb00008.x

Hopkins, J. S. (2021). To make more Covid-19 vaccines, rival drugmakers team up. *The Wall Street Journal*, 2/23/2021. Retrieved August 12, 2021, from https://www.wsj.com/articles/to-make-more-covid-19-vaccines-rival-drugmakers-team-up-11614081601

Ivanov, D. (2021). Introduction to supply chain resilience: Management, modelling, technology. Springer Nature.

Ivanov, D., Dolgui, A., Sokolov, B. (Eds.) (2019). Handbook of ripple effects in the supply chain. 1st ed. Springer International Publishing. Retrieved May 27, 2021, from https://link.springer.com/content/pdf/10.1007%2F978-3-030-14302-2.pdf

Ivanov, D., Sokolov, B., & Dolgui, A. (2014). The Ripple effect in supply chains: trade-off 'efficiency-flexibility-resilience' in disruption management. *International Journal of Production Research, 52*(7), 2154–2172. https://doi.org/10.1080/00207543.2013.858836

Keshner, A. (2021). There's a COVID-related bicycle shortage in the U.S. In *MarketWatch*, 6/4/2021. Retrieved August 4, 2021, from https://www.marketwatch.com/story/why-is-there-a-bicycle-shortage-its-got-a-lot-to-do-with-why-fireworks-are-scarce-11622751152

Kleindorfer, P. R., & Saad, G. H. (2005). Managing disruption risks in supply chains. *Production and Operations Management, 14*(1), 53–68. https://doi.org/10.1111/j.1937-5956.2005.tb00009.x

Lee, H. L. (2004). The triple-A supply chain. Harvard business review, 82(10), 102-113.

Lee, H. L., Padmanabhan, V., Whang, S. (1997). The Bullwhip effect in supply chains. In *MIT Sloan Management Review*. Retrieved September 17, 2021, from https://sloanreview.mit.edu/wp-content/uploads/1997/04/633ecdb037.pdf

Lee, H. L., Padmanabhan, V., & Whang, S. (2004). Information distortion in a supply chain: The Bullwhip Effect. *Management Science, 43*(4), 546–558. https://doi.org/10.1287/MNSC.43.4.546

Lee, H. L., & Schmidt, G. (2017). Using value chains to enhance innovation. *Productions and Operations Management, 26*(4), 617–632. https://doi.org/10.1111/poms.12665

Liu, W., Beltagui, A., Ye, S. (2021). Accelerated innovation through repurposing: exaptation of design and manufacturing in response to COVID-19. *R&D Management*. https://doi.org/10.1111/radm.12460.

Loske, D. (2020). The impact of COVID-19 on transport volume and freight capacity dynamics: An empirical analysis in German food retail logistics. *Transportation Research Interdisciplinary Perspectives, 6*, 100165. https://doi.org/10.1016/j.trip.2020.100165

Moore, S. K. (2021). How and when the chip shortage will end, in 4 charts. In *IEEE Spectrum*, 6/29/2021. Retrieved August 4, 2021, from https://spectrum.ieee.org/chip-shortage

Netland, T. (2020). A better answer to the ventilator shortage as the pandemic rages on. *World Economic Forum*. Retrieved August 13, 2021, from https://www.weforum.org/agenda/2020/04/covid-19-ventilator-shortage-manufacturing-solution/

Omezzine, F., Oruganti, V., Freitas, B., & Maria, I. (2022). Learning from crisis: Repurposing to address grand challenges. *Innovation and Development, 12*, 59–69. https://doi.org/10.1080/2157930X.2021.1930397

Paul, S., & Chowdhury, P. (2020). Strategies for managing the impacts of disruptions during COVID-19: An example of toilet paper. *Global Journal of Flexible Systems Management, 21*(3), 283–293. https://doi.org/10.1007/s40171-020-00248-4

Rodrigue, J-P. (2020). *Coronavirus impacts on trade and supply chains*. METRANS Advisory Board Meeting, April 3 2020. Retrieved November 12, 2021, from https://sites.hofstra.edu/jean-paul-rodrigue/wp-content/uploads/sites/11/2020/04/Metrans_Covid_Trade_JPR.pdf

Rogetzer, P., Nowak, T., Jammernegg, W., & Wakolbinger, T. (2019). Impact of digitalization on sustainable supply chains. In F. Luks (Ed.), *Chancen und Grenzen der Nachhaltigkeitstransformation* (pp. 131–144). Springer Fachmedien Wiesbaden.

Schwartz, J. (2021). A lesson in lumber shortages, buyer preferences and supply and demand. In *Forbes*, 6/15/2021. Retrieved August 13, 2021, from https://www.forbes.com/sites/forbesrealestatecouncil/2021/06/15/a-lesson-in-lumber-shortages-buyer-preferences-and-supply-and-demand/

Souza, K. (2020). The supply side: Walmart's 98% OTIF requirement remains a work in progress. In *Talk Business and Politics*, 11/8/2020. Retrieved August 3, 2021, from https://talkbusiness.net/2020/11/the-supply-side-walmarts-98-otif-requirement-remains-a-work-in-progress/

Svensson, G. (2000). A conceptual framework for the analysis of vulnerability in supply chains. *IJPDLM, 30*(9), 731–750. https://doi.org/10.1108/09600030010351444

Thibault, M. (2021). *Economist: Construction industry resilient despite high prices, pandemic*. Retrieved August 13, 2021, from https://www.constructiondive.com/news/construction-industry-resilient/603491/

Tribe, D. (2021). Flexibility can help car makers cope with chip supply challenge. *Engineering and Technology, 16*(2), 19. https://doi.org/10.1049/et.2021.0200

Volkswagen AG News. (2020). *COVID-19 crisis: From making cars to ventilators. Volkswagen AG News*. Retrieved August 13, 2021, from https://www.volkswagenag.com/en/news/2020/04/SEAT_starts_the_production_of_emergency_ventilators.html

World Construction Today. (2021). *Construction material shortages to continue in 2021*. Retrieved August 13, 2021, from https://www.worldconstructiontoday.com/news/construction-material-shortages-to-continue-in-2021/

Wu, X., Zhang, C., & Du, W. (2021). An analysis on the crisis of "Chips shortage" in automobile industry: Based on the double influence of COVID-19 and trade friction. *Journal of Physics, 1971*(1), 12100. https://doi.org/10.1088/1742-6596/1971/1/012100

Lydia Novoszel is Research Associate at the Institute for Transport and Logistics Management at WU (Vienna University of Economics and Business). With an international professional career in supply chain management, she incorporates practical relevance and perspectives in supply chain disruption research. Lydia has earned a master's degree in Mechanical Engineering and a master's degree in Business Administration.

Tina Wakolbinger, PhD is Professor for Supply Chain Services and Networks. She serves as Head of the Research Institute for Supply Chain Management and Deputy Head of the Institute for Transport and Logistics Management at the WU (Vienna University of Economics and Business). Her research interests lie in the modeling and analysis of complex decision-making on network systems with a focus on global issues. She serves in editorial positions in Production and Operations Management and Central European Journal of Operations Research. Her work on supply chain management and humanitarian logistics is published in renown journals.

Chapter 5
Pandemic-Related Disruptions in the Field of Freight Transportation

Stefan Schönfelder and Manuel Tuscher

Abstract The importance of transportation for innovation, growth, competitiveness and well-being is largely indisputable. Freight transportation, in particular, is a prerequisite for the functioning of modern supply chains and a key enabler for customer-oriented strategies of logistics operations.

Often, transportation systems are also acknowledged as "critical". The criticality of transport expresses itself—among others—by its special level of interdependency (with other systems), level of dependency (with human and corporate activities) and the level of infrastructural risk. As transportation systems are regularly exposed to threats and vulnerable to disruptions with far-reaching effects, they receive special attention in political approaches addressing resilience.

The COVID-19 pandemic has caused disruptions in various societal and economic areas—including transportation. COVID-19 related disruptions (caused, e.g., by lockdowns) that were accompanied by further problematic events in 2020/21 (such as the Suez Canal blockage) were in particular evident in maritime shipping, but also had effects on the other transport modes. This chapter provides a summary of those effects. It will show that the pandemic turned out to be both, a demand and supply crisis, whereas the latter aspect was dominating. This sets the pandemic apart from demand-only shocks such as the various economic crises of the past.

5.1 Introduction

The development of modern civilisations and economies as well as the genesis of globalisation is closely linked to the existence and expansion of (advanced) transportation systems ensuring low or reduced costs of interaction (Lewis, 1936; Meier-Dallach, 1979; Rodrigue, 2020). Transportation has always been an integral part of social and economic life, and its importance for innovation, growth, competitiveness

S. Schönfelder (✉) · M. Tuscher
Institute for Transport and Logistics Management, WU (Vienna University of Economics and Business), Vienna, Austria
e-mail: stefan.schoenfelder@wu.ac.at

S. Kummer et al. (eds.), *Supply Chain Resilience*, Springer Series in Supply Chain Management 17, https://doi.org/10.1007/978-3-030-95401-7_5

and well-being is largely indisputable. This holds even if methodologically the identification of clear cause-effect relationships, e.g. between transportation infrastructure investment and the economy, remains difficult (Banister and Berechman, 2000) and given the great challenges to reduce the various negative externalities caused by largely carbon-based transport operations (Van Essen et al., 2019).

The close relationship of the availability of (high-quality) transportation options and especially of its improvement with economic and social progress often touches the existence of physical networks. It also concerns the efficiency and capacity gains in passenger and freight transport operations. These are closely interwoven with connectivity as well as accessibility improvements but also with technological innovation beyond physical transportation networks. An improvement in both areas, i.e. infrastructure and operations, usually shows direct and indirect economic impacts. These are benefits for users and operators in terms of, among other things, cost and time savings, improved reliability as well as better access of firms to suppliers, consumers and labour market potential (Rodrigue, 2020).

Transportation therefore takes a key "auxiliary role" by providing essential services to firms as well as households for production, consumption and efficient labour markets. Freight transportation, in particular, is a prerequisite for functioning supply chains. Transportation is acknowledged as "the 'glue' that holds the supply chain together" and as a "key enabler for important customer-oriented strategies" such as just-in-time-delivery, for example (Coyle et al., 2016, p. 1). What shouldn't be forgotten, either, is that transport and logistics operations have themselves become an important industry that provides income for employees and company owners and that adds substantially to GDP. In Austria alone, companies in the transport industry generated gross value added at factor cost of around €15 billion in 2020 and made gross investments of almost €4 billion (Stabsabteilung Statistik der WKO, 2020).

However, like many prerequisites for the functioning of societal and economic processes, transportation is not untouchable and is exposed to risks. The history of transportation shows that natural and man-made "events" have repeatedly led to *disruptions* that have subsequently impacted those areas that rely on the availability and the reliability of transportation infrastructure as well as services (see, e.g. Zhu & Levinson, 2012). A prominent example of this was the eruption of the Eyjafjallajökull volcano in Iceland in 2010. This event caused the cancellation of 48% of European air traffic (approximately 104,000 flights) from April 15 to April 22, 2010. Figure 5.1 shows the development of flight volumes in the respective time span. Apart from thousands of passengers being stranded, international trade by air, which usually carries time-critical high-value goods, was heavily impacted. Economic losses caused by the eruption and its consequences were estimated to be around 4.7 billion US dollars (Ellertsdottir, 2014). Fortunately, regular flight operations could resume quickly after the ash cloud dissipated—or to be more exact: traffic restrictions were loosened.

This chapter serves two purposes: it places transportation in the context of "criticality" and vulnerability but mainly addresses the question of how freight and passenger transportation have been challenged by disruptions caused by the

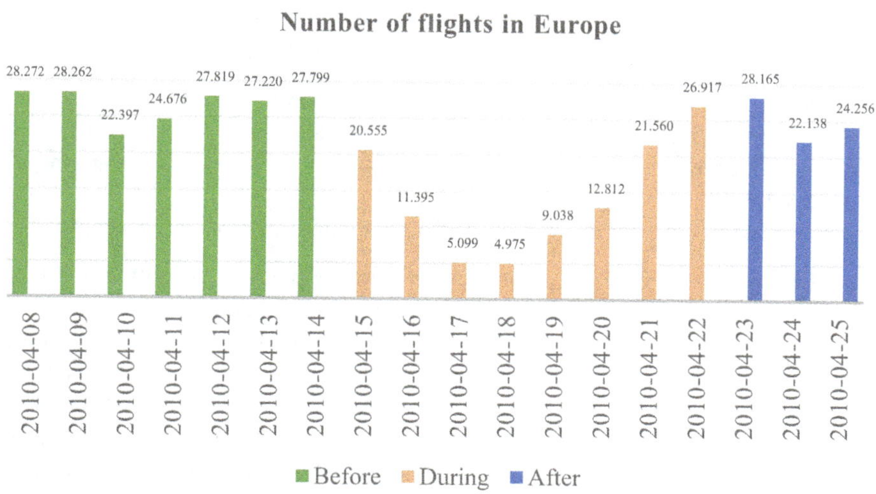

Fig. 5.1 Number of flights in Europe before, during and after the eruption of Eyjafjallajökull in 2010 (©EUROCONTROL, EUROCONTROL, 2010)

coronavirus pandemic and other events that occurred during this time period (i.e. the Suez Canal blockage). We will show that the effects were even more severe than those caused by the event discussed above but that they had different structural characteristics.

5.2 Framing the Problem: The Discussion About Critical Infrastructures and Their Protection

Acknowledging the important function of transportation for the economy and society as well as a key industry, transportation is commonly referred to as "critical infrastructure" (CI). CIs—that apart from transportation include sectors such as energy supply, information technology or media (depending on which definition is applied, see, e.g. BMI, 2015; CISA, 2021)—are predominantly highly complex and often interrelated. Transportation, for example, plays an important direct and indirect role in providing services for the lifeline or rescue services, the health system, food production and the supply of energy. It is widely agreed that CI sectors need to be protected from failure or disruption, as this would expose society to severe risks and provoke "lasting supply bottlenecks, significant disruptions to public safety or other dramatic consequences" (BSI and BBK, 2021). The protection of CIs is an important task of the different administrative levels and requires long-term and comprehensive planning (see for national approaches of the DACH-countries BMI, 2009; Bundeskanleramt, 2015; Schweizerische Eidgenossenschaft, 2017).

The discussion on critical infrastructures is not new but mainly took off in the 2000 years. It primarily intensified against the background of terrorist attacks but also severe weather events or other natural catastrophes. Criticality usually refers to a sectoral prioritization that may take into consideration the sectors'

- Level of resiliency (i.e. an infrastructure's ability to bounce back after failure).
- Level of interdependency (i.e. system interconnectedness).
- Level of dependency (i.e. how much people's daily activities revolve around the system).
- Level of infrastructure risk (i.e. potential for realization of negative events).

(Katina & Hester, 2013). Another approach to comprehend the notion of critical infrastructure is to assess the sectors' critical proportion, critical time and critical quality (Fekete, 2011). Whereas the *proportion* relates to the infrastructure's number of elements or nodes, choke points and number of services, size of population or magnitude of customers affected in case of failure, *time* is linked to duration of outage, speed of onset and specific critical time frames. Finally, *quality* concerns issues like service delivered (in terms of quality) and public trust in the quality.

The transportation system (defined as the combination of elements and their interactions, which produce the transport demand and the supply of services to satisfy this demand [according to Cascetta, 2001)] is without doubt "critical". It is highly complex, regularly exposed to threats and vulnerable to disruptions with far-reaching effects. Interruption recovery (such as the repair or restoration of infrastructure) can take weeks, months or even years (take, e.g. the restoration of the *Viadotto Polcevera* in Genova after 2018).

The causes of disruption range from extreme weather events to (unforeseeable) technical defects, strikes and sabotage. Vulnerability of the transport system is usually defined as the "susceptibility" to incidents that can result in considerable reductions in the *serviceability* of transport infrastructure (Berdica, 2002). From a more general perspective, which considers both, infrastructure and operations, transportation service characteristics or components comprise of

- *Transit time(s):* affecting the level of inventory and its associated cost.
- *Reliability:* enabling market actors to optimise service levels and minimise stock-out costs.
- Accessibility (and connectivity): enabling carriers to provide services between origin and destination.
- *Capability (as well as efficiency)* of tailor-made services.
- *Security* of the goods in transit.

(Novack et al., 2019, pp. 42 and 43). In cases of disruption, "the fundamental purpose of the transport system [. . .], i.e. its ability to provide transport services to the users is hurt, and [. . .] the adverse consequences are significant" (Mattsson & Jenelius, 2015, p. 27). The assessment of risks and the impact of disruptions on interdependent critical infrastructures also proves to be an important aspect of research and is dealt with by various researchers (e.g. Dvořák et al., 2017; Hackl et al., 2018; Patrman et al., 2019; Seppänen et al., 2018), which underlines its importance.

5.3 Crises of the Past as Major Disrupting Events and the Ongoing COVID-19 Crisis

These days, the term "crisis" is used in an inflationary manner—not the least in respect of disruptions in the field of critical infrastructures. It should, however, be clearly defined and separated from shorter-term unwelcome events for CIs, such as recapitulated by Borca et al. (2021) (based on Farazmand, 2018, and Quarantelli, 2000). They distinguish between the phenomena "emergencies", "disasters", "catastrophes" and "crises" and assign different levels of impact and influences on natural and sociotechnical systems to each of these categories.

The COVID-19 pandemic was not the first crisis to hit the transport sector. However, its scope and severity of impact can be seen as a novelty since prior events either caused only local disruptions or were time-limited in impact (such as the aforementioned volcano eruption or the collapse of a bridge). In a literature review, Borca et al. (2021) identified the following crises affecting Europe in the last 20 years.

5.3.1 Financial Crisis of 2008

The financial crisis of 2008, which was triggered by the bankruptcy of the Lehman Brothers Bank in September 2008, caused a downturn in the global economy. As an accompanying result of the reduced economic output, freight transport and traffic volumes also declined. In the maritime sector, for example, demand shrunk, caused overcapacities and thus decreasing freight rates (Jerebić & Pavlin, 2018). In combination with already ordered ships being built, overcapacity increased even further and worsened the imbalance between supply and demand (Min et al., 2009). Jerebić and Pavlin (2018) state that the effects of this imbalance are observable until today. Studies on air freight transport like Azadian (2020) and Islam (2018) showed similar results, stating that the recuperation of markets was and will be slow.

5.3.2 Migration Crisis of 2015

Fleeing from war, crises, etc. has always been an issue for humanity—the year 2015, however, was special for Europe in this respect. Due to various events and reasons, several countries opened their borders and allowed people seeking protection to enter or pass through without bureaucratic complications. However, these migratory movements also caused problems in the transport sector—especially in road freight transport. Studies by Lietuvnikė et al. (2017), Nowakowska and Tubis (2018) and Radionov and Savić (2019) report that longer waiting times at border crossings and an increase in goods damaged were reported since the beginning of the crisis. Along with uncertainties in regard to delivery requirements (in terms of punctuality), these aspects cause a loss of efficiency within supply chains.

5.3.3 Climate Crisis (Ongoing)

As the effects of human-induced climate change become increasingly visible, they are also having a growing impact on the transport sector. Even if the effects of climate change are not so directly attributable compared to other crises, there are already papers that deal with the direct effects of (mostly regional) weather extremes. For example, Gabela and Sarmiento (2020) found that the 2013 flood in Germany led to route shifts on 23% of all major roads. As a result, negative effects such as longer journeys, delays and higher fuel consumption are highly likely.

5.3.4 COVID-19 Crisis (Ongoing)

The COVID-19 pandemic has caused a crisis (or crises) in various social and economic areas—including supply chains and transportation. It is very likely that it will probably take long to recover and it has put life-sustaining systems such as health, security/safety or wealth (at least for some) under extreme risk.

The following table provides a brief overview about the timeline of the COVID-19 crisis.

2019

- December: First cases of pneumonia reported in Wuhan, Hubei Province, China.

2020

- January: Novel coronavirus discovered as cause.
- February: Hubei under quarantine; various countries restrict travel to and from China.
- March: COVID-19 declared a pandemic by WHO; drastic travel restrictions and lockdowns in multiple countries.
- June–August: Most travel restrictions lifted.
- September–November: Increasing number of cases lead to new travel restrictions.
- November–April 2021: Second and third wave of infections cause repeated lockdowns and far-reaching restrictions.
- December: First vaccines approved and administered; new virus mutation discovered.

2021

- Spread of more infectious mutations.
- Easing of restrictions due to ongoing vaccination campaign.

Undoubtedly, travel restrictions such as border closings heavily influenced freight transport. The freight transport disruption due to the COVID-19 crisis was in particular evident in global maritime shipping—with implications on the national and regional levels, too (Allianz Global Corporate & Specialty, 2021). The pandemic crisis was accompanied by a series of further problematic events, including the Suez Canal blockage of March 2021 (see below), extreme weather events and political disputes such as the China-Australia clash of 2020/2021.

5.4 Disrupting Impacts of COVID-19 on Transport Modes with a Focus on Maritime Shipping

World maritime shipping is a sensitive system that might be characterised by the circulation of containers and vessels between ports/terminals on the different continents. In addition to that, pronounced geographical asymmetries exist: in total, about 50% more full containers are sent from Asia to Europe and the USA than in the other direction. This is because Asia still takes the roles of the "workbench and the department store of the world economy". Even in normal times, empty containers pile up in Europe and the USA, which poses a challenge for return shipping to Asia. Understandably, shipping companies are hesitant to return containers without goods—as this is economically unreasonable—which is why, for example, low-value materials such as waste paper and scrap metal are transported to Asia in containers. Spare capacities in the global maritime sector are typically limited.

In the pandemic crisis (in/after spring of 2020), challenges for the maritime transport became aggravated:

1. The pandemic and the disruption of world trade started in China of all places: Due to the stringent COVID responses in China at the beginning of 2020, only few containers were shipped. This caused piling up of containers and congestion at Asian ports: only few containers arrived in Europe and the USA, and also few containers were shipped back.
2. When after approx. 2 months production in China resumed and the ports started to work more intensively, Europe and the USA went into lockdowns and discharging of the cargo took long. This again had the effect that only few containers were returned to Asia.
3. In the light of the pandemic, the shipping companies reduced their capacities as they expected weak demand in 2020.
4. As could be expected, few empty containers in Asia and too little ship capacities were available. The demand for products from Asia such as electronics, sports

equipment and health products, however, did not collapse as in other crises (such as the economic crisis of 2008/2009) but even increased compared to pre-pandemic times.

In autumn 2020 then:

1. The demand for freight transportation was much higher than the supply.
2. The supply could not be increased as quickly as needed because of a lack of containers.
3. Due to the uncertain situation continuing, the shipping companies did not necessarily want to expand their supply as prices skyrocketed (see below), and business got very profitable for the shipping companies.

Alongside port closures and border closures, also political conflicts and accidents affected the shipping industry negatively. An example was the dispute between China and Australia over the origin of the coronavirus in which China reacted by banning imports of Australian products. This resulted in ships with Australian coal (as well as wine, food, timber and barley) being stranded (Bodewein, 2020).

Another cause of disruption for maritime shipping was the accident of the 20,000 TEU container ship "Ever Given" in the Suez Canal in March 2021. The accident resulted in a blockage of the canal for almost 1 week (March 23–29) and caused a massive backlog of ships (prepared for entering the canal). Until April 3 (i.e. within 5 days), a backlog of over 400 waiting ships was cleared, while usually 40–50 ships pass the canal on average per day (Reuters, 2021). The accident underlines the last years' trend towards larger vessels, which bears the risk of incidents becoming more severe, less simple to solve and more expensive. Until August 2021, the effects of the accident were still evident, and catch-up effects just began thereafter.

In the course of the year 2020, container freight rates reached all-time highs when shipping companies charged six to ten times higher container freight rates than before the pandemic crisis. After a short period of relaxation in early 2021, the "Ever Given" incident caused freight rates to rise again. Experts estimated that supply constraints could last probably until autumn 2021 or even spring 2022. Although the share of transport costs in product prices is low (well below 10%), higher prices for final and intermediary products (such as raw materials and computer chips) are likely in the future (Dempsey et al., 2021).

Uncertainties remained even after the Suez Canal clearing and disruptions continued: new congestion at container ports occurred induced by the closure of terminals that were ordered by authorities to contain local virus outbreaks. This affected the important ports of Yantian/Shenzhen (May/June 2021) or Ningbo-Zhoushan/Eastern China (August 2021), for example, as China strongly emphasises a zero-COVID strategy. As ships tried to move to other ports (with limited capacity), the congestion spread as a chain reaction. About 300 container ships were waiting for entry into congested ports in June 2021—leading to a considerable decline in ships' schedule performance (Sea-Intelligence, 2021). Overall, the time container-ships spent waiting for berths has doubled since 2019 (The Maritime Executive, 2021). The closure of the ports in China therefore demonstrated the severe negative effects for the global movement of goods and the functioning of supply chains in particular clarity. The terminal closure in China was, however, not the first disruption but can be compared to another domino falling. Consequences of these port closures were not only visible at Asian ports, but also European ports are affected. Terminals struggle with congestion and backlogs in clearance and thus hinterland transport via rail or road as capacity cannot adapt (enough).

Despite all these circumstances, the shipping industry proved to be more resilient than some expected. Compared to 2019 the global seaborne trade declined only by 3.6% in 2020, and for 2021 a higher freight volume than 2019 is forecasted (Chambers, 2021). This shows that the industry is volatile, yet the fast recovery is closely linked to the success of worldwide vaccination programmes. While trading goods shipping recovers better than expected and the impacts appear to be limited, the car carrier segment and cruise ships have been hit much more by disruptions (Allianz Global Corporate & Specialty, 2021).

The pandemic-related maritime shipping tensions made shippers (producers) face considerable challenges in their transport decision-making. Switching from container shipping to other modes appeared to be difficult. Air transport, for example, is considerably more expensive than sea (approx. ten times more than maritime transport). In addition to that, the capacity of airfreight was significantly limited during the pandemic as about half of global airfreight is belly freight on passenger flights. Passenger transport, however, has been considerably affected by the pandemic (see below). Only few flights were operated during the various lockdowns, and even after global vaccination programmes gained momentum at the end of 2020, there was limited supply (in particular into and from China due to the country's restrictive corona regulations) (Brett, 2021). Rail could be an alternative to sea transport (e.g. the land bridge Asia-Europe), too. However, it remains a limited option for many shippers: rail accessibility and capacity are simply not comprehensive enough, and rail freight rates are usually higher than maritime shipping on the same routes. Interestingly, even road transport was discussed as an alternative to cargo shipping, though this seems somewhat bizarre considering durations of intercontinental lorry trips and potential freight rates.

In conclusion, one might ask: "What is the way out of the maritime shipping crisis?" As rail and other modes of transport promise only little relief, more supply chain/transportation resilience with less dependence on China (also Chinese production of intermediate products) among more diversity in the design of supply chain and transportation options is needed.

Not only the maritime shipping industry was hit particularly hard by the pandemic crisis, but there was also a significant upheaval in aviation. While take-off bans paralysed air traffic during the volcanic eruption in 2010, travel warnings at the beginning of the Corona crisis were initially responsible for the collapse in air traffic, followed by landing/entry bans later. As the country of origin of the pandemic was China, the decline in passenger numbers was first felt in the Middle Kingdom, where the number of seats offered fell by 75% from January 2020 to February 2020 (ICAO, 2021). However, as COVID quickly became a global problem, passenger numbers also declined rapidly in many other countries. Figure 5.2 shows the development of

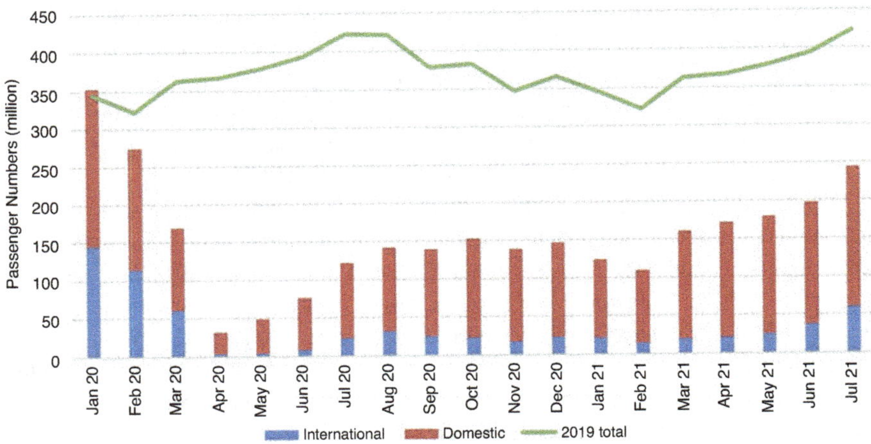

Fig. 5.2 Monthly worldwide passenger numbers (source: ICAO, 2021, ICAO Economic Analysis of COVID-19 on Civil Aviation https://www.icao.int/sustainability/Pages/Economic-Impacts-of-COVID-19.aspx)

passenger numbers in 2020/21 compared to 2019: passenger numbers in April 2020 were only around 10% of the previous year's level, for example. Though the numbers recuperated a bit and for 2020 a total passenger decline of 60% (compared to 2019) was recorded, for 2021 only a slow recovery was expected, and estimations predict passenger numbers to be around 46–49% percent lower than in 2019 (ICAO, 2021). This trend could be also confirmed for Austria, where the decrease in passenger numbers was even higher. In April and May 2020 less than 1% of the 2019 level of passengers was reported. In the entire year 2020, only one third of flights took off, and one fourth of passengers departed from Austrian airports (Statistik Austria, 2021a).

While cargo-only flights were not that heavily influenced by the crisis, the low number of flights caused problems for airfreight transport as a significant share of air cargo is transported as belly freight of passenger flights. As this reduced the available supply of air cargo capacity, air freight rates increased—similar to the maritime sector. Several airlines reacted to these constraints by operating their passenger aircraft as so-called preighters (i.e. passenger aircraft used for cargo-only). While some airlines simply left the passenger room empty, others even took a step further and demounted seats to increase loading space or simply put loading onto the seats. A share of around 13% of air freight was carried by preighters from April to December 2020 (IATA, 2021).

Whereas shipping and aviation struggled with multiple issues, road and rail transport was less influenced by the crisis at first sight. In addition, continental transport was influenced by border closures and waiting times at borders, while inland freight remained mostly untouched. For example, a Chinese study (Ho et al., 2021) found that road transport in China profited from COVID-19 as traffic volumes and turnover increased. For Austria in 2020, no growth in road transport was recorded, but, compared to aviation, the decline was comparatively low (−6.6% compared to 2019), being the strongest in the second quarter at around −15% (Statistik Austria, 2021c). The Austrian rail freight sector reported a freight volume reduction of 4.9% for 2020 with transit freight operations hardly affected with a minus of only 0.7%. Similar to road, the second quarter showed the strongest downturn of −19.4% (Statistik Austria, 2021b).

5.5 Conclusion

The pandemic and its transportation effects have hit worldwide economies like a rock—although pandemics are not entirely new events and there have been several geographically limited phenomena in the past (AIDS, swine flu, Ebola, etc.). The COVID-19 pandemic had, however, a much more severe impact on transportation and the industries as well as societal functions served by the sector. Far-reaching closures of border crossings and lockdowns of entire societies proved to be unprecedented and almost unthinkable events.

We have shown that the pandemic turned out to be both a demand and supply crisis, with the latter aspect dominating without doubt. This sets it apart from demand-only shocks such as the economic crisis of 2008 with its origins in the financial strains of the USA. Supply-side shocks, i.e. crises within transportation system triggered by capacity restrictions or the total failure of transportation services, on the other hand, have been rarer so far. The grounding of many airlines in the Northern Hemisphere after the eruption of the Icelandic volcano Eyjafjallajökull is one of such memorable (and rudimentarily comparable) events.

Acknowledging common transportation risk factors such as congestion, poor weather, strikes or capacity shortages (in the case of peak seasonal demand), many companies have long applied sophisticated transportation risk reduction strategies (Novack et al. 2019, p. 345). These are based on several steps including the identification of risks and their causes, the assessment of their probability and effects as well as the development of a risk management strategy to manage and mitigate the risks. The detailed strategies include, e.g. the usage of event management software, the employment of dynamic rerouting tools or the securing of backup capacities. These mainly proactive responses result at best in the reduction of wait time and greater reliability as well as the avoidance of major SC disruptions. This in turn can help to improve SC productivity/availability and customer satisfaction, too.

From the shipper and in particular the consignee point of view, transportation risks are manifold and can include difficulties such as the loss, damage and contamination of the product as well as security breaches (Novack et al., 2019). What is more relevant when talking about the negative effects of the pandemic, however, is delays in delivery and, above all, interruptions in the supply chain. The former touches particular time-sensitive shipments and parts needed for just-in-time deliver production, causing a domino effect and thus resulting in backlogs, delays as well as fluctuating freight rates.

References

Allianz Global Corporate & Specialty (2021). Safety and Shipping Review 2021, AGCS, Unterföhring. Retrieved from https://www.agcs.allianz.com/content/dam/onemarketing/agcs/agcs/reports/AGCS-Safety-Shipping-Review-2021.pdf

Azadian, F. (2020). Assessing the effect of urban socioeconomic factors and the financial crisis of 2008 on domestic air cargo traffic in Florida. *Transportation, 47*, 223–241.

Banister, D., & Berechman, J. (2000). *Transport investment and economic development*. Routledge.

Berdica, K. (2002). An introduction to road vulnerability: what has been done, is done and should be done. *Transport Policy, 9*, 117–127.

Bodewein, L. (2020). Machtdemonstration mit Wein. Tageschau. Retrieved from https://www.tagesschau.de/wirtschaft/weltwirtschaft/australien-mit-china-im-konflikt-101.html

Borca, B., Putz, L.-M., & Hofbauer, F. (2021). Crises and their effects on freight transport modes: A literature review and research framework. *Sustainability, 13*, 5740.

BMI. (2009). Nationale Strategie zum Schutz Kritischer Infrastrukturen (KRITIS-Strategie). Retrieved from https://www.bmi.bund.de/SharedDocs/downloads/DE/publikationen/themen/bevoelkerungsschutz/kritis.pdf;jsessionid=BEB4B857098376D74D0CF1311A776D6A.2_cid373?__blob=publicationFile&v=3

BMI. (2015). Nationale Strategie zum Schutz Kritischer Infrastrukturen (KRITIS-Strategie).

Brett D. (2021). Ongoing boost from shipping and bellyhold shortages for freighter operators. Aircargonews.com. Retrieved from https://www.aircargonews.net/airlines/freighter-operator/ongoing-boost-from-shipping-and-bellyhold-shortages/

BSI and BBK. (2021). Retrieved from https://www.kritis.bund.de/SubSites/Kritis/DE/Einfuehrung/einfuehrung_node.html

Bundeskanzleramt. (2015). Österreichisches Programm zum Schutz kritischer Infrastrukturen. Retrieved from https://www.bundeskanzleramt.gv.at/dam/jcr:bb6a1a41-eb1d-4552-96da-9b460bbc5c0b/%C3%96sterreichisches%20Programm%20zum%20Schutz%20kritischer%20Infrastrukturen%20(APCIP).pdf

Cascetta, E. (2001). Transportation systems. In *Transportation Systems Engineering: Theory and Methods. Applied Optimization* (Vol. 49). Springer.

Chambers S. (2021). Clarksons predicts seaborne trade volumes will surpass 2019 levels this year. Splash247.com. Retrieved from https://splash247.com/clarksons-predicts-seaborne-trade-volumes-will-surpass-2019-levels-this-year/

CISA. (2021). CRITICAL INFRASTRUCTURE SECTORS. Retrieved from https://www.cisa.gov/critical-infrastructure-sectors

Coyle, J. J., Langley, C. J., Novack, R. A., & Gibson, B. (2016). *Supply Chain Management: A Logistics Perspective*. Cengage Learning.

Dempsey H., Giles C., Riordan P. (2021). Shipping bottlenecks set to prolong supply chain turmoil. Financial Times. Retrieved from https://www.ft.com/content/e1263950-1173-4832-a011-ada04df1e93c

Dvořák, Z., Sventekova, E., Řehák, D., & Čekerevac, Z. (2017). Assessment of critical infrastructure elements in transport. *Procedia Engineering, 187*, 548–555.

Ellertsdottir, E. (2014). Eyjafjallajökull and the 2010 Closure of European Airspace: Crisis Management, Economic Impact, And tackling Future Risks.

EUROCONTROL. (2010). Ash-cloud of April and May 2010: Impact on Air Traffic. Retrieved from https://www.eurocontrol.int/sites/default/files/article/attachments/201004-ash-impact-on-traffic.pdf

Farazmand, A. (2018). *Global encyclopedia of public administration, public policy, and governance*. Springer International Publishing.

Fekete, A. (2011). Common criteria for the assessment of critical infrastructures. *International Journal of Disaster Risk Science, 2*(1), 15–24.

Gabela, J. G. F., & Sarmiento, L. (2020). The effects of the 2013 floods on Germany's freight traffic. *Transp. Res. Part D Transp. Environ., 82*(102), 274.

Hackl, J., Lam, J. C., Heitzler, M., Adey, B. T., & Hurni, L. (2018). Estimating network related risks: A methodology and an application in the transport sector. *Natural Hazards and Earth System Sciences, 18*(8), 2273–2293.

Ho, S. J., Xing, W., Wu, W., & Lee, C. C. (2021). The impact of COVID-19 on freight transport: Evidence from China. *MethodsX, 8*(101), 200.

IATA – International Air Transport Association. (2021). ATA Economics' Chart of the Week Freighters and Preighters – The Agility of Airline Cargo Operations. Retrieved from https://www.iata.org/en/iata-repository/publications/economic-reports/freighters-and-preighters%2D%2Dthe-agility-of-airline-cargo-operations/

ICAO – International Civil Aviation Organization. (2021). Effects of Novel Coronavirus (COVID-19) on Civil Aviation: Economic Impact Analysis. Retrieved from https://www.icao.int/sustainability/Documents/COVID-19/ICAO_Coronavirus_Econ_Impact.pdf

Islam, D. M. Z. (2018). Prospects for European sustainable rail freight transport during economic austerity. *Benchmarking Int. J., 25*, 2783–2805.

Jerebić, V., & Pavlin, S. (2018). Global Economy Crisis and its Impact on Operational Container Carrier's Strategy. *Promet Traffic Transp., 30*, 187–194.

Katina, P. F., & Hester, P. T. (2013). Systemic determination of infrastructure criticality. *International journal of critical infrastructures, 9*(3), 211–225.

Lewis, W. M. (1936). The significance of transportation to civilization. *The ANNALS of the American Academy of Political and Social Science., 187*(1), 1–6.

Lietuvnikė, M. M., Vasilienė-Vasiliauskienė, V., & Vasilis-Vasiliauskas, A. (2017). Core problems the road freight transport companies face due to the refugee crisis. *Innov. Infotechnolog. Sci. Bus. Educ., 2*, 3–9.

Mattsson, L. G., & Jenelius, E. (2015). Vulnerability and resilience of transport systems–A discussion of recent research. *Transportation Research Part A: Policy and Practice, 81*, 16–34.

Meier-Dallach, H. P. (1979). *Transport and the Challenge of Structural Change - Decentralisation and Regional Environment*. ECMT.

Min, D.; Fengqing, W.; Shibing, Z. Impact Analysis of the Global Financial Crisis on Global Container Fleet. In Proceedings of the sixth International Conference on Service Systems and Service Management, 2009: pp. 161–166.

Novack, R. A., Gibson, B. J., Suzuki, Y., & Coyle, J. J. (2019). Transportation: A Global Supply Chain Perspective.

Nowakowska, M., & Tubis, A. (2018). The impact of illegal population migration on the risk assessment of freight transport carried out by polish carriers. *Logist. Transp., 40*, 121–128.

Patrman, D., Splichalova, A., Rehak, D., & Onderkova, V. (2019). Factors influencing the performance of critical land transport infrastructure elements. *Transportation Research Procedia, 40*, 1518–1524.

Quarantelli, E. L. (2000). *Emergencies, disaster and catastrophes are different phenomena.* Disaster Research Center, University of Delaware, Newark.

Radionov, N., & Savić, I. (2019). The Impact of Irregular Migrations, Smuggling and Human Trafficking on the Land Transport Industry: The Croatian Case. *Pored. Pomor. Pravo, 173*, 103–149.

Reuters. (2021). Suez Canal shipping backlog ends, days after giant vessel freed. Retrieved from https://www.reuters.com/article/uk-egypt-suezcanal-ship-idUSKBN2BQ07T

Rodrigue, J-P, (2020) The Geography of Transport Systems, Fifth Edition, : Routledge. 456 pages. ISBN: 978-0-367-36463-2 .

Sea-Intelligence. (2021). Schedule reliability continues to be low in July 2021. Retrieved from https://www.sea-intelligence.com/press-room/92-schedule-reliability-continues-to-be-low-in-july-2021

Schweizerische Eidgenossenschaft. (2017). Nationale Strategie zum Schutz kritischer Infrastrukturen 2018–2022. Retrieved from https://www.babs.admin.ch/content/babs-internet/de/aufgabenbabs/ski/nationalestrategie/_jcr_content/contentPar/tabs/items/downloads/tabPar/downloadlist/downloadItems/73_1460987489220.download/natstratski2018-2022_de.pdf

Seppänen, H., Luokkala, P., Zhang, Z., Torkki, P., & Virrantaus, K. (2018). Critical infrastructure vulnerability—A method for identifying the infrastructure service failure interdependencies. *International Journal of Critical Infrastructure Protection, 22*, 25–38.

Stabsabteilung Statistik der WKO. (2020). DIE ÖSTERREICHISCHE VERKEHRSWIRTSCHAFT DATEN UND FAKTEN 2020, Wirtschaftskammer, Wien.

Statistik Austria. (2021a). 74,4% weinger Fluggäste im Corona-Jahr 2020. Retrieved from https://www.statistik.at/web_de/presse/125440.html

Statistik Austria. (2021b). Transportaufkommen Transportaufkommen im Schienengüterverkehr 2020 um 4,9% gesunken. Retrieved from https://www.statistik.at/web_de/presse/125831.html

Statistik Austria. (2021c). Transportaufkommen österreichischer Unternehmen im Straßengüterverkehr verringerte sich 2020 um 6,6% auf 375,6 Mio. T. Retrieved from https://www.statistik.at/web_de/presse/126100.html

Van Essen, H., van Wijngaarden, L., Schroten, A., Sutter, D., Bieler, C., Maffii, S., & El Beyrouty, K. (2019). Handbook on the external costs of transport, version 2019 (No. 18.4 K83. 131).

Zhu, S., & Levinson, D. M. (2012). Disruptions to transportation networks: A review. In D. Levinson, H. Liu, & M. Bell (Eds.), *Network Reliability in Practice. Transportation Research, Economics and Policy*. Springer.

The Maritime Executive. (2021). *Time containerships spent waiting for berths doubled in two years*. Published 16 July 2021. Retrieved September 30, 2021, from https://www.maritime-executive.com/article/time-containerships-spent-waiting-for-berths-doubled-in-two-years

Stefan Schönfelder is a transportation scientist and a university lecturer. His particular research interests are the structures and motives of travel behaviour and current transport policy issues. Stefan Schönfelder has been working in consultancy and research institutions such as the ETH Zurich, WIFO and the German Federal Institute for Research on Building, Urban Affairs and Spatial Development (BBSR) before he joined the Institute for Transport and Logistics Management at WU (Vienna University of Economics and Business) in April 2019.

Manuel Tuscher is a Ph.D.-candidate at the Institute for Transport and Logistics Management at WU (Vienna University of Economics and Business). He holds a master's degree in Information Systems and is a part of the institute since 2017. His research interest lie within the field of mobility and travel behaviour.

Chapter 6
Modern Slavery and Working Conditions in the European Trucking Industry: A Growing Threat to Supply Chain Resilience

Ki-Hoon Lee, Wolfram Groschopf, and Andreas Mossyrsch

Abstract The purpose of this paper is to uncover grey areas of modern slavery and to highlight the key challenges and opportunities of modern slavery and working conditions in European road transport. Under the increasing pressure on modern slavery in supply chains, supply chain managers and researchers have mainly focused on the focal firm and/or a buying firm without considering outsourced suppliers' activities such as transportation and logistics. To close this gap in the existing literature, the paper presents insights from the transportation and logistics field in the European Union based on an explorative online survey. The results clearly indicate the existence of modern slavery in sub-tier supplier activities in European road transportation: Short-visa holding truck drivers from non-EU Eastern Europe countries are placed in vulnerable positions where they are exploited. To manage supplier risks relating to modern slavery and working conditions, focal firms and/or buying firms need to identify and remove modern slavery risks from supply chains. Opportunities exist for supply chain risk management and investment in modern slavery reduction. More empirical evidence and theory-driven research in supply chain management are needed to facilitate the understanding and managing modern slavery risks and to contribute to supply chain resilience.

K.-H. Lee
Griffith Business School, Griffith University, Brisbane, QLD, Australia

W. Groschopf (✉)
Institute for Transport and Logistics Management, WU (Vienna University of Economics and Business), Vienna, Austria
e-mail: wolfram.groschopf@wu.ac.at

A. Mossyrsch
Camion Pro e.V., Munich, Germany

S. Kummer et al. (eds.), *Supply Chain Resilience*, Springer Series in Supply Chain Management 17, https://doi.org/10.1007/978-3-030-95401-7_6

6.1 Introduction

The multidisciplinary concept of resilience has been subject to research in various domains, focusing on psychological, social and economic phenomena (Jain et al., 2017; Ponomarov & Holcomb, 2009). In supply chain context, resilience is a relatively new research field. So far, scientific literature proposes different approaches to defining the term 'supply chain resilience'. In a comprehensive literature review, Hosseini et al. (2019) identify different definitions of supply chain resilience and conclude that, 'many definitions underscore the capability of a SC [supply chain] to recover and return to normal operations after a disruption'. Supply chain disruption refers to realised risks caused by natural disasters or manmade threats like labour strikes or terrorist attacks, highlighting vulnerabilities of single organisations, entire supply chains or global industries (Chopra & Sodhi, 2014). Vulnerabilities and possible threats to supply chain resilience need to be recognised to achieve better readiness and preparedness against unexpected disruptions (Hosseini et al., 2019). Current research on supply chain resilience focuses mainly on economic aspects like competitive advantage, outsourcing, product and information availability and economic sustainability without considering ecological or social sustainability (Jain et al., 2017; Ponomarov & Holcomb, 2009). Nevertheless, the relationship and possible trade-offs between resilience and ecological and social sustainability in supply chains form existing research gaps (Fahimnia & Jabbarzade, 2016).

Environmental sustainability in supply chains gains increasing attention within the scientific community as well as from corporate executives, but the topic of modern slavery in supply chains needs further attention. The term 'modern slavery' describes a range of exploitative practices and forced labour cases, and there is a broad consensus that such exploitation is widespread internationally. Modern slavery working conditions are exemplary for a lack of social sustainability in supply chains and impose challenges, which are often complex, vexed and partially hidden. Gold et al. (2015) define 'modern slavery in supply chains' as 'the exploitation of a person who is deprived of individual liberty anywhere along the supply chain, from raw material extraction to the final customer, for the purpose of service provision or production (p. 487)'. In particular, grey areas of exploitive working conditions in supply chain and logistics industries with multiple subcontracting like European road transport are not visible for buyers or focal firms in global supply chains.

Recognising modern slavery as a global problem and acts to begin a legislative movement to ensure that the products imported or services purchased by a company are not tainted by human rights or labour abuse occurring directly or indirectly through their supply chains. The UK Modern Slavery Act 2015 requires corporate organisations with a turnover of £36 million or more to report on modern slavery in their operations and supply chains through annual modern slavery statements (UK Government, 2015). More recently, Australia's Modern Slavery Act 2018 came into force in January 2019 requiring corporate entities with annual consolidated revenue of more than $100 million to address modern slavery risks

(Commonwealth of Australia, 2019). Many businesses are struggling to deal with the legal requirements and customer expectations that go beyond their direct operations like outsourced transport services, imposing an increasing threat to their supply chains' resilience.

6.2 Problem Framing

Modern slavery and working conditions are associated with vulnerability and extreme exploitation in supply chains. In today's globalised supply chains, focal firms and buying firms adopt cost advantages by facilitating cheap labour through their supply chains (LeBaron, 2014). As today's supply chains are often global and highly outsourced, the risk of using modern slavery labour in raw material extraction exists not only in developing countries but also developed regions. The use of unidentified or grey slavery labour in supply chains that often go beyond first-tier suppliers becomes a considerable legal and reputational risk for focal companies (Lee & Vachon, 2016).

Recent publications mainly focus on raw material extraction and processing. In this context, existing studies primarily provide insights in form of case studies and findings in fisheries, textile and garments and the cocoa sectors. Alsamawi et al. (2017) found that many workers from Southeast Asia for fishing are undocumented and obtain their position through unofficial channels paying fees to brokers. Nolan (2017) and Sreedharan and Kapoor (2018) report that buying firms' push for cheap clothing produced in shorter periods provides some grounds for developing underground in shadow factories with enforced labour. Crane (2013) also argues that the cocoa industry from West Africa, particularly in Ivory Coast, exploited child labour and forced labour for decades. The cocoa industry is an example of unequal power distribution between local farmers, which are often poor smallholders and buyers from large multinational companies (Christ et al., 2020; Manzo, 2005). Most studies report examples of modern slavery in developing countries based such as Southeast Asia and Africa where cheap, non-technical and simple labour is available for many multinational companies in developed countries.

Recent studies address social conditions in the European road transport industry. For instance, EVA (2019) provides an overview of EU social rules and national framework conditions for effective enforcement of social regulations in the road transport industry in different countries. The authors highlight legislative loopholes and fraudulent practices concluding, 'There is no just and fair level playing field (EVA, 2019, p. 69)' in European road transport. ETF (2018) provides an insight on working conditions of truck drivers in international road transport in the EU based on qualitative interviews, describing working conditions as alarming for the sector and shocking for social Europe. In accordance, AK (2016) describes working conditions in Europe's transport industry as 'borderless exploitation'.

Existing publications highlight poor working conditions and exploitative business practices using qualitative interviews and case studies. So far, supply chain resilience studies do not (a) reflect on the role and working conditions of the growing number of non-EU resident truck drivers employed in the European Union and (b) use online-based survey methods to collect information and describe the current state of social sustainability (in particular, modern slavery) in the European transport sector. To address these shortcomings, we present an example of modern slavery and working conditions of non-EU resident truck drivers in the Eastern European transport sector. The primary purpose of this study is to provide a better understanding on the key challenges and opportunities of modern slavery risks in supply chain management.

6.3 An Explorative Online Survey on Working Conditions in the European Road Transport Industry

Road transport is the dominant transport mode in EU27 freight transport, accounting for 76.3% of the total inland freight transport in 2019 (Eurostat, 2021). The European road freight transport market is strongly deregulated and internationalised, leading to an increasing share of foreign trucks and drivers operating in domestic and international road transport markets throughout the EU (Thörnquist, 2019). Truck hauling companies based in Eastern European member states gain increasing importance in the transport market. Vehicles registered in these countries performed 62% of international road transport based on ton-kilometres in the EU27 in 2019 (Amaral et al., 2021). To an increasing extent, transport companies hire drivers from non-EU countries and post them mainly to Western European countries. In 2020, almost 230,000 non-EU residents officially worked as truck drivers within the EU, mainly employed by Polish and Lithuanian companies (European Commission, 2021).

In Germany, Camion Pro e.V was founded in 2001 as a non-commercial association and protection community and has been an official association for the transport industry since 2003. Camion Pro e.V, as a protective community, has made it its mission to represent the rights and concerns of its members conscientiously and to act aggressively against the grievances of the industry in Europe. One of the authors represents Camion Pro e.V.

Based on insights from the trucking industry and on-site investigations in Eastern European countries, Camion Pro e.V conducted an online survey among non-EU resident truck drivers from Ukraine and Belarus employed by hauling companies from Eastern European EU-member states. The goal of the survey was to evaluate current working conditions, effects of COVID-19 on payment, and to identify potential modern slavery practices in this specific labour market segment.

Camion Pro e.V distributed the survey link via social media and relevant chat groups between May and July 2020 and provided YouTube videos to explain the goals of the survey and to stimulate participation on a voluntary basis. Survey and videos were provided in the Russian language. The main survey items include payment conditions (e.g. payment only for days in service), changes in working conditions under COVID-19 and potentially illegal activity requested by the employer (e.g. use of falsified documents supplied by employers, steering time violations). Out of 95 respondents, 80 respondents provided sufficient information for further analysis. The main findings from the survey are:

- Drivers operate mainly in Western European countries: 100%.
- Drivers do not receive the minimum wages applicable in the Western European country of operation: 100%.
- Employers refuse to pay the agreed salary: 91.25%.
- Salary is only paid for days in service. In case of sickness, holidays or a lack of customer demand, drivers do not receive a fixed income: 90%.
- Salary reductions were imposed on drivers since COVID-19: 77.5%.
- Drivers are at least sometimes forced to exceed the driving times: 70%.
- Employing companies provide falsified documents (e.g. falsified hotel bills to prove weekly rest periods outside trucks during police checks): 50%.

Respondents provide information on social challenges and in many cases illegal business practices along the entire working contract lifecycle. In recruitment, when Eastern European truck drivers from Ukraine and Belarus are hired, they often have to sign the contracts without understanding the content due to different language, as employers do not provide translations for newly hired drivers. Drivers are forced to sign the contracts 'blindly.' The resulting information asymmetry on contractual clauses, a lack of knowledge of applicable legal frameworks and procedures and the economic dependence established by the working contract form the basis for exploitation of the drivers.

Concerning the drivers' periods of operation, Eastern European truck drivers are usually on the road for 6–8 weeks at a time. Then they are replaced and have 2–4 weeks holiday without payment (i.e. unpaid leave). Many drivers are enforced to continue driving the trucks against their will. In some cases, drivers have to drive trucks over 3 months instead of 6 weeks. The hiring companies would not let them go home; otherwise, they would lose their jobs or at least parts of their wages. In this context, one survey respondent describes his situation as follows: 'I have been working for 17 weeks and they won't let me go home. They are also blackmailing me that if I stop my truck, I won't get the rest of my salary' (translated from Russian).

In working practice, the contracts seem to be irrelevant. Many drivers do not receive regular wages and certainly not in the agreed amount in the contract. In many cases, drivers are paid only a part of their wages, and the rest wage is withholding by the company. Besides, some drivers from Eastern Europe have a temporary and short work visa in the European Union. When it ends, the company deducts wages from accruals. To keep the job or to avoid dismissal, drivers are enforced to sign new contracts, agreeing to receive the reduced amount of wages, or to accept a pay cut. According to the survey results, Eastern European hauling companies use this business practice intensively since the beginning of the COVID-19 pandemic.

Finally, upon the termination of the employment relationship, many truck drivers report inconsistencies in the final settlement. In these cases, employers usually refuse to pay the agreed remuneration for overtime, retained salary components or allowances. At the end of the working contract, drivers have to leave the EU. Thus, they would have to claim labour rights from their country of origin. The main difficulties for drivers in this context consist of the assertion of legal claims from their country of origin in the country of the employer, high costs of legal enforcement of drivers' claims and a lack of knowledge of the legal situation. These circumstances usually result in drivers' rights not being enforceable and financial claims from working contracts, especially concerning allowances, not being re-coverable. In addition to financial issues, some respondents even report threats of slander by employers to reduce job prospects with other trucking companies.

6.4 Relevance

As truck transportation is often outsourced for economic and cost advantage purposes and subject to (multiple) subcontracting, the truck drivers have no direct formal contractual relationship with the focal firms. In Europe, truck drivers from non-EU Eastern European countries are often used in outsourced transportation and logistics services to contribute to major focal firms' economic advantages. The EU has recognised the fundamental problem of working conditions in European road transport and developed the EU Mobility Package. The goal of this reform is to enable competitive, socially fair, clean and sustainable mobility in the road transport industry (European Commission, 2017). The change in legal framework conditions through the EU Mobility Package concerning social regulations could improve specific aspects of drivers' working conditions in the long run (EVA, 2019). However, the abstract formulation of regulations was introduced, and the existence of blind spots still leaves room for illicit business practices at the drivers' expense. Besides, challenges in operational enforcement of regulations consist of the verification of compliance with the regulations as well as the enforceability of workers' rights at an international level in the different EU and non-EU countries.

The United Nations' Sustainable Development Goals (SDGs) Target 8.7 focuses on the eradication of forced labour by 2030. The target needs to be part of supply chain risk management because forced labour risks are prevalent across corporate supply chains regionally and globally. In this context, supply chain management researchers call for more actions and studies on modern slavery in supply chains as this field has been at large neglected (Gold et al., 2015; Stevenson & Cole, 2018).

6.5 Conclusion

Illegal or non-legitimate activities and documentations are current business practices in outsourced truck transportation. The subcontracted hauling companies, as employers of the truck drivers, use their power to push or enforce drivers in vulnerable and poor working conditions. Some cases involve third-party employment agencies in the supply of forced labour. The drivers' (workers') voice for fair working conditions is ignored and remains silent. The nature of modern slavery is often hidden and results in potentially severe repercussions for those who involved in labour exploitation if uncovered for warning or detection and remediation. The outsourced transportation service function is not visible in the focal firm's supply chain and at large neglected in supply chain management. The modern slavery risk for focal firms can be a high alarming risk unless grievance mechanisms and/or remediation actions are not implemented across the entire supply chain.

The study presented is not representative and has several shortcomings due to sample size, question types applied, formulation of specific questions and scaling. Nevertheless, it clearly demonstrates a viable solution approach for data collection in this specific labour market segment and shows the applicability of online surveys in this field of research.

Finally, the study reveals that truck drivers and related modern slavery risks are hidden and invisible in supply chains and constitute existing threats to supply chain sustainability and resilience. Without detecting or identifying the risks of modern slavery and working conditions from sub-suppliers, many firms are revealed to legal, economic, social and reputational risks. As companies face increasing legitimate pressure of modern slavery acts (UK, Australia, California, EU), logistics and supply chain managers should pay immediate attention to establish modern slavery risk management in supply chain management for enhanced supply chain resilience. Future research opportunities consist of the concept development for the segregation of road transport providers and schemes for the assessment and development of transport service providers to prevent operational disruptions in supply chains. The development of dynamic models for sustainability trade-off analysis could facilitate deeper insights on the effects of different approaches to mitigate modern slavery risks in supply chains and reduce supply chain vulnerability resulting from poor working conditions in European road transport. Finally, supply chain research should address possible effects from enhanced social sustainability in supply chains on supply chain resilience and contribute to multidisciplinary research development by examining the relationship between sustainability and resilience in supply chains.

References

AK. (2016). Kammer für Arbeiter und Angestellte für Wien. In Vienna Chamber of Labour (Ed.), *Borderless mobility - Borderless exploitation: Working conditions in Europe's transport industry*. Retrieved August 15, 2021, from https://akeuropa.eu/sites/default/files/main_report_en_411.pdf

Alsamawi, A., McBain, D., Murray, J., Lenzen, M. and Wiebe, K. (2017), "Case study – assessing social impacts in the seafood industry", The Social Footprints of Global Trade. Environmental Footprints and Eco-Design of Products and Processes, Springer, Singapore.

Amaral, S., Scammell, H., Pons, A., Benney, R., Niu, T., Giannelos, G., Millard, K., Tweed, J., & McKinnon, A. (2021). Assessment of the impact of a provision in the context of the revision of

Regulation (EC) No 1071/2009 and Regulation (EC) No 1072/2009 - Final Report. Retrieved August 14, 2021, from https://op.europa.eu/en/publication-detail/-/publication/b35587b8-72a1-11eb-9ac9-01aa75ed71a1
Chopra, S., & Sodhi, M. (2014). Reducing the Risk of Supply Chain Disruptions. *MIT Sloan Management Review, 55*(3), 72–80.
Christ, K., Burritt, R., & Schaltegger, S. (2020). Accounting for work conditions from modern slavery to decent work. *Accounting, Auditing & Accountability Journal, 33*(7), 1481–1504.
Commonwealth of Australia (2019), Commonwealth Modern Slavery Act 2018, Canberra.
Crane, A. (2013). Modern slavery as a management practice: exploring the conditions and capabilities for human exploitation. *Academy of Management Review, 38*(1), 49–69.
ETF. (2018). In European Transport Worker's Federation (Ed.), *Modern slavery in modern Europe*. Retrieved April 11, 2021, from https://www.etf-europe.org/resource/etf-brochure-modern-slavery-in-modern-europe/
Eurostat. (2021) "Modal split of freight transport" (defined as the percentage of each inland mode in total freight transport performance measured in tonne-kilometres. Inland freight transport modes include road, rail and inland waterways). Retrieved April 10, 2021, from http://appsso.eurostat.ec.europa.eu/nui/submitViewTableAction.do
EVA. (2019). In Europäische Akademie für umweltorientierten Verkehr gGmbH (Ed.), *Social conditions in logistics in Europe: Focus on road transport*. Retrieved April 14, 2021, from https://psl.verdi.de/++file++5d00b20c9194fb1d8bbc127f/download/Social%20Conditions%20Logistics%20in%20Europe.pdf
European Commission. (2017). Europe on the Move: Driving change for business and people. Retrieved August 14, 2021, from https://ec.europa.eu/transport/modes/road/road-initiatives_en
European Commission. (2021). Driver attestations in road freight transport 2012–2020. Retrieved July 27, 2021, from https://ec.europa.eu/transpo/sites/default/files/driver-attestations-in-road-freight-transport.pdf (europa.eu)
Fahimnia, B., & Jabbarzade, A. (2016). Marrying supply chain sustainability and resilience: A match made in heaven. *Transportation Research Part E, 91*(2016), 306–324.
Gold, S., Trautrims, A., & Trodd, Z. (2015). Modern slavery challenges to supply chain management. *Supply Chain Management: An International Journal, 20*(5), 485–494.
Hosseini, S., Ivanov, D., & Dolgui, A. (2019). Review of quantitative methods for supply chain resilience analysis. *Transportation Research Part E, 125*(2019), 285–307.
Jain, V., Kumar, S., Soni, U., & Chandra, C. (2017). Supply chain resilience: model development and empirical analysis. *International Journal of Production Research, 55*(2), 6779–6800.
LeBaron, G. (2014). Subcontracting is not illegal, but is it unethical? Business ethics, forced labor, and economic success. *The Brown Journal of World Affairs, 20*(2), 237–249.
Lee, K.-H., & Vachon, S. (2016). *Business Value and Sustainability: An Integrated Supply Network Perspective*. Palgrave.
Manzo, K. (2005). Modern slavery, global capitalism and deproletarianisation in West Africa. *Review of African Political Economy, 32*(106), 521–534.
Nolan, J. (2017). Business and human rights: the challenge of putting principles into practice and regulating global supply chains. *Alternative Law Journal, 42*(1), 42–46.
Sreedharan, L., & Kapoor, A. (2018). *Sitting on Pins and Needles*. Anti-Slavery International.
Ponomarov, S. Y., & Holcomb, M. C. (2009). Understanding the concept of supply chain resilience. *The International Journal of Logistics Management, 20*(1), 124–143.
Stevenson, M., & Cole, R. (2018). Modern slavery in supply chains: a secondary data analysis of detection, remediation and disclosure. *Supply Chain Management: An International Journal, 23*(2), 81–99.
Thörnquist, A. (2019). Truck Drivers in the Grey Area between Employment and Self-employment: Swedish Experiences. *Nordic Journal of Working Life Studies, 9*(6), 33–52.
UK Government. (2015). *Modern Slavery Act 2015*. The Stationery Office, London. Retrieved March 10, 2020, from www.legislation.gov.uk/ukpga/2015/30/pdfs/ukpga_20150030_en.pdf

Ki-Hoon Lee is a Professor of Business Sustainability at Griffith Business School, Griffith University in Australia. Through his research, Professor Lee embraces environmental, social, governance and economic challenges, integrating sustainability into the business value chain to enhance both business and societal value. With his teaching, consulting and public policy experience, Professor Lee's research and consulting expertise include corporate sustainability management, sustainable supply chain management, responsible sourcing and transparency in global supply chain, and environmental, social and governance (ESG) in supply chain performance management.

Wolfram Groschopf is an assistant professor at the Institute for Transport and Logistics Management at WU (Vienna University of Economics and Business). Previously he worked as a senior lecturer at WU Vienna, as a management consultant in Austria and as an IT-project manager in Belgium. His research focuses mainly on ecological and social sustainability in transport, digitalization in logistics and supply chain management, and e-commerce.

Andreas Mossyrsch is a former transport operator, founder and board member of the professional association Camion Pro, with which he is also involved in the fight against economic crime and social dumping. In addition, as an investigative journalist, he conducted several undercover research projects in Germany and Eastern Europe, during which he succeeded in uncovering central connections to organised crime in the transport industry. Mossyrsch is also a co-author of several scientific studies on economic crime in the transport industry, among others for the Swiss government.

Part II
Measuring Resilience

Chapter 7
Enhancing Supply Chain Resilience Through Incorporating Business Continuity Management Systems

Felix Tuczek

Abstract Predictable and unpredictable disruptions of supply chains are omnipresent. This has led to an increased interest in methods and tools to handle disruptions. A possible solution to reduce the impact of disruptions to organizations is the implementation of a business continuity management system (BCMS). The objective of a BCMS is to continue the delivery of products and services within an acceptable time frame at predefined capacity during disruption. This manuscript, therefore, presents the content of a BCMS referring to the well-recognized standards ISO 22301 and the corresponding standard of the Federal Office for Information Security (BSI) in Germany. The central element of an BCMS is the business impact analysis and for this reason it is discussed in detail. Finally, the BCMS is set into the broader field of supply chain resilience. It is important to consider the supply side to achieve resilience.

7.1 Introduction

Supply chain disruptions have been omnipresent recently. Critical infrastructure such as an oil pipeline in the USA (Krauss, 2021) and even hospitals were shut down after attacks with ransomware, for instance, in Duesseldorf (Ernst, 2020). Apart from cyberattacks, other events like the ship blocking the Suez Canal bring about disruptions of supply chains (Ziady, 2021). Currently, the pandemic outbreak interrupts material flows, and moreover employees are absent due to restrictions in movement and diseases (Allianz Global Corporate & Specialty, 2021). Thus 94% of all companies suffered disruptions due to the pandemic outbreak. In addition, cyberattacks have risen during the lockdowns around the globe (Garatti & Dib, 2020).

In order to cope with these pressing topics, companies are striving to become resilient throughout the supply chain. Yet we focus on the resilience of a single company without outlining the consequences on the entire supply chain in detail. A

F. Tuczek (✉)
Stuttgart, Germany

S. Kummer et al. (eds.), *Supply Chain Resilience*, Springer Series in Supply Chain Management 17, https://doi.org/10.1007/978-3-030-95401-7_7

myriad of definitions of the term resilience exists (Chen et al., 2020). In the present paper, however, we follow the definition of the International Standardization Organization (ISO). Here, organizational resilience is defined as "ability of an organization to absorb and adapt in a changing environment" (ISO-22316, 2017). Thus, an increased degree of resilience enables companies to anticipate and respond to threats and opportunities emerging from sudden or gradual changes in companies' environment (ISO-22316, 2017). Promising practices for enhancing resilience are discussed such as collaboration and contingency planning (Tang & Musa, 2011). In the present paper, we focus on establishing a business continuity management system (BCMS) according to ISO 22301:2019. Business continuity encompasses the "capability of an organization to continue the delivery of products and services within acceptable time frame at predefined capacity during disruption" (ISO-22301, 2019). The management system provides the frame to achieve the respective objective. ISO defines a management system as "a set of interrelated or interacting elements of an organization to establish policies and objectives and processes to achieve those objectives." The scope of this management system can cover the entire organization or parts of the organization. The elements of an organization include, for instance, roles or organizational structure. A management system can address several disciplines (for instance, quality, environment, and BCM) or a single discipline (ISO-22301, 2019).

In the subsequent section, therefore, we show the main characteristics of the ISO 22301 standard. We begin with elucidating the current state of adopting BCMS. Then we outline the standard ISO 22301:2019 with its core elements for achieving business continuity. Afterward, BCMS is embedded into concepts of supply chain resilience. The paper ends with the summary.

7.2 Current State of Adopting Business Continuity Management Systems

The implementation of a BCMS is required by law for critical infrastructure and sector-specific regulations, for instance, in Germany the IT Security Act. Country-specific guidelines and certification options are available. One possibility to comply with legal requirements is to certify with ISO 22301 (BSI-CD-200-4, 2021; ISO-22301, 2019). The adoption of certifiable ISO standards yields various benefits, for instance, increased confidence in organizations with reliable systems (Tuczek et al., 2018) just like a BCMS.

ISO 22301 was first published in 2012. Since 2012, the adoption rate has increased worldwide. In 2019, 1693 valid certificates were issued. This represents the tenth most often used ISO management standard worldwide (first place: ISO 9001 with nearly 900,000 certificates) (ISO-Survey, 2019). Current data considering the consequences of COVID-19 are not available so far (this paper was written in spring 2021). In order to complete the picture on ISO certificates capturing business continuity, it is important to take a look at ISO 27001 (information security management systems). According to this standard, the implementation of a BCM is mandatory, yet the use of other standards than ISO 22301 is possible for achieving information security continuity (ISO/IEC-27001, 2013). For instance, companies certifying with ISO 27001 implement a BCM compliant to ISO 27031 or BSI 100-4. Due to the dissemination of IT into business processes, the implementation of ISO 27001 and ISO 22301 simultaneously is considered useful for yielding increased resilience and synergy effects in terms of integrated management systems (Appendix summarizes ISO standards considered in this paper).

A disruption is defined as an "event, whether anticipated (e.g., labor strike or hurricane) or unanticipated (e.g., a blackout or earthquake), that causes an unplanned, negative deviation from the expected delivery of products or services according to an organization's objectives." As outlined in the introduction to this paper, ISO 22301 aims to develop a BCMS to prepare for, provide, and maintain controls and capabilities for managing an organization's overall ability to continue to operate during disruptions (ISO-22301, 2019).

Scientific research on BCM has been scarce so far (Wieteska, 2018). However, research underscores the positive impact of BCM implementation on competitive advantages, supply chain cooperation, and recovery time (Montshiwa et al., 2016).

7.3 Establishing a Business Continuity Management System

ISO 22301:2019 is structured in accordance with the ISO High-Level Structure (HLS) applying the plan, do, check, and act (PDCA) cycle. This structure ensures a degree of consistency with other management standards such as ISO 9001 and ISO 14001 facilitating the integration of different management systems. Relevant to certification are the clauses 4–10. The plan phase of the PDCA encompasses clauses 4–7. In these clauses, the organization and its internal and external context are under scrutiny in order to ensure the BCMS meets its requirements. Further, the role of top management as well as planning actions and supportive elements to establish a BCMS are addressed. The do phase of the PDCA cycle is reflected in clause 8. This is the central part of the BCMS and discussed subsequently. Clause 9—the check phase of the PDCA—consists of the measurement options for a BCMS and the corresponding management review. Finally, clause 10 addresses the continuous improvement of the BCMS (ISO-22301, 2019).

As already mentioned, clause 8 is the core element of a BCMS. The six elements of business continuity management as described in ISO 22301:2019:

- Operational planning and control encompass planning, implementation, and controlling of processes to meet the requirements.
- Business impact analysis (BIA) and risk assessment: The BIA process aims to analyze the impact over time of a disruption on the organization. The risk assessment captures risks that could lead to a disruption. The risk assessment is

often conducted as part of risk or information security management. BIA and risk assessment lay the foundation for building business continuity strategies.

- Business continuity strategies and solutions: Identification and evaluation of different paths to achieve business continuity enable organizations to choose from suitable options of preventing disruptions and treat disruptions that take place. The organization assesses the different strategy options in terms of their parameters such as costs or recovery time and selects the appropriate option.
- Business continuity plans and procedures: This element of the BCMS captures the implementation and maintenance of a response structure facilitating timely warning and communication to relevant interested parties. The business continuity plans are documented information guiding an organization through the disruption.
- Exercise program: Organizations implement and maintain a program of exercising and testing. This ensures that business continuity strategies and solutions are complete, current, and appropriate.
- Evaluation of business continuity documentation and capabilities: The organization is to evaluate the documentation (e.g., business continuity plans, testing procedures) at planned intervals and when necessary due to changing circumstances.

Even though all aspects of ISO 22301:2019 and elements of business continuity management are helpful and important, the heart of a BCMS is the business impact analysis (BIA). This statement is also underscored empirically (Montshiwa et al., 2016).

7.3.1 Business Impact Analysis (BIA)

According to ISO 22301:2019, the scope of the BCMS is already defined in the plan phase of the PDCA cycle. Conducting BIA is positioned in the do phase of the PDCA and is employed within the previously defined scope of the BCM. The result of the BIA determines which business processes and resources are time-critical. Further, the threshold of unacceptable impact to the organization is set. This leads to define the boundaries, levels, and duration of emergency operations. The impact of a disruption over time increases. Impact (or damage) categories are, for instance, financial loss due to fines, penalties, lost profits or diminished market share (BSI 100-4, 2009).

Several ways to conduct a business impact analysis (BIA) are applied (e.g., ISO/TS 22317:, 2015, BSI CD 200-4). Subsequently, the way to conduct a BIA is presented according to BSI 100-4. Like other standards (e.g., ISO 27031:, 2013; ISO/TS 22317:, 2015), this is a well-recognized standard. An advantage of this standard is the continuous reference to information security management, yet addressing other disruptive events such as shortfalls in delivery additionally. Further it provides detailed guidelines free of charge supporting the easy access to BCM

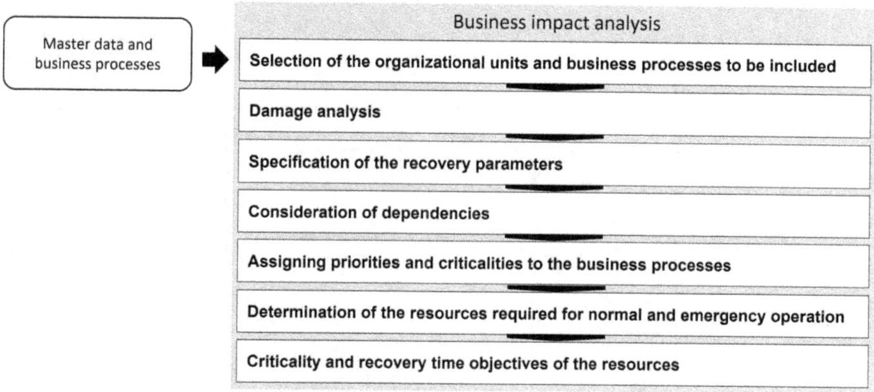

Fig. 7.1 Overview of a business impact analysis (source: ISO 100-4, 2009)

(BSI-100-4, 2009). Currently, the revised version has been published as a draft in German only (BSI-CD-200-4, 2021). The content of the BIA, however, remains almost the same in both BSI standards.

Figure 7.1 depicts the steps of conducting a business impact analysis. Before starting the BIA, an overview of all relevant business processes in the organization is needed. If this is not available, the overview must be created or updated. Additionally, master data of the organization (e.g., locations) are needed.

Step 1: Selection of the organizational units and business processes to be included—Within the scope of the BCMS, some business processes are not critical to organization. These processes do not need further examination.

Step 2: Damage analysis—Examination of potential damage to an organization when individual business processes fail. In addition to the amount of the damage, the chronological sequence of damage is especially important.

Step 3: Specification of the recovery parameter—Based on the chronological sequence of damaging events and the amount of damage expected, the maximum tolerable period of disruption, the recovery time objective, and the recovery level for each business process are specified.

- The recovery level and the process capacity required for stable emergency operation (e.g., 60% capacity) must also be specified in addition to the time of recovery.
- The maximum tolerable period of disruption (MTPD) of a process designates the time frame in which the process must be recovered so that the organization does not enter a phase in which its ability to survive is threatened in the short term or long term.
- The recovery time objective (RTO) specifies the time in which the process is intended to be recovered.
- The time frame specified for the RTO must be lower than the maximum tolerable period of disruption.

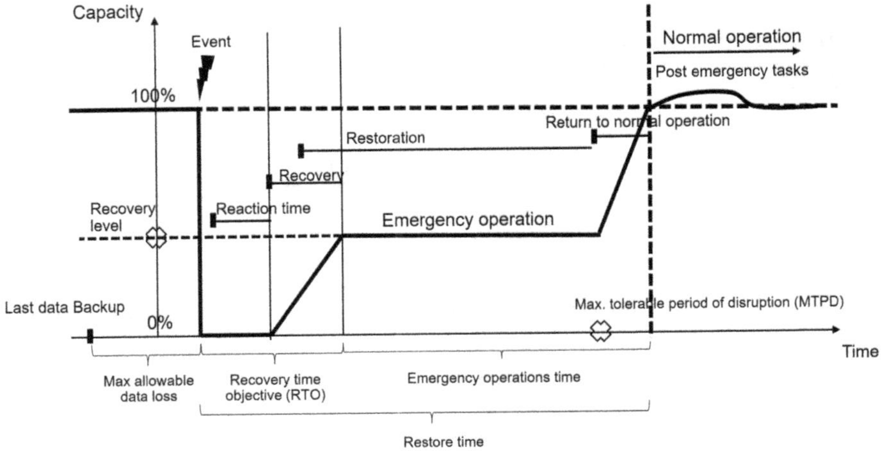

Fig. 7.2 Recovery parameters (source: BSI 100-4, 2009)

These KPIs are central to the concept of business continuity and visualized in Figure 7.2.

Step 4: Taking dependencies into account—The recovery parameters are specified individually for each process. In this step, interdependencies between business processes are analyzed, and the availability requirements are adjusted if necessary.

Step 5: Prioritization and criticality of the business processes—Based on the data available for recovery and the resulting damage, the order in which the business processes will be recovered and the criticality of each process are specified. To do this, the criticality categories and their boundaries must be defined.

Step 6: Determining which resources are required for normal and emergency operations—To be able to develop continuity strategies and specify preventive measures, it is necessary to identify the resources used by the critical business processes. The types of resources and the capacity required for normal operation and for emergency operation must be determined.

Step 7: Criticalities and recovery time objectives of the resources—Finally, the recovery and restoration time objectives of the resources used by the critical processes as well as their criticalities are determined. The restoration time objective is the time from the interruption of the process until the start of normal operations (BSI-100-4, 2009).

7.4 Linkage Between BCMS and Supply Chain Resilience

In this section, the linkage of business continuity to the field of supply chain resilience is discussed threefold. First, the BCM is embedded into a taxonomy of supply chain resilience. Second, ISO standards with relevance to supply chain resilience are presented. Third, the influence of suppliers on supply chain resilience is reviewed.

Supply chain resilience can be defined "as the ability of a supply chain to decrease the likelihood and/or impacts of possible disruptions, and to reduce the restoring and resuming times" (Falasca et al., 2008). Based on this definition, it can be derived that supply chain resilience has several dimensions with appropriate resilience strategies (Namdar et al., 2021):

- Anticipation: Detection of disruptions in advance, e.g., information-sharing.
- Preparation: Decrease response time (e.g., supply chain continuity team) or assess/reduce likelihood of an incident, e.g., risk management process.
- Robustness: Reduce disruption impact (e.g., strategic stock and slack, redundancy) or avoid disruptions, e.g., supplier selection.
- Recovery: Resumption of disrupted processes, e.g., recovery plans.

The business continuity management system presented captures preparation in terms of establishing organizational structure to respond to disruption. Further, robustness is increased through establishing continuity strategies based on the BIA results. Finally, recovery plans are central to BCMS. Overall, the discussed BCM standards in this paper underscore the need to take into account supply chain processes and especially suppliers.

Apart from ISO 22301, further standards consider supply chain resilience. ISO/TS 22318 provides guidance for extending the BCM addressed in ISO 22301 to supply chain continuity. This standard, therefore, focuses on relationships to suppliers in order to assure continuity of supply. In opposite to ISO 22301, the standard ISO/TS 22318 is not certifiable (ISO/TS-22318, 2015). ISO 28001 addresses security management systems for supply chains. It requires organizations to assess their business environment and derive appropriate security measures. Currently, ISO 28001 is under revision by Technical Committee ISO/TC 292, which also worked on ISO 22301. The revised version will be structured accordingly to the high-level structure to align with other management system standards. ISO 28001 is certifiable (ISO-28001, 2007). As already mentioned in this paper, ISO 22301 complements ISO 27001 (information security). Intersections to business continuity is obvious in ISO 20000 (IT Service Management). This standard is originated in ITIL, with the practice "service continuity management" embedded in the service value chain (ITIL-4, 2019).

In order to react to the growing risk of business disruptions, companies initiate business continuity management followed by developing suppliers (Allianz Global Corporate & Specialty, 2021). This is reasoned with the domino effect caused by disruption of supply. In manufacturing companies, the production processes cause the most disruptions (Wieteska, 2018b). Therefore, reliable and robust suppliers are of special interest. A myriad of criteria for supplier selection are applied. However, the BCM capabilities of candidate suppliers have not been considered in supplier selection approaches so far. Even though approaches focusing on resilience are scarce, components to achieve resilience—such as flexibility—are widely implemented as a criterion for supplier selection (Tuczek & Wakolbinger, 2018).

7.5 Summary

In this paper a business continuity management system (BCMS) is presented. A BCMS sets a structured approach for organizations with the objective to continue the delivery of products and services within an acceptable time frame at predefined capacity during disruption. The heart of a BCMS is the business impact analysis which is the process of analyzing the impact over time of a disruption on the organization. After presenting the steps to conduct a business impact analysis, the BCMS and related standards are embedded into the field of supply chain resilience.

Appendix

Table 7.1 provides an overview of ISO standards discussed in this paper. Also relevant to business continuity management is BSI 100-4 (this standard is currently under revision)

Table 7.1 ISO standards considered in this paper

ISO standard	Title	Category
ISO/IEC 27001	Information technology—security techniques—information security management systems—requirements	Management system standard—certifiable
ISO/IEC 27031	Information technology—Security techniques—guidelines for information and communication technology readiness for business continuity	Guideline
ISO 22301	Security and resilience—business continuity management systems—requirement	Management system standard—certifiable
ISO 22313	Societal security—Business continuity management systems—Guidance	Guideline
ISO 22316	Security and resilience—organizational resilience—principles and attributes	Guideline
ISO/TS 22317	Societal security—business continuity management systems—guidelines for business impact analysis (BIA)	Guideline
ISO/TS 22318	Societal security—business continuity management systems—guidelines for supply chain continuity	Guideline
ISO 28001	Security management systems for the supply chain—best practices for implementing supply chain security, assessments and plans—requirements and guidance	Management system standard—certifiable
ISO/IEC 20000-1	Information technology—service management—Part 1: service management system requirements	Management system standard—certifiable
ISO 9001	Quality management systems—requirements	Management system standard—certifiable
ISO 14001	Environmental management systems—requirements with guidance for use	Management system standard—certifiable

References

Allianz Global Corporate & Specialty. (2021). Allianz risk barometer - identifying the major business risks for 2021. https://www.agcs.allianz.com/news-and-insights/reports/allianz-risk-barometer.html.

BSI-100-4. (2009). *BSI Standard 100–4- Business Continuity Management.* Federal Office for Information Security (BSI).

BSI-CD-200-4. (2021). BSI-Standard 200–4- Business Continuity Management (Community Draft). Bonn: Bundesamt für Sicherheit in der Informationstechnik.

Chen, L.; Dui, H.; Zhang, C. (2020). A resilience measure for supply chain systems considering the interruption with the cyber-physical systems. Reliability Engineering and System Safety (199).

Ernst, A. (2020). Polizei ermittelt nach Hacker-Angriff in einem Todesfall. Sueddeutsche Zeitung, https://www.sueddeutsche.de/panorama/duesseldorf-uniklinikum-erpressung-hacker-angriff-1.5035140

Falasca, M.; Zobel, C. W.; Cook D. . (2008). A decision support framework to assess supply chain resilience. Proceedings of the 5th International ISCRAM Conference, 596–605.

Garatti, A.; Dib, G. (2020). Global supply chain survey - In search of post Covid-19 resilience. Euler Hermes, Allianz.

ISO/IEC-27001. (2013). *Information Technology - Security Techniques - Information Security Management Systems - Requirements.* International Organization for Standardization.

ISO/TS-22317. (2015). *Societal Security - Business Continuity Management Systems - Guidelines for Business Impact Analysis (BIA).* International Organization for Standardization.

ISO/TS-22318. (2015). *Societal Security - Business Continuity Management Systems - Guidelines for Supply Chain Continuity.* International Organization for Standardization.

ISO-22301. (2019). *Security and Resilience - Business Continuity Management Systems - Requirements.* International Organization for Standardization.

ISO-22316. (2017). *Security and Resilience - Organizational Resilience - Principles and Attributes.* International Organization for Standardization.

ISO-28001. (2007). *Security Management Systems for the Supply Chain - Best Practices for Implementing Supply Chain Security, Assessments and Plans - Requirements and Guidance.* International Organization for Standardization.

ISO-Survey. (2019). 1._ISO_Survey_2019_results_-_Number_of_certificates_and_sites_per_country_and_the_number_of_sector_overall. https://isotc.iso.org/livelink/livelink?func=ll&objId=18808772&objAction=browse&viewType=1

ITIL-4. (2019). *ITIL Foundation-ITIL* (4th ed.). AXELOS Limited.

Krauss, C. (2021). Hackers and Climate Change Threaten U.S. Energy Independence. New York Times. https://www.nytimes.com/2021/05/18/business/energy-environment/colonial-pipeline-security-weather.html

Montshiwa, A. L., Nagahira, A., & Ishida, S. (2016). Modifying business continuity plan (BCP) towards an effective auto-mobile business continuity management (BCM): A quantitative approach. *Journal of Disaster Research, 11*, 691–698.

Namdar, J., Torabi, S., Sahebjamnia, N., & Pradhan, N. (2021). Business continuity-inspired resilient supply chain network design. International Journal of. *Production Research, 59*, 1331–1367.

Tang, C., & Musa, S. (2011). Identifying risk issues and research advancements in supply chain risk management. *International Journal of Production Economics, 133*, 25–34.

Tuczek, F., & Wakolbinger, T. (2018). A meta-analysis of sustainable supplier selection approaches. In H. Qudrat-Ullah (Ed.), *Innovative Solutions for Sustainable Supply Chains* (pp. 55–79). Springer International Publishing AG.

Tuczek, F., Castka, P., & Wakolbinger, T. (2018). A review of management theories in the context of quality, environmental and social responsibility voluntary standards. *Journal of Cleaner Production, 176*, 399–416.

Wieteska, G. (2018). Business Impact Analysis of supply chain disruptions. 8th International Conference on Management, Economics and Humanities, 110–119). Barcelona, Spain.

Wieteska, G. (2018b). The domino effect- disruptions in supply chains. *LogForum, 14*, 495–506.

Ziady, H. (2021). Global shipping was in chaos even before the Suez blockage. Shortages and higher prices loom. CNN. https://edition.cnn.com/2021/03/26/business/global-shipping-supply-chains/index.html

Felix Tuczek works as an IT-Consultant and as a manager for Integrated Management Systems. He runs projects in various industries such as automotive and insurance. Felix has earned a Ph.D. at the Institute for Transport and Logistics Management at WU (Vienna University of Economics and Business). In his scientific work, he focused on sustainability, supplier selection, and ISO management standards.

Chapter 8
Measuring and Fostering Supply Chain Resilience in the Humanitarian Context

Jonas Stumpf, Niklas Jaeschke, Maria Besiou, and Lisa Rustemeier

Abstract The severe impact of the COVID-19 pandemic has brought the consequences of supply chain disruptions into our everyday life. Organizations operating in the humanitarian space are confronted with supply chain risks in the majority of their programs. Building and strengthening supply chain resilience, in particular in the context of humanitarian operations, is critical. However, it is also a complex, time and resource intense undertaking. To tackle this challenge we present a proven approach that helps gaining fact-based knowledge on supply chain vulnerabilities and lays the foundation for impactful supply chain investments. We recommend a thorough analysis of the operating environment and the contextual factors by tapping into tools such as the "Country Logistics Resilience Indicator" tool. Ultimately, building resilience requires smart, sustainable, and long-term investment plans. To develop such investment plans and maximize the investment impact, HELP Logistics and KLU have benefitted from existing preparedness frameworks that highlight the relevance of considering both intra- and inter-organizational supply chain investments.

J. Stumpf (✉)
HELP Logistics, Schindellegi, Switzerland
e-mail: jonas.stumpf@kuehne-stiftung.org

N. Jaeschke
HELP Logistics, Nairobi, Kenya

M. Besiou
Kuehne Logistics University, Hamburg, Germany

L. Rustemeier
Otto Group, Hamburg, Germany

S. Kummer et al. (eds.), *Supply Chain Resilience*, Springer Series in Supply Chain Management 17, https://doi.org/10.1007/978-3-030-95401-7_8

8.1 Introduction

Supply chains are the backbone of humanitarian operations and lifeline for sustainable economic development (Lewin et al., 2018). The growing interconnectedness in today's world combined with accelerating change processes has created a dynamic and complex environment that makes organizations and their supply chains vulnerable to a multitude of operational and environmental risks. In 2020, the world was severely affected by COVID-19, but how has the pandemic affected the supply chains? A survey carried out by HELP Logistics in July 2020 with 76 representatives of the logistics sector in East Africa found that the COVID-19 pandemic has been causing severe transport capacity restrictions, higher cost, and longer lead times for humanitarian operations in the region (O'Sullivan et al., 2020). In this chapter, we discuss the supply chain risks humanitarian actors are facing and outline a practical approach to evaluate and strengthen their resilience.

8.2 Supply Chain Risks, Disruptions, and Resilience

According to Pfohl (2002), there is no universal classification of supply chain risks. For this chapter, we follow Christopher and Peck (2004), who differentiate between three categories of risk that contain subcategories and produce a total of five categories (Fig. 8.1): risks that are internal to the organization (process and control risks), risks that are external to the organization but internal to the supply chain network (demand and supply risks), and risks that are external to the network (environmental risks).

Supply chain risks are very much present in humanitarian operations. We list some examples below (Table 8.1).

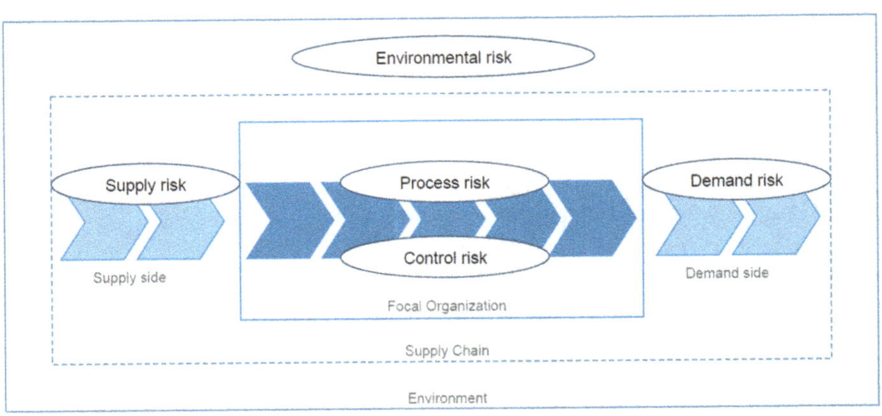

Fig. 8.1 Supply chain risk classification by Christopher and Peck (2004)

Table 8.1 Supply chain risk taxonomy and examples

Risk category	Examples
Environmental risks	Security issues in terms of theft of supplies as well as security risks for aid workers; weather conditions such as flooding making transport corridors impassable or damaging supplies during storage or handling; government regulations affecting specific supplies, areas, or organizations; financial constraints at donor level reducing funds for operations
Supply risks	Suppliers affected by disaster or becoming obsolete; transport corridors affected by disaster or/and overloaded with large volume of relief supplies; high demand and competition for supplies in the immediate aftermath of a disaster
Process and control risks	Poor IT infrastructure limits information exchange and hampers planning and managing of a response; no or poorly defined processes, guidelines, and standards slow down operation in particular at the early stage of a response; insufficient supply chain knowledge of staff increases risk for mistakes all along the supply chain from planning to distribution; unclear roles and responsibilities and weak coordination between departments increase potential for conflicts and frustration, duplication of efforts, and delays in decision-making process; wrong order quantities or the lack of safety stocks may lead to stock-outs and failure to deliver
Demand risks	High uncertainty on the actual occurrence of the disaster (in terms of time, location, and scale of devastation) that triggers the needs and also high uncertainties on the needs in the immediate aftermath (what, where, and how much is needed)

Any of the risks presented can lead to severe disruptions in the supply chain. Wagner and Bode (2008) define a supply chain disruption as "the combination of (1) an unintended, anomalous triggering event that materializes somewhere in the supply chain or its environment, and (2) a consequential situation which significantly threatens normal business operations of the firms in the supply chain." A disrupted or even collapsing supply chain in an emergency relief program leads to extensive costs and late deliveries, with the consequence of prolonged and aggravated suffering for the affected population (Blecken, 2010; Lewin et al., 2018).

Reducing and avoiding risks of supply chain disruptions should therefore be of utmost interest to any actor operating in the humanitarian space. In this context, the concept of supply chain resilience is gaining increasing attention in research and practice (e.g., Day, 2014; Dubey, 2019; Scholten et al., 2014; Zobel & Khansa, 2014).

Wieland and Durach (2021) describe supply chain resilience as "the capacity of a supply chain to persist, adapt, or transform in the face of a change." Subsequently, building or strengthening supply chain resilience can ultimately reduce vulnerability to disruptions (Tang, 2006; Wagner & Bode, 2008).

However, in spite of increasing attention by researchers and practitioners alike, our experience has shown that most humanitarian organizations still lack formal supply chain risk management processes.

At the same time, the recent COVID-19 pandemic served as a reminder of the importance of comprehensive risk management and resilience in humanitarian supply chains. The evaluation of the resilience level and the identification of critical bottlenecks are essential prerequisites for any effort that aims at strengthening supply chain resilience in the long run (Christopher & Peck, 2004; Ponomarov & Holcomb, 2009).

8.3 Evaluating Supply Chain Resilience

Lessons from industrial supply chains include gathering data to improve transparency and risk awareness and to inform decision-makers on the level of resilience in the supply chain. Collecting such data usually takes on an organization/operation-centric approach and includes demand and demand variability, sourcing decisions, supplier capacity, lead times, inventory policy, etc. However, when evaluating potential risks (see Table 8.1) and supply chain resilience, the internal view is necessary but not sufficient. Organizations can hugely benefit from looking outside of their own boundaries at the environment they operate in. While there are many different methods to do so, we have found it practical to adopt well-established macro-indicators.

For instance, research has shown that there is a clear relationship between logistics performance indicators of a country and the impact of a disaster (Haavisto, 2012; Vaillancourt & Haavisto, 2016). The studies demonstrate that the lower the performance indicators are, the more vulnerable the country is in terms of number of people affected (Vaillancourt & Haavisto, 2016), which translates into higher demand risks for organizations operating in that context.

The Kuehne Logistics University (KLU), World Food Programme, and HELP Logistics developed and implemented a "Country Logistics Resilience Indicator" tool that combines 24 indicators to identify supply chain risks and evaluate resilience levels from a country perspective. The datasets are presented in interactive dashboards (see screenshot in Fig. 8.2) that are made available to interested practitioners and researchers on the HELP Logistics website (https://www.help-logistics.org/our-services/tools/country-logistics-resilience-indicators).

Between 2017 and 2020, HELP Logistics and KLU applied the indicator tool in numerous large-scale supply chain analysis projects with their humanitarian partners in Kenya, Madagascar, South Sudan, Zimbabwe, and Burundi. These projects aimed to assess the level of resilience of critical supply chains during different emergencies such as disease outbreaks or large-scale movements of displaced people. The tool has proven to be an asset in these projects and was used to compare indicators of the country under study with regional and global average as well as selected benchmark countries. Comparatively low scores and outliers often point at potential supply chain vulnerabilities and can direct further analyses.

In the Republic of Zimbabwe, for example, the indicator tool was applied to study potential supply chain vulnerabilities in the case of a large cholera outbreak. The tool showed that the country scores particularly low for the category "logistics performance" as well as the indicators "local supplier quality," "production process

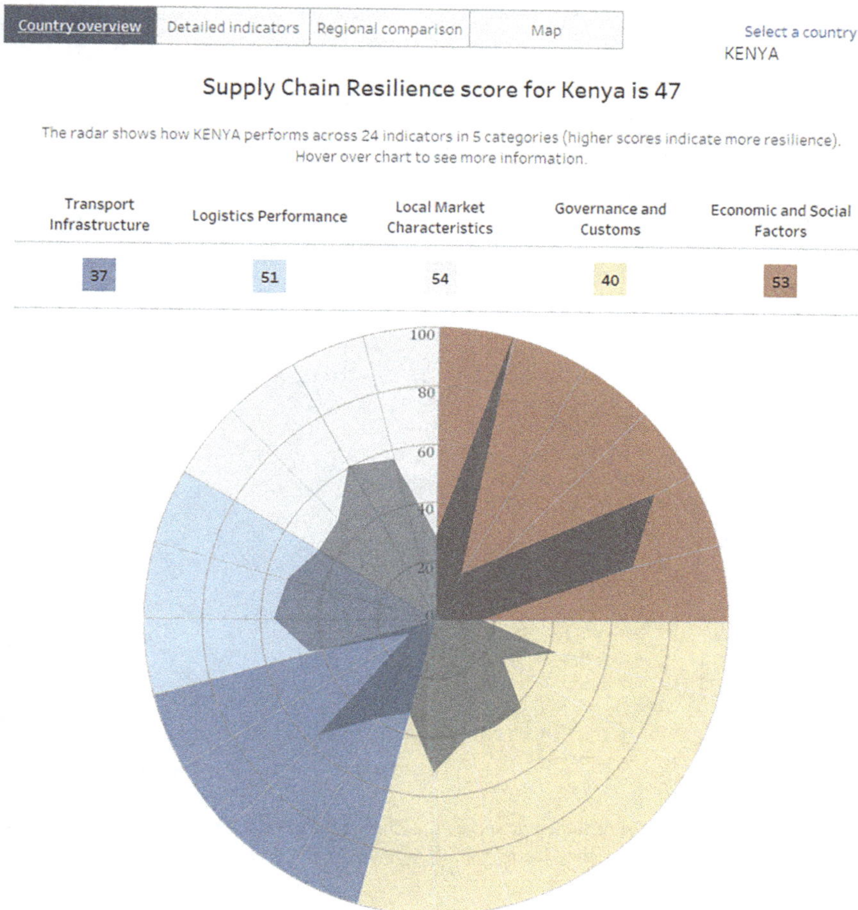

Fig. 8.2 Country Logistics Resilience Indicators (country overview). Visualization based on data from WEF, FAO, and World Bank

sophistication," "burden of customs procedure," and "access to nonsolid fuel" (see Fig. 8.3). Poor local supplier quality and production process sophistication contribute to the fact that local availability of supplies such oral rehydration salts, which are urgently needed during a cholera outbreak, is often unstable in the country. Importing supplies from neighboring or international markets can be a lengthy process due to inefficient customs procedures. The effective and timely distribution of supplies within the country is impeded by insufficient infrastructure capacity and quality as well as the low competence and quality of logistics providers, often leading to long lead times with high variability. Moreover, reflecting the low score in "access to nonsolid fuel," Zimbabwe had faced repeated fuel crises, which poses a further risk to supply chains, especially during disease outbreaks where fuel demand is usually increased.

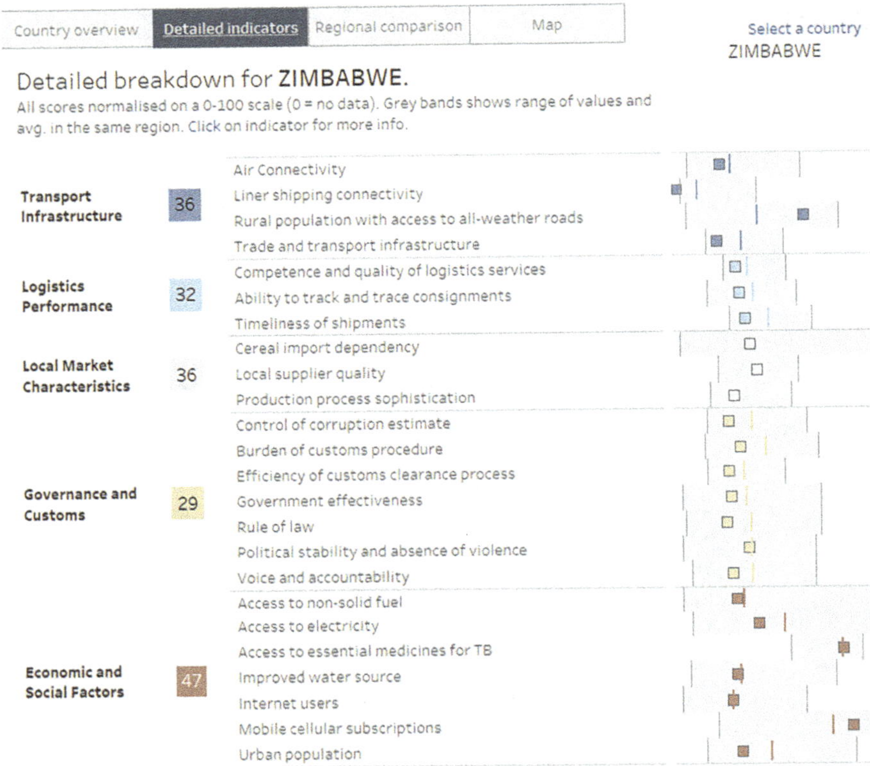

Fig. 8.3 Detailed overview of indicator scores for Zimbabwe in relation to other countries in the region. Visualization based on data from WEF, FAO, and World Bank

A simulation model was built around the cholera scenario to analyze the supply chain for essential medical supplies during the outbreak. The results echoed the findings of the indicator tool. For example, the simulation demonstrated that at day 160 after the outbreak, only 18% of the total demand was met because of shortcomings in the available procurement, transport, storage, and fuel capacities.

In Burundi, the indicator tool was applied to study the resilience of a food supply chain for refugee camps (see Fig. 8.4).

A particularly interesting finding in this study was related to the two low-ranking indicators “rural population with access to all-weather roads” and “local supplier quality.” Bringing in the food from neighboring Tanzania or Uganda by road takes up to 30 days, putting the timely and uninterrupted delivery to the camps at risk. Those findings supported ongoing negotiations with donors on the revitalization of the lake Tanganyika corridor, which has the potential to speed up the importation of food by up to 20 days while saving transportation costs, ultimately making the transport system in the region more efficient, more effective, and more resilient. This would benefit both humanitarian and commercial supply chains: “The proposed Lake Tanganyika Transport Corridor Development Project will boost regional

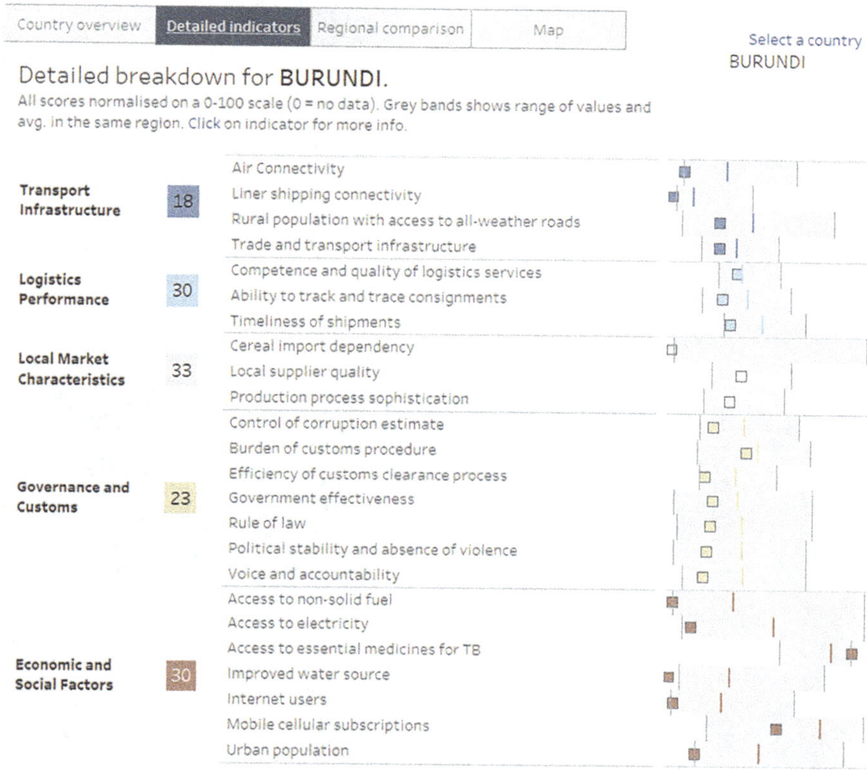

Fig. 8.4 Detailed overview of indicator scores for Burundi in relation to other countries in the region. Visualization based on data from WEF, FAO, and World Bank

integration and significantly reduce trade costs between riparian countries (Burundi, DRC, Tanzania and Zambia). Multimodal links with Central Corridor roads and railways will provide greater transport connectivity with other countries in the sub-region, such as Uganda and Rwanda. The project will therefore unlock Lake Tanganyika's potential as an inland waterway and provide a platform that would link the Northern (Mombasa in Kenya), Central (Dar-es-Salaam in Tanzania) and Southern (Mpulungu in Zambia/Durban in South Africa) Road Corridors. Given its geostrategic location, it has significant economic potential, fostering trade in a wide range of agricultural and fishery products and building materials. Bujumbura (Burundi) and Mpulungu (Zambia) ports, as well as Kigoma (Tanzania) and Kalemia (DRC) ports, are some of the main ports of Lake Tanganyika" (African Development Bank Group, 2019).

The tool can also be used to identify countries that might be particularly vulnerable to disruptions in global supply chains. The COVID-19 pandemic serves as a recent example, which certainly impacted economies and supply chains on a global level. However, developing countries are at risk of being hit the hardest and suffering disproportionately since they have "less resources to protect themselves against this dual health and economic crisis" (UNCTAD, 2020; USGLC, 2021). A recent survey

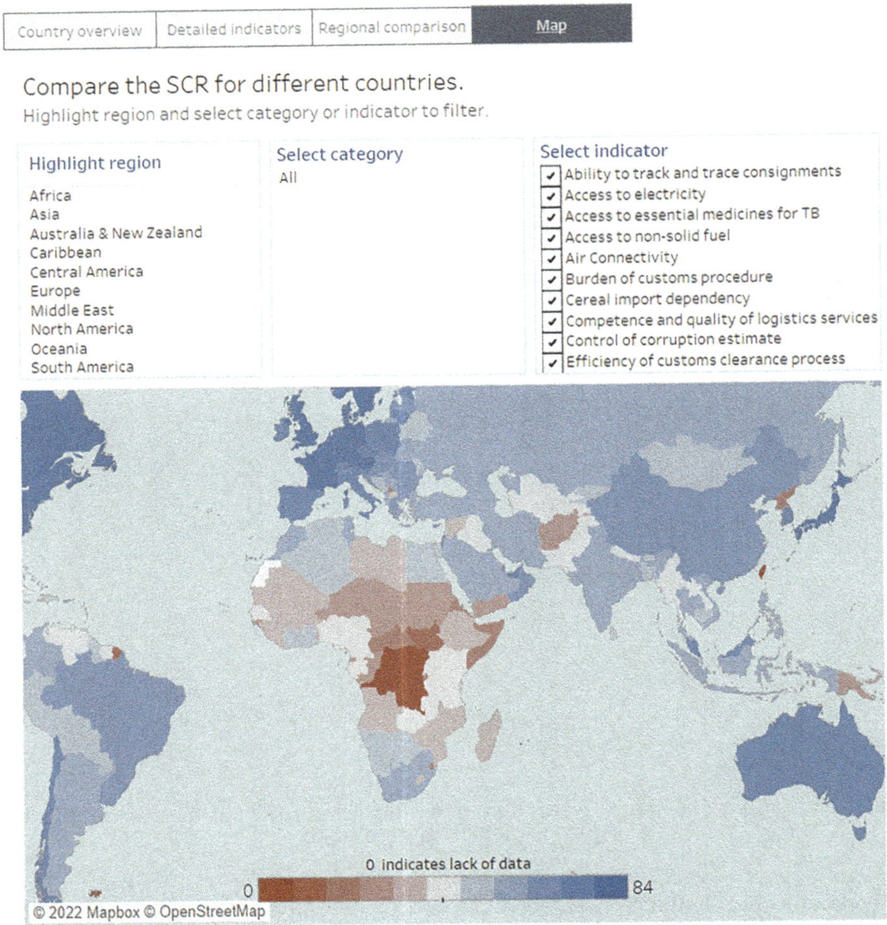

Fig. 8.5 Global comparison of logistics resilience indicators. Visualization based on data from WEF, FAO, and World Bank

conducted by HELP Logistics on the impact of COVID-19 on the (humanitarian) logistics sector in East Africa (O'Sullivan et al., 2020) demonstrates that the pandemic and subsequent measures imposed by governments and logistics companies have resulted in severe disruptions in supply chains across the region and affected the mobility, livelihoods, and food security of many people (WFP, 2020; IOM and WFP, 2020). The dependence on external markets paired with long shipment times and lengthy customs procedures in particular resulted in a significant reduction in supply chain capacities (especially in air transport, road transport, and warehouse staff), extreme increases in lead times (43% of responses indicate a lead time increase of more than 10 days), and higher logistics costs (65% of respondents reported cost increases of over 10%).

The survey results clearly fall in line with the picture painted by the tool, with comparatively low corresponding scores in the region (Fig. 8.5).

Bolstering supply chains starts with understanding risk, vulnerability, and resilience. The evident lack of formal supply chain risk management processes requires a practical approach that humanitarian organizations can use to evaluate the resilience of their supply chains. This approach should combine the internal view with an evaluation of the operating environment and the contextual factors that make supply chains susceptible to vulnerabilities. Relying on well-established macro-indicators, the indicator tool presents a valuable contribution that practitioners can leverage when evaluating supply chain resilience.

8.4 Building Supply Chain Resilience

A thorough evaluation of supply chains and operating environments usually exposes gaps, bottlenecks, and potential for improvement. Realizing this potential and strengthening supply chain resilience often requires large-scale investments. Such investments need to be carefully planned and should show a positive expected return on investment (RoI) in terms of costs, lead times, and other organization-specific priorities.

Between 2017 and 2020, HELP Logistics and KLU conducted RoI studies with Action Contre la Faim (ACF) (Help Logistics et al. 2017), Save the Children International (Help Logistics et al., 2018a), UNICEF (Help Logistics et al., 2019), and the International Federation of Red Cross and Crescent Societies (IFRC) (Help Logistics et al., 2018b). The studies demonstrated that building supply chain capacities prior to a disaster bears tremendous potential for humanitarian organizations to save cost and time. We found that operational response costs could be reduced by around 40% and the lead times by up to 75%. However, the maximum impact was only achieved in case the investments had enough time to fully unfold their potential before the disaster hit and if the investments were done in a holistic and complementing way, rather than in isolation from each other.

For many years, humanitarian organizations, donors, and researchers have been calling for more efforts to strengthen emergency preparedness (British Government, 2019; Jahre & Jahre, 2019; Lewin et al., 2018; OECD, 2017; Van Wassenhove, 2006). However, in spite of huge potential benefits, relatively few resources have been going into supply chain preparedness and resilience (Jahre et al., 2016; Kunz et al., 2013). One of the reasons for this situation is the lack of using standardized frameworks (Jahre et al., 2016), which makes it difficult for the relevant stakeholders such as humanitarian organizations, governments, and donors to find common ground and formulate joint strategies.

Indeed, based on HELP Logistics' and KLU's experience with the RoI studies and other comprehensive capacity building programs carried out over the last few years, we strongly recommend organizations to build their investment plans on existing supply chain preparedness frameworks such as Van Wassenhove (2006), Kunz et al. (2013), and Jahre et al. (2016). The framework from Jahre et al. (2016)

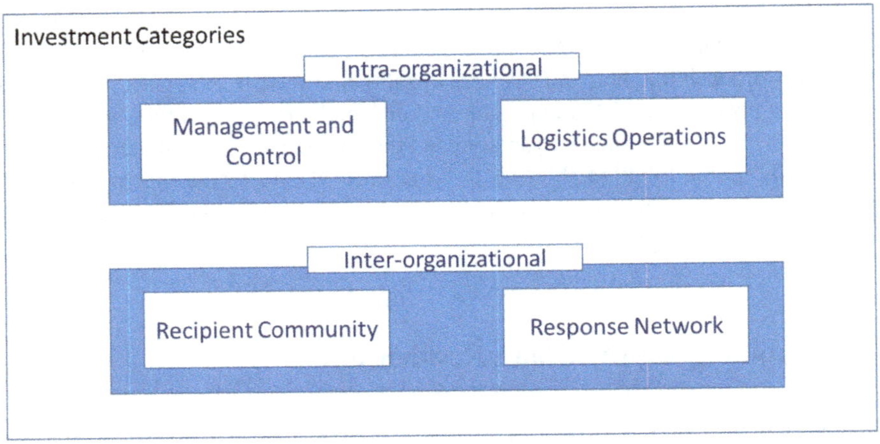

Fig. 8.6 Preparedness investments categories (Jahre et al., 2016)

corresponds particularly well with the discussion in this chapter of supply chain risk, disruptions and resilience. The framework captures intraorganizational (management and control and logistics operations) and interorganizational (recipient community and response networks) investments that are addressing the internal risks as well as the supply network risks outlined by Christopher and Peck (2004) (Fig. 8.6).

Following the findings of the indicator tool and the simulation in Zimbabwe (see example above), concrete action plans and investment proposals were formulated corresponding to the different categories shown above. For instance, strategic prepositioning of relief items (intraorganizational/logistics operations) was suggested to counter the volatile local availability and long lead times in the country, in combination with a strategic fuel reserve for the distribution of these items during a cholera outbreak. Actions to engage with logistics service providers and set up long-term agreements with implementing organizations were put forward (intraorganizational/logistics operations) to mitigate bottlenecks in transportation and warehousing and allow for rapid capacity extensions during emergencies. A capacity strengthening plan was recommended for human resources across the supply chain to improve process execution, speed, quality, and coordination (intra- and interorganizational).

In Table 8.2 we summarize some of the key investments analyzed in HELP and KLU's supply chain analysis projects and RoI studies and outline how they contributed to more resilient supply chains in the humanitarian context.

Table 8.2 Preparedness investments building supply chain resilience

Investment activity	Investment category	Risk classification	Resilience indicator	Impact generated (resilience built)
Human resource capacity building through trainings, streamlined processes, and system support	Intraorganizational/ management and control	Process and control risks	Competency and quality of logistics service	Reduce dependence on (costly) international deployments; improved skill and competence level enhances overall supply chain capacity and prepares staff to better handle disruptive events
Pre-positioning of relief items	Intraorganizational/ logistics operations	Supply risk	Local supplier capacity and production process sophistication	Reduced impact of limited production capacities and lengthy procurement processes at early stage of relief response
Supplier management (market assessments and establishment of frameworks)	Intraorganizational/ logistics operations	Supply risk	Local market characteristics	Better understanding of local market; quicker, cheaper, and more procurement of relief items in country
Relationship management with national governments	Interorganizational/ response network	Environmental and demand risks	Efficiency of customs clearance process and burden of customs procedure	Reduced process time for imported relief items
Capacity building at municipality level	Interorganizational/ recipient community	Demand risks	Trade and transport infrastructure Rural population with access to all weather roads	Better and swifter understanding of needs; tapping into available capacities in affected areas (e.g., storage facilities, support for distribution process)

8.5 Conclusion

The severe impact of the COVID-19 pandemic has brought the consequences of supply chain disruptions into our everyday life. Organizations operating in the humanitarian space are confronted with supply chain risks in the majority of their programs. Building and strengthening supply chain resilience, in particular in the context of humanitarian operations, is critical. However, it is also a complex, time- and resource-intense undertaking. To tackle this challenge, we present a proven approach that helps gain fact-based knowledge on supply chain vulnerabilities and lays the foundation for impactful supply chain investments. We recommend a thorough analysis of the operating environment and the contextual factors by tapping into tools such as the "Country Logistics Resilience Indicator" tool. Ultimately, building resilience requires smart, sustainable, and long-term investment plans. To develop such investment plans and maximize the investment impact, HELP Logistics and KLU have benefitted from existing preparedness frameworks that highlight the relevance of considering both intra- and interorganizational supply chain investments.

Country Logistics Resilience Indicators. Visualization by HELP Logistics Based on the Following Data Sources

Food and Agriculture Organization of the United Nations (FAOSTAT): Cereal import dependency ratio.

The World Bank: Liner Shipping Connectivity Index 2019: United Nations Conference on Trade and Development, Review of Maritime Transport 2010.

The World Bank: Access to clean fuels and technologies for cooking (% of population): World Bank, Sustainable Energy for All (SE4ALL) database from WHO Global Household Energy database.

The World Bank: Access to electricity (% of population): World Bank Global Electrification Database from "Tracking SDG 7: The Energy Progress Report" led jointly by the custodian agencies: the International Energy Agency (IEA), the International Renewable Energy Agency (IRENA), the United Nations Statistics Division (UNSD), the World Bank and the World Health Organization (WHO).

The World Bank: Individuals using the Internet (% of population): International Telecommunication Union (ITU) World Telecommunication/ICT Indicators Database.

The World Bank: Mobile cellular subscriptions (per 100 people): International Telecommunication Union (ITU) World Telecommunication/ICT Indicators Database.

The World Bank: People using safely managed drinking water services (% of population): WHO/UNICEF Joint Monitoring Programme (JMP) for Water Supply, Sanitation and Hygiene.

The World Bank: Rural Access Index: World-Measuring Rural Access: Update 2017/18 (English). Washington, D.C.: World Bank Group.
The World Bank: Tuberculosis treatment success rate (% of new cases): World Health Organization, Global Tuberculosis Report.
The World Bank: Urban population (% of total population): United Nations Population Division. World Urbanization Prospects: 2018 Revision.
The World Bank: Worldwide Governance Indicators 2018.
World Bank and Turku School of Economics, Logistic Performance Index Surveys 2018.
World Economic Forum, The Global Competitive Report 2017–2018.
World Economic Forum, The Global Competitiveness Report 2019. Data Source: International Air Transport Association (IATA) (data received through direct communication).

References

African Development Bank Group. (2019). https://www.afdb.org/en/documents/multinational-lake-tanganyika-transport-corridor-development-project-phase-i-rehabilitation-bujumbura-port-project-appraisal-report#:~:text=The%20proposed%20Lake%20Tanganyika%20Transport,DRC%2C%20Tanzania%20and%20Zambia
Blecken, A. (2010). A Reference Task Model for Supply Chain Processes of Humanitarian Organisations. Kuehne Foundation Book Series on Logistics (18). Haupt.
British Government. (2019). https://devtracker.dfid.gov.uk/projects/GB-1-203044
Christopher, M., & Peck, H. (2004). Building the Resilient Supply Chain. *The International Journal of Logistics Management, 15*(2), 1–14.
Day, J. M. (2014). Fostering emergent resilience: The complex adaptive supply network of disaster relief. *International Journal of Production Research, 52*(7), 1970–1988.
Dubey, R. (2019). Resilience and agility: The crucial properties of humanitarian supply chain. *Handbook of Ripple Effects in the Supply Chain*, 287–308.
Haavisto, I. (2012). Disaster impact and country logistics performance. In G. Kovács & K. Spens (Eds.), *Relief Supply Chain Management for Disasters: Humanitarian Aid and Emergency Logistics* (pp. 208–225). Business Science Reference.
Help Logistics AG, Kuehne Logistics University and Action Contre la Faim, 2017. Supply Chain Expenditure & Preparedness Investment Opportunities. https://logcluster.org/document/help-logistics-ag-kuehne-university-acf
Help Logistics AG, Kuehne Logistics University and IFRC, 2018a. Supply Chain Expenditure & Preparedness Investment Opportunities. https://logcluster.org/document/help-logistics-ag-kuehne-logistics-university-ifrc
Help Logistics AG, Kuehne Logistics University and Save the Children International, 2018b. Investing in Supply Chain Preparedness. https://logcluster.org/document/help-logistics-ag-kuehne-logistics-university-and-save-children-international
Help Logistics AG, Kuehne Logistics University and UNICEF (through the GLC), 2019. Investing in Supply Chain Preparedness. https://logcluster.org/document/help-logistics-ag-kuehne-logistics-university-unicef
Jahre, M., Pazirandeh, A., & Van Wassenhove, L. N. (2016). Defining logistics preparedness: a framework and research agenda. *Journal of Humanitarian Logistics and Supply Chain Management., 6*(3), 372–398.

Jahre, M. and Jahre, M. (2019). Logistics Preparedness and Response: A Case of Strategic Change. Villa et al. (eds.), Decision-making in Humanitarian Operations: 3–29.

Kunz, N., Reiner, G., & Gold, S. (2013). Investing in disaster management capabilities versus pre-positioning inventory: A new approach to disaster preparedness. *International Journal of Production Economics., 157*, 261–272.

Lewin, R., Besiou, M., Lamarche, J. B., Cahill, S., & Guerrero-Garcia, S. (2018). Delivering in a moving world. . .looking to our supply chains to meet the increasing scale, cost and complexity of humanitarian needs. *Journal of Humanitarian Logistics and Supply Chain Management., 8*(4), 518–532.

OECD. Organisation for Economic Co-operation and Development. (2017). https://www.oecd.org/development/humanitarian-donors/docs/financingpreparedness.pdf

O'Sullivan, C., Jaeschke, N. and Bensolomon, B. (2020). COVID-19 Impact on Supply Chains in East & Southern Africa. https://www.help-logistics.org/fileadmin/user_upload/Dateien_HELP/documents/report/COVID-19_Supply_Chain_Impact_E_S_Africa_2020-10.pdf

Pfohl, H.-C. (2002). *Risiko- und Chancenmanagement in der Supply Chain: proaktiv – ganzheitlich – nachhaltig*. Erich Schmidt Verlag.

Ponomarov, S. Y., & Holcomb, M. C. (2009). Understanding the concept of supply chain resilience. *The International Journal of Logistics Management, 20*(1), 124–143.

Scholten, K., Scott, P., & Fynes, B. (2014). Mitigation processes–antecedents for building supply chain resilience. *Supply Chain Management: An International Journal, 19*(2), 8.

Tang, C. S. (2006). Robust strategies for mitigating supply chain disruptions. *International Journal of Logistics, 9*(1), 33–45.

UNCTAD (2020). Impact of COVID-19 Pandemic on Trade and Development. Transitioning to a new normal. https://unctad.org/system/files/official-document/osg2020d1_en.pdf, 61, 93.

UN International Organisation for Migration (IOM) and World Food Programme (WFP) (2020). Populations at risk: Implications of COVID-19 for hunger, migration and displacement. https://docs.wfp.org/api/documents/WFP-0000120687/download/

UN World Food Programme (WFP) Regional, Bureau for East Africa (2020). Situation Update #3. Retrieved September, 2020, from https://reliefweb.int/sites/reliefweb.int/files/resources/WFP%20East%20Africa%20Situation%20Report%20%20%233%2C%2029%20September%202020.pdf

USGLC (2021). US Global Leadership Coalition. https://www.usglc.org/coronavirus/economies-of-developing-countries/

Vaillancourt, A., & Haavisto, I. (2016). Country logistics performance and disaster impact. *Disasters, 40*, 262–283. https://doi.org/10.1111/disa.12146

Van Wassenhove, L. N. (2006). Blackett Memorial Lecture. Humanitarian aid logistics: supply chain management in high gear. *Journal of the Operational Research Society, 57*(5), 475–489.

Wagner, S. M., & Bode, C. (2008). An Empirical Examination of Supply Chain Performance Along Several Dimensions of Risk. *Journal of Business Logistics, 29*(1), 307–325.

Wieland, A., & Durach, C. F. (2021). Two perspectives on supply chain resilience. *Journal of Business Logistics*. https://doi.org/10.1111/jbl.12271

Zobel, C. W., & Khansa, L. (2014). Characterizing multi-event disaster resilience. *Computers & Operations Research, 42*, 83–94.

Jonas Stumpf obtained his Masters in Logistics and International Management from the University of Mannheim in 2009. Before he joined the Kühne Foundation, he worked at the United Nations World Food Programme (WFP) where he conducted supply chain analyses and provided training courses at headquarters and various field offices in the Central and Eastern Africa region. From 2013 to 2016, he began HELP Logistics operations in Asia where he established a broad network of humanitarian actors. In his current role as HELP's Director Global Programs and CHORD's Operations Manager, he focuses on the design, development, and coordination of education, research, and consulting services for global partners.

Niklas Jaeschke is a senior supply chain consultant at HELP Logistics, a program of the Kühne Foundation. He obtained a M.Sc. in Business Administration and Mechanical Engineering from RWTH Aachen University in Germany and wrote his master thesis on supply chain resilience in the humanitarian context. Before joining HELP Logistics in 2017, he worked as a management consultant at P3 Group where he was involved in a number of large-scale digital transformation projects.

Maria Besiou is a Dean of Research and a Professor of Humanitarian Logistics at Kühne Logistics University. She received her Ph.D. in Mechanical Engineering and Operations Management from the Aristotle University of Thessaloniki (AUTH) in Greece. Before joining KLU she worked as a Postdoctoral Research Fellow at INSEAD, France. She serves in Editorial positions in the Decision Sciences Journal, the Journal of Humanitarian Logistics and Supply Chain Management, and the Production and Operations Management (POM). She has published her work on humanitarian logistics in renown journals with special focus on humanitarian operations.

Lisa Rustemeier holds a master's degree in supply chain management. She currently works as a Senior CR Manager for the Otto Group and is a co-founder of Invest2Change, a start-up dedicated to scale sustainable solutions in supply chains. Prior to this, she worked for several organizations in the field of humanitarian logistics and port logistics.

Chapter 9
The Value of Artificial Intelligence for More Resilient Supply Chains

Isabell Claus and Matthias Szupories

Abstract Even before the beginning of the COVID-19 pandemic, the need for reallocation of international supply chains became apparent. Then, the COVID-19 pandemic and the slowdown or disruption of supply chains in many industries and companies showed the dependency and interconnectedness. The former focus mainly on costs is no longer adequate. Strategies must consider the increasing demand with regard to social, political and ecological requirements. It rapidly became critical to maximize productivity by reducing uncertainties in any area. To manage the increased complexity, the rise in costs and the necessary speed, supply chain managers must benefit from technological advances that allow them to receive up-to-date and ready-to-act-on information. The use of Artificial Intelligence (AI) in various management tasks from planning to executing and beyond will soon become a standard because human capacities are no longer able to achieve the necessary enterprise-wide visibility into all aspects of the supply chain with granularity and methodologies at scale. Use cases are numerous. AI goes beyond rule-based automation of existing processes. It means a comprehensive redesign of processes with the aim of improved quality of information processing, faster responsiveness and ultimately resilience.

9.1 Introduction

Even before the beginning of the COVID-19 pandemic, the need for reallocation of international supply chains became apparent: firstly, customers in many industries increasingly demanded at least a minimum level of local or national added value. This is characterized on the one hand by the awareness and demand of consumers and on the other hand by the political necessity and the will to keep added value in

I. Claus (✉)
thinkers.ai, Vienna, Austria
e-mail: isabell.claus@thinkers.ai

M. Szupories
Business Management, Studienzentrum Hohe Warte, Vienna, Austria

S. Kummer et al. (eds.), *Supply Chain Resilience*, Springer Series in Supply Chain Management 17, https://doi.org/10.1007/978-3-030-95401-7_9

the country and therewith to keep employment and tax revenue high in order to secure prosperity. Secondly, procurement faced ever new, more demanding technical and ecological regulations and standards for several years: manufacturing companies need to ensure that certain material compliance requirements, related import requirements[1] and operating regulations are complied with, for example, REACH[2] and ROHS[3] as cross-sector regulations. If they do not comply, goods are no longer allowed to enter a country or a region. In addition, requirements for ecological production increased with high speed and pressure from society and governments, for example, in the context of material retention and waste (water, raw materials, recyclability) or in terms of pollutant emissions during production processes, for transport routes or for the manufactured good during its entire life cycle. Direct taxes and levies on users and manufacturers as well as indirect penalties such as higher refinancing costs on financial markets due to the ecological footprint are measures which companies now need to take into account. Last but not least, social conditions were much more in focus than in the past and companies need to actively avoid unsustainable social or ecological burdens. Passing these risks on to suppliers is not an option anymore; child labour or minimum wages are examples.

The COVID-19 pandemic and the slowdown or disruption of supply chains in many industries and companies showed the dependency and interconnectedness to everyone and also the immense influence of the availability of materials for almost every value creation process. Increasing bankruptcies in the supplier industry, squeezed margins and disrupted transport routes needed to be compensated for by expensive ad hoc procurement. If the above-mentioned stricter and manifold requirements for products and producers are also taken into consideration, the need for reorganization of supply chains is apparent.

[1]Material compliance requirements with the observance of environmental and international regulations intend to restrict or prohibit the use of various substances and materials in products. The governmental goal is always about to protect nature, human beings and animals from harmful substances and prevent the uncontrolled exploitation of restricted resources. Therefore, companies must observe and follow numerous national and international regulations regarding material compliance that contain many specific or time-limited exemptions for various uses of the regulated substances.

[2]The EU REACH regulation is valid for the European Economic Community (EU + Norway, Iceland and Liechtenstein) and contains specific regulation concerning the registration, evaluation, authorization and restriction of chemicals (REACH). This is controlled by the European Chemicals Agency. Various obligations occur depending on the role in the supply chain.

[3]The ROHS EU Directive (2011/65/EU) is valid for the European Imio since 2019 and contains the restriction of the use of certain hazardous substances in electrical and electronic equipment. That means equipment which is dependent on electric currents or electromagnetic fields in order to work properly and equipment for the generation, transfer and measurement of such currents and fields and designed for use with a voltage rating not exceeding 1000 volts for alternating current and 1500 volts for direct current. The Directive does not apply to means of transport for persons or goods or non-road mobile machinery made available exclusively for professional use.

9.2 Problem Framing

Resuming these developments, the former focus mainly on costs is no longer adequate: the single sourcing principle needs to change towards a more local and own (intermediate) production, at least duo supply principles and a realignment of the supply chain depending on customers, production and procurement markets. Strategies must consider the increasing demand with regard to social, political and ecological requirements which need to be fulfilled, which will change further and which will intensify onwards. The margin for errors is rapidly shrinking. Overall, this means a massive increase in complexity and a much higher need for up-to-date and ready-to-act-on information for supply chain managers, while speed in decision-making, in operations, in reducing cycle times and in continuous improvement is key.

9.3 Solution

Disruptive change is going on and companies need to react in a very dynamic and highly competitive environment with increased competition also due to the connected digital world. COVID-19 accelerated this situation much more than any other factor. It rapidly became critical to maximize productivity by reducing uncertainties in any area. To manage the increased complexity, the rise in costs and the necessary speed, supply chain managers must benefit from technological advances that allow them to receive up-to-date and ready-to-act-on information. The use of artificial intelligence (AI) in various management tasks from planning to executing and beyond will soon become a standard because human capacities are no longer able to achieve the necessary enterprise-wide visibility of all aspects of the supply chain with granularity and methodologies at scale.

9.3.1 Examples of Use Cases

AI can analyse and interpret huge datasets quickly, providing timely guidance on forecasting supply and demand. A high number of input variables resulted in very time-consuming tasks and a high tendency for error before. The combination of machine intelligence and human intelligence should be focused for competitive advantage and resilience at the same time.

Use cases for AI are manifold: supply chain monitoring and continuous analysis of suppliers, risk analyses, procurement market monitoring, internal process analyses, network management, impact analysis and quantification (including social and ecological factors), smart planning, end-to-end visibility, unlocking fleet management efficiencies or streamlining enterprise resource planning. Moreover, intelligent algorithms can predict and discover new consumer habits and forecast seasonal demand—on the one hand an important measure to minimize costs of overstocking and on the other hand an anticipation of future customer demand trends.

Efficient and safe processes are another goal: AI can assist in ensuring a smooth journey for customers or solve issues around it more quickly and accurately than humans can. AI can simplify complex procedures and speed up work. Moreover, AI can also analyse workplace safety data and inform manufacturers about any possible risks.

AI-based systems and tools for such a diverse set of use cases are either already available or should be developed in cooperation with specialized vendors according to the individual needs of a company. It is recommended to develop basic internal know-how, which is necessary for the evaluation of such technologies and their use in daily work, in order to ensure using the full potential of AI-based solutions. In many companies, this know-how is gathered through a collaboration with innovation departments.

An example illustrates a use case for demand forecasting: during the COVID-19 pandemic, prices of many raw materials changed massively. This was not only because of, e.g. difficulties in logistics but also because of political actions such as new customs duties or announcements of import/export bans. Still, demand needed to be met, raw materials needed to get supplied from other countries or regions, prices went up and supply within these markets was disrupted. Companies in various sectors struggled to cope with the situation, and end customers cancelled or delayed orders because of sudden price increases, which resulted not only from supply and demand reasons but also from speculation as a side effect on top. Early warning signals were of utmost importance to manage the situation as best as possible. However, signals such as announcements of new export bans were hidden in masses of unstructured data (text), e.g. in various languages on the web. While it is impossible for humans to read and filter all these data for relevant information, AI can do this: in various languages and untiringly no matter how many millions of datasets it has to check. AI is trained once and is then able to prequalify data in order to deliver only relevant information to a user. Complexity is reduced, and humans are enabled to handle the information flood, to focus on analysing and to take quick and data-based action (Fig. 9.1).

9.3.2 *Relevance*

Conventional, rule-based software quickly reaches its limits when it comes to managing complex and dynamic tasks. This is where AI delivers an advanced solution. It enables to analyse heterogeneous data that is relevant in the supply chain management context, it reduces masses of information from millionfold sources to the essentials, sketches relationships and hidden patterns and automizes to release employees from repetitive tasks. Thus, AI reduces complexity to an amount a human being is able to cope with and contributes to the goals of

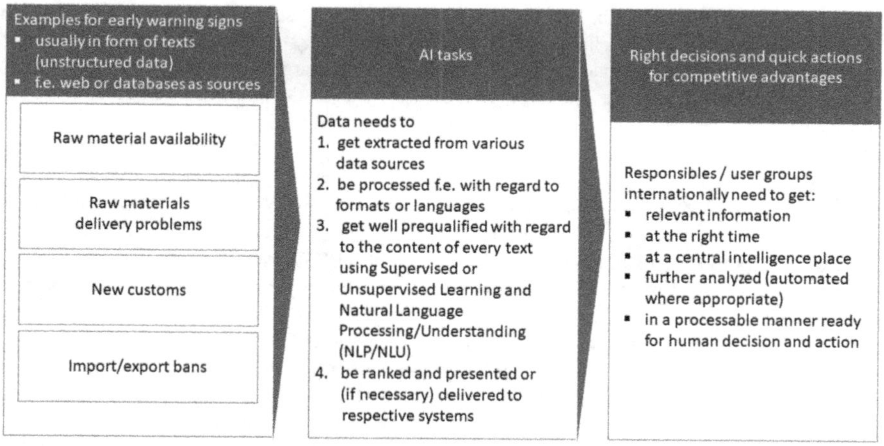

Fig. 9.1 Example use case "demand forecasting"

competitiveness, flexibility and improved risk management—all of them necessary to manage the current change and complex environment in supply chain management in various industries.

9.4 Conclusion

Resilience is also a matter of timely information, which in turn is the basis for timely decisions and reactions to any kind of change or problem. As of today, many companies lack key actionable insights to drive timely decisions that meet expectations with the necessary speed and agility.

In this respect the COVID-19 pandemic highlighted the problems and established sensitivity and a good understanding of the impact on supply chains, and contingency plans can help manufacturing companies deal with uncertainties better than before this extraordinary time.

Furthermore, the status quo of supply chains has become so complex that the ability of AI to sift through large amounts of scattered information to detect patterns and quantify trade-offs at a scale, much better than what is possible with conventional systems, needs to be exploited: designing a more resilient supply chain means to take action on manifold issues, while at the same time the number of employees remains limited and costs continue to be a constraining factor. Thus, technological advances and automation need to be focused to successfully manage complexity and speed. Use cases are numerous and should, if necessary, be discussed with innovation departments. AI goes beyond rule-based automation of existing processes. It means a comprehensive redesign of processes with the aim of improved quality of information processing, faster responsiveness and ultimately resilience.

Isabell Claus is a managing director and co-founder of thinkers.ai. The company is specialized in AI-based web search engine technology for the B2B sector. As a serial tech entrepreneur she was a part of the co-founders and management team of one of the largest cybersecurity companies in Europe, which was one of the Top100 fastest growing companies in the EMEA region for five consecutive years. Isabell Claus was awarded as "Entrepreneur of the Year 2020" in Austria. She studied business sciences and international business at the Vienna University of Economics and Business including a doctorate in international finance. She studied abroad at Harvard University, London School of Economics, Singapore Management University and Dubai University College.

Matthias Szupories works in the automotive sector at DEUTZ AG and before for brands like Peugeot, Sixt, MAN, Volkswagen Financial Services for many years in expert and management functions. He is a Senior Vice President for Central Sales and Marketing as well as a Regional Head of the second-largest sales region of Deutz AG. In his focus is the increase of customer satisfaction, building up new business models and in turn increasing revenues and EBIT. He also holds various supervisory board functions. As an advocate of dual education he finished his Diploma at FHDW in Bergisch Gladbach (Germany) and his Doctorate at the Pan-European University in Vienna and Bratislava in the research field of industrial economy. Since 2013, he works as a lecturer at FHDW, at the Automotive Center of Prof. Stefan Bratzel and as a visiting lecturer at other universities.

Chapter 10
Applying Blockchain Technologies for Increasing Supply Chain Resilience

Martin Hrušovský, Gerald Reiner, and Alfred Taudes

Abstract Managing supply chains in globalized world brings many challenges for the responsible managers due to the increasing number of disruptions and uncertainty. Although many experts have been calling for increasing the resilience of supply chains, surveys show that the implementation of resilience strategies in companies is lacking behind. One of the reasons for this might be the lack of transparency and information sharing between different supply chain actors. Whereas information sharing might help to reduce uncertainty and improve supply chain visibility, the risk of revealing too much information and potential data leakages to competitors result in reluctance of the companies to share information. This chapter describes potential risks and problems related to information sharing and presents blockchain technology concepts as a possible solution for these problems. The chosen concepts, including smart contracts, zero-knowledge proofs, homomorphic encryption, and secure multi-party computation, are shortly introduced and their possible applications for quality management, planning tasks, tracking & tracing, and other areas are discussed.

10.1 Introduction

Managing supply chains in a globalized world brings many challenges for the responsible managers, planners, and decision-makers responsible. As discussed by Mack et al. (2016), the increasing random variability of, e.g., demand, prices, or supply, increases the uncertainty for future predictions that are the basis for planning and execution of all supply chain activities. As a result, the decisions are becoming more ambiguous, and their short-term and long-term impacts on the complex and interconnected supply chains (SCs) cannot be evaluated easily. This can also be illustrated by challenges in, e.g., the automotive industry, where past decisions in

---

M. Hrušovský (✉) · G. Reiner · A. Taudes
Institute for Production Management, Department of Information Systems and Operations Management, WU (Vienna University of Economics and Business), Vienna, Austria
e-mail: martin.hrusovsky@wu.ac.at

S. Kummer et al. (eds.), *Supply Chain Resilience*, Springer Series in Supply Chain Management 17, https://doi.org/10.1007/978-3-030-95401-7_10

combination with unexpected disruptions might lead to production shutdowns in the next few months due to missing parts, such as semiconductors or rubber (Coppola, 2021; Daly, 2021).

Since the frequency of SC disruptions has been increasing in recent years (Ho et al., 2015), there have been many calls from experts as well as strategies developed in the academic literature for increasing the resilience of supply chains (see, e.g., Christopher & Peck, 2004; Pettit et al., 2019). However, as noted by Van Hoek (2020), who summarized the results of current surveys among hundreds of procurement managers, the implementation of these concepts in practice is still lacking behind, as a substantial part of the surveyed companies worldwide did not have any resilience strategies that would help them to identify possible disruptions of their operations and implement efficient solutions for dealing with them. One of the reasons for this situation might be the lack of SC transparency and information-sharing between the different SC actors (Forde, 2020; Van Hoek, 2020). This is caused by the fact that companies are involved in multiple SCs, and, therefore, revealing too much sensitive data might negatively influence the position of the supplier in relationship to its competitors or to the negotiation partner. As an example, if the partner sees that the inventory level of the supplier is too high, which might be caused by, e.g., low sales, it might give him more power in price negotiations (Sahai et al., 2020). Furthermore, Ried et al. (2021) addressed in their study a related issue: "Information leakages—the unauthorized sharing of an organization's information with another organization—are a growing concern in today's supply chains, but remain relatively underexplored."

In order to overcome these problems, innovative technologies that enable information-sharing without revealing too much information might be applied. One of the possibilities is the blockchain technology, which has been successfully applied mainly for tracking and tracing purposes (see examples in Sahai et al., 2020). Moreover, this technology offers also other concepts that might be relevant for SC collaborations and information-sharing, but have not been widely used until now. Therefore, the aim of this article is to present these concepts and identify possible fields of application within the SC management context. In order to do so, we first describe potential problems with a negative influence on SC resilience, later we introduce the basic blockchain concepts, and at the end we present possible solutions to the described problems offered by blockchain concepts.

10.2 Problem Framing

Today's globalized SCs have to cope with a variety of risk sources internal or external to the SC that can be divided into different categories. A common approach found in the literature (Christopher & Peck, 2004; Lee, 2002; Wagner & Bode, 2006) is to distinguish, among other things, between demand-side and supply-side risks.

When looking at demand-side risks, we can distinguish between disruptions in the physical distribution of goods (ripple effect) and disruptions arising from demand uncertainty and forecast inaccuracy (Ivanov et al., 2014; Wagner & Bode, 2006). In the latter case, an important issue is the bullwhip effect, which arises from small fluctuations in demand that propagate through the whole supply chain and are intensified by information distortion and insufficient information-sharing (Lee et al., 1997).

In contrast, supply-side risks are related to supplier management, purchasing and production. In this context, companies need to be aware of the ripple effect that is observed if a disruption does not impact only one SC partner but cascades to other stages and negatively influences the performance of the whole SC (Dolgui et al., 2018). Although the frequency of such disruptions is usually rather low, resilience plans for mitigating these risks need to be prepared due to their high impact.

In order to increase SC resilience, it is recommended to firstly identify the potential risks and prepare appropriate mitigation strategies. This requires a suitable SC design with built-in redundancies and extended capacities instead of focusing only on efficiency and one supplier, allowing flexibility and an alternative delivery path if a certain part of the SC is affected (Christopher & Peck, 2004). Another important element is close cooperation of all SC actors involved, which requires information-sharing that helps to reduce uncertainty (Van Hoek, 2020). Hand in hand with this goes SC visibility, which gives an overview of the relationships and communication lines as well as the current state of the SC (e.g., performance of actors or inventory levels) (Christopher & Peck, 2004). In this way companies can identify potential reasons for demand fluctuations, which helps to avoid high volatilities arising from the bullwhip effect or to identify potential signs of disruption that could be resolved before it propagates as described by the ripple effect (Dolgui et al., 2018). As an example, sharing quality data from the production of a certain part could help to identify potential quality problems in an early stage and avoid expensive product failures or repairs if this problem is discovered only after the final product has been put into usage (Enns, 1996). However, sharing this data might also reveal details about the production process itself which the supplier does not want to share with his/her customers. As a consequence, companies are reluctant to share information with partners, which decreases the effectiveness of the implemented resilience strategies. Therefore new methods are needed which would enable sharing only the necessary data without revealing sensitive information. One possibility to achieve this could be the blockchain technology with its various concepts.

10.3 Solution

Although mainly known from the discussion about cryptocurrencies, blockchain technology can bring added value to many other areas, including also SC management. In general, blockchain can be defined as a distributed peer-to-peer database network which keeps track of transactions between its users using asymmetric encryption (Min, 2019). Transactions are aggregated into blocks by so-called miners and connected into blockchains which are then replicated for the users of the network (Bartsch et al., 2018). Since the transaction data is not stored centrally, it provides high security against possible hacker attacks, and the recorded history of transactions gives an overview of all changes, which can be useful for tracking and tracing purposes (Min, 2019). Moreover, the blockchain technology includes several concepts that facilitate collaboration and information-sharing between the users.

The first application facilitates the execution of contracts that can be defined in form of smart contracts. Smart contracts are computer programs that define a set of rules for possible situations and enforce their execution in an automated way (Min, 2019). This enables to define and negotiate procedures for different states of the systems in advance and follow them automatically if such a state is detected, which saves time, increases transparency, and contributes to better monitoring of the system. Mohanta et al. (2018) show multiple examples of possible application of smart contracts in healthcare, finance, or SCs.

To solve the problem of sharing too much data, SC partners can use the zero-knowledge proof. This cryptographic method enables the user to prove to another user that he/she possesses certain information or that certain information is true without revealing the information itself or any additional information (Lavrenov, 2019). The potential usage areas for this concept are very broad, including not only SCs (Sahai et al., 2020) but also, e.g., e-voting (Panja & Roy, 2018).

Besides looking at the type of the exchanged data, it is also important to focus on the data encryption and security of the data exchange. Homomorphic encryption is a method which allows to encrypt data and then send it to other users which can perform operations on ciphertext without ever decrypting the data (Thaine, 2018). In this way data of different users can be compared, or even data operations on untrusted computers can be performed without revealing the real data to anybody who does not own the decryption key (Fontaine & Galand, 2007).

The last concept presented in this article is secure multiparty computation, which is a method that enables to combine data from multiple users and perform computational operations on them without sharing the data of individual users between each other or with some central authority computing the results. A simple example shown by Inpher (2021) would be to calculate an average salary of multiple employees without sharing the information about their real salaries between them. Further possible applications are discussed by Zhao et al. (2019).

10.4 Relevance

The concepts used in blockchain technology that were presented in the previous chapter might be relevant for several applications in the SC context, which can contribute to better information-sharing and coordination of SC actors and in this way improve overall resilience. Therefore we present here some of the possible future applications that are summarized in Table 10.1.

Table 10.1 Application of blockchain concepts in an SC context

Concept	Supply chain application
Smart contract	Ripple effect prevention/response real-time planning Disaster management Supplier coordination
Zero-knowledge proof	Quality management Tracking and tracing of product origin Inventory level information
Homomorphic encryption	Big data and optimization problems Supplier selection
Secure multiparty computation	Bullwhip effect prevention Benchmarking

The implementation of smart contracts could bring advantages especially in situations where a fast reaction is needed after the occurrence of a disruption to avoid the ripple effect. In order to increase the resilience of the system and to decrease the time needed to recover from the disruption, it is advisable to prepare mitigation strategies and reactions to different scenarios in advance. However, even if such strategies are defined, still a lot of communication between the involved parties is needed. If smart contracts were implemented, the process could be automated and follow the defined steps automatically, checking, e.g., necessary preconditions and without the need to wait for approval from a responsible manager responsible. This could help in real-time transport planning where due to a disruption in the transport network, a new alternative route needs to be found (Hrušovský et al., 2021). There it is often necessary to call alternative service providers and check if they have available capacities for the planned change. Using smart contracts, the system would automatically find the best option and conduct all the necessary steps for replanning. Another application could be in humanitarian SCs, where disaster management capabilities are often built in order to be prepared for potential disasters in a certain region (Kunz et al., 2013). However, when the disaster strikes and a fast delivery of relief supplies is needed, there are often delays due to extensive customs clearance that could potentially be reduced by introducing smart contracts in advance. Last but not least, smart contracts could be used for monitoring and coordination of suppliers, e.g., to automatically inform suppliers in the automotive industry that they might not need to deliver their parts until a certain deadline if the delivery of other parts is delayed and therefore the production cannot be started on time.

Zero-knowledge proofs can be used to build trust between partners and to ensure that a certain criterion in a process is met without revealing the detailed information about that process. Using this technology, a supplier could prove to its customer that certain quality criteria have been met without revealing data about the production process itself. In addition to that, tracking the origin and all the changes made on a product could be ensured, which is gaining importance in many industries, e.g., in food or steel production (Ledger Insights, 2020; Nurgazina et al., 2021). As an example, the company FVT is developing a system based on blockchain technology and sensors that should enable customers to verify authenticity for tangible products for purchasing and trading purposes (FVT, 2021). A similar principle can be applied to plastic bottles in the beverage industry, where tokenization of the bottles could offer incentives for higher recycling rates and improve the quality of the collected material, which in turn could lead to plastic waste reduction (Pulsfort et al., 2021). Moreover, zero-knowledge proofs could be also used to check whether a supplier has sufficient inventory available for fulfilling a certain order without obtaining the information about the exact inventory level.

Solving difficult optimization problems or simulating future development scenarios is necessary for efficient SC coordination. This requires extensive computational power, which might not be affordable for all participants. Therefore, homomorphic encryption could be applied for encrypting the data needed to solve these problems and cloud computing could be used to provide the necessary computational capacity. Encrypted data could be used to compare the performance of different suppliers and to perform automated supplier selection, avoiding the risk that unauthorized persons could get access to the detailed suppliers' data.

Very often there are situations in which comparisons based on aggregated data are useful, e.g., if performance indicators have to be compared across different companies within a certain industry in order to create benchmarks, i.e., best in class. Introducing secure multiparty computation here could increase the willingness of the companies to participate in such surveys and bring benefits for all of them since the benchmark used for comparisons would be much more significant if a higher number of participants are included. A better coordination of forecasts and information-sharing could be achieved within the individual SCs if data from each actor is encrypted and combined, which would help to prevent the bullwhip effect.

10.5 Conclusion

Building resilience in SCs is necessary for improving their performance and ability to react to the increasing number of disruptions. Even though this has been often emphasized in the literature in the last few years, the practical implementation of the proposed measures is lacking behind. Collaboration of SC partners and information-sharing between them are important factors in this context and therefore they need to be encouraged using innovative technologies. As our overview shows, there are multiple possibilities for integrating blockchain technologies into SC operations that need to be further investigated so that the overall performance and resilience of SCs can be improved.

References

Bartsch, F., Neidhardt, N., Nüttgens, M., Holland, M., & Kompf, M. (2018). Anwendungsszenarien für die Blockchain-Technologie in der Industrie 4.0. *HMD Praxis der Wirtschaftsinformatik, 55*, 1274–1284.

Christopher, M., & Peck, H. (2004). Building the Resilient Supply Chain. *International Journal of Logistics Management, 15*(2), 1–13.

Coppola, G., 2021. The Next Shortage That's Making the Auto Industry Nervous. Retrieved May 13, 2021, from https://www.bloomberg.com/news/newsletters/2021-04-14/supply-chains-latest-rubber-shortage-worries-the-auto-industry

Daly, J., 2021. A big little problem: How to solve the semiconductor shortage. Retrieved May 18, 2021, from https://www.ibm.com/blogs/industries/global-semiconductor-shortage-solutions/

Dolgui, A., Ivanov, D., & Sokolov, B. (2018). Ripple effect in the supply chain: An analysis and recent literature. *International Journal of Production Research, 56*(1–2), 414–430.

Enns, S. T. (1996). Analysis of process improvement path using rapid modeling. *Total Quality Management, 7*(3), 283–292.

Fontaine, C., & Galand, F. (2007). A survey of homomorphic encryption for nonspecialists. *EURASIP Journal on Information Security, 013801*. https://doi.org/10.1155/2007/13801

Forde, M., 2020. 60% of procurement leaders say lack of transparency is a risk, survey finds. Retrieved May 18, 2021, from https://www.supplychaindive.com/news/procurement-leaders-transparency-risk/571847/

FVT, 2021. The Verification solution. Retrieved July 15, 2021, from https://www.futureverification.com/product.html

Ho, W., Zheng, T., Yildiz, H., & Talluri, S. (2015). Supply chain risk management: A literature review. *International Journal of Production Research, 53*(16), 5031–5069. https://doi.org/10.1080/00207543.2015.1030467

Hrušovský, M., Demir, E., Jammernegg, W., Van Woensel, T., 2021. Real-time disruption management approach for intermodal freight transportation. Journal of Cleaner Production, Vol. 280, Part 2. https://doi.org/10.1016/j.jclepro.2020.124826

Inpher, 2021. What is Secure Multiparty Computation. Retrieved May 21, 2021, from https://inpher.io/technology/what-is-secure-multiparty-computation/

Ivanov, D., Sokolov, B., & Dolgui, A. (2014). The Ripple effect in supply chains: trade-off 'efficiency-flexibility-resilience'in disruption management. *International Journal of Production Research, 52*(7), 2154–2172. https://doi.org/10.1080/00207543.2013.858836

Kunz, N., Reiner, G., & Gold, S. (2013). Investing in disaster management capabilities versus pre-positioning inventory: A new approach to disaster preparedness. *International Journal of Production Economics, 157*, 261–272. https://doi.org/10.1016/j.ijpe.2013.11.002

Lavrenov, D., 2019. A Zero-Knowledge Proof: Improving Privacy on a Blockchain. Retrieved May 21, 2021, from https://www.altoros.com/blog/zero-knowledge-proof-improving-privacy-for-a-blockchain/

Ledger Insights, 2020. RIDDLE&CODE partners with S1Seven for blockchain-based metals certification, traceability. Retrieved May 22, 2021, from https://www.ledgerinsights.com/riddlecode-s1seven-blockchain-steel-traceability-metals-certification/

Lee, H. L. (2002). Aligning supply chain strategies with product uncertainties. *California Management Review, 44*(3), 105–119.

Lee, H. L., Padmanabhan, W., & Whang, S. (1997). The Bullwhip effects in supply chains. *MIT Sloan Management Review, 38*(3), 93–102.

Mack, O., Khari, A., Krämer, A., & Burkart, T. (Eds.). (2016). *Managing in a VUCA World*. Springer International Publishing.

Min, H. (2019). Blockchain technology for enhancing supply chain resilience. *Business Horizons, 62*, 35–45.

Mohanta, B.K., Soumyashree, S.P., Debasish, J., 2018. An overview of smart contract and use cases in blockchain technology. 9th International Conference on Computing, Communication and Networking Technologies. https://doi.org/10.1109/ICCCNT.2018.8494045.

Nurgazina, J., Pakdeetrakulwong, U., Moser, T., & Reiner, G. (2021). Distributed ledger technology applications in food supply chains: A review of challenges and future research directions. *Sustainability, 12*, 4206. https://doi.org/10.3390/su13084206

Panja, S., & Roy, B. K. (2018). A secure end-to-end verifiable e-voting system using zero knowledge based blockchain. *IACR Cryptology ePrint Archive, 2018*, 466.

Pettit, T. J., Croxton, K. L., & Fiksel, J. (2019). The evolution of resilience in supply chain management: A retrospective on ensuring supply chain resilience. *Journal of Business Logistics, 40*(1), 56–65. https://doi.org/10.1111/jbl.12202

Pulsfort, J., Polt, R., Wankmüller, C., Reiner, G., 2021. The impact of blockchain-enabled tokenization on plastic waste: an empirical study. Paper submitted to EurOMA 2021 Conference.

Ried, L., Eckerd, S., Kaufmann, L., & Carter, C. (2021). Spillover effects of information leakages in buyer–supplier–supplier triads. *Journal of Operations Management, 67*(3), 280–306. https://doi.org/10.1002/joom.1116

Sahai, S., Singh, N., Dayama, P., 2020. Enabling Privacy and Traceability in Supply Chains using Blockchain and Zero Knowledge Proofs. 2020 IEEE International Conference on Blockchain (pp. 134–143). https://doi.org/10.1109/Blockchain50366.2020.00024.

Thaine, P., 2018. Homomorphic Encryption for Beginners: A Practical Guide (Part 1). Retrieved May 21, 2021, from https://medium.com/privacy-preserving-natural-language-processing/homomorphic-encryption-for-beginners-a-practical-guide-part-1-b8f26d03a98a

Van Hoek, R. (2020). Research opportunities for a more resilient post-COVID-19 supply chain – closing the gap between research findings and industry practice. *International Journal of Operations & Production Management, 40*(4), 341–355. https://doi.org/10.1108/IJOPM-03-2020-0165

Wagner, S. M., & Bode, C. (2006). An empirical investigation into supply chain vulnerability. *Journal of Purchasing & Supply Management, 12*, 301–312.

Zhao, C., Zhao, S., Zhao, M., Chen, Z., Gao, C.-Z., Li, H., & Tan, Y. (2019). Secure multi-party computation: Theory, practice and applications. *Information Sciences, 476*, 357–372.

Martin Hrušovský, Ph.D., is a teaching and research associate at the Institute for Production Management at WU (Vienna University of Economics and Business). He also did his Ph.D. at the institute in years 2013–2018 and holds a master's degree in Supply Chain Management from WU Vienna. In his research, he is currently dealing with mathematical optimization models for transport planning and fleet sizing including uncertainty using stochastic methods and simulation. Besides that, his research interests include risk management and sustainability in supply chains as well as Physical Internet and its implementation in the areas of transportation and SCM.

Gerald Reiner holds a Magister Degree, a doctorate degree, and Habilitation in Business Administration from WU (Vienna University of Economics and Business). After being a full professor in Production and Logistics Management in Neuchatel (2007–2014) and in Klagenfurt (2014–2018), in 2018 he joined WU as a full professor in Operations Management at the Institute for Production Management. His research interests include various topics of supply chain and operations management, including, e.g., inventory management, humanitarian logistics, or circular supply chains.

Alfred Taudes holds a doctoral degree in Business Administration from WU (Vienna University of Economics and Business), a Magister Degree in Management Information Systems from Vienna University, and a Ph.D. from WU Vienna in both fields. After assistant professorships at WU in the areas of Operations Research and Applied Informatics he was a visiting professor at Universities

Augsburg, Münster, Essen, and Tsukuba, Japan and joined WU in 1993. There he coordinated large-scale research projects such as WWTF-project "Integrated Demand and Supply Chain Management" and the Special Research Area Adaptive Models in Economics and Management Science. His actual research interests are on the impact of Digitalization on Operations Management and on Cryptoeconomics, where he heads a WU Research Institute on this topic.

Part III
Achieving Resilience

Chapter 11
Policy Options for Strengthening Resilience to Achieve Strategic Autonomy for Austria in a Disrupted World

Michael Böheim

Abstract The COVID-19 pandemic has given the question of the resilience of international supply and value chains considerably more weight in economic policy. In the political discussion, (re)localisation towards national production ("reshoring") plays a very prominent role and often overrides the other economic policy options for strengthening resilience to achieve strategic autonomy. Given the interconnectedness of the world economy large-scale relocation of production and technologies is neither realistic nor desirable. Based on the concept of open strategic autonomy developed by the European Commission a framework for strengthening resilience to achieve strategic autonomy for Austria as a small open economy is presented. Critical raw materials, key enabling technologies, projects of common European interest (IPCEI) and critical goods are identified as central focal points in this respect. Policy options according to the principles of subsidiarity for Austria in cooperation with its European partners include smart (re)localisation according to dynamic competitive advantages as well as strategic stockpiling and the consideration of supply security in public procurement.

11.1 Introduction

The world economy is organised along global value chains according to the principle of comparative competitive advantages. This leads to a pronounced specialisation of national economies and a concentration in the production of certain goods in certain (few) countries. This international division of labour creates welfare gains for all economies involved but also mutual dependencies. Although global value chains are

M. Böheim (✉)
Austrian Institute of Economic Research (WIFO), Vienna, Austria

Institute for Economic Policy and Industrial Economics, WU (Vienna University of Economics and Business), Vienna, Austria

Scientific Commission, Ministry of Defence, Vienna, Austria
e-mail: michael.boeheim@wifo.ac.at

S. Kummer et al. (eds.), *Supply Chain Resilience*, Springer Series in Supply Chain Management 17, https://doi.org/10.1007/978-3-030-95401-7_11

characterised by maximum efficiency and productivity through minimisation of warehousing within the framework of just-in-time logistics, they are (as a result) also very susceptible to disruptions, as the COVID-19 pandemic has shown. As a direct consequence, the (previously) neglected question of stability and resilience of global value chains and, going further, the question of stronger economic independence and strategic autonomy moved to the centre of the (economic) political discussion.

This article is based on WIFO research first conducted by Klien et al. (2021) and then further developed by Böheim et al. (2021a). After introductory remarks (Sect. 11.1), this article is devoted to clarifying the complex concepts of "strategic autonomy" and "resilience" in the political and economic context (Sect. 11.2). Furthermore, key enabling technologies, projects of common European interest (IPCEI) and critical goods are treated as central focal points of a concept of (open) strategic autonomy (Sect. 11.3). Based on this, policy options according to the principles of subsidiarity for Austria in cooperation with its European partners are outlined (Sect. 11.4), and finally conclusions are drawn (Sect. 11.5).

11.2 Open Strategic Autonomy

The member states of the European Union in general and Austria in particular are among the winners of globalisation (cf. Sachs et al., 2020). Despite the evident economic advantages, a latent critique of globalisation has manifested itself since the end of the 1990s. Against the backdrop of this critique of globalisation, which in its scientifically oriented form certainly addresses problem areas correctly, it makes sense to critically question the concept of globalisation by focusing more on previously neglected questions of strategic autonomy and the resilience of the Austrian and European economies.

The COVID-19 pandemic has given the question of the resilience of international supply and value chains even more weight in economic policy. For example, a surge in demand led to bottlenecks in protective equipment (masks, gloves) and medical technology (respirators). In addition to the excess demand, export restrictions in individual EU countries even led to a temporary restriction of free trade in goods within the European single market.

Although the COVID-19 crisis is the occasion for the current discussion on the regionalisation of value and supply chains, the issue of the international distribution of production is by no means new. The relocation of production and globalisation of value chains has also been intensively discussed and researched in the technology sector for many years. An interim conclusion of these research strands is that the resilience of value chains can also have a significant influence on the location decisions of companies (cf. Antràs, 2016).

In contrast to autarky, the complete self-sufficiency of an economy, which can neither be implemented effectively nor efficiently in a globalised world order based on the division of labour, we are guided by the concepts of open strategic autonomy

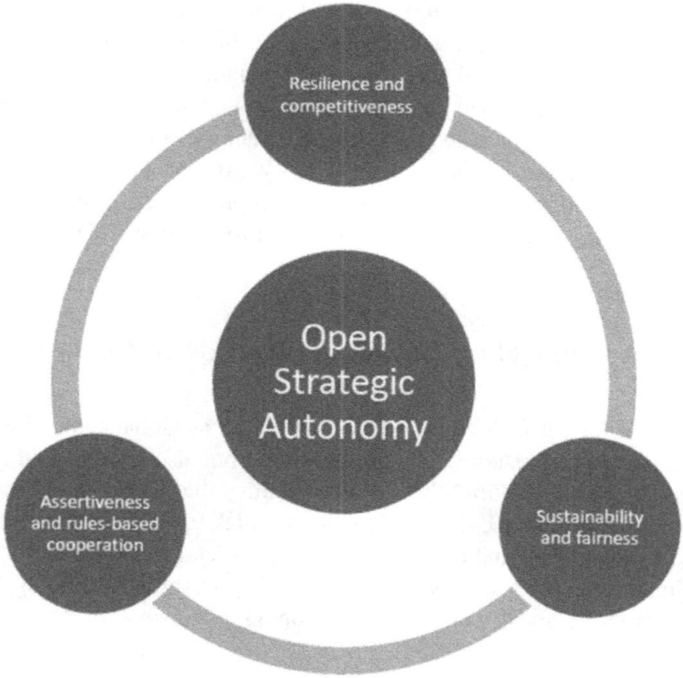

Fig. 11.1 The concept of open strategic autonomy, Q: European Commission (2021b)

(European Commission, 2021a) and economic resilience, which are described as a "new compass for EU policy" (European Commission, 2020c) and a "policy option" (European Commission, 2021b).[1]

The concept of open strategic autonomy is "anti-protectionist" at its core, building on the importance of (fundamental) openness and aligned with the EU's commitment to free and fair trade with well-functioning, diversified and sustainable global value chains (European Commission, 2021b). Open strategic autonomy comprises three constituent elements (Fig. 11.1).

Strengthening the resilience and competitiveness of the European economy requires open and undistorted access to global markets, including new market access opportunities and open trade flows for the benefit of the economy and society. As a modern economy is organised along globalised value chains based on the division of labour and comparative competitive advantage, strengthening economic resilience must start with the design of global competitive conditions (European Commission, 2021b). In this context, strategic autonomy is understood as the ability of an economy to set its own (economic) policy priorities and make decisions, as well as

[1]The concept of strategic resilience developed by the European Commission (2020b) as part of the Foresight Agenda comprises the four dimensions of social and economic, geopolitical, environmental and digital resilience.

the institutional, political and material conditions to implement them in cooperation with third parties or, if necessary, independently. This understanding encompasses the entire spectrum of political action, i.e. the foreign, security and defence policy dimension as well as the economic policy dimension. Autonomy is always relative. Politically, it is about an increase in the ability to act, i.e. a process, not an absolute state. Autonomy means neither self-sufficiency nor isolation or a rejection of alliances. It is not an end in itself but a means to protect and promote a country's own values and strategic interests (adapted from Lippert et al., 2019).

11.3 Focal Points of a Concept of Strategic Autonomy

The European Union is facing major challenges, such as global competition and the need to use energy and resources efficiently, due to but also apart from the COVID-19 pandemic, which is currently also dominating the economic policy debate. Investment in research and innovation is essential to address these challenges while helping to develop and deploy solutions to societal challenges such as health, energy, climate, etc. Critical raw materials and key enabling technologies (KETs/ATIs) are essential focal points for developing a concept of (open) strategic autonomy.

11.3.1 Critical Raw Materials

Critical raw materials are essential inputs in the production or supply of critical products and/or technologies. Since 2011, the European Commission has published an updated list of critical raw materials every 3 years. The current list, dating from 2020, includes a total of 30 materials (in alphabetical order): antimony, barite, bauxite, beryllium, borate, fluorspar, gallium, germanium, graphite, hafnium, indium, cobalt, coking coal, lithium, magnesium, natural rubber, niobium, platinum metals, phosphorus, phosphorite, scandium, rare earths (LREE, HREE), silicon metal, strontium, tantalum, titanium, vanadium, bismuth and tungsten (European Commission, 2020d).

The supply of many critical commodities is heavily concentrated in a few countries, including politically unstable and authoritarian regimes, which again substantially exacerbates the EU's dependence (Fig. 11.2).

For three sectors classified as strategically important (renewable energy, e-mobility and aerospace), a total of 25 raw materials were analysed by the European Commission (2020c) in terms of their supply risk as part of a future study (Foresight Study) for nine technology fields involved. According to the study, rare earths (LREE, HREE) are subject to the highest supply risk and magnesium, niobium, germanium, borates and scandium to a high supply risk (Fig. 11.3).

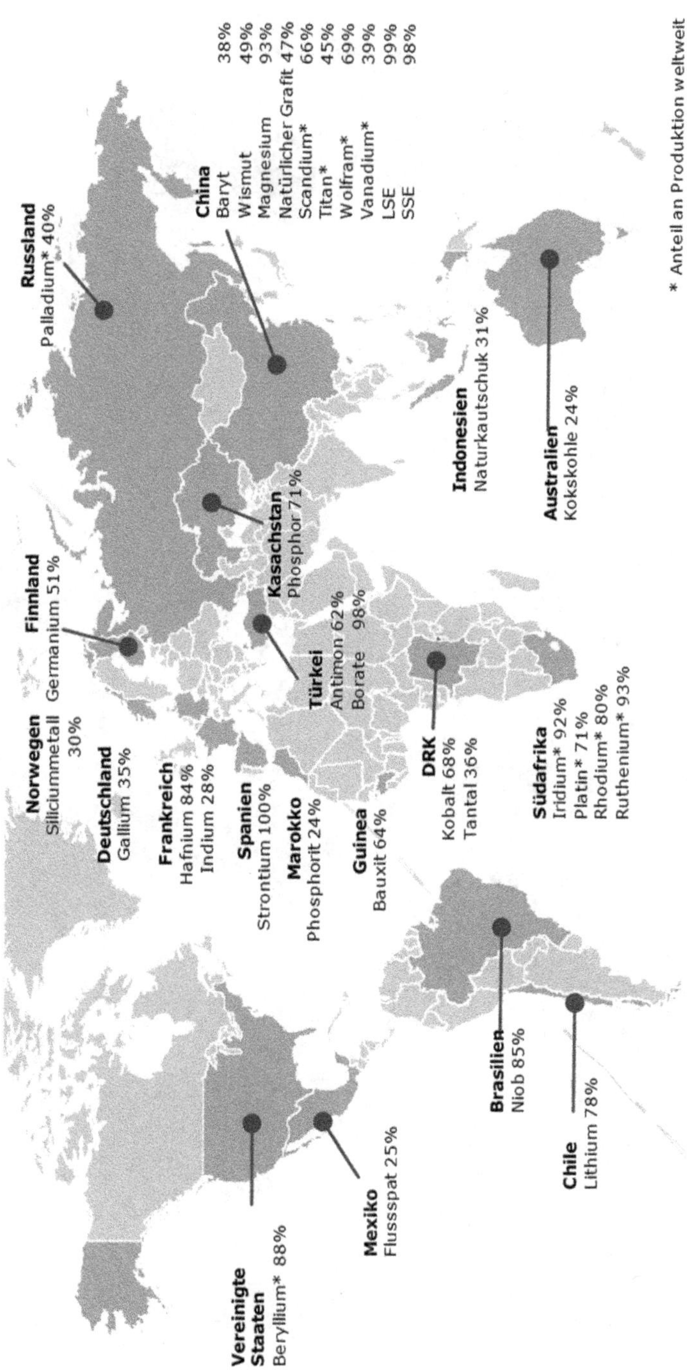

Fig. 11.2 Countries supplying critical raw materials to the EU, source: European Commission (2020d)

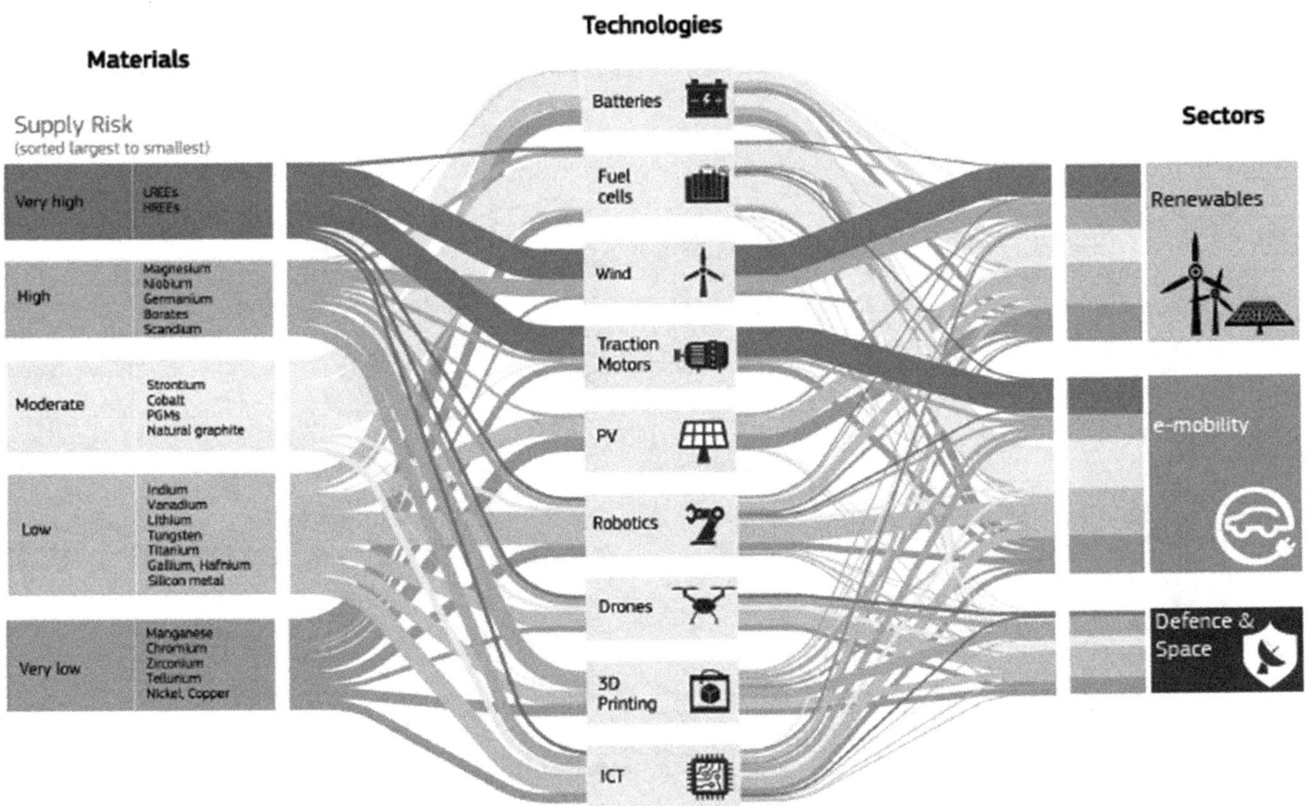

Fig. 11.3 Critical raw materials, technologies and strategically important economic sectors, source: European Commission (2020c)

11.3.2 Key Enabling Technologies

As a starting point for innovation and industrial policy measures, the European Commission already identified so-called key enabling technologies (KETs) in 2009 (European Commission, 2009). KETs are understood to be knowledge-intensive cross-sectional technologies with a high R&D intensity, fast innovation cycles, high investment expenditure and highly qualified employment (Fig. 11.4). KETs enable innovation in processes, goods and services throughout the economy and are of systemic relevance. As cross-cutting technologies, they are multidisciplinary and span many technology areas with a trend towards convergence and integration. KETs significantly support innovation efforts in many sectors of the economy.

KETs are the essential technology building blocks underpinning Europe's (aspirational) global leadership position in various sectors, especially in high value-added, high-technology products and services (European Commission, 2017).

Not quite a decade later, a further development of the definition of KETs was proposed (European Commission, 2018), where under the title "KETs 4.0", which takes account of the digital transformation, mainly a restructuring of the previous system – grouping of the KETs into three supergroups "production technologies", "digital technologies" and "cybertechnologies" – took place, and, apart from two (marginal) adjustments, the original KETs were essentially retained. While the first adjustment concerned the expansion from the narrowly(er) defined "biotechnology" to the broader "life sciences", two new categories were introduced with "artificial intelligence" and "digital security and connectivity" (Fig. 11.5).

In a final step, the concept of key enabling technologies (KETs) was further developed into Advanced Technologies for Industry (ATI) (European Commission, 2020a).

ATIs essentially represent a further specification and greater differentiation of KETs, in that 16 cutting-edge technologies are now explicitly addressed (Fig. 11.6).

According to the European Commission's vision, ATIs could be priorities for European industrial policy because they enable process, product and service innovation across the economy, thus promoting industrial modernisation and structural change.

1. Advanced manufacturing technologies
2. Advanced materials
3. Nanotechnology
4. Micro-/Nano-Electronics
5. Industrial biotechnology
6. Photonics

Fig. 11.4 Key enabling technologies (KETS), Q: European Commission (2009)

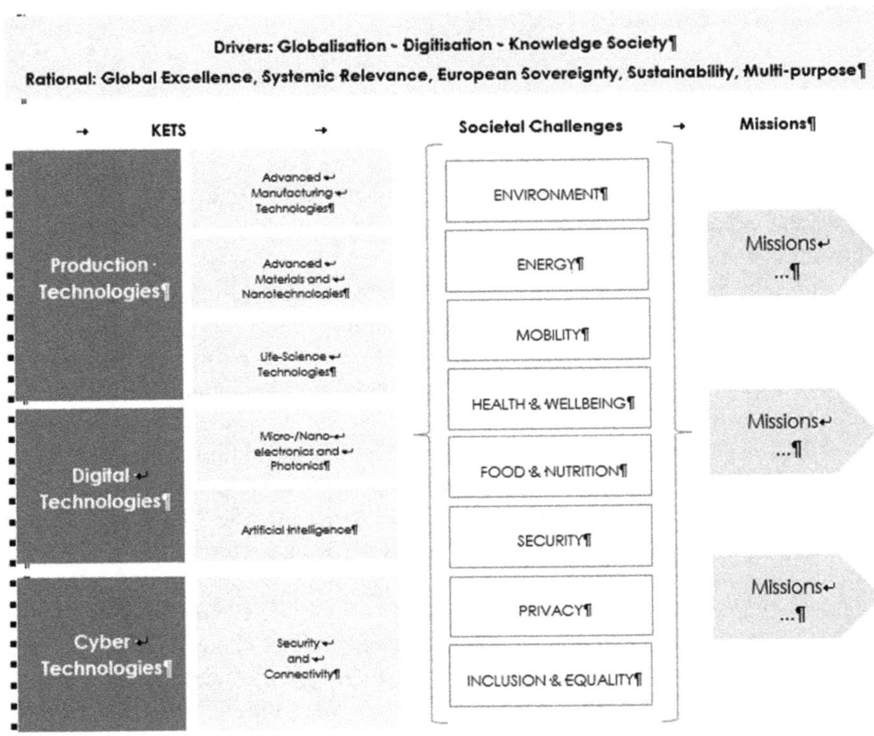

Fig. 11.5 KETs 4.0, Q: European Commission (2018)

1. Advanced materials
2. Advanced manufacturing
3. Artificial intelligence
4. Augmented and Virtual Reality
5. Big Data
6. Blockchain
7. Cloud technologies
8. Connectivity
9. Industrial biotechnology
10. Internet of Things
11. Micro- and nanoelectronics
12. Mobility
13. Nanotechnology
14. Photonics
15. Robotics
16. Security

Fig. 11.6 Cutting-edge technologies within the framework of Advanced Technologies for Industry (ATI), Q: European Commission (2020a)

11.3.3 Maintaining a Fair Global Level Playing Field

KETs or ATIs are key technologies which, together with the raw materials identified as critical, are of crucial importance for the (future) economic development of economic areas. If European industry does not have full access to KETs/ATIs and critical raw materials under fair global conditions, economic development is only possible to a limited extent, and a loss of competitiveness is the inevitable consequence.

Investments in these technology areas have the potential to increase competitiveness at the microeconomic level of companies as well as at the macroeconomic level of economies, to increase employment and to support sustainable economic growth. Due to their inherent potential and their great importance for economic and social development, KETs/ATIs, together with critical raw materials, have a key function in formulating a concept of strategic autonomy. Only if an economic area has secure access to key technologies and critical raw materials can the economy and society fully participate in future economic development and unfold their economic potential.

Strengthening resilience while preserving the anti-protectionist core of European economic policy “as a new compass for EU policy” (European Commission, 2020e) is of paramount importance in formulating a concept of (open) strategic autonomy (European Commission, 2021a).

The EU is one of the most open economies in the world, and its member countries are among the beneficiaries of globalisation. The EU attracts a high level of investment from its trading partners in third countries. However, this openness appears to be increasingly challenged by external trade practices, including subsidies, which distort the level playing field for EU companies. A global level playing field seems to be less and less guaranteed (Böheim et al., 2021b).

The EU advocates open international markets and is committed to providing market access to the European single market for (certain) goods and services. On the other hand, many European companies face difficulties in gaining access to the markets of non-EU countries. Some trading partners have maintained or introduced protectionist or discriminatory measures that affect EU companies. Subsidies granted to non-EU companies by their home governments are (so far) not subject to EU state aid control and can be detrimental to EU companies here. In response, the EU is taking action in several areas to ensure a level global playing field and increase market opportunities for European companies in the world market.

In this context, EU competition rules in general and the EU state aid framework in particular play an important role in ensuring fair conditions for companies in the single market. Subsidies by member states have always been subject to the strict EU state aid rules in order to avoid distortions of competition in the internal market. Neither the US nor China has a restriction on the granting of subsidies comparable to the EU state aid framework. State aid granted by non-EU governments to companies in the EU appears to have an increasingly negative impact on competition in the internal market, but does not fall under EU state aid control. There are a growing number of cases where foreign subsidies appear to have facilitated the takeover of EU companies or distorted the investment decisions, market activity or pricing policies of their recipients or distorted tendering in public procurement to the detriment of non-subsidised companies.

Against this background, the European Union is trying to form alliances with important strategic partners (e.g. with the USA and Japan) in order to address these problems at the multilateral level (WTO). Beyond these long-term economic diplomacy initiatives, however, an effective short- to medium-term update of the EU's economic policy instruments also seems urgently needed.

According to the European Commission's vision, ATIs could be priorities for European industrial policy because they enable process, product and service innovation across the economy and thus promote industrial modernisation and structural change. Bundling the development and promotion of critical enabling technologies in cross-member state cooperation programmes led to the development of the industrial policy instrument of "Important Projects of Common European Interest (IPCEI)".

11.3.4 Important Projects of Common European Interest (IPCEI)

Compared to the framework conditions for (the award of state) subsidies in the USA and China, the competition-oriented European state aid law is significantly more restrictive. Against the backdrop of the challenges arising from the digital and green transformation, the EU state aid framework is increasingly also seen as a substantial disadvantage for European companies in global competition. Since the (self-imposed) restriction of state aid in the EU is also increasingly viewed critically from an industrial policy perspective, an instrument under state aid law[2] was developed with the "Important Projects of Common European Interest (IPCEI)" for the targeted promotion of industrial areas of strength and for strengthening European competitiveness (Deffains et al., 2020).

An IPCEI must be a significant, highly innovative ("beyond the state of the art") research and development project supported by several member states, or a fundamental product or process innovation ("R&I IPCEI"), or a project of major importance for the EU's environment, energy or transport strategy ("infrastructure IPCEI"). In addition, there must be serious cases of market and system failure and positive externalities ("spillovers") of the project must be demonstrated. According to the intentions of the European Commission, IPCEI should be an essential part of a "new European industrial policy". With this instrument, projects of outstanding pan-European importance should be able to be funded, where the handling lies essentially with the member states and companies involved in the project, while the approval is carried out by the European Commission. The companies enter into consortia with other companies along specified technology fields. So far, (only) three IPCEIs have been approved, one each in the key technology areas of microelectronics and batteries for the development of strategic value chains and one pure infrastructure project. Further IPCEIs are in preparation in the areas of batteries, hydrogen and reduction of CO2 emissions (Pender & Polt, 2020).

---

[2] Under state aid law, IPCEIs are exceptions to the general prohibition of state aid in Art. 107 TFEU. Each IPCEI requires individual notification by the European Commission (DG Competition).

11.4 Options for Strengthening Resilience at the Corporate and Political Levels

Improved resilience requires the cooperation of all key actors involved. Specific options for action can be derived in particular at the levels of companies and politics.

11.4.1 Corporate Level

Securing one's own business model in the long term is an urgent strategic task for the management of every company. At the operational level, strengthening operational resilience is an integral part of implementing corporate strategy. An increase in (long-term) resilience will regularly go hand in hand with a reduction in (short-term) efficiency. Since resilience-increasing measures burden the company's results, at least in the short term, international competitiveness can suffer. Depending on the sector-specific and company-specific risk potential as well as the respective costs, a company faces the challenge of assessing the trade-off between long-term resilience and short-term efficiency for its own competitive position (VBW, 2020).

Resilience as a corporate task can be divided into static resilience and dynamic resilience. Which type of resilience a company should strive for should be assessed on the basis of the (desired) security of supply. Companies with a high level of static resilience are able to bridge disruptions in the value chains within the company through redundancies. Since the uncertainty is comparatively low, it is easier to plan and prepare for. If, on the other hand, value chains show greater uncertainty, a proactive approach would be associated with (too) high costs, and it may make more sense for a company to strive for dynamic resilience. Companies with dynamic resilience are characterised by a high level of adaptability and speed in the event of an unforeseen disruption to their value chains.

Companies aiming for high static resilience will (have to) mainly resort to supply chain specific measures such as multiple sourcing and inventory management. Both measures have a positive impact on resilience through higher redundancy and flexibility. However, an increase in inventories is often only suitable for particularly critical intermediate goods due to the company's internal costs, while multiple sourcing generally achieves a diversification of the supplier structure. In order to strengthen the dynamic resilience of a company, investments in the IT infrastructure (supplemented by ongoing risk analyses and elaborate contingency plans) are of central necessity in order to ensure a high level of internal adaptability supported by automation. Personnel-specific measures complement both resilience concepts.

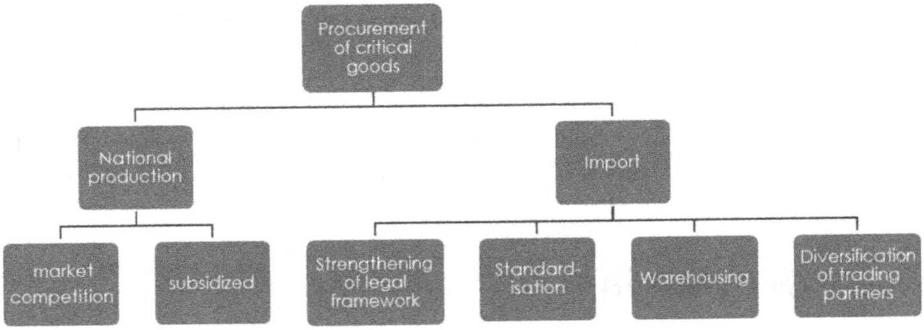

Fig. 11.7 National production vs. import in the procurement of critical goods, Klien et al. (2021)

11.4.2 Political Level

In a (continental) European-style market economy, the state is basically limited to shaping the framework conditions, unless there are market failures or strategic political interests. Political interests take precedence over economic considerations and are therefore beyond the scope of economic calculation. Only market failure can be meaningfully assessed with the methods of economics. According to economic theory, state intervention is only justified if there is market failure and the concrete state intervention can also eliminate this market failure (Böheim, 2011). This core principle of microeconomics also applies mutatis mutandis to the preservation of the resilience and competitiveness of a business location.

Fundamental economic policy options concerning the provision of critical goods can be derived from the resolution of the seemingly polar decision between import and domestic production (Fig. 11.7).

The interest of economic policy should be focused primarily on the availability of critical technologies and goods to secure the supply of one's own population. By what means (import or national production) should be secondary in this objective function, as long as the primary objective of security of supply is achieved. A given objective should be achieved by the most appropriate means. The policy should be fundamentally neutral towards the different instruments that (can) be used to achieve the goal. It comes down to developing the right policy mix according to the assessment of the trade-off between efficiency and resilience.

In the political discussion, (re)localisation towards national production ("reshoring") plays a very prominent role and often overrides the other economic policy options. However, these high expectations of reshoring cannot withstand a "reality check". By and large, these high expectations are mere political wishful thinking, and a large-scale relocation of production and technologies is largely unrealistic. (Raised) expectations of large-scale relocation to Austria or the EU due to economic and technological factors, especially digital technologies, are most likely not realisable in the short to medium term. The evidence available so far is limited and only points to a weak trend of reshoring to the EU before COVID-19, for example, due to automation and additive manufacturing or due to quality issues and the importance of market proximity. These processes were essentially driven by internal company decisions based on business considerations rather than political considerations of overarching goals such as technological sovereignty and strategic autonomy (European Parliament, 2021).

(Re-)localisation will be one of several instruments that can help to ensure security of supply, but it is certainly not an economic policy “all-purpose weapon”. The assessment of reshoring must be carefully examined on a case-by-case basis. In principle, reshoring can make a contribution in the following two constellations: firstly, with regard to increasing the security of supply of critical COVID-19 products, and, secondly, in securing and expanding the EU’s technological sovereignty in the pursuit of greater strategic autonomy in a changing international order.

Any economic policy measure must be tailored to the specific circumstances of the relevant product market. Given the diversity and the very specific nature of global value chains, there can be no general policy approach to reshoring. It should also be noted that the success of policy measures to promote reshoring as applied in other countries such as the USA, the UK and Japan has been limited. It is therefore crucial that the policies applied and the respective role played by reshoring in these policies are adapted to the specific characteristics of product or technology, given the overall policy objective to be achieved.

The public sector can support (re)localisation in a variety of ways. Starting points should in any case be the suitability of a (critical) product for reshoring on the one hand and comparative locational advantages on the other. Reshoring can be promoted directly through sector-specific policies and indirectly through horizontal policies. Sector-specific, direct policies include obligations for companies to source domestically or to use domestic production or financial incentives to relocate production. Horizontal, indirect policies include measures that make international trade and transport more expensive, such as CO_2 levies, tariff preferences for (re-) localised products or due diligence obligations for companies to increase the resilience and robustness of their supply chains (European Parliament, 2021).

In principle, following the principles of the EU framework, preference should be given to horizontal instruments, as they tend to have a less distortive effect on competition. This includes, in particular, subsidies that proactively support the digital and green transformation of the economy and society. These policies can also make a substantial contribution to the incentive-compatible (re)localisation of the production of critical goods and technologies. Public procurement can also have a supporting effect at the horizontal level, which could be realigned in terms of supply security and resilience by giving preference to purchasing from suppliers who, on the one hand, submit to special due diligence obligations in order to increase the resilience and robustness of their supply chains and/or, on the other hand, undertake to use local production capacities or to procure primary products from regional suppliers.

On the side of production location, the fundamental question arises as to whether national production can be competitive under market economy conditions or whether state subsidies are necessary. This is relevant both from a legal perspective (state aid law) and due to different economic policy accompanying measures.

Business location and international trade take place on the basis of comparative locational advantages. The question of possible state reactions to the production (decisions) of companies therefore also depends significantly on the national economic structure. For a small open economy like Austria, a concept of strategic autonomy at the national level makes no sense, so that the assessment, especially in the economic field, must at least be based on a supranational framework. In cooperation with other member states and under the coordination of the European Union, however, the development and expansion of national production capacities can also be possible location policy options for Austria.

In principle, a production settlement under market economy competition conditions is the preferred variant. However, if purely private sector production is not profitable, it could be subsidised by the public sector. In the European Union, there is a fundamental ban on the granting of state aid that distorts competition on the internal market. Exceptions, such as the promotion of research, development and innovation, require special justification and are regulated in so-called frameworks on state aid. Important Projects of Common European Interest (IPCEI) also falls into this category as a new instrument for the implementation of industrially motivated guidelines of overriding European interest. These instruments, which seek to prevent a subsidy race among the member states, should not be undermined under the guise of supply critical goods and strategic technologies.

In accordance with the principles of public procurement law, public purchase guarantees can help to ensure a minimum utilisation of (otherwise) unprofitable production facilities. In European competition, this means that in public tenders, price takes a back seat to other award criteria. This would require a promotion of the "best offer principle" and a repression of the "cheap offer principle" (Hölzl et al., 2017). In the case of standardised goods, price increases are to be expected, ceteris paribus. The overpayment represents (a kind of) "security of supply premium" that guarantees quick access to locally produced supply critical goods in the event of a short-term increase in demand. Here, less efficiency is exchanged for more resilience. Consideration should therefore be given to including the "increase in resilience" as a further award criterion to be assessed in addition to price in the "best offer principle".

However, the promotion of reshoring through financial incentives for companies, in particular through subsidies and/or tax breaks, should only be used on a subsidiary basis, provided that either the strategic technological importance or the relevance for the security of supply of the sector or product in question has been clearly demonstrated and that no other economic policy instrument that is equally efficient and less distortive of competition is available. European competition law, which is relatively restrictive with regard to subsidies, could be interpreted more flexibly if one of the two conditions is fulfilled—especially in order to create a level playing field with China and the USA (European Parliament, 2021).

If production does not take place in Austria (for whatever reason), critical goods must be procured from abroad, and a diversification of suppliers both at the level of the companies and at the level of the countries of origin should be strived for in any case. The former counteracts market concentration, the latter geopolitical dependence. For reasons of close ties in political, legal and economic dimensions, trading partners from the European Union should be preferred. The closer the trading partner, the shorter the transport routes, and the faster these goods can be delivered to Austria.

Although just-in-time production is particularly efficient, it is also particularly vulnerable to disruptions in the supply chain. Stockpiling more than the minimum is inefficient in the short term because it causes additional costs, but it increases the resilience of production in the event of a crisis. How this trade-off between efficiency and resilience is dealt with must be assessed on a case-by-case basis. Where a significant increase in resilience can be realised with the abandonment of comparatively little efficiency, state incentives for companies can achieve a major leverage effect.

Even if national siting of critical products is the declared policy goal, it is unlikely that the entire supply chain will be fully integrated. And even against the background that not all critical products are suitable for national production, it makes sense to consider a bundle of measures to strengthen the resilience of supply chains that work in a complementary way to achieve the goal of greater strategic autonomy. From stockpiling critical products, greater standardisation of products and components, to broader diversification of trading partners (countries), there are a number of options to reduce the risks of high import dependency.

From stockpiling critical products, greater standardisation of products and components, to broader diversification of trading partners (countries), there are a number of options to reduce the risks of high import dependency.

Warehouses on one's own territory allow access to hoarded inventory at any time. Strategic stockpiling can therefore be an alternative to (relocating the) production of critical products (Baldwin & Freeman, 2020; Felbermayr & Görg, 2020). However, stockpiling is a costly undertaking, especially if the stored products have an expiry date or quickly become obsolete due to short product cycles (e.g. due to technological change), as unused stock has to be discarded and renewed. For this reason, standardised products with a long or unlimited shelf life, such as protective masks, disposable gloves, etc., are particularly suitable for strategic stockpiling. The storage of critical products such as medicines with short expiry dates therefore requires sophisticated management in order to keep costs as low as possible. If stockpiling is not carried out by the public sector itself, private companies such as pharmaceutical manufacturers and distributors would have to be compensated for the additional costs with subsidies so that stockpiling is economically viable. In addition to an obligation to stockpile (including compensation of costs), positive incentives for stockpiling by private companies could be implemented. In this regard, the use of public procurement to preferentially procure from manufacturers and distributors that commit to minimum stockpiling and the granting of financial incentives to selected manufacturers and distributors that commit to holding fixed stocks of critical products could be considered. Due to their complexity, the contribution of stockpiling to security of supply could prove limited. The extensive use of stockpiling measures should therefore be limited to cases where there is no manufacturing in the EU and building domestic manufacturing capacity would be excessively costly (European Parliament, 2021).

At the (high) political level, the strengthening of the legal framework for fair world trade (WTO) and a diversification of trading partner countries (trade and cooperation agreements) can be promoted in the long term. Greater standardisation of goods (through international standardisation) can reduce the complexity of procurement in the medium term, which is likely to have a cost-reducing effect.

11.5 Conclusion

Global supply chains are important drivers of productivity growth and international competitiveness (Jenny, 2020; Amiti & Konings, 2007). Austria as a business location benefits greatly from this global economy organised on the basis of the division of labour (Falk & Wolfmayr, 2008; Egger et al., 2001; Kratena & Wüger, 2001). The increasing digitalisation and automation of production opens up new opportunities to increase efficiency in local, automated manufacturing, which favours the shortening of supply chains (repatriation (of parts) of production). The (short-term) supply problems in global value chains as a result of the COVID-19 pandemic have also increased concerns about the vulnerability of global supply chains and dependence on individual suppliers. They are influencing risk assessment at the government level in relation to the security of supply of critical products and are also likely to play an increasing role in corporate risk assessment. This reassessment could also lead to domestic or more European-oriented production gaining in importance, especially in the area of critical products. Considerations of relocating production ("reshoring") should in any case be based on the suitability of the products and technologies on the one hand and on the comparative competitive advantages of the location on the other.

Whether (re)localisation is the best measure to increase resilience and security of supply with critical products and technologies must be assessed in consideration of other measures. Strategic stockpiling and the consideration of supply security in public procurement are further instruments for an effective policy mix.

References

Amiti, M., & Konings, J. (2007). Trade liberalization, intermediate inputs and productivity. *American Economic Review, 97*(5), 1611–1638.

Antràs, P. (2016). *Global production. Firms, contracts and trae structure*. Princeton University Press.

Baldwin, R, & Freeman, R. (2020, April 01). *Supply chain contagion waves: Thinking ahead on manufacturing 'contagion and reinfection' from the COVID concussion*. VoxEU.org.

Böheim, M. (2011). Die Privatisierung öffentlichen Eigentums als Instrument der Wirtschaftspolitik: Privat- versus Staatsei-gentum an Unternehmen – theoretische Grundlagen. *WIFO-Monatsberichte, 84*(9), 593–604.

Böheim, M., Jaeger, T., Meyer, B., & Kopetzki, M. (2021a). *Vorschläge für einen zukunftsorientierten EU-Beihilferahmen, Stu-die im Auftrag des Bundeskanzleramts (BKA) und des Bundesministeriums für Digitalisierung und Wirtschaftsstand-ort (BMDW)*. WIFO.

Böheim, M., Braito, N., Ceccanti, D., Fina, D., Huynh-Olesen, D., Jacob, C., & Kubovicová, K. (2021b), *Foreign subsidies and public procurement, in-depth analysis*. The INTA Committee, European Parliament.

Deffains, B., d'Ormesson, O., & Perroud, T. (2020). *Competition policy and industrial policy: For a reform of European Law*. Foundation Robert Schuman.

Egger, P., Pfaffermayr, M., & Wolfmayr-Schnitzer, Y. (2001). The international fragmentation of the value-added chain: The effects of outsourcing to Eastern Europe on productivity and wages in Austrian manufacturing. *The North American Journal of Economics and Finance, 12*(3), 257–272.

European Commission. (2009, September 30). *Communication "Preparing for our future: Developing a common strategy for key enabling technologies in the EU", COM(2009) 512 final.*

European Commission. (2017, September 13). *Communication "Investing in a smart, innovative and sustainable industry: A renewed EU industrial policy strategy," COM(2017)479 final.*

European Commission. (2018). *Re-finding industry. Defining innovation.*

European Commission. (2020a). *Advanced technologies for industry – Methodological report.*

European Commission. (2020b, September 09). *2020 strategic foresight report. Strategic foresight – Charting the course towards a more resilient Europe, COM(2020) 493 final.*

European Commission. (2020c). *Critical raw materials for strategic technologies and sectors in the EU. A foresight study.*

European Commission. (2020d, September 09). *Communication 'Critical raw materials resilience: Charting a path towards greater Security and Sustainability', COM(2020) 474 final.*

European Commission. (2020e, May 27). *Communication "Europe's moment: Repair and prepare for the next generation", COM(2020) 456 final.*

European Commission. (2021a, January 19), *Communication 'The European economic and financial system: fostering openness, strength and resilience', COM(2021) 32 final.*

European Commission. (2021b, February 18). *Communication 'Trade policy review - An open, sustainable and assertive trade policy', COM(2021) 66 final.*

European Parliament. (2021, March). *Post Covid-19 value chains: Options for reshoring production back to Europe in a globalised economy, Study requested by the INTA committee, PE 653.626.*

Falk, M., & Wolfmayr, Y. (2008). *International outsourcing and productivity growth, FIW-Studie des Österreichischen Insti-tuts für Wirtschaftsforschung im Auftrag des Bundesministeriums für Wirtschaft und Arbeit.*

Felbermayr, G., & Görg, H. (2020). Die Folgen von Covid-19 für die Globalisierung. *Perspektiven der Wirtschaftspolitik, 21*(3), 263–272.

Hölzl, W., Böheim, M., Klien, M., & Pichler, E. (2017). *Das öffentliche Beschaffungswesen im Spannungsfeld zwischen Billigst- und Bestbieterprinzip*. WIFO-Studie im Auftrag der Wirtschaftskammer Österreich.

Jenny, F. (2020). Economic resilience, globalization and market governance: Facing the Covid-19 test. *CEPR Covid Economics, 3*(1), 64–78.

Klien, M., Böheim, M., Firgo, M., Reinstaller, A., Reschenhofer, P., & Wolfmayr, Y. (2021). *Stärkung der Unabhängigkeit des Wirtschaftsstandortes Österreich bei kritischen Produkten*. WIFO

Kratena, K., & Wüger, M. (2001). *Real trade costs, fragmentation and employment*. WIFO Working Papers 144, WIFO.

Lippert, B., von Ondarza, N., & Perthes, V. (Eds.). (2019). *Strategische Autonomie Europas.* Akteure, Handlungsfelder, Ziel-konflikte.
Pender, M., & Polt, W. (2020). *Important Projects of Common European Interest (IPCEI) als Instrument einer neuen euro-päischen Industrie- und Innovationspolitik, Inputpapier für das Projekt "Neue Industrie-, Innovations- und Tech-nologiepolitik" im Auftrag des Rates für Forschung und Technologie-entwicklung (RFTE).*
Sachs, A., Funke, C., Kreuzer, P., & Weiss, J. (2020). *Globalisierungsreport 2020. Wer profitiert am stärksten von der Globa-lisierung?* Bertelsmann Stiftung.
VBW. (2020). *Verbesserung der Resilienz der bayerischen Wirtschaft.*

Michael Böheim has been a senior economist at the Austrian Institute for Economic Research (WIFO) in the research area "Industrial Economics, Innovation and International Competition" since 1997. Since 2002, he has acted as a certified expert witness to the Austrian Cartel Court and he was a member of the Austrian Competition Commission from 2002 to 2018. He has 25 years project-relevant experience as researcher, consultant and university lecturer as well as an author of 100+ publications on industrial, competition and regulatory economics and policy. His expertise as a project manager includes serving the European Commission in various projects. Michael has studied economics, law and philosophy at Karl-Franzens-University Graz with research study visits to the UK and the USA; He holds master's degrees in Economic Sciences, Law and Philosophy as well as a doctoral degree in Economic Sciences. Cf. https://www.wifo.ac.at/michael_boeheim

Chapter 12
Managing Supply Chain Resilience for Sustainability in an Uncertain World: Challenges and Solutions

Ki-Hoon Lee

Abstract Supply chain resilience and economic, environmental, and social sustainability challenges are highly vulnerable and uncertain. Under the unprecedented supply chain disruption caused by epidemics such as COVID-19, many organisations face new challenges of shifting situation, managing volatility of information, and coordinating supply chain structures. During the pandemic crisis, corporations are presented with an opportunity to reconsider their global supply chain management and accelerate their capabilities for the long-term sustainability in managing current and future challenges. Corporate leaders and supply chain managers have major tasks to reduce supply chain uncertainty and risks, while balancing supply chain resilience and sustainability performance. By addressing the key question 'can supply chain resilience and sustainability help companies survive and recover for business sustainability and continuity?', this chapter presents important solutions and opportunities for corporate leaders and supply chain managers. This paper also offers new insights on how supply chain resilience and sustainability help companies to manage complex interdependency and related risks in supply chain.

12.1 Introduction

Over the past few decades, sustainability in supply chain management has drawn much attention from both academics and industry. To achieve sustainability, companies need to address interconnected environmental, social, and financial goals and performance in the supply chain. An increasing number of companies have adopted sustainability practices to improve the environmental and social performance of their businesses and corporate supply chains (Lee & Vachon, 2016). Unexpectedly, the COVID-19 pandemic hit the world. The pandemic emerged as a healthcare crisis, but soon it was identified as an unprecedented cause of the supply chain crisis at a global scale and scope. We witnessed how the COVID-19 affected the corporate

K.-H. Lee (✉)
Griffith Business School, Griffith University, Brisbane, QLD, Australia
e-mail: ki-hoon.lee@griffith.edu.au

S. Kummer et al. (eds.), *Supply Chain Resilience*, Springer Series in Supply Chain Management 17, https://doi.org/10.1007/978-3-030-95401-7_12

supply chain and its sustainability performance under a vulnerable and uncertain supply chain environment. The unprecedented supply chain disruption caused by the COVID-19 pandemic has had severe operational and financial outcomes such as demand drop and surge, supply shortage, inventory placement challenges, and reduced productivity (Govindan et al., 2020). Moreover, the pandemic is not only a global health crisis but also an economic and social crisis. The pandemic has created an unprecedented adverse condition in labour-intensive supply chains (e.g. apparel, mining, agriculture sectors) in developing economies of the world, which is known as 'modern slavery' in the supply chain. The COVID-19 has disrupted the supply chain on a global scale. Over 90% of Fortune 1000 companies have experienced supply chain disruptions due to the COVID-19 pandemic (Kilpatrick & Barter, 2020). Increased border controls and customs regulations result in longer waiting times, and lack of capacity for the long-haul and last-mile fulfill-ment make the challenges extreme since they have been a vital lifeline to support the response, keeping essential medical supplies, food, and other key necessities to meet demand where they're needed the most (Bastug & Yercan, 2021).

While the impacts of the pandemic on the global supply chain are increasingly high, scholars and practitioners have argued that epidemic outbreaks happen unpredictably, and the impacts on the supply chain have long-term disruption. The businesses and supply chains are probably the most sensitive to market changes and disruption. Thus, there is an urgent need for the corporate leaders and supply chain managers to explore new ways or approaches that support the supply chain against current and future global disruptions. During the pandemic crisis, corporations are presented with an opportunity to reconsider their global supply chain management and accelerate their capabilities for the long-term sustainability in managing current and future challenges. Corporate leaders and supply chain managers have major tasks to reduce supply chain uncertainty and risks, while balancing supply chain resilience and sustainability performance.

To address the corporate challenges and possible solutions, this paper brings the timely approaches to reduce the supply chain risks while increasing supply chain resilience and sustainability under the uncertain business environments.

12.2 Key Problems

Sustainability is a long-term commitment and poses several challenges for corporate leaders and supply chain managers. To achieve and operationalise sustainability, they need to address interconnected environmental, social, and financial objectives in the supply chain (Michelle & Walinga, 2017). Thus, supply chain leaders seek to reduce the negative impacts of supply chain management and to improve the triple bottom line of sustainability performance (Vargas et al., 2018; Lee & Vachon, 2016). Companies also seek to mitigate supply chain risks and vulnerabilities from unexpected disruptions by utilising supply chain resilience. A supply chain resil-ience is about the supply chain ability to absorb disturbances and retain and grow its function and structure in the face of disruptions (Jabbarzadeh et al., 2018; Pettit et al., 2010).

In 2020, most firms experienced an unprecedented series of disruptions and shocks caused by the COVID-19 pandemic in the global supply chain. Obviously, the pandemic has immensely affected all areas of the economy and society raising a series of new challenges for academics and practitioners. One of the key challenges is:

Can supply chain resilience and sustainability help companies survive and recover for business sustainability and continuity?

Supply chain resilience has been extensively studied in the literature from strategic and operational perspectives in the light of severe disruptions such as natural disasters and the COVID-19 pandemic. Recent disasters (extreme weather conditions, bushfires, pandemic crisis) have demonstrated dramatic consequences of unexpected disruptions on supply chains, such as production facility shutdowns, hampered productivity and timely delivery, shortages of safety stocks, and inventories. Such consequences inevitably make a negative impact on the market and customers and the long-term sustainability of the company.

As corporate leaders and supply chain managers face the current challenges—and are about to face future challenges—of sustainability, the immediate challenge for supply chain managers is how to establish or utilise resilience in the supply chain to mitigate risks and negative impacts. One of the key areas in this regard is the interface between resilience and sustainability in supply chains. Firms have extensively incorporated sustainability dimensions and performance measures into their supply chain management. Lee and Vachon (2016) describe business sustainability as 'embracing environmental, social and economic challenges by integrating sustainability into the business value chain to enhance both the business and the societal value (p. 25)'. Although the studies on sustainability in supply chain management differ across the scopes and methods, they commonly argue that the adoption and implementation of sustainable supply chain management are to maintain business continuity and to secure both business and societal value in order to reduce the long-term risks of the supply chain. Business continuity is an organisation's ability to maintain essential functions during and after severe disruptions and the key characteristic of supply chain resilience.

The pandemic situation motivates many firms to rethink about their current supply chain and consider adopting long-term sustainability in managing future disruptions like outbreaks. There is a significant need to find new approaches that can support supply chain against future global disruptions (van Remko, 2020).

12.3 Solutions and Opportunities in Supply Chain Resilience for Sustainability

To answer the question 'can supply chain resilience and sustainability help companies to survive and recover for business sustainability and continuity?', the first step is to identify how to incorporate resilience and sustainability in supply chain management.

Negri et al. (2021) conducted a systematic literature review on 'integrating sustainability and resilience in the supply chain', and discovered a lapse in the connection between supply chain sustainability and resilience. In most cases, the two concepts (i.e. sustainability and resilience) are separated and independently applied in supply chain. Their findings indicate that there is a strong need to strengthen the link between sustainability and resilience and to incorporate both in supply chain management. Resilience and sustainability in supply chain aim to boost business stability and reduce delays and costs in the production and distribution processes under uncertain business environments; both resilience and sustainability in supply chain management ensure efficient operational as well as economic performance, risk management, quick responses to uncertain environments, and achievement of sustainability practices. It is not easy to utilise operational and structural efficiencies in short/long term and sustainability performances under uncertain business environment. To provide practical solutions, I propose two solutions to consider.

Solution 1: Establishing efficient supply chain resilience and sustainability in line with effective supply chain risk management

Supply chain resilience and sustainability are directly relevant to supply chain risk management. As supply chain disruption may have short and long-term negative effects with environmental, social, and economic risks and challenges, it is important to establish efficient supply chain resilience and sustainability from supply chain risk management. As global outsourcing activities have made supply chain more complex and less controllable, disruptions in a global supply chain may make an impact on the entire supply chain. Due to the COVID-19 pandemic, recent semiconductor chip shortage caused global car production to slow down, and global semiconductor shortage seems to continue to stifle car makers. Traditionally receiving chips on a just-in-time basis for car manufacturers, and global makers (Volkswagen, GM, Ford, Honda, Hyundai, Nissan, Fiat) have all been affected by the parts shortage, as available chipsets are allocated to personal electronics products over the automobile industry. In the short term, tensions between car manufacturers and semiconductor makers (e.g. TSMC, Samsung Electronics) seem to continue. Relating to sustainability risks, economic and environmental risks are often caused by the tension between competing sustainability objectives. For example, with increasing consumer demands on electric vehicles and strict climate change regulations, global car makers face the challenge of producing green cars, which will reduce carbon emissions and climate change risks in the long term, but they cannot respond efficiently due to the shortage of chip sets with high prices for car production. To respond to this type of disruption quickly, efficient supply chain resilience and sustainability should be established in line with supply chain risk management. Supply chain risk management present two types of risks—operational risks and disruption risks. Ivanov (2018) described operational risks as high-probability-low-impact risks such as demand fluctuations and amplification of demand variation on production and ordering quantities in supply chains (i.e. bullwhip effect) and disruption risks as low-probability high-impact risks such as natural disasters, man-made catastrophes, political crises, and the COVID-19 pandemic (i.e. ripple effect). The bullwhip effect is often caused by a small operational deviation and is expected to be amplified in the upstream supply chain. Dolgui et al. (2020) describes the ripple effect as 'a downstream propagation of the downscaling in demand fulfilment in the supply chain as a result of a severe disruption (p. 1286)'. As disruption risks result in structural dynamics in supply chain, the performance impact of this risk is potentially huge. A recent study from Jabbour et al. (2020) investigated efficient disruption risk management capacity under the COVID-19 pandemic and found that risk management capacity enables the companies and organisations to follow the approaches in line with the creation of continuous risk assessment owing to the long-run effects of the crisis.

A good example is how COVID-19 in Wuhan, China, affected global supply chains. Wuhan has been an industrial base for global high technology (optoelectronic technology, pharmaceuticals, biology engineering, and environmental protection) and manufacturing (automotive, steel and iron manufacturing) industries. Over 200 of the Fortune Global 500 firms have a presence directly in Wuhan and over 900 Tier 1 and Tier 2 suppliers of the Fortune 1000 operate in the impacted area. Visibility to only Tier 1 suppliers is unlikely to be sufficient for many firms looking to manage supply chain resilience and sustainability from risk management perspective. Clearly the pandemic brought huge economic, environmental, and social sustainability challenges in forms of conflicting goals and/or a tension between competing goals. For example, when implementing supply chain resilience and sustainability management, its societal impact on well-being of humans and environments should be seriously considered, more importantly finding a balance between economic growth and social sustainability.

To operationalise the solution 1, companies may set key focus areas including (1) rationalise the strategic link between corporate sustainability goals and supply chain operations. Many global firms have continuously pursued high-level sustainability targets with limited key Tier 1 suppliers in their global supply chain. For example, Nestlé claims that they can 'share sustainable consumption and steward resources for future generations'. While Nestlé set high-level sustainability goals and targets, the full scale of multitier suppliers have been slow to adopt to Nestlé's creating shared value (CSV). Therefore, global firms' sustainability goals and strategies should be well reflected and actioned in supply chain resilience and sustainability management with multitier suppliers' participation. (2) Elucidate the extended supply network with high visibility to key Tier 2 suppliers and beyond, which will impact key Tier 1 supplier order fulfilment performance and supply chain resilience. It will provide maximum time and flexibility to work with key Tier

1 suppliers to actively amend and/or redesign supply chain plans to keep operational running at high efficiency. By doing this, companies can manage efficiently 'bullwhip effects' and 'ripple effect' in supply chain resilience and sustainability management. (3) As supply chain disruption may have short- and long-term negative effects with environmental, social, and economic risks and challenges, resilient and sustainability supply chain should include total costs under disruption risks to enhance sustainability performance of the supply chain, which will allow corporate decision-makers to predict the expected total cost with sustainability in the supply chain management.

Solution 2: Localising with circular economy to establish resilient and green supply chain.

Globalised supply chain has been very popular with the increased use of subcontracting and outsourcing. Both subcontracting and outsourcing have become more prevalent due to several reasons including the increased sophistication of components and parts, advanced manufacturing processes, the desire to have more flexible capacity to respond to demands, cost savings and lean/just-in-time (JIT) based minimum stocks, and inventories. From environmental supply chain management, lean production with reduced wastes and high operational efficiencies has resulted in superior economic and environmental performance in the past decades. However, the COVID-19 outbreak exposed the vulnerability of overreliance on lean and JIT production and delivery system (Choi, 2020). To reduce supply chain risks from global subcontracting and outsourcing, companies need to consider building resilient local supply and production systems instead of global outsourcing and subcontracting in future.

A recent example demonstrates how localisation within circular economy can enhance resilience in supply chain management. Apple, Inc., had a serious shortage in its shipments of parts and components to their global assembly plants due to the governments'-imposed shutdown in China. In Apple's global operations, lean and JIT production and delivery system have been well practiced saving costs and delivery time. However, G2 (US and China) trade war and related actions, which began in 2018, directly impacted Apple's global supply chain. It exposed the shortcomings of a globalised production system whose supply chains and logistics are complexly configured but operationally limited. To tackle the challenge, localisation with circular economy tools and applications can offer practical solutions. That is, by applying circular economy strategies characterised by resource circularity, secondary use of products, local sourcing of input materials, optimised logistic chains, and reverse logistics, Apple, Inc., can reuse components of 'used' or 'old' phones with the support from digital technology-based traceability that will allow the customers to make an informed decision on phone purchase or replacement.

From green supply chain and circular economy perspective, environmentally and economically sound supply chain configurations have been debated for a decade. The reverse logistics for secondary materials and waste products, which can be further enabled by digital technologies (e.g. blockchain, Internet of Things), can facilitate smart production and logistics system (Sarkis et al., 2020). For example, knowing the location of materials and components through real-time tracking and traceability makes local sourcing efficient and easier. Similarly, building local resilient supply and production is likely to be accelerated by the pandemic and international trade regionalisation. The new cabinet of President Joe Biden in the United States has already called for localising the supplier base of major semi-conductors in the US territory, and more political and institutional pressures in localisation will be set for many global companies. Replacing the entire global sourcing will not be possible, but it is to be reduced to rebalance global and local sourcing and subcontracting to develop resilient supply chain through digital platforms and circular economy approach. In attempt to link resilience and sustainability in supply chain management, localisation and circular economy can support to develop resilient local supply and production for focal firms and final manufacturing firms. As per the concept of circular economy, it can provide localised inputs materials and resources from products at the end of life for new product development and/or production, the opportunities of reuse, refurbishment, remanufacture and recyclability (4Rs), and environmental supply chain management will be enhanced for the entire supply chain. Utilising 4Rs, circular economy, for example, can facilitate locally sourced e-wastes and plastic wastes to support localised and resilient green supply chain. Such a circular economy solution can fortify local suppliers' capability to provide locally sourced materials and resources for products and production purposes, which result in superior environmental and economic supply chain performance.

12.4 Conclusion

An increasing number of companies experience unexpected disruptions on supply chains such as production shutdowns under the pandemic. Companies attempt to create more resilient supply chains by reconsidering subcontracting and outsourcing activities without losing their sustainability commitment and performance in their supply chain management. This paper argues that how supply chain resilience and sustainability help companies to manage complex interdependency and related risks in supply chain.

As the pandemic continues, the substantial impacts on sustainability are unknown. Resilient supply chain is relatively new and an emerging field as a part of supply chain risk management. The impacts from disruption risk bring structural changes or dynamics to the entire supply chain, and corporate leaders and supply chain managers seek more resilient supply chain. Research on the intersection of supply chain resilience and sustainability is nascent and calls for more rigorous development. This paper provides two solutions to tackle supply chain problems (resilience and sustainability related risks): first, establishing efficient supply chain resilience and sustainability in line with effective supply chain risk management, and second, localising with circular economy to establish resilient and green supply chain. It is expected that the proposed solutions can motivate researchers to develop rigorous conceptual and empirical evidences and trigger new development and changes in supply chain design and management practices to utilise supply chain resilience and sustainability.

References

Bastug, S., & Yercan, F. (2021). An explanatory approach to assess resilience: An evaluation of competitive priorities for logistics organizations. *Transport Policy, 103*, 156–166.

Choi, T. (2020). Innovative "bring-service-near-your-home" operations under Corona virus (COVID-19/SARS-CoV-2) outbreak: Can logistics become the messiah? *Transportation Research Part E: Logistics and Transportation Review, 140*, 101961.

Dolgui, A., Ivanov, D., & Rozhkov, M. (2020). Does the ripple effect influence the bullwhip effect? An integrated analysis of structural and operational dynamics in the supply chain. *International Journal of Production Research, 58*(5), 1285–1301.

Govindan, K., Mina, H., & Alavi, B. (2020). A decision support system for demand management in healthcare supply chains considering the epidemic outbreaks: A case study of coronavirus disease 2019 (COVID-19). *Transportation Research Part E: Logistics and Transportation Review, 138*, 101967.

Ivanov, D. (2018). Revealing interfaces of supply chain resilience and sustainability: A simulation study. *International Journal of Production Research, 56*(10), 3507–3523.

Jabbarzadeh, A., Fahimnia, B., & Sabouhi, F. (2018). Resilient and sustainable supply chain design: Sustainability analysis under disruption risks. *International Journal of Production Research, 56*(17), 5945–5968.

Jabbour, A., Jabbour, C., Hingley, M., Vilalta-Perdomo, L., Ramsden, G., & Twigg, D. (2020). Sustainability of supply chains in the wake of the coronavirus (COVID-19/SARS-CoV-2) pandemic: Lessons and trends. *Modern Supply Chain Research and Applications, 2*(3), 117–122.

Kilpatrick, J., & Barter, L. (2020). *COVID-19: Managing supply chain risk and disruption*. Deloitte.

Lee, K.-H., & Vachon, S. (2016). *Business value and sustainability: An integrated supply network perspective*. Palgrave.

Michelle, I., & Walinga, J. (2017). The creative imperative: The role of creativity, creative problem solving and insight as key drivers for sustainability. *Journal of Cleaner Production, 140*, 1872–1884.

Negri, M., Cagno, E., Colicchia, C., & Sarkis, J. (2021). Integrating sustainability and resilience in the supply chain: A systematic literature review and a research agenda. *Business Strategy and the Environment, 30*(7), 2858–2886.

Pettit, T., Fiksel, J., & Croxton, L. (2010). Ensuring supply chain resilience: Development of a conceptual framework. *Journal of Business Logistics, 31*(1), 1–21.

Sarkis, J., Cohen, M. J., Dewick, P., & Schröder, P. (2020). A brave new world: Lessons from the COVID-19 pandemic for transitioning to sustainable supply and production. *Resources, Conservation and Recycling, 159*, 104894.

van Remko, H. (2020). Research opportunities for a more resilient post-COVID-19 supply chain – Closing the gap between research findings and industry practice. *International Journal of Operations and Production Management, 40*(4), 341–355.

Vargas, J. R. C., Mantilla, C. E. M., & de Sousa Jabbour, A. B. L. (2018). Enablers of sustainable supply chain management and its effect on competitive advantage in the Colombian context. *Resources, Conservation and Recycling, 139*, 237–250.

Ki-Hoon Lee is a Professor of Business Sustainability at Griffith Business School, Griffith University in Australia. Through his research, Professor Lee embraces environmental, social, governance and economic challenges, integrating sustainability into the business value chain to enhance both business and societal value. With his teaching, consulting and public policy experience, Professor Lee's research and consulting expertise include corporate sustainability management, sustainable supply chain management, responsible sourcing and transparency in global supply chain, and environmental, social and governance (ESG) in supply chain performance management.

Chapter 13
Supply Chain Resilience in the Fourth Industrial Revolution

Muhammad Azmat, Shehzad Ahmed, and Muhammad Shujaat Mubarik

Abstract The unusual and dynamic global political situation, man-made and natural disasters, and an upsurge in economic instability internationally are some of the key factors disrupting the global business operations and their supply chains. Similarly, a new dimension known as the fourth industrial revolution is inducing a rapidly changing technological world and its adoption race has also started showing its impact on company's value chains and started setting new standards by creating technological competitive advantages. Therefore, it is imminent for companies to brace themselves for technological, organizational, and environmental changes. Recent events like the COVID-19 pandemic has perfectly showcased the fragility of businesses operations and over-reliance on global supply chains. Nonetheless, a similar situation has also taught us that being resilient, flexible, and agile in such unprecedented circumstances could be beneficial for the organizations. Thus, this chapter precisely articulates the importance of resilience entering into the fourth industrial revolution and presents, how supply chain visibility, collaboration, flexibility, and control could be the ingredients of the winning recipe for businesses. Furthermore, Industry 4.0 promises to revolutionize how the supply chain operates. It provides companies with several predictive capabilities of their supply chains helping them to mitigate and anticipate any risk or disruption caused by the changes in the external environment. Thus, resilience combined with Industry 4.0 could redefine corporations' operations and supply chain forever.

M. Azmat (✉)
Department of Engineering Systems and Supply Chain Management (ESSCM), College of Engineering and Physical Sciences, Aston University, Birmingham, UK
e-mail: Muhammad.Azmat@wu.ac.at

S. Ahmed
School of Business & Creative Industries, University of the West of Scotland, Paisley, UK

M. S. Mubarik
College of Business Management, Institute of Business Management (IoBM), Karachi, Pakistan

S. Kummer et al. (eds.), *Supply Chain Resilience*, Springer Series in Supply Chain Management 17, https://doi.org/10.1007/978-3-030-95401-7_13

13.1 Introduction

"From a 'lost generation' of disillusioned young people, to long-term financial crisis and even state collapse, the world could be feeling the fallout of the COVID-19 crisis for years to come" World Economic Forum (2021).

Businesses have been facing catastrophic events, disruptions and volatilities since the inception of the first firm on the earth; however, the way novel coronavirus SARS-CoV2 (commonly known as COVID-19) pandemic has hit the businesses is unprecedented and unmatchable. To date, COVID-19 has become the largest disruptive event in human history, which has unequivocally disrupted the economic spectrum across the globe. According to Congressional Report Service (CRS) (2021, p. 1), "...economic crisis [due to COVID-19] that affected the $90 trillion global economy beyond anything experienced in nearly a century. Further, it is reported," the loss of global economic output between 2020 and 2025 as a consequence of the pandemic would total $28 trillion" (p. 13). Experts believe that the volume of these losses could have been reduced if the world economies worked on their resilience. Further, it is claimed that one of the major causes of the extolling business losses could be the lack of resilient supply chains. Therefore, it has created concern among practitioners and scholars to identify as to how a firm's supply chain resilience (SCRE) can be improved to encounter massive supply chain disruptions and bounce back effectively (Pettit et al., 2019; Mubarik et al., 2021). Ambulkar et al. (2015), defines SCRE as "The capability of the firm to be alert to, adapt to, and quickly respond to changes brought by a supply chain disruption," while SCRE empowers the system to reinstate its original or a new, more desired state after experiencing inevitable risks (Carvalho & Cruz Machado, 2007; Jüttner & Maklan, 2011). Furthermore, it also ensures the continuity of operational and logistical activities, such as delivery to the final destination (Pettit et al., 2019; Ambulkar et al., 2015).

The temporary disruptive events have low probability and high impacts, which are difficult to anticipate and handle traditionally and imply a certain level of turbulence across the whole supply chain (Pettit et al., 2019; Ralston & Blackhurst, 2020). Such events can lead to financial loss, market share loss, reputation loss, deterioration in share value or lost/missed market opportunities (Jüttner & Maklan, 2011; Morisse & Prigge, 2017). Industry 4.0 (I4.0) and intelligent systems offer improved supply chain performance through digitisation (Luthra et al., 2020). By restructuring the system and employing the resources effectively, firms can achieve greater flexibility in their processes and keep the systems capable of dealing with the changes in the external environment (Kalsoom et al., 2020; Ahmed et al., 2021). I4.0 systems and approaches bring a technology-driven proactive mechanism of dealing with the fluctuations in the external environment. This system can play a crucial role in uplifting the resilience of a supply chain manifold.

Despite the plethora of literature on I4.0, the questions about how I4.0 could contribute to SC resilience, the artefact of such a system, and how a firm can adopt I4.0-driven-resilience are yet to be comprehensibly addressed. This acts as an impetus for the present study, leading us to explore the role of I4.0 in SC resilience.

In doing so, we introduce attributes and characteristics of I4.0-driven SCRE. The study takes a qualitative approach and reviews the available literature to synthesise the characteristics and attributes of I4.0-driven supply chain. The synthesis of this chapter can pave the way to undertake further research to explore how I4.0 could be capitalised on for effective SCRE and sustainability. The chapter has been divided into four major sections. Section 13.2 briefly delineates the historical evolution and dimensions of I4.0. It is followed by a discussion on the linkage of I4.0 and supply chain management in Sect. 13.3. This section paves the way to discuss I4.0 in the context of SCRE in Sect. 13.4. Section 13.5 provides concluding remarks.

13.2 Industry 4.0: Evolution and Dimensions

The world has witnessed three evolutionary phases since industrialisation. These industrial revolutions brought about some radical changes in the practices followed by the industry in manufacturing the products and services (Kalsoom et al., 2020; Luthra et al., 2020; Morisse & Prigge, 2017). All these revolutionary changes helped the firms increase their productivity several times (Fig. 13.1).

The term I4.0 is used for the fourth iteration of the industrial revolution. It emerged in 2011 in Germany to label the strategic German industrial policy that fostered the computerisation of manufacturing (Kalsoom et al., 2020; Leitão et al., 2016). Since its inception, I4.0 has greatly influenced industrial systems over the past few years. Similarly, previous technological advancements have led to severe disruptions and caused paradigmatic changes in economies as a whole (Ivanov et al., 2019; Luthra et al., 2020). Therefore, it is significant to understand the previous three industrial revolutions for an in-depth comprehension of the fourth industrial revolution. The first industrial revolution laid the foundation for industrialisation. In the second industrial revolution, the concept of intricate automation emerged. It was followed by the third industrial revolution, which coined the idea of flexible automation. In the fourth industrial revolution, modern information and communication technologies appear as a significant breakthrough (Ivanov et al., 2019; Atif et al., 2021). These innovative technologies include integrating industrial automation, modern manufacturing (3D printing, intelligent production, remote operations, human-computer interaction, etc.) and data networks (Mubarik et al., 2021; Atif et al., 2021). I4.0-driven technological innovations such as the Internet of Things (IoT), artificial intelligence (AI), machine-to-machine communication, big data analytics (BDA) and cyber-physical system (CPS) bring decentralisation in business processes (Basl, 2017; Atif et al., 2021). I4.0, through CPSs and Internet, creates a business environment where employees, devices, machinery and enterprise systems are interconnected (Basl, 2017).

Furthermore, I4.0 introduces a new frontier for the world economy by influencing many industries and impacting how goods are produced, sold and serviced (Ralston & Blackhurst, 2020). It does so by applying digital technologies such as big data, simulation, additive manufacturing, autonomous robots and vehicles, horizontal/

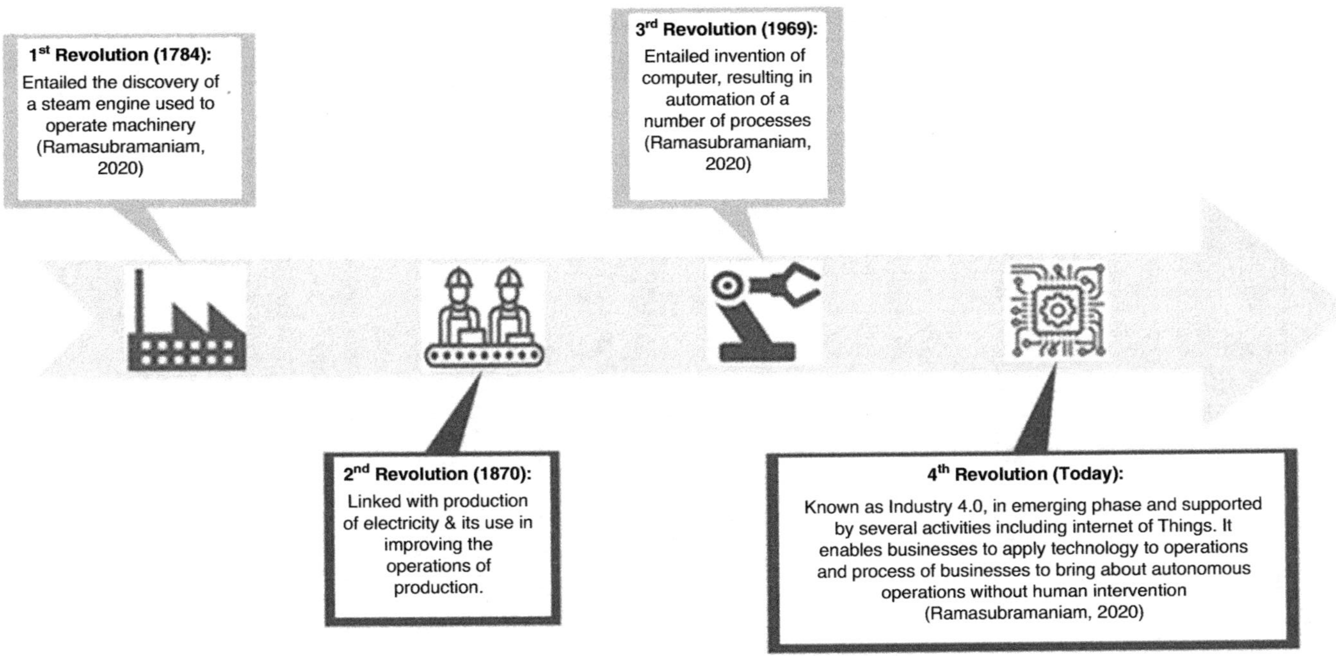

Fig. 13.1 Industrial revolutions

vertical system integration, blockchain and cybersecurity, augmented and virtual reality, cloud, fog and edge technologies and Internet of Things (IoT) (Kuo & Kusiak, 2019; Vernadat et al., 2018). The basic principle of I4.0 is that it creates intelligent networks along the entire supply chain by autonomously connecting machines, digital operations and systems (Ahmed et al., 2021; Kuo & Kusiak, 2019). Moreover, I4.0 also assists intelligent systems that autonomously utilise and integrate human interaction but avoid unnecessary human management and oversight (Kuo & Kusiak, 2019).

The concept of I4.0 entails intelligent and automated operations such as data analytics by converging the global operations of different industries, including manufacturing, computer technologies and network connectivity (Morisse & Prigge, 2017). This fourth industrial revolution characterises intricate, well-integrated and complex networks of production and delivery systems and processes (Morisse & Prigge, 2017; Verdouw et al., 2015). The I4.0 revolution had brought the firm's focus towards restricting their systems and organisation according to the needs and wants of the customers (Mubarik et al., 2021; Morisse & Prigge, 2017). I4.0 technologies make it easier for the management to access large volumes of data and make rational decisions backed by in-depth analysis and reasoning, making decision-making more accessible and transparent (Ivanov et al., 2019; Morisse & Prigge, 2017; Kalsoom et al., 2020). These technologies help the firms enhance the operations of their value chains by bringing about greater integration and coordination among the constituents of the value chain (Ahmed et al., 2021; Ivanov et al., 2019). It also helps in bringing the costs down and employing resources efficiently and effectively. I4.0 is based on the development and implementation of the latest digital technologies and highly coordinated vertical as well as horizontal integration (Al-Talib et al., 2020; Lee & Lee, 2015). Implementation of I4.0 demands changes in the production and delivery systems to reduce the delivery times and achieve greater levels of customer satisfaction by fulfilling customer demands more rapidly Lee & Lee, 2015). The companies are transforming their structural units by developing smaller and decentralised production units rather than large centralised units to cater to the demands of the local customers at relatively minor costs and shorter delivery times (Al-Talib et al., 2020; Lee & Lee, 2015).

I4.0 is a new avenue for the success of global economies. The concept of I4.0 has changed the way goods and services are developed, sold and offered (Ralston & Blackhurst, 2020). I4.0 is the integrated coordination system between machines, processes and methods of different firms operating in a business environment (Ralston & Blackhurst, 2020). The underlying concept of I4.0 states that firms can develop creative and digital solutions to support the operations of the supply chains by bringing about autonomous coordination among the systems and machines (Ralston & Blackhurst, 2020; Ivanov et al., 2019). In addition, I4.0 seeks to achieve greater levels of customer satisfaction by fulfilling their requirements and bringing autonomy in the way the machines, systems and processes are connected and operated.

Moreover, this concept accedes to increasing coordination among different business activities and developing digital networks to enhance synergy among all the supply chain actors that aim to produce and deliver goods to meet the customers' demands (Ralston & Blackhurst, 2020). Thus, the concept of I4.0 entails an intelligent system designed to cope with the changes in the external environment of the business by utilising effective solutions that integrate human interactions. Such systems, however, do not need human supervision for their operation and management (Kuo & Kusiak, 2019; Ralston & Blackhurst, 2020).

13.3 Industry 4.0 and Supply Chain Management

In the context of supply chain management, I4.0 provides efficient resources and flexible integration of customers and business partners (Fallahpour et al., 2017). It visualises that the products and equipment are interlinked in supply chains (Brandon-Jones et al., 2014). They communicate, exchange, collect and analyse data through the Internet and processes in the system using cyber-physical systems (CPS). For connecting physical devices and computational assets, CPS is understood as transformative technology (Leitão et al., 2016). I4.0 improves supply chain performance and promises to enhance the resilience of the supply chains to disruptive events (Ralston & Blackhurst, 2020). The ability to handle disruptions is the key to resilience (Ambulkar et al., 2015). The critical factor in SCRE is the system's ability to adapt and reconfigure to mitigate the continuity of risks in supply chain operations (Ivanov et al., 2021). The traditional system's complex supply chain risks are too simplistic (Pettit et al., 2019). Therefore, for superior supply chain performance, an intelligent strategy is need of the hour. On the one hand, I4.0 will make the industry more efficient and flexible, while on the other hand, it will improve the functionality of the existing products (Kalsoom et al., 2020; Ahmed et al., 2021).

Adopting I4.0 could improve the supply chain functions and bring several benefits to the firms' value chain. Therefore, to utilise the maximum potential of I4.0, the manufacturing industries in developed countries are embracing technological advancements extensively (Brandon-Jones et al., 2014; Mccoll-kennedy et al., 2015; Vernadat et al., 2018). Moreover, in recent years, through real-time tracking and transparency among actors, I4.0 has streamlined and facilitated the flow of information across different organisations and entities. It enabled effective communication among different supply chain actors and avoided unnecessary delays due to a lack of transparency (Ahmed et al., 2021; Kalsoom et al., 2020). I4.0 establishes the possibility of autonomous linkages between the different operations of the firm and between firms. It enables production, enhanced flow of the information across the departments, efficient distribution and delivery of the final goods and/or services to the customers (Mccoll-kennedy et al., 2015). In a few ways, the digital connection between the businesses acts like complex adaptive systems. In a supply chain, the benefits of implementing I4.0 include faster processes, streamlined operations, smooth flow of information and effective communication, greater accuracy, greater resilience, more flexibility and granularity (Kuo & Kusiak, 2019; Ralston & Blackhurst, 2020). The granularity aspect of I4.0 arises from identifying the types and nature of the products and services that customers want and the ability to fulfil individual orders and making deliveries (Hess et al., 2014; Kuo & Kusiak, 2019; Ralston & Blackhurst, 2020). Stated otherwise, the core concept of I4.0 lies in the ability of the firms to standardise the processes of their supply chains and strive to achieve economies of scale. At the same time, the order customisation takes place only and when necessary (Mccoll-kennedy et al., 2015).

Hence, it is evident that introducing I4.0 technologies to the supply chains will bring numerous advantages to the businesses, including flexibility, reduction in costs and elimination of inefficiencies and inaccuracies (Al-Talib et al., 2020; Ivanov et al., 2021).

13.4 Industry 4.0 and Supply Chain Resilience

The term resilience is extensively used in business, economics and engineering (Morisse & Prigge, 2017). It can generally be defined as the ability of a system to maintain the original state under the challenging circumstances of the external environment (Ismail et al., 2011). On the level of an organisation, resilience is defined as the ability of a firm to maintain its original state and recover from the disruptions caused by the external environment (Ambulkar et al., 2015; Ismail et al., 2011). The disruptive risks posed to the operations of the businesses are characterised by events that are less probable to occur but leave a substantial impact on the operations of the business. Such events are often difficult to be anticipated and prepare for in advance (Jüttner & Maklan, 2011). Disruptive risks can endanger the business in many ways, including a decrease in the market share, loss of the image, reduced value generation and threat to the firm's capabilities (Ambulkar et al., 2015; Jüttner & Maklan, 2011. I4.0 equips businesses with capabilities to deal with turbulent times and keep the organisation on the right track (Ivanov et al., 2019). Achieving resilience in the supply chain operations helps the firms achieve better performance and gain a competitive advantage (Pettit et al., 2019; Ambulkar et al., 2015).

I4.0 epitomises the digital and autonomous linkages within and between the firms (Alicke et al., 2016). These links optimise the production process and make operations more accurate and flexible (Kuo & Kusiak, 2019; Atif et al., 2021). The flexible aspect caters for the need of the clients and ensures timely delivery. Supply chain resiliency to cope with unprecedented changes is a hallmark. I4.0 and intelligent systems not only help in mitigating actual disruptions but also proactively avoid future troubles. Resilience to supply chain disruptions needs continuous monitoring of the system to reconfigure necessary resources Ambulkar et al. (2015). The I4.0 key initiatives include decentralisation, virtualisation, interoperability, modularity, service orientation and real-time capabilities to build resilience through automated supply chain processes (Gupta et al., 2021).

Furthermore, I4.0 promotes decentralisation that can help in better usage of available resources. For instance, virtualisation can decrease industrial waste by increasing recycling opportunities. Interoperability can help improve and enhance the machine life cycle, modularity allows for better usage of industrial assets and service orientation can elevate final products. Adapting as required during unanticipated disruption is the key to SCRE Ambulkar et al. (2015). I4.0 promises to enhance the functioning of the supply chains, making them more resilient to tackle disruptions effectively (Ralston & Blackhurst, 2020). Ambulkar et al. (2015) stated that the ability to adapt to the changes in the external environment is the key to the success of the supply chains, and resilience helps the supply chains to adapt to the changes and disruptions occurring in the business environment. The interaction between the risks that supply chains is vulnerable to and the implementation of digital technology is significant (Ralston & Blackhurst, 2020). In this sense, to efficiently deal with the disruptions, reconfiguring the functions and operations of the supply chain is the key to achieve resilience and help the firms achieve connectivity, flexibility and continuity in the operations of their supply chains (Ralston & Blackhurst, 2020; Ivanov et al., 2019). SCRE enables the supply chains to adapt to the external environment without harming the business operations. I4.0 plays a significant role in helping the supply chains be resilient (Ivanov et al., 2019; Ralston & Blackhurst, 2020). Traditional supply chain systems are too simple to deal with the modern complexities, uncertainties and disruptions in the global supply chains (Ralston & Blackhurst, 2020). Hence, employing innovative and digitalised systems is the key to the efficient management of the supply chains (Ralston & Blackhurst, 2020).

Employing I4.0 and digital systems in the supply chains helps the firms achieve greater resilience in the operations of their supply chains. A significant reason for it is because autonomy is utilised (Ralston & Blackhurst, 2020). I4.0 is recognised as the fourth evolutionary stage of the industrial revolution (Kalsoom et al., 2020; Ralston & Blackhurst, 2020). Technological advancements in businesses' ways have disrupted production, industry trends and economic conditions (Hess et al., 2014). I4.0 comprises an integrated and digitalised system of production backed by an efficient communication system between businesses, business environments and customers (Ralston & Blackhurst, 2020; Atif et al., 2021). The firms implementing I4.0 can share information regarding any operations of the value chain with other business segments. For example, the information regarding the production operations can be shared with the distribution function in real time to support decision-making and achieve efficiency (Vernadat et al., 2018). The real-time sharing of information supported by I4.0 brings numerous advantages to the business, including meeting the customers' demands more efficiently and predicting future demands (Mccoll-kennedy et al., 2015; Ralston & Blackhurst, 2020).

Moreover, to be resilient, the supply chains need to consistently monitor the changes in the environment and develop the ability to reconfigure the supply chains' sources if any changes or disruptions occur in the external environment (Ambulkar et al., 2015). Therefore, the ability of the supply chains to adapt to the changes in the external environment is attributed to resilience. This discussion was also acceded by Ivanov et al. (2019) and Ralston and Blackhurst (2020). They studied that SCRE is the ability of the supply chains to maintain their primary forms by relying on the adaptive systems as the external environment is susceptible to changes all the time. I4.0 promises to develop resilience and adaptation abilities across all partners of the supply chains. Therefore, it is essential to explore I4.0 in the resilience of the supply chains as they face disruptions (Ivanov et al., 2019; Ralston & Blackhurst, 2020).

There is some evidence stating that the resilience of the supply chains can be enhanced by reducing the reliance on other firms (Ambulkar et al., 2015; Hess et al., 2014; Ralston & Blackhurst, 2020). Studies targeting traditional supply chains state that relationships between firms can lead to greater resilience; however, firms need to develop connections with other firms, not relationships with the employees (Ambulkar et al., 2015; Ralston & Blackhurst, 2020). I4.0 ideology proposes that firms reduce reliance on workers and adopt automated processes and systems to achieve their objectives (Ambulkar et al., 2015). Therefore, the following subsection proposes some key characteristics that enable firms to reduce their dependence on other actors and deal with the disruptions in the supply chains using I4.0.

Supply chain visibility is considered an essential requisite for SC resilience. One of the significant examples highlighting the need for visibility is the horse meet scam of TESCO. According to Brooks et al. (2017, p. 1), "beef meat was fraudulently adulterated with horse meat causing widespread recalls and subsequent investigations across both retail and foodservice markets in the European Union (EU)." I4.0 technologies offer an effective solution to such problems by helping companies to map their supply chain. I4.0-driven supply chain mapping allows a firm to visualise an upstream supply chain. It further helps to zoom in on the business processes and preamp any such issue proactively, contributing to SC resilience of the firm.

In the past major supply chain disasters like a failure of Nike's planning system, resulting in 10 million revenue shortfalls; inventory management disaster in 2001, substantially decreasing its stock prices; or Hershey Foods 1999 order management failure had fatal impacts upon the firms' fate (Supply Chain Digest, 2006). I4.0 technologies can also help to encounter such disasters effectively.

13.4.1 *Industry 4.0 for Resilient Supply Chain: Attributes and Characteristics*

The characteristics of resilience help the firm attain competitiveness in the market and mitigate the disruptions caused in the supply chains (Pettit et al., 2019; Ralston & Blackhurst, 2020; Vernadat et al., 2018). Traditional supply chain practices impact SCRE in several ways (Ralston & Blackhurst, 2020). These factors include the higher costs, inaccuracies and extensive risks that the traditional supply chains are vulnerable to (Pettit et al., 2019). In addition, before adopting I4.0 in managing the businesses' supply chains, data used to be shared with a single supply chain partner; this raised several questions on the transparency of the data and information (Kuo & Kusiak, 2019). Al-Talib et al. (2020) and Pettit et al. (2019) highlight the following attributes of resilient supply chains:

13.4.1.1 Visibility

According to Al-Talib et al. (2020), visibility refers to transparency and accurate and reliable information sharing among the supply chain actors. As visibility increases along a supply chain, the trust among different partners increases, resulting in greater confidence among the stakeholders regarding the performance of the business. I4.0 equips the supply chains to enhance their visibility (Al-Talib et al., 2020). It enhances the ability of a supply chain to track the products, check the status of the deliveries, improve the flow of information and make the processes more efficient. Visibility improves the real-time sharing of information among the supply chain partners and increases the levels of customer satisfaction. For example, RFID tracks can enhance the visibility of the supply chain activities (Al-Talib et al., 2020; Ivanov et al., 2021).

13.4.1.2 Collaboration

Effective sharing of information across different supply chain activities results in reduced risks and a more remarkable ability to deal with the disruptions impacting the operations of the supply chain. Therefore, efficient communication and better visibility help reduce threats posed to the operations of the supply chains and improve the supply chain performance (Al-Talib et al., 2020; Ivanov et al., 2021). Moreover, collaboration refers to access to information and required knowledge among different supply chain actors (Al-Talib et al., 2020). Since resilience demands a holistic approach and can only be enhanced if all the components of a supply chain can effectively deal with the disruptions, it is necessary to ensure greater collaboration and equal access to the information among all the partners (Al-Talib et al., 2020; Ivanov et al., 2021). Implementing I4.0 gives rise to transparency and entails sharing data among all supply chain partners in real time. In traditional supply chains, visibility of the data and information was also a significant issue—due to the unavailability of data in real time, there were higher chances of errors and uncertainties across the supply chains. This lack of transparency, complexity and uncertainty gave rise to many supply chains issues, such as mistakes in delivering and distributing the goods resulting in the waste of valuable resources and time (Ambulkar et al., 2015). Implementation of I4.0 revolutionised the business model of the supply chains and brought about greater accuracy in the operations (Al-Talib et al., 2020; Pettit et al., 2019; Ivanov et al., 2021; Ahmed et al., 2021).

13.4.1.3 Flexibility

Similarly, flexibility entails the ability of a supply chain to deal with any disruptions or changes in the external environment without taking any negative impact on its operations and processes (Al-Talib et al., 2020), in other words, the reconfiguration of the systems, processes and products according to the customer's demands (Al-Talib et al., 2020; Ivanov et al., 2021). Furthermore, as the connectivity of all the actors of the supply chain increases, the flexibility of the supply chain increases, simplifying the sharing of information among all the partners, ultimately leading to greater levels of customer satisfaction (Al-Talib et al., 2020; Mccoll-kennedy et al., 2015; Ahmed et al., 2021). Furthermore, by introducing I4.0 in the operations of the supply chains, their process can be made more efficient and flexible to avoid any damage caused by the disruptions (Al-Talib et al., 2020; Ahmed et al., 2021).

The digitalised supply chains equipped with the technologies of I4.0 directly impact the flexibility. For example, the digital contracts between different parties allow technology-supported transactions by employing the Internet of Things (Ahmed et al., 2021; Kalsoom et al., 2020). Furthermore, by expanding the collaboration and extending the connectivity among other supply chain players, the firms can achieve greater flexibility, which positively impacts the performance of the supply chains (Al-Talib et al., 2020). Thus, supply chain connectivity helps the firms increase flexibility and effectively deal with the changes in the external environment. Moreover, flexibility brings numerous advantages to the firm, including better quality of the products and services, more excellent responsiveness, rapid delivery and distribution, greater production levels, etc. (Closs et al., 2005). Therefore, to be more flexible in effectively dealing with the disruptions, a supply chain must depict higher velocity and speed to manage the operations across different activities. Hence I4.0 enabled SCRE is an arguably better solution to deal with disruption risks.

13.4.1.4 Control

SCRE cannot be explained in an exhausted manner without discussing control and connectedness among the different supply chain actors. Control can be defined as the impact that a supply chain possesses, which enables it to deal with the catastrophic impact of any disruption or unforeseen situation affecting the operations of a supply chain. This is the essence of SCRE since it measures the ability of a supply chain to deal with disruptions (Al-Talib et al., 2020). Real-time monitoring and data sharing in I4.0 enable better control and quality assessment across the supply chain operations (Verdouw et al., 2015). Control in the supply chain activities eliminates the need for human intervention and supervision (Verdouw et al., 2015). To augment a supply chain's productivity while reducing costs, businesses must implement effective control measures (Verdouw et al., 2015). I4.0 can help achieve better control outcomes and predict the changing patterns of the external environment (Verdouw et al., 2015). The costs associated with the control measures of the supply chains can be reduced by employing Internet of Things technology (Verdouw et al., 2015).

SCRE is compulsory to deal with the disruptions in the short run and become agile and robust in the long run (Lee & Lee, 2015; Ralston & Blackhurst, 2020). Visibility, collaboration, flexibility and control are the significant characteristics of resilient supply chains (Ralston & Blackhurst, 2020). There is scarce literature discussing the significance of the Internet of Things and digital technologies in achieving SCRE (Lee & Lee, 2015; Ralston & Blackhurst, 2020). However, to achieve SCRE by successfully employing I4.0, effective collection, handling and data analysis should be the primary concern for the firm managers (Ahmed et al., 2021). Redesigning the supply chains by employing I4.0, the supply chain managers can attain greater SCRE by overcoming the weaknesses in the conventional supply chain management techniques. Replacing the outdated practices and systems of supply chain management with the intelligent, digital techniques and implementations of I4.0, the managers can achieve greater flexibility in the operations of the supply chain and collaboration among all the supply chain partners (Ahmed et al., 2021; Closs et al., 2005).

13.5 Conclusion

I4.0 seeks to align and establish a cyber-physical link between different supply chain functions, such as manufacturing, logistics, distribution and information sharing (Ivanov et al., 2021; Ahmed et al., 2021). Previously, numerous unsuccessful attempts to explore the various perspectives targeting the concern regarding availing the firm's information technology and data analytics capabilities to identify the future trends and demands have been made (Ivanov et al., 2021;). However, I4.0 has revolutionised how the supply chain operates (Ahmed et al., 2021). It has provided several predictive capabilities to the supply chains to mitigate and anticipate any risk or disruption caused by the changes in the external environment (Ahmed et al., 2021; Closs et al., 2005). The autonomous system provides heads up regarding any approaching disruption and makes arrangements in advance. The real-time monitoring and efficiently managed information sharing system have made the supply chains more resilient to the changes (Ahmed et al., 2021). Implementing an advanced technological system influences the operations of the supply chains from multidimensional perspectives, hence promising resilient supply chains (Ahmed et al., 2021). Innovative technologies equip the supply chains with the capabilities necessary to deal with external shocks and disruptions without undergoing severe changes in their structures and systems (Lee & Lee, 2015). For instance, smart scheduling methods help the supply chains achieve greater flexibility (Ivanov et al., 2021; Lee & Lee, 2015).

Both practitioners and researchers agree that I4.0 can enable firms to be more efficient and innovative. The I4.0 revolution has transformed the global economic structure and made it imperative for organisations to adopt its developments.

Initiatives of I4.0 offer strong foundations to evaluate the resilience of their supply chain and assist firms in making appropriate strategies to improve it. SCRE and digital technologies can magnify the inefficiencies in the micro part of the entire supply chain, which will help firms be more resilient. Thus, I4.0 can effectively play an instrumental role in controlling the supply chain chaos and losses. I4.0 and intelligent systems have obvious merits to combat supply chain risks and positively impact SCRE. Nevertheless, firms need to be more careful when enacting I4.0 initiatives as the supply chain represents a network of related activities. Building resilience at one node of a supply chain influences the overall SCRE.

References

Ahmed, S., Kalsoom, T., Ramzan, N., Pervez, Z., Azmat, M., Zeb, B., & Ur Rehman, M. (2021). Towards supply chain visibility using internet of things: A dyadic analysis review. *Sensors., 21*(12), 4158. https://doi.org/10.3390/s21124158

Alicke, K., Rexhausen, D., & Seyfert, A. (2016) *Supply chain 4.0 in consumer goods*. Mckinsey & Company, (exhibit 1), pp. 1–11. Retrieved from https://www.Mckinsey.Com/Industries/Consumer-Packaged-Goods/Our-Insights/Supply-Chain-4-0-In-Consumer-Goods

Al-Talib, M., Melhem, W. Y., Anosike, A. I., Garza Reyes, J. A., Nadeem, S. P., & Kumar, A. (2020). Achieving resilience in the supply chain by applying IoT technology. *Procedia CIRP, 91*, 752–757. https://doi.org/10.1016/J.Procir.2020.02.231

Ambulkar, S., Blackhurst, J., & Grawe, S. (2015). Firm's resilience to supply chain disruptions: Scale development and empirical examination. *Journal of Operations Management, 33–34*, 111–122. https://doi.org/10.1016/J.Jom.2014.11.002

Atif, S., Ahmed, S., Wasim, M., Zeb, B., Pervez, Z., & Quinn, L. (2021). Towards a conceptual development of Industry 4.0, servitisation, and circular economy: A systematic literature review. *Sustainability, 13*(11), 6501. https://doi.org/10.3390/su13116501

Basl, J. (2017). Pilot study of readiness of Czech companies to implement the principles of Industry 4.0. *Management and Production Engineering Review, 8*(2), 3–8. https://doi.org/10.1515/Mper-2017-0012

Brandon-Jones, E., Squire, B., Autry, C. W., & Petersen, K. J. (2014). A contingent resource-based perspective of supply chain resilience and robustness. *Journal of Supply Chain Management, 50*(3), 55–73. https://doi.org/10.1111/Jscm.12050

Brooks, S., Elliott, C. T., Spence, M., Walsh, C., & Dean, M. (2017). Four years post-horsegate: An update of measures and actions put in place following the horsemeat incident of 2013. *NPJ Science of Food, 1*(1), 1–7.

Carvalho, H., & Machado, V. C. (2007). Designing principles to create resilient supply chains. In *IIE annual conference. Proceedings* (p. 186). Institute of Industrial and Systems Engineers (IISE).

Closs, D. J., Swink, M., & Nair, A. (2005). The role of information connectivity in making flexible logistics programs successful. *International Journal of Physical Distribution and Logistics Management, 35*(4), 258–277. https://doi.org/10.1108/09600030510599922

Congressional Report Service (CRS). (2021). *Global economic effects of COVID19*. Retrieved from https://Fas.Org/Sgp/Crs/Row/R46270.Pdf

Fallahpour, A., et al. (2017). A predictive integrated genetic-based model for supplier evaluation and selection. *International Journal of Fuzzy Systems, 19*(4), 1041–1057. https://doi.org/10.1007/S40815-017-0324-Z

Gupta, H., Kumar, A., & Wasan, P. (2021). Industry 4.0, cleaner production and circular economy: An integrative framework for evaluating ethical and sustainable business performance of manufacturing organisations. *Journal of Cleaner Production, 295*, 126253. https://doi.org/10.1016/J.Jclepro.2021.126253

Hess, T., Legner, C., Esswein, W., Maaß, W., Matt, C., Österle, H., Schlieter, H., Richter, P., & Zarnekow, R. (2014). Digital life as a topic of business and information systems engineering? *Business and Information Systems Engineering, 6*(4), 247–253. https://doi.org/10.1007/S12599-014-0332-6

Ismail, H. S., Poolton, J., & Sharifi, H. (2011). The role of agile strategic capabilities in achieving resilience in manufacturing-based small companies. *International Journal of Production Research, 49*(18), 5469–5487. https://doi.org/10.1080/00207543.2011.563833

Ivanov, D., Dolgui, A., & Sokolov, B. (2019). The impact of digital technology and industry 4.0 on the ripple effect and supply chain risk analytics. *International Journal of Production Research, 57*(3), 829–846. https://doi.org/10.1080/00207543.2018.1488086

Ivanov, D., Blackhurst, J., & Das, A. (2021). Supply chain resilience and its interplay with digital technologies: Making innovations work in emergency situations. *International Journal of Physical Distribution and Logistics Management, 51*(2), 97–103. https://doi.org/10.1108/IJPDLM-03-2021-409

Jüttner, U., & Maklan, S. (2011). Supply chain resilience in the global financial crisis: An empirical study. *Supply Chain Management, 16*(4), 246–259. https://doi.org/10.1108/13598541111139062

Kalsoom, T., Ramzan, N., Ahmed, S., & Ur-Rehman, M. (2020). Advances in sensor technologies in the era of smart factory and industry 4.0. *Sensors, 20*(23), 6783. https://doi.org/10.3390/s20236783

Kuo, Y. H., & Kusiak, A. (2019). From data to big data in production research: The past and future trends. *International Journal of Production Research, 57*(15–16), 4828–4853. https://doi.org/10.1080/00207543.2018.1443230

Lee, I., & Lee, K. (2015). The internet of things (IoT): Applications, investments, and challenges for enterprises. *Business Horizons, 58*(4), 431–440. https://doi.org/10.1016/J.Bushor.2015.03.008

Leitão, P., Colombo, A. W., & Karnouskos, S. (2016). Industrial automation based on cyber-physical systems technologies: Prototype implementations and challenges. *Computers in Industry, 81*, 11–25. https://doi.org/10.1016/J.Compind.2015.08.004

Luthra, S., Kumar, A., Zavadskas, E. K., Mangla, S. K., & Garza-Reyes, J. A. (2020). Industry 4.0 as an enabler of sustainability diffusion in supply chain: An analysis of influential strength of drivers in an emerging economy. *International Journal of Production Research, 58*(5), 1505–1521. https://doi.org/10.1080/00207543.2019.1660828

McColl-Kennedy, J. R., Gustafsson, A., Jaakkola, E., Klaus, P., Radnor, Z. J., Perks, H., & Friman, M. (2015). Fresh perspectives on customer experience. *Journal of Services Marketing*. https://doi.org/10.1108/JSM-01-2015-0054

McLennan, M. (2021). *The Global Risks Report 2021* (16th ed.). World Economic Forum.

Morisse, M., & Prigge, C. (2017). Design of a business resilience model for industry 4.0 manufacturers. *Twenty-Third Americas Conference on Information Systems., 2017*, 1–10.

Mubarik, M. S., Naghavi, N., Mubarik, M., Kusi-Sarpong, S., Khan, S. A., Zaman, S. I., & Kazmi, S. H. A. (2021). Resilience and cleaner production in industry 4.0: Role of supply chain mapping and visibility. *Journal of Cleaner Production, 292*, 126058. https://doi.org/10.1016/j.jclepro.2021.126058

Pettit, T. J., Croxton, K. L., & Fiksel, J. (2019). The evolution of resilience in supply chain management: A retrospective on ensuring supply chain resilience. *Journal of Business Logistics, 40*(1), 56–65. https://doi.org/10.1111/Jbl.12202

Ralston, P., & Blackhurst, J. (2020). Industry 4.0 and resilience in the supply chain: A driver of capability enhancement or capability loss? *International Journal of Production Research, 58*(16), 5006–5019. https://doi.org/10.1080/00207543.2020.1736724

Supply Chain Digest. (2006, Sep 11). *The 11 greatest supply chain disaster.* Retrieved from https://www.scdigest.com/assets/reps/scdigest_top-11-supplychaindisasters.pdf

Verdouw, C. N., Beulens, A. J. M., Reijers, H. A., & Van Der Vorst, J. G. A. J. (2015). A control model for object virtualisation in supply chain management. *Computers in Industry, 68,* 116–131. https://doi.org/10.1016/J.Compind.2014.12.011

Vernadat, F. B., Chan, F. T. S., Molina, A., Nof, S. Y., & Panetto, H. (2018). Information systems and knowledge management in industrial engineering: Recent advances and new perspectives. *International Journal of Production Research, 56*(8), 2707–2713. https://doi.org/10.1080/00207543.2018.1454615

Muhammad Azmat is an Assistant Professor in Logistics and SCM at the Department of Engineering Systems and Supply Chain Management at Aston University, UK. He comes from a Business and Management background, with a Ph.D. in logistics and supply chain management and a master's in supply chain management from WU (Vienna University of Economics and Business). Besides, he is also an alumnus of the Oxford Leadership Program, Transport Study Unit, University of Oxford. Dr. Azmat has developed hybrid research interests in his brief academic career, which fall right in the center of disruptive technologies, consumers' perspectives, innovative business applications, and traditional supply chain issues in commercial and humanitarian sectors. Dr. Azmat has published his scientific research with publishers like Emerald, Springer, MDPI, and others. Some of his most cited works could be found in Logistics Journal, Asian Journal of Sustainability and Social Responsibility, Supply Chain Forum, and Journal of International Humanitarian Action.

Shehzad Ahmed is a Programme Leader for MSc Logistics and Supply Chain Management (LSCM) at the University of the West of Scotland (UWS). In addition, he is involved in undergraduate and postgraduate teaching and research. He obtained his Ph.D. in Logistics and Supply Chain Management, from the University of Hull, UK. Previously, he has done MSc Logistics and Supply Chain Management from Hull and a Master in Operations and Information Management from the University of the Punjab, Pakistan. Dr. Shahzad's research interest includes but is not limited to Supply Chain Risk and Resilience, Strategies for broader adoption of ICT, Cloud Computing and Industry 4.0 in Logistics and Circular Supply Chain Management.

Muhammad Shujaat Mubarik is a Professor and Dean of the College of Business Management (CBM), Institute of Business Management (IoBM), Karachi. He holds a Ph.D. in Industrial Organization from the University of Malaya. His areas of interest are supply chain management, intellectual capital, and sustainability economics. He has more than 60 research papers published in journals of high repute, including Technological Forecasting and Social Change journal, Journal of Cleaner Production, International Journal of Production Research, Business Strategy and Environment, etc. He also has Springer Handbook on Dynamics of Intellectual Capital in the Current Era to his credit, which is the only handbook that covers IC from a South Asian perspective. Dr. Mubarak has also contributed various book chapters in the international best-selling handbooks; prominent among them are Palgrave's Handbook on Cross-Cultural Negotiation and The Palgrave Handbook of Corporate Sustainability in the Digital Era. He regularly appears on TV shows to share his opinion on national and international economics and business affairs.

Chapter 14
Resilient Supply Chain Network Design: An Overview of Optimization Models

Najmesadat Nazemi and Sophie N. Parragh

Abstract Recent disruptive events have revealed the vulnerability of today's global supply chains and put supply chain resilience into focus. This chapter presents an overview of the literature on optimization models for resilient supply chain network design. We categorize the models first based on proactive and reactive resilience strategies. Then, two sections are dedicated to covering different risk treatment approaches and commonly considered objective functions, respectively. Following a discussion of the research gap and to provide additional insights into modeling aspects concerning risk treatment and mitigation strategies, a bi-objective two-stage stochastic capacitated facility location model is presented. It is used to design a responsive and resilient network which is robust against facility disruptions and demand fluctuations. Different levels of fortification investments in facilities and the option of inventory sharing are considered as resilience strategies, and the conditional value-at-risk is employed as a risk measure. The latter allows to incorporate various risk preferences of decision-makers. To analyze the trade-off relationship between the concurrent goals of resilience and responsiveness, the model is applied to two test cases. The computational study shows the importance of considering random events already in the planning phase and how different risk mitigation strategies can be combined.

14.1 Introduction

Supply chain network design (SCND) decisions are strategic decisions and directly affect supply chain (SC) performance. They concern the decisions on the number, location, and capacity of facilities to provide goods and services to predetermined customers. This also involves the decisions on the selection of suppliers and/or subcontractors. Due to today's global and complex environment, supply chain

N. Nazemi · S. N. Parragh (✉)
Institute of Production and Logistics Management, Johannes Kepler University Linz, Linz, Austria
e-mail: sophie.parragh@jku.at

S. Kummer et al. (eds.), *Supply Chain Resilience*, Springer Series in Supply Chain Management 17, https://doi.org/10.1007/978-3-030-95401-7_14

networks perform under numerous unexpected incidents in an unstable state. Therefore, it is of utmost importance to consider risk when designing a supply chain to overcome relevant uncertain events. Tang (2006) classifies supply chain risks into two categories: operational risks and disruption risks. Operational risks refer to business-as-usual fluctuations such as demand or supply uncertainty, whereas disruption risks are arising from unforeseen natural (e.g., earthquake) or manmade (e.g., terrorist attacks) disasters occurring in the system. It is crucial to design a robust supply network that is resilient to disruptions and responsive regarding business-as-usual fluctuations through risk mitigation strategies at the design level.

SC risk management attempts to protect SCs against disruptive events by mitigating the risks. There are different proactive and reactive mitigation strategies to cope with SC disruptions and increase SC resiliency (Hohenstein et al., 2015). Proactive strategies aim to protect the SC in the pre-disruption stage, whereas reactive actions focus on SC adaptation when a disaster strikes, i.e., the post-disaster stage (Dolgui et al., 2020). Resilience in an SC is defined as the ability to bounce back from a disruption (Sheffi, 2007). Redundancy and contingent recovery plans are two major elements that shape resilience theory in operations research (Hosseini et al., 2019). We provide a brief overview of the optimization models proposed in the SCND literature that explore redundancy and/or recovery as the resilience mitigation options. To this end, we reviewed journal papers published between 2010 and 2021. Google Scholar and Web of Science were the main databases used to identify the papers in peer-reviewed journals written in English. The keyword search in the titles, keywords, and abstracts was conducted using Boolean keyword combinations of ("supply chain" OR "supply chain network design" *or* "facility location") *and* ("disruption" *or* "resilience*"). Qualitative papers were excluded and those that contain at least one optimization model of SCND with the inclusion of disruption risks, and resilience strategies were selected. This analysis resulted in 21 journal papers, which are listed in Table 14.1.

Below, we first categorize these papers according to proactive and reactive mitigation strategies. Second, we analyze them with a focus on their risk treatment approaches. Lastly, the most commonly considered objective functions are discussed. Then, after highlighting the research gap, we present a bi-objective two-stage stochastic capacitated facility location model under disruption as an example.

14.2 Literature Review

In this section, we introduce different proactive and reactive resilience strategies, and we classify the papers accordingly. Furthermore, we present widely used risk measures and objective functions employed in the reviewed papers.

Table 14.1 Characteristics of surveyed supply chain network design optimization models under disruption

	Resilience strategy							Risk treatment			Objective		
	Proactive					Reactive		Risk-neutral	Risk-averse				
	FF	PI	AC	BS	MS	OPR	IS	Expected value	Robustness	CVaR	M	S	R
Lim et al. (2010)	*					*		*			*		
Azad et al. (2013)	*					*	*	*			*		
Meena and Sarmah (2013)					*			*			*		
Azad et al. (2014)	*					*	*	*		*	*		
Sadghiani et al. (2015)					*			*			*		
Fahimnia and Jabbarzadeh (2016)			*			*		*			*	*	
Hasani and Khosrojerdi (2016)	*	*			*				*		*		
Jabbarzadeh et al. (2016)	*						*		*		*		
Fazli-Khalaf and Hamidieh (2017)			*			*			*		*	*	
Khalili et al. (2017)		*	*	*		*				*	*		*
Fahimnia et al. (2018)			*			*			*		*	*	
Jabbarzadeh et al. (2018)			*	*	*			*			*	*	
Namdar et al. (2018)				*	*					*	*		
Ni et al. (2018)		*	*	*		*		*			*		
Elluru et al. (2019)			*			*		*			*		
Hatefi et al. (2019)	*			*							*		*
Snoeck et al., (2019)		*	*			*				*	*		
Fattahi et al. (2020)	*					*		*			*		
Yan and Ji (2020)				*		*		*			*		
Alikhani et al. (2021)	*	*	*		*		*	*			*		
Wang and Yao (2021)						*		*			*		
This work	*						*			*	*		*

FF: facility fortification; PI: pre-positioned inventory; AC: additional capacity; BS: backup supplier; MS: multiple sourcing; OPR: operational reassignment; IS: inventory sharing; M: monetary; S: sustainability; R: responsiveness

14.2.1 Proactive Strategies

The actions which are considered in the pre-disruption phase to reduce SC vulnerabilities are proactive strategies. Through these strategies, the SC can be proactively improved to cope with a possible disruptive event. The most common proactive strategies, referred to as *redundancy* and *flexibility* resilience strategies (Snyder et al., 2016), are listed below:

- Facility fortification: this strategy is defined as the investment in the facilities (e.g., installation of emergency equipment and implementation of preventive maintenance) to make them partially or fully non-disruptable. The higher the level of fortification is, the higher the facility protection against disruption (e.g., Snyder & Daskin, 2005; Lim et al., 2010; Azad et al., 2013, 2014; Hasani & Khosrojerdi, 2016; Jabbarzadeh et al., 2016; Hatefi et al., 2019; Fattahi et al., 2020; Alikhani et al., 2021).
- Pre-positioned inventory: additional inventory can be held in the form of safety stock either upstream or downstream in the network to create adaptive capabilities (e.g., Hasani & Khosrojerdi, 2016; Jabbarzadeh et al., 2016; Hatefi et al., 2019; Fattahi et al., 2020; Alikhani et al., 2021).
- Additional production capacity: it enables the SC to cope with lost capacities to continue to operate (e.g., Fahimnia & Jabbarzadeh, 2016, Fazli-Khalaf & Hamidieh, 2017, Khalili et al., 2017, Fahimnia et al., 2018, Jabbarzadeh et al., 2018, Ni et al., 2018, Elluru et al., 2019, Snoeck et al., 2019, Alikhani et al., 2021).
- Backup suppliers are those that are assumed to be located in safe places. They can serve the customers in emergencies when the primary facility/supplier is not available (e.g., Khalili et al., 2017; Jabbarzadeh et al., 2018; Namdar et al., 2018; Ni et al., 2018; Hatefi et al., 2019; Yan & Ji, 2020).
- Dual or multiple sourcing: the customers are served by multiple sources instead of a single supplier. This strategy enables risk reduction by decreasing the number of critical paths and sources (e.g., Meena & Sarmah, 2013, Sadghiani et al., 2015, Hasani & Khosrojerdi, 2016, Jabbarzadeh et al., 2018, Namdar et al., 2018, Alikhani et al., 2021).

14.2.2 Reactive Strategies

While the proactive strategies focus on the pre-disruption phase, the aim of reactive strategies is to increase SC contingency and recover the system by its adaptation to the post-disruption phase. The widely considered post-disruption strategies include (Aldrighetti et al., 2021):

- Operational reassignment: it consists of rerouting and assignment of the customer to the secondary facility/transportation links when the primary ones are disrupted (Lim et al., 2010, Azad et al., 2013, 2014, Fahimnia & Jabbarzadeh, 2016, Fazli-

Khalaf & Hamidieh, 2017, Khalili et al., 2017, Fahimnia et al., 2018, Ni et al., 2018, Elluru et al., 2019, Snoeck et al., 2019, Fattahi et al., 2020, Yan & Ji, 2020, Wang & Yao, 2021).

- Inventory/good sharing: it happens between a reliable facility and partially disrupted facilities after a disruption occurs. Although the sharing strategy may increase the inventory cost for each facility, the share can be considered as the safety stock in the system (Azad et al., 2013, 2014; Jabbarzadeh et al., 2016; Alikhani et al., 2021).

14.2.3 Risk Treatment

The majority of the surveyed literature on resilient SCND uses stochastic optimization with a risk-neutral attitude to deal with randomness in their study both in the single and two-stage form (e.g., Lim et al., 2010; Azad et al., 2013, 2014; Meena & Sarmah, 2013; Sadghiani et al., 2015; Fahimnia & Jabbarzadeh, 2016; Hasani & Khosrojerdi, 2016, Jabbarzadeh et al., 2018, Ni et al., 2018, Elluru et al., 2019, Fattahi et al., 2020, Yan & Ji, 2020, Alikhani et al., 2021, Wang & Yao, 2021). The expected value is the considered risk measure in a risk-neutral approach. The assumption in this approach is that the underlying distribution functions of the random variables are known.

Some studies take decision-makers' risk preferences into account to hedge against a disruption (Jabbarzadeh et al., 2016; Fazli-Khalaf & Hamidieh, 2017; Fahimnia et al., 2018; Khalili et al., 2017; Namdar et al., 2018; Snoeck et al., 2019). Robustness concepts and conditional value at risk (CVaR) are two widely used risk measures to reflect different risk attitudes of a policy-maker within the models. Robustness measures are often applied in the form of either a minimax criterion or p-robustness. Minimax robust optimization minimizes the worst-case outcome, whereas p-robustness minimizes the cost for the nominal scenario (without disruption) while bounding the regret for each scenario by p. The regret is defined as the difference between the cost of the solution in a scenario and the cost of the optimal solution for that scenario (see, e.g., Fahimnia et al., 2018).

CVaR is defined as the conditional expected value exceeding the VaR at the confidence level of α ($\alpha \in [0, 1)$) where VaR(α) is the targeted cost based on the α-percentile of costs (see, Rockafellar & Uryasev, 2000). The closer the value of α to one, the more risk-averse is the policy-maker. CVaR can be incorporated in a constraint (e.g., Azad et al., 2014) or the objective function (e.g., Khalili et al., 2017; Snoeck et al., 2019).

14.2.4 Objective Functions

The majority of SC resilience papers consider cost-oriented objectives and mainly focus on minimizing cost or maximizing profit. The most commonly considered components of a monetary objective are pre-disaster-related costs, setup cost, fixed cost, transportation cost, holding cost, and ordering cost, and post-disaster-related ones, rerouting cost and reassignment cost (e.g., Lim et al., 2010; Azad et al., 2013, 2014; Meena & Sarmah, 2013; Sadghiani et al., 2015; Fahimnia & Jabbarzadeh, 2016; Hasani & Khosrojerdi, 2016; Jabbarzadeh et al., 2016; Fazli-Khalaf & Hamidieh, 2017; Khalili et al., 2017; Fahimnia et al., 2018; Jabbarzadeh et al., 2018; Namdar et al., 2018; Ni et al., 2018; Elluru et al., 2019; Hatefi et al., 2019; Snoeck et al., 2019; Fattahi et al., 2020; Yan & Ji, 2020; Alikhani et al., 2021; Wang & Yao, 2021).

Some studies also employ sustainability factors, including social and environmental impact in addition to resilience to design SC networks. Furthermore, also responsiveness criteria have been considered in different forms in the literature, such as maximizing demand satisfaction or minimizing the recovery time after a disruption. In the reviewed papers, the authors consider these factors in addition to resilience cost in a multi-objective framework. Fahimnia and Jabbarzadeh (2016) propose a tri-objective model considering the minimization of a monetary goal, maximization of a social score, and an environmental score as the objectives. Hatefi et al. (2019) introduce a bi-objective model for SCND under disruption. The first objective aims at minimizing total cost and the second one maximizes responsiveness. They use the recovery time as a responsiveness factor for rapid recovery from a disruption.

14.3 Research Gap Analysis

The recent worldwide COVID-19 outbreak showed that although the literature on resilience in SCND is scientifically rich, it still needs to be scrutinized further (Ivanov & Dolgui, 2021). More than 60 percent of the analyzed literature considers a risk-neutral approach to measure the risk imposed on an SC by a disruption. However, since most disruptions are low-likelihood but high-impact events in a system, it might be more pragmatic to consider a (more) risk-averse measure. In addition, there is potential in exploring the trade-off between resilience, sustainability, and responsiveness. Further promising future research directions can be found in the recent survey by Aldrighetti et al. (2021).

In the following sections, based on the work of Jabbarzadeh et al. (2016) we contribute to this literature by presenting a bi-objective two-stage capacitated facility location problem. We take resilience and responsiveness into account, which are important factors for designing a robust supply chain network. A bi-objective framework, by identification of Pareto-optimal solutions, helps a decision-maker to learn more about the trade-offs among these two objectives. Uncertainties in demand and capacity are dealt with by incorporating the CVaR approach.

14.4 Problem Definition

The capacitated facility location problem considered incorporates resilience strategies into the work of Nazemi et al. (2021) and adds the risk of random disruptions at facilities, assuming demand and also capacity uncertainties. The assumption is that facilities can be fully or partially disrupted. However, there are possibilities to fortify and harden them either fully or partially against the potential disruption risks. Various fortification levels depend on the amount of monetary investments in facilities. An example of such investments is the installation and implementation of infectious disease control measures to prevent disabling workers in disruptions like the recent COVID-19 outbreak (Araz et al., 2020). Another example is to acquire and install advanced protection systems to mitigate the risk of deliberate attacks to the warehouses of the World Food Programme running to deliver food aid in war-torn Yemen (Nat, 2018).

First, we formally define the CVaR measure that we use in our mathematical formulation. Then, a bi-objective mixed integer linear program for the capacitated facility location problem considered under operational and disruption risk is presented.

14.4.1 *CVaR*

To cope with parameter uncertainty, as mentioned in the introduction, we consider a two-stage stochastic risk-averse optimization model using the widely applied risk measure function named conditional value at risk (CVaR). The CVaR at confidence level $\alpha \in [0, 1)$ of a random variable X is defined as follows (Rockafellar & Uryasev, 2000):

$$\text{CVaR}_\alpha(X) = \min\left\{\eta + \frac{1}{1-\alpha} E\left([X-\eta]_+\right), \eta \in \mathbb{R}\right\}, \tag{14.1}$$

where $[z]_+ = \max\ \{z, 0\}$, $z \in \mathbb{R}$. In this study, we characterize the uncertainty in parameters via a finite discrete set of random equiprobable scenarios ($s \in S$, $S = \{1, \ldots, N\}$). It is worth mentioning that this formulation is equivalent to the two-stage stochastic approach (risk-neutral) when $\alpha = 0$ and, it is equivalent to the two-stage robust approach (risk-averse) for a sufficiently large value of α, $\alpha \longrightarrow 1$.

14.4.2 Model Formulation

The considered facility location problem is formulated on a graph $G = (V, A)$, where V is the set of all nodes including customers ($k \in K$) and potential facility locations and A is the set of arcs. The potential facilities are split into reliable facilities ($i \in I$) and unreliable ones ($j \in J$) with different fortification levels ($f \in F$). One assumption is that a reliable facility is fully fortified and its capacity (CR_i) is unfailable against disruptions. However, the capacity of unreliable facilities which are partially fortified (CU_j) is subject to disruptions. In this study, we assume a good sharing policy at the time of disruption, i.e., the reliable facilities can share their inventory with the affected unreliable facilities. Coverage levels ($\psi(d_{ik})$ and $\psi(d_{jk})$) are assumed for each reliable as well as unreliable facility, i.e., customers can only be covered by a facility if their distance ($d_{ik,}$ respectively, d_{jk}) is less than or equal to a certain threshold (d_{max}) (then $\psi(d_{ik})$, respectively, $\psi(d_{jk})$ is equal to 1 and equal to 0, otherwise). Additionally, demand of customers (D_k^s), and percentage of capacity loss (a_{jf}^s) in unreliable facilities when a disaster occurs are considered uncertain and as such depending on scenario $s \in S$. The first-stage decisions concern the selection of reliable facilities ($x_i \in \{0, 1\}$) and unreliable ones ($y_{jf} \in \{0, 1\}$), in combination with a fortification level f, with given fixed costs (γ_i^R and γ_{jf}^U, respectively), and the available budget for inventory transfers from reliable to unreliable facilities (B). These decisions have to be taken before the realization of the uncertain parameters. The second-stage decisions are the assignments of customers $k \in K$ to the selected facilities either reliable ($r_{ik}^s \in \{0, 1\}$) or unreliable ($u_{jk}^s \in \{0, 1\}$) ones and the number of items delivered from reliable facilities to unreliable ones (T_{ij}^s), which are determined based on the first-stage decisions and realized uncertain data and are therefore scenario dependent. We formally define the considered problem as a bi-objective two-stage stochastic program with a CVaR objective and we present it in its deterministic equivalent form:

$$\min \ f_1 = \sum_{j \in J} \sum_{f \in F} \gamma_{jf}^U y_{jf} + \sum_{i \in I} \gamma_i^R x_i + B \tag{14.2}$$

$$\min \ f_2 = \eta + \frac{1}{(1-\alpha)} \frac{1}{N} \sum_{s \in S} w^s \tag{14.3}$$

$$s.t. \quad x_v + \sum_{f \in F} y_{vf} \leq 1 \quad \forall v \in V \backslash \mathrm{K} \tag{14.4}$$

$$\sum_{i \in I} x_i \geq 1 \tag{14.5}$$

$$\sum_{i \in I} \sum_{j \in J} \sum_{f \in F} y_{jf} (c_{ij} T_{ij}^s) \leq B \quad \forall s \in S \tag{14.6}$$

$$w^s \geq \sum_{k \in K} D_k^s - \sum_{j \in J} \sum_{k \in K} D_k^s u_{jk}^s - \sum_{i \in I} \sum_{k \in K} D_k^s r_{ik}^s - \eta \quad \forall s \in S \tag{14.7}$$

$$r_{ik}^s \leq \psi(d_{ik}) x_i \quad \forall i \in I, k \in K, s \in S \tag{14.8}$$

$$u_{jk}^s \leq \sum_{f \in F} \psi(d_{jk}) y_{jf} \quad \forall j \in J, k \in K, s \in S \tag{14.9}$$

$$\sum_{j \in J} u_{jk}^s + \sum_{i \in I} r_{ik}^s \leq 1 \quad \forall k \in K, s \in S \tag{14.10}$$

$$\sum_{k \in K} D_k^s u_{jk}^s \leq \sum_{f \in F} CU_j y_{jf} \quad \forall j \in J, s \in S \tag{14.11}$$

$$\sum_{k \in K} D_k^s u_{jk}^s \leq \sum_{i \in I} T_{ij}^s + (1 - \sum_{f \in F} a_{jf}^s y_{jf}) CU_j \quad \forall j \in J, s \in S \tag{14.12}$$

$$\sum_{j \in J} T_{ij}^s + \sum_{k \in K} D_k^s r_{ik}^s \leq CR_i x_i \quad \forall i \in I, s \in S \tag{14.13}$$

$$x_i \in \{0, 1\} \quad \forall i \in I. \tag{14.14}$$

$$y_{jf} \in \{0, 1\} \quad \forall j \in J, f \in F \tag{14.15}$$

$$u_{jk}^s \in \{0, 1\} \quad \forall j \in J, k \in K, \ s \in S \tag{14.16}$$

$$r_{ik}^s \in \{0, 1\} \quad \forall i \in I, k \in K, s \in S \tag{14.17}$$

$$B \geq 0 \tag{14.18}$$

$$T_{ij}^s \geq 0 \quad \forall i \in I, j \in J, s \in S \tag{14.19}$$

$$w^s \geq 0 \quad \forall s \in S \tag{14.20}$$

$$\eta \in \mathbb{R} \tag{14.21}$$

The first objective (14.2) minimizes the total cost including the location of reliable and unreliable facilities with different fortification levels and the budget for transportation costs for shipment of items from reliable facilities to unreliable ones after the occurrence of a disruption (resilience-related criteria), and the second one (14.3) minimizes the CVaR of the unmet demand of the customers (responsiveness-related criterion). Constraints (14.4) and (14.5) are the first-stage constraints. Constraints (14.4) indicate that at most one facility can be located in each node. Constraints (14.5) show that at least one reliable facility should be open. Constraints (14.6) set the budget on the transportation costs. Constraints (14.7)–(14.13) represent the associated second-stage constraints under realization of each scenario $s \in S$. Constraint (14.7) is the necessary CVaR constraint. The auxiliary real variables w^s represent the excess values as introduced in (14.1) to derive the deterministic equivalent of the CVaR formulation. Constraints (14.8), (14.9), and (14.10) ensure that each customer k is only covered at most once within the coverage radius of the located facilities. Constraints (14.11) ensure that the capacity of unreliable facility j is not exceeded. Constraints (14.12) guarantee that the covered demand with facility j cannot be higher than the available capacity of the located facility at this node plus the amount of items transported from the reliable facility to this node. Constraints (14.13) guarantee the capacity limit of reliable facilities, and finally, constraints (14.14)–(14.21) determine the domain of decision variables.

Note that the proposed model is nonlinear because of the term $y_{jf}T_{ij}^{s}$ in (14.6). However, it can be easily linearized by introducing a new nonnegative variable L_{ijf}^{s} and the following set of constraints:

$$L_{ijf}^{s} \geq T_{ij}^{s} + M\left(y_{jf} - 1\right) \qquad \forall i \in I, j \in J, f \in F, s \in S. \tag{14.22}$$

14.5 Bi-objective Framework

In this paper, we employ the well-known ϵ-constraint method (Laumanns et al., 2006) to generate *Pareto-optimal (efficient)* solutions. A Pareto-optimal solution has the property that the value of one objective cannot be improved without deteriorating the value of the other objective. The ϵ-constraint method generates efficient solutions step by step. In each iteration, one of the objective functions is used as the main objective, and the other is restricted by a constraint with an allowable bound. It starts by finding the efficient solution corresponding to one of the endpoints of the Pareto frontier. Then, the algorithm enumerates the remaining Pareto frontier, generating one efficient solution per non-dominated point in each iteration. Weakly efficient solutions are avoided by applying lexicographic optimization. As shown in Algorithm 1, the ϵ-constraint is iteratively adapted with regard to the first objective, where we consider the second objective as the main objective. We set the value of ϵ equal to 1 in each iteration.

Algorithm 1. ϵ-constraint method

$L \leftarrow \emptyset$
ϵ-constraint $\leftarrow f_1 \leq \infty$
repeat
$x \leftarrow$ *solveMIP(lexmin(*f_2, f_1*),* ϵ*- constraint)*
$L \leftarrow L \cup x$
ϵ-constraint $\leftarrow f_1 \leq f_1(x) - \epsilon$
until MIP cannot be solved
return L

14.6 Computational Study

We apply our model embedded into the ϵ-constraint scheme to data adapted from the region of Thies in western Senegal (obtained from Tricoire et al. (2012)). This region consists of 32 rural areas where each consists of several villages (demand nodes). The demand nodes are also assumed to be potential locations to open facilities. For each instance, we consider ten sample scenarios, which differ with respect to demand as well as potential disruptions, and three possible levels of fortification investments—full (F), moderate (M), and low (L). The opening cost of a reliable facility (F) is assumed to be 80% of the given opening cost in the dataset. The opening costs for unreliable facilities (M and L) are assumed to be 50% and 25% of the opening cost of a reliable facility (F), respectively. Additionally, the capacity of unreliable facilities is set equal to 50% of a reliable facility. Unit transportation cost from reliable facilities to unreliable ones (c_{ij}) is equal to 0.5% of the distance between them. We assume the capacity given in the dataset to be the capacity of unreliable facilities. The potential capacity loss percentages a^s_{jf} in case of a disruption are uniformly generated in (0.35, 0.55) and (0.5, 0.75) for M and L, respectively. The ϵ-constraint method has been implemented in C++ using the Concert Technology component library of IBM ®ILOG ®CPLEX ®12.9 as a MIP solver where multi-threading is disabled.

To provide some insight into the problem, we now take two of the instances, the Cherif Lo instance with nine nodes and the Notto Gouye Diama instance with ten nodes. These instances can be solved in less than 5 min. Table 14.2 gives seven sampled efficient solutions for different levels of α for Cherif Lo. Solution 1 is related to the case where f_1 is at its best value, while solution 7 has the same role for f_2. The results show that when we move from solution 1 to 7, the resilience cost increases (f_1), where the CVaR of unmet demand decreases (f_2), i.e., the responsiveness increases. We note that even for the same cost value, the decisions which facilities to open or fortify may be different for different levels of α. In the most conservative setting ($\alpha = 0.9$), f_2 optimizes the uncovered demand for the worst possible outcome. This means that e.g., if solution 1 ($\alpha = 0.9$) is implemented, in the worst case, the uncovered demand will amount to 1316. In a risk-neutral setting ($\alpha = 0$), the value of f_2 gives the uncovered demand on average across all scenarios, and the worst case uncovered demand may be higher than for more conservative solutions, obtained with $\alpha = 0.7$ or $\alpha = 0.9$, with the same or similar cost (f_1).

We also conduct a comparison between the solutions obtained by our CVaR approach at $\alpha = 0.7$, the risk-neutral model ($\alpha = 0$), the risk-averse model ($\alpha = 0.9$), and the average deterministic model, i.e., considering just one averaged scenario in the model. The Pareto frontiers are explored by fixing the first-stage solutions obtained from each of the models and plugging them into the second stage of the

Table 14.2 Trade-off comparison for different α-levels for the Cherif Lo instance with nine nodes

α-level	0.1		0.7		0.9	
Solution	f_1	f_2	f_1	f_2	f_1	f_2
1	4000	1064.33	4000	1264.00	4000	1316
2	5612	794.33	5828	908.33	5160	1099
3	6728	539.78	6868	638.67	6868	653
4	7988	266.33	7988	461.67	8248	448
5	9032	130.11	9032	224.00	9868	252
6	10326	57.11	10959	57.67	10960	88
7	12179	0.00	12179	0.00	12179	0

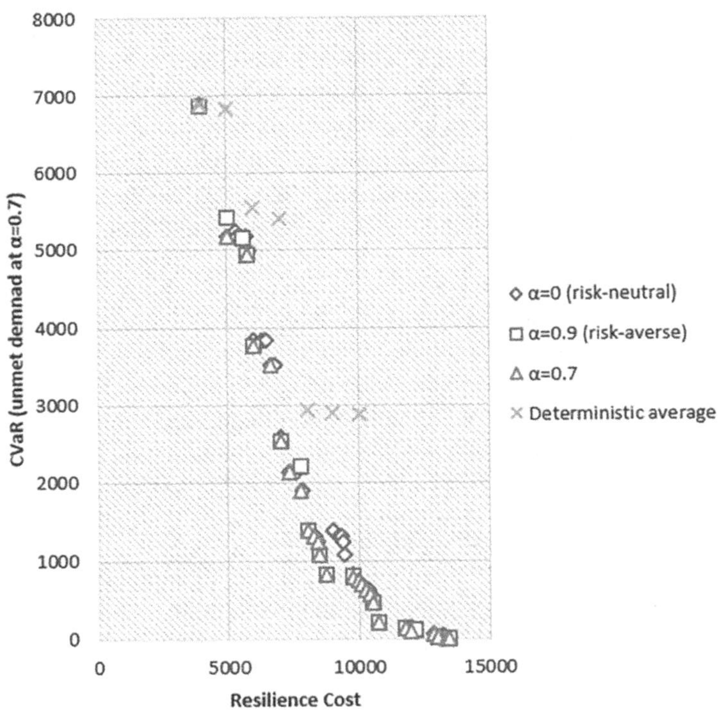

Fig. 14.1 Pareto frontiers for the Notto Gouye Diama instance with 10 nodes

CVaR model. They are depicted in Fig. 14.1 for Notto Gouye Diama. It shows that the distribution of Pareto points along the Pareto frontier is very similar for different α-levels, whereas they dominate the Pareto solutions generated in the case of the deterministic model. The quantity of difference between the values of the obtained solutions is the cost of ignoring risk.

Figure 14.2 illustrates the optimal selected facilities with different fortification levels (first-stage decisions) and the assignment as well as good sharing decisions

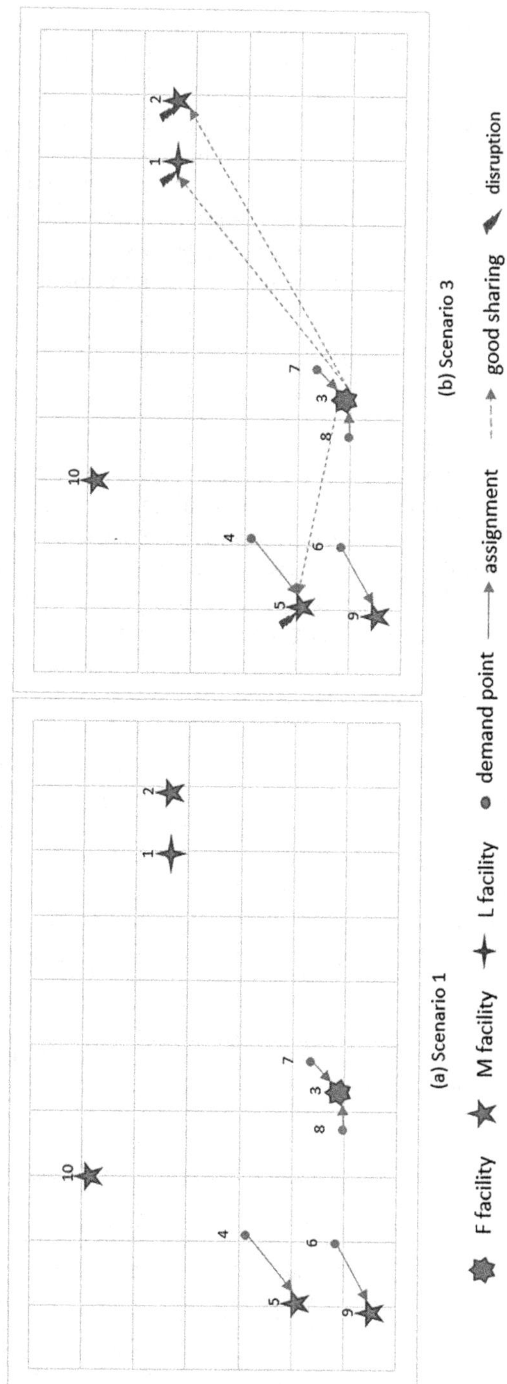

Fig. 14.2 Comparison of the optimal decisions for the efficient solution of the Notto Gouye Diama instance with 10 nodes with $f_1 = 13409$ and f_2 $(\alpha = 0.7)$= 0, for **(a)** scenario 1 and **(b)** scenario 3

(second-stage decisions) for the model at $\alpha = 0.7$ for two different scenarios. For the sake of illustration, we take the efficient solution where all of the demand is covered ($f_2 = 0$). We compare the second-stage decisions for scenarios 1 and 3 (out of ten considered scenarios). The first-stage decisions (investment in facilities and transportation budget) are the same for all scenarios – they are implemented before potential disruptions as well as demand realizations. We observe that for this small instance, in the case of a disruption in scenario 3, three of the unreliable facilities require inventory sharing. The necessary goods are foreseen to be provided by the reliable facility. This shows how proactive (such as facility fortification) and reactive (such as good sharing) resilience strategies can be combined.

14.7 Conclusion

In this paper, we first provide an overview of mathematical models in the resilient SCND literature. We categorize them based on their respective resilience strategies, risk measures, as well as objective functions. This analysis shows that there is still potential to investigate further combinations of resilience strategies. Further research could also aim at exploring sustainability and responsiveness factors in addition to resilience in a multi-objective framework. Then, for illustration purposes, we model and solve a bi-objective location-allocation facility location problem that is subject to disruption and operational risks. The main assumption is that facilities can be fortified to different levels with various amounts of investments and an inventory sharing policy may be implemented. The first objective aims at minimizing the cost, whereas, the second objective maximizes responsiveness by minimizing the amount of unmet demand. The CVaR is considered as a risk function to cope with uncertainty. Moreover, we employed the ϵ-constraint method due to its simplicity to address the bi-objective nature of our problem.

There are potentials to extend the model, e.g., by exploring further resilience strategies, or heuristic or matheuristic solution procedures to solve also large-scale instances in reasonable computation time.

Acknowledgments The authors want to thank Tricoire et al. (2012) for having provided us with the Senegal data sets and Walter J. Gutjahr for his valuable comments.

References

Aldrighetti, R., Battini, D., Ivanov, D., & Zennaro, I. (2021). Costs of resilience and disruptions in supply chain network design models: A review and future research directions. *International Journal of Production Economics, 2021*, 108103.

Alikhani, R., Torabi, S. A., & Altay, N. (2021). Retail supply chain network design with concurrent resilience capabilities. *International Journal of Production Economics, 234*, 108042.

Araz, O. M., Choi, T. M., Olson, D., & Salman, F. S. (2020). Data analytics for operational risk management. *Decision Sciences, 51*(6), 1316–1319.

Azad, N., Saharidis, G. K., Davoudpour, H., Malekly, H., & Yektamaram, S. A. (2013). Strategies for protecting supply chain networks against facility and transportation disruptions: An improved benders decomposition approach. *Annals of Operations Research, 210*(1), 125–163.

Azad, N., Davoudpour, H., Saharidis, G. K., & Shiripour, M. (2014). A new model to mitigating random disruption risks of facility and transportation in supply chain network design. *The International Journal of Advanced Manufacturing Technology, 70*(9–12), 1757–1774.

Dolgui, A., Ivanov, D., & Sokolov, B. (2020). Reconfigurable supply chain: The X-network. *International Journal of Production Research, 58*(13), 4138–4163.

Elluru, S., Gupta, H., Kaur, H., & Singh, S. P. (2019). Proactive and reactive models for disaster resilient supply chain. *Annals of Operations Research, 283*(1), 199–224.

Fahimnia, B., & Jabbarzadeh, A. (2016). Marrying supply chain sustainability and resilience: A match made in heaven. *Transportation Research Part E: Logistics and Transportation Review, 91*, 306–324.

Fahimnia, B., Jabbarzadeh, A., & Sarkis, J. (2018). Greening versus resilience: A supply chain design perspective. *Transportation Research Part E: Logistics and Transportation Review, 119*, 129–148.

Fattahi, M., Govindan, K., & Maihami, R. (2020). Stochastic optimization of disruption-driven supply chain network design with a new resilience metric. *International Journal of Production Economics, 230*, 107755.

Fazli-Khalaf, M., & Hamidieh, A. (2017). A robust reliable forward-reverse supply chain network design model under parameter and disruption uncertainties. *International Journal of Engineering, 30*(8), 1160–1169.

Hasani, A., & Khosrojerdi, A. (2016). Robust global supply chain network design under disruption and uncertainty considering resilience strategies: A parallel memetic algorithm for a real-life case study. *Transportation Research Part E: Logistics and Transportation Review, 87*, 20–52.

Hatefi, S. M., Moshashaee, S. M., & Mahdavi, I. (2019). A bi-objective programming model for reliable supply chain network design under facility disruption. *International Journal of Integrated Engineering, 11*(6), 80–92.

Hohenstein, N. O., Feisel, E., Hartmann, E., & Giunipero, L. (2015). Research on the phenomenon of supply chain resilience: A systematic review and paths for further investigation. *International Journal of Physical Distribution & Logistics Management.*

Hosseini, S., Ivanov, D., & Dolgui, A. (2019). Review of quantitative methods for supply chain resilience analysis. *Transportation Research Part E: Logistics and Transportation Review, 125*, 285–307.

Ivanov, D., & Dolgui, A. (2021). OR-methods for coping with the ripple effect in supply chains during COVID-19 pandemic: Managerial insights and research implications. *International Journal of Production Economics, 232*, 107921.

Jabbarzadeh, A., Fahimnia, B., Sheu, J. B., & Moghadam, H. S. (2016). Designing a supply chain resilient to major disruptions and supply/demand interruptions. *Transportation Research Part B: Methodological, 94*, 121–149.

Jabbarzadeh, A., Fahimnia, B., & Sabouhi, F. (2018). Resilient and sustainable supply chain design: Sustainability analysis under disruption risks. *International Journal of Production Research, 56*(17), 5945–5968.

Khalili, S. M., Jolai, F., & Torabi, S. A. (2017). Integrated production–distribution planning in two-echelon systems: A resilience view. *International Journal of Production Research, 55*(4), 1040–1064.

Laumanns, M., Thiele, L., & Zitzler, E. (2006). An efficient, adaptive parameter variation scheme for metaheuristics based on the epsilon-constraint method. *European Journal of Operational Research, 169*(3), 932–942.

Lim, M., Daskin, M. S., Bassamboo, A., & Chopra, S. (2010). A facility reliability problem: Formulation, properties, and algorithm. *Naval Research Logistics (NRL), 57*(1), 58–70.

Meena, P. L., & Sarmah, S. P. (2013). Multiple sourcing under supplier failure risk and quantity discount: A genetic algorithm approach. *Transportation Research Part E: Logistics and Transportation Review, 50*, 84–97.

Namdar, J., Li, X., Sawhney, R., & Pradhan, N. (2018). Supply chain resilience for single and multiple sourcing in the presence of disruption risks. *International Journal of Production Research, 56*(6), 2339–2360.

Nat, K. (2018). *Countless to suffer from hunger globally in war torn regions as food deprivation through aid impediment cripples civilian lives: A yemeni focus*. Retrieved from https://theowp.org/countless-to-suffer-from-hunger-globally-in-war-torn-regions-as-food-deprivation-through-aid-impediment-cripples-civi

Nazemi, N., Parragh, S. N., & Gutjahr, W. J. (2021). Bi-objective facility location under un-certainty with an application in last-mile disaster relief. *Annals of Operations Research*. https://doi.org/10.1007/s10479-021-04422-4

Ni, N., Howell, B. J., & Sharkey, T. C. (2018). Modeling the impact of unmet demand in supply chain resiliency planning. *Omega, 81*, 1–16.

Rockafellar, R. T., & Uryasev, S. (2000). Optimization of conditional value-at-risk. *Journal of Risk, 2*, 21–42.

Sadghiani, N. S., Torabi, S. A., & Sahebjamnia, N. (2015). Retail supply chain network design under operational and disruption risks. *Transportation Research Part E: Logistics and Transportation Review, 75*, 95–114.

Sheffi, Y. (2007). *The resilient enterprise: Overcoming vulnerability for competitive advantage*. Zone Books.

Snoeck, A., Udenio, M., & Fransoo, J. C. (2019). A stochastic program to evaluate disruption mitigation investments in the supply chain. *European Journal of Operational Research, 274*(2), 516–530.

Snyder, L. V., & Daskin, M. S. (2005). Reliability models for facility location: The expected failure cost case. *Transportation Science, 39*(3), 400–416.

Snyder, L. V., Atan, Z., Peng, P., Rong, Y., Schmitt, A. J., & Sinsoysal, B. (2016). OR/MS models for supply chain disruptions: A review. *IEE Transactions, 48*(2), 89–109.

Tang, C. S. (2006). Perspectives in supply chain risk management. *International Journal of Production Economics, 103*(2), 451–488.

Tricoire, F., Graf, A., & Gutjahr, W. J. (2012). The bi-objective stochastic covering tour problem. *Computers & Operations Research, 39*(7), 1582–1592.

Wang, M., & Yao, J. (2021). Intertwined supply network design under facility and transportation disruption from the viability perspective. *International Journal of Production Research, 2021*, 1–31.

Yan, S., & Ji, X. (2020). Supply chain network design under the risk of uncertain disruptions. *International Journal of Production Research, 58*(6), 1724–1740.

Najmesadat Nazemi is a doctorate student at the Institute of Production and Logistics Management at Johannes Kepler University Linz. She has earned a master's degree in Socio-Economic Systems Engineering with focus on Operations Research from the University of Tehran, Iran. Her research interests include multi-objective optimization, optimization under uncertainty, and their applications in humanitarian logistics.

Sophie N. Parragh is a professor and head of the Institute of Production and Logistics Management at Johannes Kepler University Linz. She holds a Ph.D. in Management and a habilitation in Business Administration. She currently serves as an associate editor at several prestigious journals and as a program director of JKU's Economic and Business Analytics master's degree program. She is an author of various publications in renown journals, such as Transportation Science and INFORMS Journal on Computing, with special focus on vehicle routing and multi-objective optimization.

Part IV
Resilience in Theory and Practice

Chapter 15
Resilient Supply Chains: A Practical Guide for Successful Implementation

Gregor Gluttig

Abstract Creating resilient supply chains is not an option, but a prerequisite in order to master the challenges ahead. Gregor Gluttig shares his knowledge on building resilient supply chains with best practices from different industries. A practical guide for supply chain executives on how to prepare for upcoming disruptions in global supply chains is presented. A 6-step approach illustrates the key tasks required to transform to a resilient supply chain. It is also shown how advanced technologies such as AI and control towers can be used to provide full visibility into supply chains. These tools enable companies to be proactive by predicting where and when a supply chain disruption is most likely to occur. However, the importance of both digital solutions and a skilled organisation is also emphasised. The key to success lies in enabling organisations and employees to use the processes and tools described.

15.1 Introduction

As observant citizens who regularly consume current news, all of us are sensitised to the increasing importance of resilient supply chains. Due to complex global supply networks, which can lead to a higher chance of interruption, supply chain networks have been brought into focus.

Global shortages of available containers, a huge cargo ship stranded in the Suez Canal causing huge financial costs due to delayed deliveries or production stops at major car manufacturers forced by the global semiconductor shortage—these are just a few of the latest examples that companies are facing.

In theory a resilient supply chain is able to anticipate, respond to, and recover fast from unexpected disruptions—enabling a company to achieve and sustain a competitive advantage.

G. Gluttig (✉)
TenglerGluttig Consulting, Vienna, Austria
e-mail: g.gluttig@tenglergluttig.com

S. Kummer et al. (eds.), *Supply Chain Resilience*, Springer Series in Supply Chain Management 17, https://doi.org/10.1007/978-3-030-95401-7_15

But how can global players prevent or mitigate interruptions and respond to unexpected events in real time?

15.2 Increasing Complexity

A well-known example using the production of computers illustrates how many spheres in a supply chain are vulnerable: metals are imported from South America; rare earths are mined in China; and components such as chips, keyboards and LCD screens are made in Southeast Asia, China, and the USA. The major assemblies are manufactured in the USA, Taiwan, Japan and the Philippines, and the final assembly and inspection is done in Chongqing. The finished products are shipped worldwide from Chongqing and Shenzhen to the end customer, e.g. in Italy. Within all these transport routes, vessels, production sites, warehouses, borders, etc., there is a risk of supply disruption.

15.3 Examples of Mitigation Activities to Exhibit/Demonstrate Supply Chain Resilience During COVID-19

Some companies have used the coronavirus crisis to demonstrate how SC (supply chain) resilience can work with small adaptations, depending on whether the country was before, or already within, a lockdown phase. (It is important to understand in which phase of the disaster we currently are.)

For example, in a pre-lockdown phase, it is critical to prepare for the potential of closed transportation routes. Managers need to assess the readiness of their logistics service provider and consider alternative transportation modes.

This activity has been applied, for example, by an Austrian manufacturer of windows. The company established new transport routes and modes before the first lockdown in Greece and used rail transport instead of transport by ferry. They also leveraged their long-standing supplier relationships to prepare properly. As a result, they were able to increase their orders by 15% (compared to pre-lockdown) despite just-in-time deliveries.

During a lockdown, there might be different priorities. For example, companies might need to adapt and put an emphasis on their process to match demand with available capacity. This process—known as sales and operations planning—was already in place at a British car manufacturer. Prior to the coronavirus outbreak, this process was conducted monthly; within the first lockdown, execution meetings shifted to a weekly or even daily basis. As a foundation, the company had visibility of material availability for 2 weeks. This increase in forecasting frequency and immediate development of backup scenarios helped to avoid supply bottlenecks, even though most of its suppliers were located in China.

15.4 After the Crisis Is Before the Crisis

Even after the coronavirus crisis, supply chains will continue to face global risks in the near future.

In the World Economic Forum's Global Risk Report 2020, infectious diseases are rated lower in terms of likelihood and impact than climate-related risks. No one can imagine it today, but compared to coronavirus, extreme weather events and climate change have much greater impacts on the supply chain and are highly likely to occur. Impacts include crop failures, shifting of growing areas, damaged facilities and transportation routes.

Climate action failure (meaning failure to meet climate targets such as a drastic reduction in CO_2 emissions) is considered the risk with the highest impact. And we all realise how difficult it is for all countries to pull together.

15.5 How to Prepare for the Upcoming Disruptions?

The transformation to a resilient supply chain is not a matter of weeks. It needs good preparation and consistent implementation.

Therefore, a step-by-step approach is necessary, from identifying and categorising relevant risks to simulating the impact of countermeasures and embedding the governance.

The following six-step approach illustrates the key tasks required to transform to a resilient supply chain (Fig. 15.1).

15.5.1 Step 1: Risk Identification with AI-Powered Risk Monitoring

Within phase 1, AI-powered risk monitoring and notification software can help. This software analyses social media and news using artificial intelligence. From this it can monitor specific risks at selected supply chain nodes such as suppliers, ports, transportation routes, etc. In real time and sometimes predictively, a company is notified when risks occur. Political and labour unrest (strikes, demos, etc.), and financial and legal risks (bankruptcies, licence revocations, etc.) can be monitored, as can workplace accidents and CSR incidents (industrial accidents, pandemics, etc.). Alerting time is often days or weeks before the potential risk occurs. For

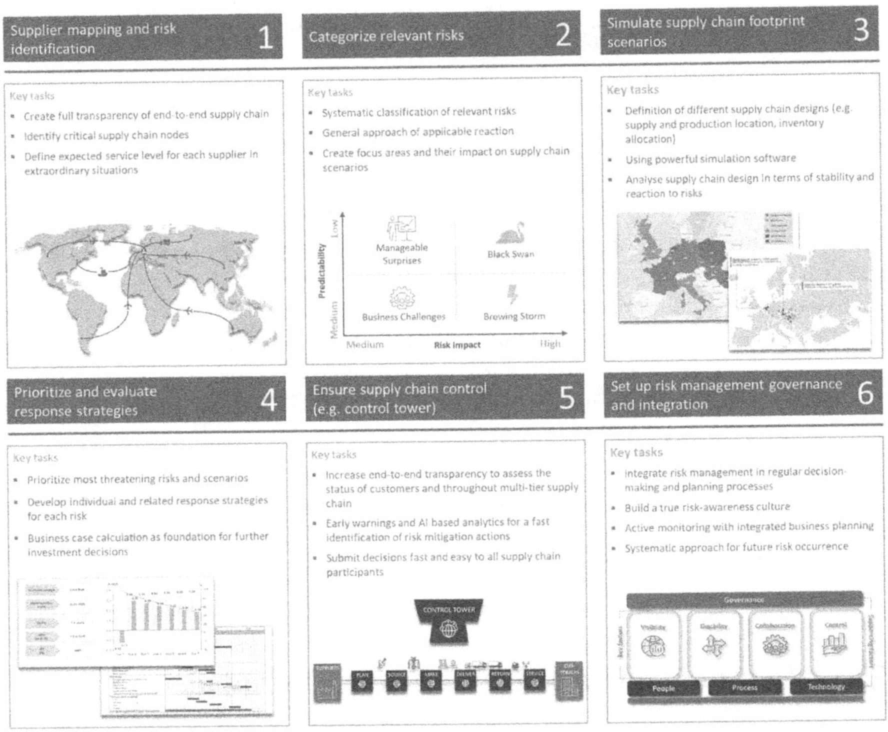

Fig. 15.1 Six-step approach, source: TenglerGluttig Consulting

example, port strikes were already foreseen 18 days in advance. Even demonstrations were predicted 3 days before they took place. Unpredictable events are reported after the shortest possible time, e.g. explosions at the supplier within 2 min.

15.5.2 *Step 2: Different Risk—Different Measure*

The example of a German manufacturer of medical technology shows how different countermeasures depend on how risk is categorised. This company produces pumps for infusion solutions and has identified Brexit as a relevant risk. The risk is relatively easy to forecast but has a huge impact—in risk management jargon, a so-called brewing storm. Because higher tariffs are expected on finished products than on their components, the response has been to move locally certain finishing/assembly production steps for the UK market.

In addition, the company has identified natural disasters in Southeast Asia as an important risk—some of their suppliers for pump parts are located in Malaysia. These risks are difficult to predict but have major effects and are synonymous with the 'black swan' category. Coronavirus is also one of them. As a countermeasure, the company revised its inventory strategy and massively increased stock levels of strategically important components. Where possible, it pursues a dual-sourcing strategy.

Selecting the right countermeasure is strategically important, as it is often quite cost-intensive. Therefore, each measure must be part of an in-depth impact analysis.

15.5.3 Steps 3 and 4: The Impact Simulation

The example of the medical technology manufacturer that wanted to relocate its production to the UK perfectly illustrates the impact this decision could have. In a simulation, the effects on the following parameters should be analysed:

- Where in GB should the site be located, and which subsidiary produces which components (since there was a second plant in Wales)?
- How does the warehouse structure change for the distribution of parts in GB to and from the production site?
- From which location can the manufacturer ship, how far and how fast, and how does that fit with the customers' delivery time requirements?
- How does the new setup affect freight costs and inventory levels?
- Which customers should be served from which warehouse or which production location?

To properly answer all these questions, powerful simulation software is required. Scenarios are used to compare the effects and search for the overall optimum. The key is to have the right data available to feed the simulation software.

15.5.4 Step 5: Ensure Supply Chain Control with Control Towers?

In the supply chain world, there is some hype around control towers, sometimes also called command centres, and with good reason. So, what is behind it?

Supply chain managers have been dreaming about ensuring real-time control in supply chains for decades. The good news is that with digital transformation and new technologies, these software platforms are available. The bad news is that they are often not affordable for midsize and small businesses.

With a control tower, disruptions are quickly identified in a supply chain and action scenarios are provided. All participants in the supply chain are included and integrated in one system.

The following example illustrates how such a platform works (Fig. 15.2).

Imagine that one of the trucks of the German producer on the way to its customer breaks down in Ukraine. As a result, the customer order cannot be fulfilled. The

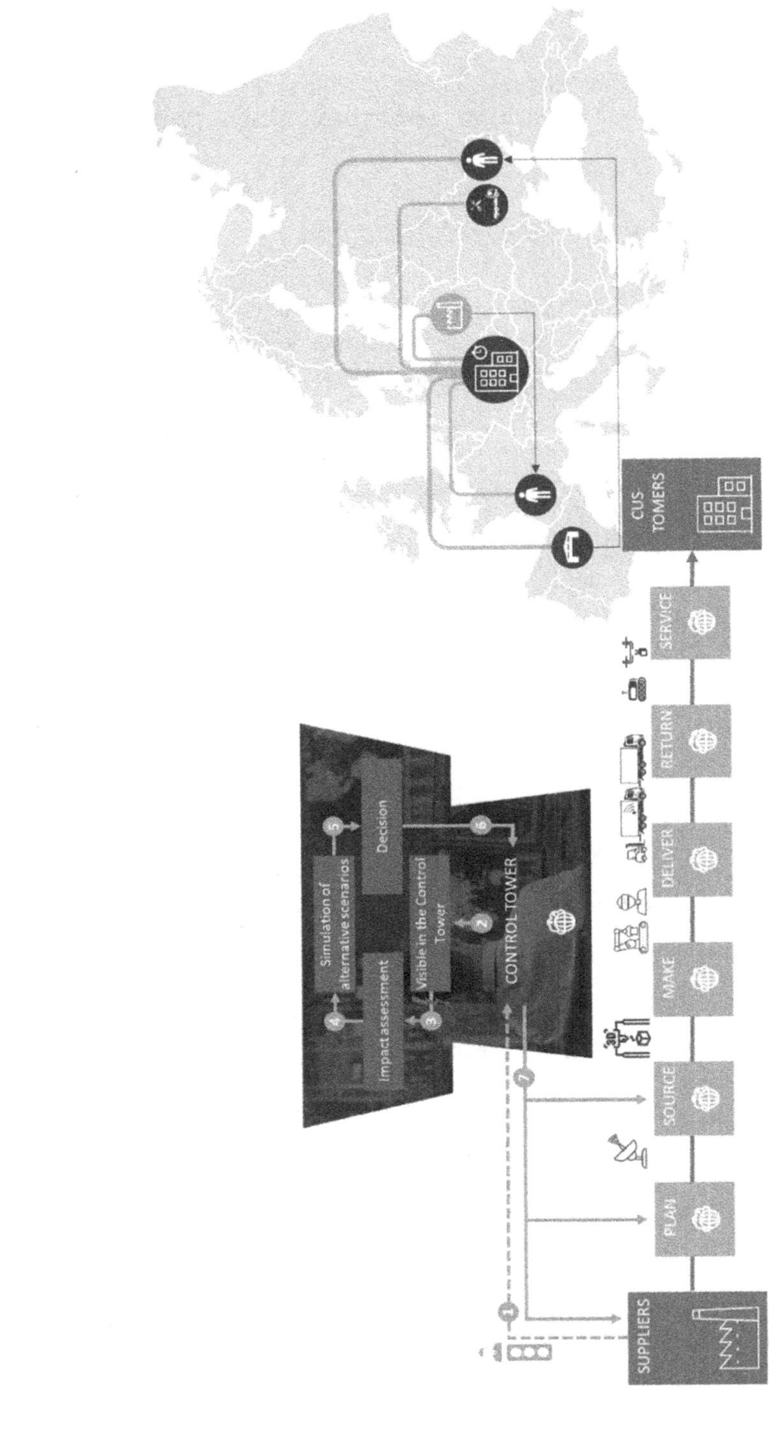

Fig. 15.2 Operating principle of Control Towers, source: TenglerGluttig Consulting

control tower shows in real time that these goods are also stored in another warehouse in Spain. The goods are already reserved for a customer in France, but the control tower immediately gives the information that the plant in Poland can replenish the goods for the French customer quickly enough and without changing the production schedule. In this way, all service level agreements (SLAs) made with the customers can be met. Supported by real-time data, the dispatcher becomes more of a manager than an administrative employee.

15.5.5 Step 6: Embedment Within the Organisation

One way to integrate the management of risks within an organisation is to implement an integrated business planning process. Through integrated business planning, future problem areas, such as delivery bottlenecks, can be identified at an early stage.

The basis for this is a rolling monthly planning cycle for the upcoming 12–18 months. Together with all affected areas (such as sales, purchasing, production and controlling), gaps between prognosis and available capacity are identified and various options of how to close them are weighed up. Decisions are made together, in accordance with clear rules and KPIs for the best interest of the entire company.

15.6 Conclusion

Creating resilient supply chains is not an option but a prerequisite in order to master the challenges ahead. Digitisation and new software tools can help. But the success of any supply chain digitisation project depends on the maturity of the tools and processes, as well as overall organisational readiness. Companies need an open culture that is willing to change the environment. Supply chain resilience also goes hand in hand with new processes in the organisation. A full commitment to these new processes at all levels, clear roles and responsibilities and the introduction of process-mining KPIs to control the supply chain are critical.

So, to enable resilient supply chains with the help of digital solutions, the supply chain must fulfil certain requirements. The success of supply chain digitalisation does not depend on the right tool and the IT infrastructure. Rather, the focus should be on employees and culture, processes and organisational structure. Digitisation projects are primarily organisational transformations that usually take much more time than implementing IT requirements itself. Employees need to develop digital skills. To ensure this, all relevant stakeholders should be involved in the conceptual design at an early stage and full support from top management should be guaranteed. In addition, employees must receive comprehensive training. The topic of people enablement and training should be addressed at the very beginning.

In a nutshell: To cope with the new challenges, you need both digital solutions and a skilled organisation. By following these recommendations, the desired benefits of a resilient supply chain, such as increasing customer service levels in a volatile environment at low costs, can be achieved.

Gregor Gluttig is the founder and managing partner of TenglerGluttig—The Supply Chain Minds. He studied industrial engineering and today gives talks on supply chain digitisation and lectures at universities on risk management. Having previously worked as a logistics coordinator at REWE, an assistant to the executive board at Railcargo, and a Director of the in-house consulting firm Gebrüder Weiss in Vienna, he has extensive supply chain experience. During his many years as a consultant at Barkawi and later at TenglerGluttig, he managed several SCM transformation projects in various industries, such as pharmaceuticals, construction, logistics service providers, automotive and retail.

Chapter 16
What Really Works: A Practitioner's Critical Review on Supply Chain Resilience Research

Christian Hammer

Abstract This chapter shares a practitioner's view on supply chain resilience research. Recurrent critical opinions from the practice field state that problems in academic research are too theoretical and limited to be used in real-world. Besides this, the scientific focus on applying historic data results in findings that are being outdated for the changing environment of the business context. Based on the author's practical implementation of research practices in different supply chain settings, it can be concluded that these applications prove relevant and supportive for real-world business settings. For the coordination of supply and demand, aligning internally and accepting supply chain management was a vital step. In addition, the application of the latest planning solutions to optimize the match between supply and demand while reducing demand variability has also turned out to be the right choice. Supply chain flexibility can still be enhanced, for example stock buffers can serve as measures for availability and business continuity.

16.1 Introduction

In the summer of 2013, I handed in my dissertation on the topic of "Matching supply and demand in the chemical industry during turbulent times" to professors Kummer and Wakolbinger at the Institute for Transport and Logistics Management. The aim for the dissertation project was to research an area with high practical relevance and investigate "real" industry problems. My findings should provide guidance to companies struggling with disruptions in their supply chains and the ever-increasing need to react more flexibly to sudden changes of supply and demand.

I remember many heated discussions with my practitioner colleagues from that time. Could the outcome of a Ph.D. study be relevant to practitioners? Even more, could it be applied seamlessly in a business environment? Basically, the line of

C. Hammer (✉)
Biconi Ventures, Singapore, Singapore

S. Kummer et al. (eds.), *Supply Chain Resilience*, Springer Series in Supply Chain Management 17, https://doi.org/10.1007/978-3-030-95401-7_16

reasoning of many of my practitioner colleagues can be summarized into two main messages:

- Academic research would be by far too theoretical and of limited use to solve real-world problems.
- Even if I would be lucky enough to solve an issue with practical relevance, academic business research would be looking at historic data and as such it would be outdated and not of relevance for an environment characterized by ever-changing business dynamics.

It was clear to me that these arguments were not completely pointless, and they were constant reminder and motivation for me to be as relevant to supply chain practice in my studies as possible. Did I succeed? Eight years later is a good time for me to challenge and review my thesis with the practitioner's view that I now have. We definitely have seen many disruptions in global supply chains in these years, so it truly was a good period for the field test.

16.2 Research Findings: Was That All Just Dreary Theory?

My research has investigated how a better match of supply and demand during turbulent times can be achieved. An ongoing effort to reduce demand variability and increase supply chain flexibility was identified as a promising approach and an extensive list of practices, and their situation-specific implementation requirements was presented. An empirical study, consisting of three in-depth case studies with leading specialty chemical companies, tested the applicability of these practices and complemented the theoretical discussion of the improvement measures with additional improvement ideas and factors for implementation success. Figure 16.1 presents the framework for improved supply chain fit during turbulent times that was developed as part of the research study.

Research suggested ensuring internal alignment first to eliminate any mismatch or disruption that might arise from inside the organization. In a second step, reducing demand variability as much as possible was proposed. The measures in this area were grouped into the following approaches: cross-supply chain information sharing, demand shaping, and product portfolio management. Only in the last step, increasing supply chain flexibility—the most expensive measure—was proposed. The flexibility practices can be roughly categorized into these approaches: supply chain synchronization, cycle time reduction, provision of buffers, and capacity allocation.

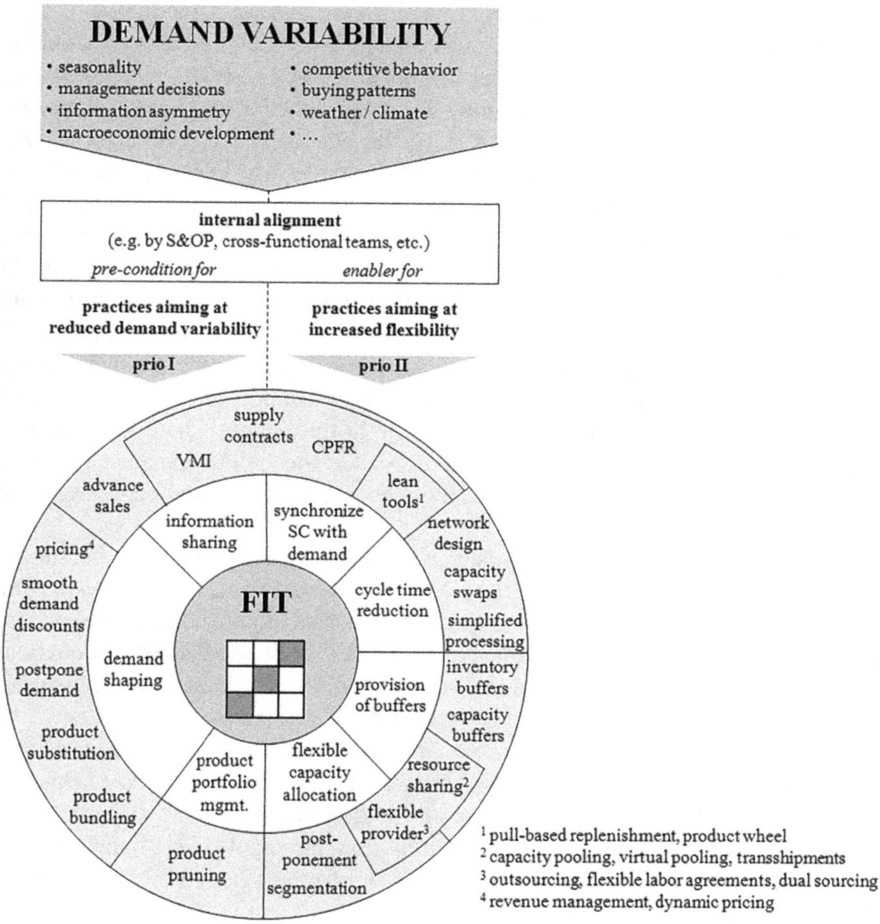

Fig. 16.1 Framework for achieving improved supply chain fit during turbulent times (Hammer, 2013)

16.3 The Hour of Truth: What Has Actually Worked During the Eight-Year Field Trial?

Right after my Ph.D. project was completed, I continued my professional career as a practitioner and joined a large multinational chemical company where I had the pleasure to build up and lead the global Supply Chain Excellence initiative. All that time I had my "bible" with me—eager to implement some of my research suggestions in my new environment.

At the beginning of my time with the company, we have seen a massive mismatch between supply and demand driven by internal misalignment. Sales forecasts were highly inaccurate, and updates were seldom shared with Operations. Our factories—on the other hand—were incentivized on production efficiency. We produced huge volumes—typically of the wrong products—in long and rigid production cycles. Supply chain was left outside of the decision-making process, basically focusing on warehousing, transportation, and order fulfilment. It took a major effort to change this. We had a lot of resistance from the sales and production teams, but with a few cooperative managers, we ran pilot projects, and ultimately the first business units saw the huge benefits of internal alignment from the newly implemented Sales & Operations Planning process. Product availability significantly increased, while inventories were reduced to healthy levels and—other than feared by many manufacturing managers—production efficiency remained on high levels and in many plants even improved. This was the tailwind that we needed to push through a major global initiative. All business units on a global scale finally implemented the new way to work. Massive process improvements were put in place, and new supply chain teams were in charge of sales and operations planning, and the entire process was supported by an advanced system. A role in the Supply Chain Management team also became a sought-after position for sales and production managers that were eager to advance their career opportunities—something that would have been unthinkable of a few years earlier.

Finding 1: The huge benefits we have seen from internal alignment, the implementation of an advanced S&OP and cross-functional teams, fully supports the claim of my earlier research findings to ensure internal alignment first to eliminate any mismatch or disruption. Implementing Sales & Operations Planning throughout the corporation has probably been my most important supply chain project so far, and it has prepared the stage for all further supply chain improvements. It was also our first step to reduce variability and enable the "large ship" to react much more flexibly to external events. Establishing this sort of internal alignment also helped us to overcome some huge external disruptions in the years to come.

While we were enjoying higher profitability from the supply chain improvements put in place, we were soon in the midst of a substantial external crisis. Oil prices plummeted from 100$ per barrel in 2014 to just half of that in 2015. Being a major supplier to the oil and gas sector, we were hit hard. Exploration projects were stopped and upstream operations needed to focus on efficiency. Demand for our products has changed completely and our good internal alignment was a life saver at that time as it allowed us to react significantly faster than our competition. And again, many of my previously researched practices found some use in managing a real-life crisis. Product pruning was one of our first activities. The market was demanding lower cost products and was accepting a lower yield. We reduced our product portfolio of highly customized, high-yield, but also highly priced products significantly. Products with low demand or high demand variability were pruned, and demand was bundled to more standardized products. This in turn allowed us to run our supply chain efficiently and offer lower prices in return—as demanded by the market at that time.

We also continued our way to improve information availability. Technology matured and so did the general mindset in the industry, but even with new silver bullets like "Integrated Business Planning," "Supply Chain Control Towers," "Real-time Demand Sensing," etc., the general concept remains the same: improve visibility and use that information to match supply and demand as much as possible. Cross-company information sharing certainly remained to be a challenge, but where trustful partnerships were in place, we have seen many improvements by sharing demand signals, forecasts, orders, and inventory information across supply chains. Paired with the abilities of modern planning software, this can do some real magic. Also, even where we did not receive information from our supply chain partners, modern technology did help with predictive scenario planning.

Finding 2: Information sharing remains the number one goal in running our supply chains efficiently and effectively. Many of the practices researched in my thesis did prove relevant in practice and also the sequence in which they were applied follows my previous suggestion. While the concepts I have described in my thesis remain valid and relevant, modern planning solutions are so much more powerful than they were 8 years ago to predict, prevent, and resolve disruptions and add tremendous new opportunities to increase visibility—by collaborative sharing or predictive forecasting. Applying new planning solutions has paid back very much to us, and I am constantly scouting for any further promising innovations.

Can modern planning solutions with all the increased visibility perform the entire magic of supply chain management? Would there even be any more flexibility needed? The practitioner's answer is clearly a "yes," especially in the chemical industry with its long cycle times. We have introduced the product wheel approach very successfully. By doing so, cycle times have been significantly reduced due to optimized changeover times. However, more importantly, we have reserved flexible slots for MTO products and were able to fulfil unexpected demand without interrupting production plans and schedules. Other measures that helped us with staying flexible were product postponement and capacity swaps in our global manufacturing network. Also, here, advanced planning solutions have helped us very much to articulate the requirements for flexibility, to optimize the system, and to streamline processes that ensured the effectiveness of the intended flexibility gains.

Finding 3: Despite improved visibility, we needed to respond flexibly to sudden changes in demand—as well as changes of our own supply situation. Not all the researched flexibility practices have been applied by myself, but product wheel, capacity swaps, and postponement strategies were most effective—especially when combined with advanced supply chain planning solutions. I do expect supply chain flexibility to gain even more importance in the future as customer expectations in terms of service levels and availability are getting higher and competition is getting tougher.

After changing the mindset of our organization toward intensive internal alignment and coordination, after improving planning capabilities tremendously and after reducing the cycle time in our supply chains, the remaining flexibility "insurances" built into our supply chains seemed obsolete. Would we need all the buffers in the supply chain still? Inventory at multiple echelons in the supply chain and idle capacity, all seem to be nothing else than waste. Being a Lean Six Sigma Black Belt myself, I have been fighting overstocking and capacity buffers for many years. However, experience has taught me some different lessons. Despite all the planning technology, artificial intelligence, and machine learning, global supply chains are still not as predictable as we think. The supply chains I had been looking after had seen completely unpredicted supply and demand changes, some of them happening pretty much with immediate effect; we have seen major interruptions from political conflicts, currency, and raw material crises with major impacts on supply and demand. We have seen whole markets going into lockdowns during the COVID-19 pandemic with suppliers and our own plants temporarily closed, borders blocked, and ports congested. Furthermore, major transportation routes have seen interruptions by shortage of capacity, and—as I am writing this article—the Suez Canal has just been blocked by the grounding of a large container ship. Despite all of this, we have been able to fulfil almost all our orders during these crises and supply chain interruptions and I have been eternally thankful to my colleagues from the commercial teams that insisted to have our safety stock calculations adjusted for some extra buffers.

Finding 4: In my research, I concluded that the days of holding large stocks of inventory are over. Firms could not afford to tie up cash in inventories anymore. While this has certainly some truth in it and is in line with mainstream thinking, inventory buffers still remain to be very powerful to solve short-term supply chain interruptions, and I will continue to use inventory smartly but also generously to ensure business continuation during disruptions.

16.4 Conclusion: Did My Research Pass the Field Trail?

In the past 8 years, I was able to apply surprisingly many of the practices researched in my Ph.D. project in various supply chain settings. I would definitely say that "my bible" has passed its field trial and has been helpful in many cases. I'm really happy about that and got many thumbs-up from my colleagues who previously challenged the relevance of my research for solving real-life business issues. Many practices have proven to be successful and have remained relevant, despite steep technological advancements. Also the implementation sequence was important. The game changer for us was internal alignment and the acceptance of SCM as the coordinator of supply and demand. Reducing demand variability in a second step also has proven to be the right choice. The openness to invest into state-of-the-art planning solutions has certainly been a big plus in optimizing the matching of supply and demand in tough times. I will also continue to be an early implementer of new supply chain innovations in this area. The third category—supply chain flexibility—is still very much needed and powerful especially when blended in with modern technology. However, despite all the computing power and artificial intelligence, in times of massive supply disruptions, the layman's wisdom of keeping buffers still is a strong measure to ensure availability and business continuity.

Reference

Hammer, C. (2013). *Matching supply and demand in the chemical industry during turbulent times - a multi-case investigation on practices to improve supply chain fit by reducing demand variability and increasing supply chain flexibility, Dissertation*. WU Vienna University of Economics and Business.

Christian Hammer is a consultant, an entrepreneur, and a venture capitalist. He holds a Ph.D. in Supply Chain Management from WU (Vienna University of Economics and Business) and has supported many Fortune 500 and DAX 30 companies in driving their Supply Chain Excellence strategies.

Chapter 17
Delphi Study on Supply Chain Resilience

Lydia Novoszel, Alexander M. Geske, Sebastian Kummer, and Tina Wakolbinger

Abstract This newly conducted Delphi Study investigates supply chain resilience amid the current corona virus supply chain challenges. Participants with commercial and humanitarian supply chain background from academia and practise share their insights on supply chain activities as well as capabilities. Best practices to cope with the disruptions are gathered and clustered in the areas of visibility, agility, flexibility, collaboration, and people. To further develop academic research the study outlines future research opportunities in the field of supply chain resilience.

17.1 Introduction

The global COVID-19 pandemic sparked and accelerated research activities in the area of supply chain resilience. First surveys indicate visible implications amid the crisis for commercial supply chains. Seventy-three percent of commercial supply chains in the USA experienced changes in their supply and 75% in their production and distribution (Alicke et al., 2020). Besides, 10% of corporations got positively impacted (Balleer et al., 2020).

Also, humanitarian supply chains are getting impacted by the global pandemic. Almost all (99%) of humanitarian organizations applied changes to their operations, and 93% got impacted due to actions by authorities (ACAPS, 2020), and higher needs from beneficiaries (ReliefWeb, 2021).

Looking into the specifics for Austria, companies from various industries mentioned to have 46% cancelled orders, 17% challenges with supply, 15% delayed customer payments, and 14% difficulties to find employees during the second wave of COVID-19 lockdown in Fall 2020 (WIFO, 2021).

These dynamics call for supply chains to adapt to changing circumstances, with supply chain resilience being an approach to support this. In order to incorporate

L. Novoszel (✉) · A. M. Geske · S. Kummer · T. Wakolbinger
Institute for Transport and Logistics Management, WU (Vienna University of Economics and Business), Vienna, Austria
e-mail: Lydia.novoszel@wu.ac.at

S. Kummer et al. (eds.), *Supply Chain Resilience*, Springer Series in Supply Chain Management 17, https://doi.org/10.1007/978-3-030-95401-7_17

qualitative data into supply chain resilience research, an online Delphi Study was conducted among practitioners and academics between June and August 2021.

This chapter describes results of this Delphi study. For the purpose of this study, we base our supply chain resilience definition on the NRC (National Research Council 2012) which considers resilience as "the ability to prepare and plan for, absorb, recover from, and more successfully adapt to adverse events." For more details on the term resilience, please refer to Chap. 1.

The chapter is structured as follows: The first section describes the research method "Delphi Study." The research questions are introduced in the following section. The next part describes the study design. The results of the Delphi Study linked to the research questions are described thereafter. The summary describes the findings, highlights limitations, and provides an outlook of future research opportunities.

17.2 Research Method: Delphi Study

The Delphi Study was chosen as a qualitative research method to solicit input from a geographically spread group of people via an online platform. The target was to obtain feedback and perspectives on supply chain resilience from within the supply chain community.

The Delphi method was established in 1963 by Dalkey and Helmer in the context of the RAND corporation for forecasting (Dalkey & Helmer, 1963). It is a qualitative research method to use input from a group of people who are geographically dispersed. It is based on the assumption of strength in numbers: more people will more likely get to a more valid conclusion than one person alone (because they challenge assumptions and outcomes). The target is to get an aligned consensus on a specific topic.

The main characteristics of the Delphi method are anonymity, geographical distance of the participants, and iteration. The study is conducted via virtual means, like virtual platforms, online surveys, and email. The participating experts do not have knowledge about the other attendees and do not meet in person. This ensures anonymity, with the advantage of no social or group pressure (Hasson et al., 2000). At the same time, it enables people in different locations to contribute their knowledge to a topic (Rowe & Wright, 1999). The participants are confronted with multiple iterations on a topic based on the group's feedback. It enables the attendees to change their perspective and assessment without fear of "losing their face" (Rowe & Wright, 1999, p. 354).

The study is mainly used for decision-making and alignment, forecasting and assessing trends, and formulating best practices. Hasson et al. (2000, p. 1009) highlight four research objectives that call for the use of the Delphi: "to explore or expose underlying assumptions or information leading to differing judgements; to seek out information which may generate a consensus on the part of the respondent group; to correlate informed judgements on a topic spanning a wide range of disciplines; and to educate the respondent group as to the diverse and interrelated aspects of the topic."

The aim of the method is to generate an aligned understanding of the topic in question. The sequential steps are as follow: formulate the research questions, select the expert panel, and execute the questionnaire rounds with several iterations until consensus is reached. Between the various rounds and at the end, a consensus analysis has to be conducted. This feedback is the input for the following iteration. The expert panel selection targets size and qualification. The larger the group, the larger the amount of data generated. A heterogeneous group with different perspectives is preferred to generate a holistic understanding of the topic and a vivid discourse. The Delphi method does not follow statistical criteria of representation but focuses on the qualifications of the expert panel (Powell, 2003). Qualifications can be characterized in various dimensions, such as disciplines, skills, organizations, tenure in the field, presentations held, and publications in the academic literature (Okoli & Pawlowski, 2004). Confidence in expertise is an indicator that can influence the probability of changing the response (Rowe & Wright, 1999). Besides expertise, demographics of the panel including geographical distribution or representation should be well described in the documentation of the study (Schmidt, 1997). Access to Internet and email is a prerequisite for participating in the survey, which might be relevant in the humanitarian sector for people out in the field. In order to keep the attention of the attendees during the iterative rounds, it is important to understand the motivating factors for busy experts. The response rate during the entire survey is a quality criterion for the study. Okoli and Pawlowski (2004, p. 10) highlight incentives for people to participate as follows: "being chosen in a diverse but selective group; the opportunity to learn from the consensus building; and increasing their own visibility in their organization and outside."

Before sending out the first round of the questionnaire, it is advisable to pretest it. The Delphi Study itself takes 45 days to 5 months. There seems to be an agreement on three rounds. However, the decision over the number of rounds is largely pragmatic and depends on the definition of consensus and when it is reached, or the response rate drops (Powell, 2003; Okoli & Pawlowski, 2004; Schmidt, 1997; Hasson et al., 2000).

The classic first round covers open questions and unstructured opinions. Content text analysis of the qualitative responses summarizes the outcome. Rounds two and three are follow-ups on the previous rounds' results. There, the outcome of round one is presented to the experts as a quantitative structured questionnaire. The results are statistically summarized with mean/median and upper/lower quartiles (Rowe & Wright, 1999; Schmidt, 1997). These central tendencies and levels of dispersion indicate information about the collected opinion (Hasson et al., 2000). The survey attendees are asked to adjust and provide feedback and are asked for reasons why they are outside of the upper or lower quantile.

There does not seem to exist a consistent agreement on the definition and level of consensus to aim for. However, various options are discussed. For example, percentage levels of agreement, the stability of the response, or Kendall's W-coefficient is applied. There appear to be limited standards on the report-out of the overall findings of the Delphi method outcome (Rowe & Wright, 1999; Hasson et al., 2000; Schmidt, 1997; Powell, 2003).

Based on the general approach to conduct a Delphi Study, there are different types described in literature. The multi-round eDelphi uses web-based tools to conduct the survey. The real-time Delphi uses virtual means to immediately react to the results of the other participants. This means that every participant reacts to the different reactions on hand. The policy Delphi and modified Delphi are based on literature reviews (Powell, 2003; Hasson et al., 2000). The ranking type Delphi by Schmidt (1997) defines the three rounds explicitly: first, brainstorm for important factors to discover the issues; second, prioritize the most important issues; and third, rank the list of important factors (Schmidt, 1997; Okoli & Pawlowski, 2004).

Various tools are available to support the researcher in conducting the Delphi survey. In general, the activities of participant administration, sending out the survey and analyzing the responses, can be done manually. There are benefits in using a Delphi software and focusing on the content of the answers rather than the survey administration and analytics. Aengenheyster et al. (2017) compare and categorize different software tools available on the market. The Appendix compares four different online tools based on the selection criteria from Aengenheyster et al.

For this Delphi study, the software providers were chosen based on an online search regarding researchers' feedback. The information was requested via email with a request for information outlining the targets and cornerstones of the study. Based on the feedback, two virtual meetings were conducted with the two top-ranked software providers identified based on the fit of the selection criteria to the study design. The decision was taken considering ease of implementation and cost-efficiency.

17.3 Research Questions

This study aims to contribute to the growing body of work on resilience amid the COVID-19 pandemic. As mentioned earlier, the National Research Council's definition for resilience (2012), "the ability to prepare and plan for, absorb, recover from, and more successfully adapt to adverse events," is used for the study.

The aim of the first area is to understand how different supply chain activities were challenged amid two different lockdown periods linked to the global COVID-19 pandemic in spring 2020 and fall/winter 2020/2021. The activities are based on Chopra and Sodhi (2004).

- *Research Question 1*: How challenging were different supply chain activities during spring/winter 2020/2021?

For the second research question, relevant capabilities (Brusset & Teller, 2017) to adhere to disruptions are explored in different crisis situations. For more details of different supply chain resilience capabilities, please refer to Chap. 1. The definitions of the capabilities is mainly synthesized from Christopher and Peck (2004) and Pettit et al. (2010). The target was to understand the relevance of the described capabilities in different phases, potentially see a development over time, and get an indication about future relevance.

- *Research Question 2*: How are visibility, agility, flexibility, and collaboration capabilities ranked in terms of impact in different crisis situations (financial crisis, COVID-19, future)?

The third area of interest is supply chain best practices. These are configurations, technologies, or knowledge to perform a set of processes to gain a better result (Supply Chain Council, 2010). The aim was to gather insights from supply chain professionals to investigate impactful supply chain resilience best practices.

- *Research Question 3*: Which supply chain resilience best practices are most impactful?

Finally, gathering input for research opportunities from a group of practitioners gives insights into relevant topics and can spark further research projects or validate ongoing research. The Delphi Study can be used as a mean to gather insights to forecast and assess trends (Hasson et al., 2000).

- *Research Question 4*: Which research opportunities exist in the field of supply chain resilience?

17.4 Study Design

This study was conducted from June to August 2021. After defining the research focus, we derived the research questions and selected the Delphi software (edelphi.org) provider to support the administration of the study. Next, we phrased the questions for the different rounds of the Delphi Study and conducted a pretest with four different experts from the academic and practical supply chain field. The feedback from the pretest was considered for the final questionnaire setup. The target panel for the Delphi Study was an international mix of practitioners and academics with expertise in commercial or humanitarian supply chain management to cover a wide array of supply chain resilience perspectives. In order to achieve a heterogeneous composition of the group, a broad invitation initiative covering representatives of various industries (e.g., automotive, transport, consultancy, humanitarian organizations, and universities) and countries with a focus on Europe was started. The Delphi Study was conducted in two iterative rounds based on the adjusted ranking-type Delphi approach. The first round had a mixture of open and closed questions to introduce the panel to the topic. The second round gave the opportunity to adjust answers from the first round and evaluate topics gathered from the previous round.

The questionnaire consisted of four different sections. The first one gathered background information of the participants, and the others followed the research questions. As part of the descriptive information, questions related to academic/practical field, commercial versus humanitarian supply chain, years of professional experience, current job title, geographical responsibility, and supply chain functional areas were raised with single or multiple choice, drop-down, and open text fields. The content questions were formulated as open and closed questions using ranking and Likert scale answering formats. For more details on the respective questions and question types, please refer to the results section of this chapter. In addition, the questionnaire had a real-time comment function.

In the first round, taking place from June 23rd to July 20th, 2021, 44 respondents submitted their answers. During the second round, from July 28th to August 21st, 2021, thirteen answers where submitted. The study was finalized after the second round, due to the drop in responses as it could be anticipated that a third round would not have been successful.

The panel (based on round 1 data with 44 answers) consisted of 75% academics and 25% practitioners. Around 80% attributed their main responsibility to commercial supply chains and 20% to humanitarian. Most of the experts are based in Europe, followed by North America. The experts represented a tenure of up to 45 years in the field. Examples of current job titles are University Professor and Chair, CEO, or Vice President. From a functional perspective, the majority of the panel is active in the field of supply chain strategy and design followed by transportation and routing. The heterogeneous composition of the panel builds a good basis for a Delphi Study design, but the limited (complete) responses indicate a limited significance for the quantitative results of the study. This might also be due to the time when the study was conducted in summer, the busyness of the experts amid the ongoing COVID-19 pandemic, and the new developments linked to supply chain resilience. Originally, a focus group to sum up the Delphi Study results was planned. However, due to pandemic-induced travel limitation in corporations, it was not executed. In the results section of the study, the quantitative evaluations should mainly provide basic indications and cannot be considered as statistically significant. Consensus was not defined as target of the study.

17.5 Assessment of Current Supply Chain Challenges

The next section describes the questions and results from the Delphi Study linked to the first research question that addressed how challenging different actions were during COVID-19. Eleven actions were synthesized based on Chopra and Sodhi (2004).

The panel was asked to assess challenges for each action during two different time frames on a five-point Likert scale (Joshi et al., 2015). The two time periods indicate the first and second lockdowns or major disruptions due to COVID-19 infection rates and government restrictions. The exact question was, "How challenging did you consider the following activities in the two different time periods?" The five-point Likert scale descriptions are from 1 (not challenging) to 5 (very challenging). The results were analyzed based on the average across all participants for each action and each time frame.

In the first round, 41 panelists shared their perspectives. For the spring time frame (first lockdown wave in Europe during March to May 2020), the top three perceived

Table 17.1 Results assessment of supply chain challenges

Activities	Mar 2020–May 2020	Nov 2020–Jan 2021
Forecasting supply patterns	4.08 (4.20)	3.23 (3.73)
Developing supplier portfolios	3.38 (3.66)	3.08 (3.34)
Implementing and/or adapting sales and operations planning cycles	4.15 (4.02)	3.31 (3.24)
Planning scenarios for production	3.85 (3.80)	3.15 (3.34)
Collaborating with logistics service providers (e.g. 3PL, 4PL)	3.31 (3.54)	3.31 (3.29)
Planning and/or adjusting of transport routes and/or modes	3.92 (3.80)	3.54 (3.32)
Forecasting demand patterns	4.00 (3.98)	3.15 (3.29)
Collaborating with customers	3.31 (3.54)	2.92 (3.00)
Developing and/or adapting sales channels (e.g. online platform)	3.46 (3.41)	3.00 (2.95)
Prioritizing customer orders	3.77 (3.44)	3.08 (3.15)
Developing products and driving innovation	3.62 (3.46)	3.38 (3.34)

challenging activities were forecasting supply patterns (4.20), implementing and/or adapting sales and operations planning cycles (4.02), and forecasting demand patterns (3.98). During the fall/winter time frame (second lockdown in Europe during November 2020 to January 2021), forecasting supply patterns still seems to be considered most challenging. The second most challenging activity is developing products and driving innovation. Developing supplier portfolios is considered the third most challenging mitigation activity. Overall, there is some indication for a trend that the named activities are considered less challenging in the fall/winter time frame (3.71) than in the spring time frame (3.27). Table 17.1 shows the results (calculated averages) of the (first) and second round of the Delphi Study.

17.6 Impact of Supply Chain Capabilities During Different Crisis Situations

Research question 2 aims to investigate how visibility, agility, flexibility, and collaboration capabilities are ranked in terms of relevance in different crisis situations (financial crisis, COVID-19, and the future)? For more detailed background information about supply chain capabilities, please refer to Chap. 1. For the purpose of this study, the following descriptions of agility, flexibility, visibility, and collaboration were used to provide a general understanding for the participants.

- *Agility* describes the ability on a strategic level to respond to unpredictable (and sometimes erratic) changes or disruptions in the supply chain in a quick, smooth, and cost-efficient manner. It is the ability to transform a turbulent business environment into a business opportunity on a strategic level.

- *Flexibility* is the ability of a supply chain to quickly adjust to changing requirements of partners and external factors. It allows relocating resources or changing processes when needed.
- *Visibility* describes the capability of having a transparent view of the supply chain structure and processes both upstream and downstream. It allows detecting variations from plans in a timely manner and reacting effectively and appropriately to these variations.
- *Collaboration* describes the ability of different entities to work on a common goal when planning and executing their operations to obtain a mutual benefit. Information sharing and synchronized decisions are essential for collaboration.

Three different periods are compared, in order to understand the development of the concept over time. The financial crisis in 2008 is considered to be mostly a demand crisis (Jüttner & Maklan, 2011), whereas the ongoing COVID-19 pandemic shows combinations of supply, demand, and infrastructure disruptions (Ivanov, 2020). The third aspect is linked to the future assessment of supply chain capabilities (Hausman & Ruud, 1987). The question is formulated in terms of ranking the different items.

Table 17.2 shows the results of the ranking question in the Delphi questionnaire. The results are the outcome of the first round with 44 answers. We consider this result more meaningful than the second round with only twelve responses. The results do not give a clear (statistical) indication of a (aligned) perception, as due to the low number of answers and high deviation. Using the weighted average of the answers from the first round, visibility and agility ranked highest with respect to their relevance for supply chain resilience in the three different time frames.

In summary, it can be observed that the participants ($N = 44$) of the study rank the defined supply chain capabilities in the order of visibility, flexibility, agility, and collaboration for the financial crisis in 2008. For the global ongoing COVID-19 crisis, the ranking is as follows: agility, visibility, flexibility, and collaboration. For future situations, the ranking is assed similarly in the following order: agility, visibility, collaboration, and flexibility. It is interesting to see that visibility is considered highly important in all 3 periods. Moreover, agility seems to increase in attention for the COVID-19 pandemic and the future. Additional research could investigate more details with respect to these observations.

Table 17.2 Results ranking of supply chain capabilities

Financial crisis	COVID-19	Future
1. Visibility	1. Agility	1. Agility
2. Flexibility	2. Visibility	2. Visibility
3. Agility	3. Flexibility	3. Collaboration
4. Collaboration	4. Collaboration	4. Flexibility

17.7 Best Practices for Supply Chain Resilience

To answer the third research question, in the first round of the Delphi questionnaire, the open question "Please share your best practices that you applied during the COVID-19 crisis in order to sustain supply chain resilience. You maybe want to link it to one of the four capabilities: agility, flexibility, visibility or collaboration. Please describe the outset situation, the solution and if possible the result. (approx. 5 sentences)" was formulated in order to get information for research question 3. More than 40 best practices were described. The input was synthesized by using NVivo software and consolidated in four iteration steps.

Figure 17.1 visualizes the words used in the best practices in a word cloud. Verbs that stand out are establish, identify, consider, find, and set. Supply chain functions are mentioned, such as planning, transport, supply, and production. Speed, time, processes, scenario, and needs are terms with high occurrence.

The following section covers the synthesized best practices allocated to the four supply chain capabilities: visibility, flexibility, agility, and collaboration. In addition, a section for people and skills encompasses respective cross-functional capabilities.

Agility

- Shorten supply chain by sourcing closer to production/market or reducing tiers of the supply chain
- Improve strategic supply chain steering (and understand the levers)
- Consider a circular/closed-loop supply chain perspective
- Create strategic distribution hubs per transport mode (e.g., air-shipments)
- Understand the speed of the supply chain network, where can it be accelerated or slowed down, and consider it for scenario planning
- Identify and mobilize new suppliers
- Establish multiple sourcing for critical parts
- Establish in-house production for critical parts
- Set up safety stocks for critical parts
- Apply agile IT system development to quickly adapt to needs (e.g., interfaces)

Flexibility

- Build capabilities to identify disruptions and their implications
- Build contingency plans for identified bottlenecks and critical elements
- Replace expected value-based planning with scenario planning
- Adjust planning horizons and switch between scenarios/plans
- Find alternative products to produce (e.g., hand sanitizers, PPE) to support the community and use your capacity
- Implement 3D printing in supply chains
- Use virtualized services
- Reserve transport capacities
- Consider multi- and intermodal transport

Fig. 17.1 Word cloud of best practices

Visibility

- Proactively map your supply chain including critical nodes, bottleneck, and lead times to analyze risk exposure and impact of changes in demand/supply
- Develop early warning systems
- Simulate mitigation actions (e.g., nearshoring) to estimate costs for mitigation actions and propagation effects (bullwhip/ripple) for different time horizons
- Investigate speed/time for information sharing, decision-making, and realistic lead times for key parts/products (speed to recover of supplier/customer)
- Strategically invest in digital competences (human and hardware) to achieve real-time data availability (e.g., dashboards, shipment tracking)
- Implement real-time data exchange along the supply chain
- Use quantitative models such as system dynamics approaches or simulation methods to identify balancing and reinforcing processes, perform scenario analyses, assess variance and risk, and identify optimization potential

Collaboration

- Establish strategic partnerships with committed supply chain stakeholders
- Set up regular management cycles with most relevant customers/suppliers; establish trust, transparency of decision-making, and early information of partners
- Identify bottlenecks together with supply chain partners and jointly find solutions
- Collaborate among departments within your company to find new ways of working together when faced with shortages (e.g., people, products, etc.)

- Align purchasing, production, logistics, and sales for joint collaborative planning
- Practice effective and efficient communication flow/management (e.g., with control/command centers/towers), and share information openly
- Use common KPIs for all relevant stakeholders to understand and share
- Set up contractual agreements with suppliers and forwarders that include clarity for shortages and service agreements that are not met
- Understand the financial situation of critical supply chain partners and potentially adjust with advance payments/payment terms to account for disruption

People and Skills
- Focus on safety for your employees
- Be open for new ideas/changes
- Establish home-office regulations that support people and business needs
- Communicate steps in a clear manner to all impacted employees
- Be creative (without "respecting" standards and "normal" workflow)
- Take time to learn from experience
- Speed up decision-making processes
- See opportunities to adapt processes and digital needs that are made visible by disruptions, and act upon them

The outcome of this synthesis was the input for the second Delphi round. There, the panel was asked to evaluate the best practices regarding their impact on a five-point Likert scale. "Which impact do the following best practices have on the supply chain resilience of your organization? Likert scale 1 (no impact) to 5 (very high impact)."

In the area of supply chain agility, the following best practices were considered most impactful by the twelve respondents: shorten supply chain, apply agile IT system development, and understand the speed of the supply chain network.

For flexibility, evaluating the average of thirteen answers, the top three out of nine impactful best practices are: build capabilities to identify disruptions and their implications, build contingency plans, and consider multi- and intermodal transport.

On average, twelve experts considered the following three best practices for visibility as most impactful: proactively mapping the supply chain including critical nodes, bottlenecks, and lead times to analyze risk exposure and impact of changes in demand/supply, strategically investing into digital competences (human and hardware) to achieve real-time data availability (e.g., dashboards, shipment tracking), and implementing real-time data exchange along the supply chain.

For the collaboration dimension, twelve responses were collected. Five out of nine best practices get fairly similar average and median scores. The most impact seems to have establishing strategic partnerships with committed supply chain stakeholders. The next impactful activity seems to be linked to practicing effective and efficient communication flow; managing communication, for example, via control/command centers/towers; and sharing information openly. The next best practices seem to be seen equally impactful by the responding panelists: set up regular management cycles with most relevant customers/suppliers; establish trust, transparency of decision-making, and early information of partners; identify bottlenecks together with supply chain partners and jointly find solutions; and use common KPIs for all relevant stakeholders to understand and share.

The 'people and skills' dimension was added for best practices that could not be allocated to specific supply chain resilience capabilities and seem more cross-functional. Thirteen answers were received in this dimension. Based on the average impact assessment, four out of eight best practices can be highlighted: be open for new ideas and changes; see opportunities to adapt processes and digital needs that are made visible by disruptions and act upon them; communicate steps in a clear manner to all impacted employees; and take time to learn from experiences.

In summary, the study enables to synthesize a wide array of best practices for supply chain professionals for supply chain resilience. The low response rate in the second round does not allow for highly robust conclusions, yet it gives some indications on the most impactful best practices:

- Shorten supply chain and applying agile IT system development
- Build capabilities to identify disruptions and their implications
- Proactively map your supply chain to analyze risk exposure and impact of changes in demand/supply, and strategically invest in digital competences to achieve real-time data availability
- Establish strategic partnerships with committed supply chain stakeholders
- Be open for new ideas/changes

17.8 Research Opportunities

The last section of the Delphi questionnaire dealt with future research opportunities, linked to research question 4. The first round gathered input from the panel by asking the open question "Which topics do you consider most relevant (for companies or academia) to establish a resilient supply chain for the future?" More than 70 individual comments were submitted. This input was synthesized by coding different answers utilizing NVivo software.

The research opportunities for supply chain resilience according to the panel were the following:

- Supply chain resilience evaluation and measurement
- Interplay between resilience and supply chain sustainability (including circularity, closed-loop supply chains, and social sustainability)
- People's resilience capabilities to steer through multiple disruptions
- Relationship and collaboration management considering supply chain and company stakeholders
- Digital supply chain tools to assess and manage dynamic, relevant supply chain risks
- Supplier management for dynamic environments
- Glocalization, re-shoring and mass customization

- Contract design for supply chain partners to prepare for/react to disruptions
- Trade-offs between costs and benefits of mitigation actions (e.g., excess stock)
- Scalability of mitigation actions
- Measures to facilitate employee motivation and work-life-balance

The summarized research opportunities were used as input for the second Delphi round. There, the experts evaluated the research opportunities on a five-point Likert scale regarding the relevance for supply chain resilience.

Thirteen participants responded to the question. Based on the average rating of the answers, digital supply chain tools, glocalization, and interplay between resilience and supply chain sustainability are considered to be the most relevant research opportunities.

17.9 Summary of Study Results

The Delphi Study was conducted during the summer period of 2021, after approximately 18 months of the COVID-19 pandemic and its implications on supply chains. The target was to gain additional practical insights from supply chain professionals in the commercial and humanitarian sectors. The results from the first and second rounds of the Delphi Study summarize their experiences and assessments with regard to supply chain resilience and its implications on combatting supply chain disruptions and crisis situations. The outcome gives insights into the ongoing perception of the topic.

In summary, the most challenging activity during the first (spring 2020) and the second lockdown (winter 2020/2021) was forecasting supply patterns. The most impactful resilience capabilities in the financial crisis, during COVID-19, and potentially for the future are: visibility, agility and agility, respectively. Best practices for achieving supply chain resilience are plentiful. The five capabilities with the highest evaluation are shorten supply chain and apply agile IT system development; build capabilities to identify disruptions and their implications; proactively map your supply chain and invest in digital competences to achieve real-time data availability; establish strategic partnerships with committed supply chain stakeholders; and be open for new ideas and changes. One of the most relevant research opportunities to establish a resilient supply chain in the future could be digital supply chain tools to assess and manage dynamic, relevant supply chain risks.

The study sparks further interest in the topic of supply chain resilience and can be used for future research. For example, the questionnaire could be applied in a different settings to gather additional insights from the field. The relevance of the synthesized best practices could be further tested in an empirical setting.

17.10 Limitations

The Delphi method is subject to various points of criticism (Hasson et al., 2000). The main question evolves around the controversy, whether the study can be repeated with the same outcome. The reliability, validity, and objectivity of the research method have to be observed and formalized by the researcher. A "[. . .] clear decision trail that defends the appropriateness of the method to address the problem selected, choice of expert panel, data collection procedures, identification of justifiable consensus levels and means of dissemination and implementation [. . .]" (Powell, 2003, p. 380) is the basis for a solid scientific outcome of the Delphi method. Compared to other interactive group and qualitative interactive procedures, the Delphi method is facing the same challenges (Rowe & Wright, 1999). The advantage is the geographic independence of the attendees.

The Delphi method, as a group facilitated survey approach to reach consensus, is based on the assumption that a group of experts achieves a more solid answer to a problem than an individual. In expert rounds, it can be observed that after 12–15 iterations with various people, the answers tend to repeat themselves (Guest et al., 2006). Whereas consensus is the target, it bears the question on risk of conformity over consensus (Rowe & Wright, 1999). Clarity on the framework and how the findings are to be judged together with the fit of the method to the research question are the baseline. Careful selection of the panelist/experts with clearly defined qualification criteria is essential. In summary, documenting the elements of the survey design and layout for the readers is essential.

For this specific Delphi Study to better understand supply chain resilience amid the COVID-19 pandemic, the methodological limitations apply. Due to the large number of invitations (approximately 3000 people initially invited), a sample selection bias can be limited. However, the responding panelists could have been self-selecting due to closeness to the study researcher group. Due to the limited number of responses over both rounds (44 in the first round and 13 in the second round), neither stability of results nor a solid trend toward consensus of the topic could be observed. The study authors would like to emphasize the low response rate and no statistical significance. The results can provide food for thought and indicative insights for ongoing perceptions of supply chain resilience amid the COVID-19 pandemic.

References

ACAPS. (2020, June 10). *COVID-19 impact on humanitarian operations*. Retrieved February 8, 2021, from https://www.acaps.org/special-report/covid-19-impact-humanitarian-operations

Aengenheyster, S., Cuhls, K., Gerhold, L., Heiskanen-Schüttler, M., Huck, J., & Muszynska, M. (2017). Real-time Delphi in practice—A comparative analysis of existing software-based tools. *Technological Forecasting and Social Change, 118*, 15–27. https://doi.org/10.1016/j.techfore.2017.01.023

Alicke, K., Gupta, R., & Trautwein, V. (2020). *Resetting supply chains for the next normal.* Retrieved February 8, 2021, from https://www.researchgate.net/publication/347437401_Resetting_supply_chains_for_the_next_normal/link/5fdb707645851553a0c47cba/download

Balleer, A., Link, S., Menkhoff, M., & Zorn, P. (2020). *Demand versus supply: Price adjustment during the Covid-19 pandemic | VOX, CEPR Policy Portal.* Retrieved February 8, 2021, from https://voxeu.org/article/demand-versus-supply-price-adjustment-during-covid-19-pandemic

Brusset, X., & Teller, C. (2017). Supply chain capabilities, risks, and resilience. *International Journal of Production Economics, 184*, 59–68. https://doi.org/10.1016/j.ijpe.2016.09.008

Chopra, S., & Sodhi, M. S. (2004). Supply-chain breakdown. *MIT Sloan Management Review, 46*(1), 53–61.

Christopher, M., & Peck, H. (2004). Building the resilient supply chain. *International Journal of Logistics Management, 15*(2), 1–14. https://doi.org/10.1108/09574090410700275

Dalkey, N., & Helmer, O. (1963). An experimental application of the DELPHI method to the use of experts. *Management Science, 9*(3), 458–467. https://doi.org/10.1287/mnsc.9.3.458

Guest, G., Bunce, A., & Johnson, L. (2006). How many interviews are enough? *Field Methods, 18*(1), 59–82. https://doi.org/10.1177/1525822X05279903

Hasson, F., Kenney, S., & McKenna, H. (2000). Research guidelines for the Delphi survey technique. *Journal of Advanced Nursing, 32*(4), 1008. https://doi.org/10.1046/j.1365-2648.2000.01567.x

Hausman, J. A., & Ruud, P. A. (1987). Specifying and testing econometric models for rank-ordered data. *Journal of Econometrics, 34*(1–2), 83–104. https://doi.org/10.1016/0304-4076(87)90068-6

Ivanov, D. (2020). Predicting the impacts of epidemic outbreaks on global supply chains: A simulation-based analysis on the coronavirus outbreak (COVID-19/SARS-CoV-2) case. *Transportation Research. Part E, Logistics and Transportation Review, 136*, 101922. https://doi.org/10.1016/j.tre.2020.101922

Joshi, A., Kale, S., Chandel, S., & Pal, D. (2015). *Likert scale: Explored and explained. BJAST, 7* (4), 396–403. https://doi.org/10.9734/BJAST/2015/14975

Jüttner, U., & Maklan, S. (2011). Supply chain resilience in the global financial crisis: An empirical study. *Supply Chain Management, 16*(4), 246–259. https://doi.org/10.1108/13598541111139062

Metodix Ltd. (2021). *eDelphi*. Retrieved October 26, 2021, from https://www.edelphi.org/

National Research Council. (2012). *Disaster Resilience: A National Imperative*. The National Academies Press. https://doi.org/10.17226/13457

Okoli, C., & Pawlowski, S. D. (2004). The Delphi method as a research tool: An example, design considerations and applications. *Information & Management, 42*(1), 15–29. https://doi.org/10.1016/j.im.2003.11.002

Pettit, T. J., Fiksel, J., & Croxton, K. L. (2010). Ensuring supply chain resilience: Development of a conceptual framework. *Journal of Business Logistics, 31*(1), 1–21. https://doi.org/10.1002/j.2158-1592.2010.tb00125.x

Powell, C. (2003). The Delphi technique: Myths and realities. *Journal of Advanced Nursing, 41*(4), 376–382. https://doi.org/10.1046/j.1365-2648.2003.02537.x

ReliefWeb. (2021). *International Activity Report 2020 - World*. Retrieved February 8, 2021, from https://reliefweb.int/report/world/international-activity-report-2020

Rowe, G., & Wright, G. (1999). The Delphi technique as a forecasting tool: Issues and analysis. *International Journal of Forecasting, 15*(4), 353–375. https://doi.org/10.1016/S0169-2070(99)00018-7

Schmidt, R. C. (1997). Managing Delphi surveys using nonparametric statistical techniques. *Decision Sciences, 28*(3), 763–774. https://doi.org/10.1111/j.1540-5915.1997.tb01330.x

Supply Chain Council. (2010). *Supply chain operations reference model*. Version 10.0. The Supply Chain Council, Inc. SCOR: The Supply Chain Reference ISBN 0-615-20259-4 (binder)

WIFO. (2021). *Beeinträchtigungen der Geschäftstätigkeit, Liquidität und staatliche Hilfen in der zweiten COVID-19-Welle. Ergebnisse der fünften Sonderbefragung zur COVID-19-Krise im Rahmen des WIFO-Konjunkturtests vom Februar 2021 - WIFO*. Retrieved August 18, 2021, from https://www.wifo.ac.at/jart/prj3/wifo/main.jart?rel=de&reserve-mode=active&content-id=1528640199418&publikation_id=66980&detail-view=yes

Lydia Novoszel is Research Associate at the Institute for Transport and Logistics Management at the WU (Vienna University of Economics and Business). With an international professional career in supply chain management, she incorporates practical relevance and perspectives in supply chain disruption research. Lydia has earned a master's degree in Mechanical Engineering and a master's degree in Business Administration.

Alexander M. Geske is Research Associate at the Institute for Transport and Logistics Management at the WU (Vienna University of Economics and Business). He has earned a bachelor's degree in International Business Administration and a master's degree in Supply Chain Management. With a professional career in the transportation industry, Alexander combines the practical and academic perspective.

Sebastian Kummer is the Head of the Institute for Transport and Logistics Management at the WU (Vienna University of Economics and Business) as well as an Endowed Chair Professor at the Jilin University in Changchun, China. Previously he was Professor at the TU Dresden and worked at the WHU, Vallendar, where he received his Ph.D. Prof. Kummer is responsible for program development and teaching in the fields of transportation, logistics, and supply chain management. He carries out numerous successful research and practice projects for industrial and commercial companies and for transport and logistics service providers. He supports numerous transport and logistic tenders. His publication list includes more than 180 publications, including leading textbooks.

Tina Wakolbinger Ph.D., is Professor for Supply Chain Services and Networks. She serves as Head of the Research Institute for Supply Chain Management and Deputy Head of the Institute for Transport and Logistics Management at the WU (Vienna University of Economics and Business). Her research interests lie in the modeling and analysis of complex decision-making on network systems with a focus on global issues. She serves in editorial positions in Production and Operations Management and Central European Journal of Operations Research. Her work on supply chain management and humanitarian logistics is published in renown journals.

Part V
Supply Chain Resilience in Different Functional Areas

Chapter 18
Commodity Price Risks: Strategies to Increase Supply Chain Resilience

Matthias Zillner

Abstract The uncertainty of the future development of commodity prices is one of the main risk sources in manufacturing. Although these so-called commodity price risks are mentioned frequently in general supply chain risk research, there is very little research that focuses on them. This article is about the mitigation of these risks. It provides, based on the current research state, a comprehensive overview of strategies to increase supply chain resilience to commodity price risks. They range from well-known measures, like warehousing, forward contracting, and financial hedging, to some less frequently described, like contract diversification, price formulas, and recycling. In total 17 strategies, from the departments of procurement and finance, but also from production and sales side, were found and are described and compared to each other in this article. Thus, managing commodity price risks efficiently seems to be a cross-functional task that requires in-depth knowledge and information from all across the supply chain.

18.1 Introduction

This article focuses on one of the oldest and at the same time largest threats in a business context: the uncertainty of commodity prices. After a short introduction, this article provides an overview of strategies to increase supply chain resilience to the so-called commodity price risks. These strategies range from well-known measures, like warehousing and financial hedging, to some less frequently described, like contract diversification and recycling. This chapter is based on the dissertation by Zillner (2020). Already in the first markets, emerging in ancient Mesopotamia, participants were exposed to fluctuating grain, goat, and copper prices (Poitras, 2013; Polanyi, 1968; Weber, 2008). Now, 6000 years later, commodity prices are still anything but stable, and thus almost every business around the world, from farmers to grocery stores to metal miners to airlines, is affected. The origin and

M. Zillner (✉)
Merit Commodity Management GmbH, Merit Group, Vienna, Austria
e-mail: matthias.zillner@meritgroup.at

S. Kummer et al. (eds.), *Supply Chain Resilience*, Springer Series in Supply Chain Management 17, https://doi.org/10.1007/978-3-030-95401-7_18

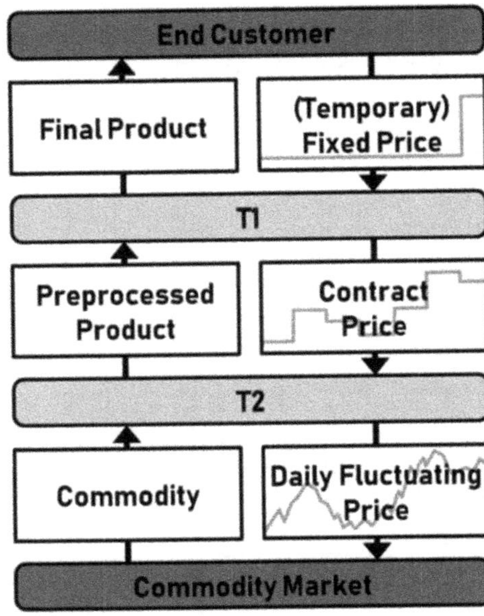

Fig. 18.1 Commodity price risks in a supply chain. Note: Two companies (T1 and T2) transform a commodity into a final product. As prices on commodity markets fluctuate daily and end customer pricing is usually fixed for a certain period of time, the companies have a price risk

distribution of the so-called commodity price risks (or "risks due to changes in raw material prices") in a supply chain are illustrated in Fig. 18.1.

The aim of a supply chain is to generate value by producing demanded products from commodities. If the final end customer pays a price for the product that is fixed for a certain period of time, then the supply chain necessarily has a "commodity price risk": This means that at least one of the participants in the supply chain has to absorb the fluctuations of the commodity prices, till the end customer's price (maybe) can be adapted (Gaudenzi et al., 2018; Kouvelis et al., 2018; Moser et al., 2017). Or in other words, the supply chain's (economic) success depends on the commodity price development. How the risk is distributed between the supply chain members depends on the contracts between them (Babich & Kouvelis, 2018; Zhang et al., 2014).

Other risks relating to the raw material, such as quality, quantity, or transportation risks, are not addressed in this article.

18.2 Research State

The importance of commodity price risks for supply chains is mainly because of their potential for very large financial damage, well known in both academia and practice: For example, in the "2016 BDO Manufacturing Risk Factor Report," commodity price risks are ranked as the third most important risks out of 25 (BDO USA LLP, 2016). In a survey in the German-speaking manufacturing industry, the 96 participants rated the importance of commodity price risks on average as 6.7 on a scale from 1 (unimportant) to 10 (very important) (KPMG International, 2007). Also, 90% of small and mid-sized US manufacturers interviewed report raw material cost uncertainty as their top concern (Manikas & Kroes, 2016). As mentioned above, the importance of commodity price risks, among other things due the anticipation of rising prices as well as rising volatilities, is also described by academic researchers like Buhl et al. (2011), Hofmann (2011), and Xiaofeng et al. (2017).

Given this high importance and awareness, it is remarkable that current investigations, e.g., by Babich and Kouvelis (2018), Fischl et al. (2014), and Gaudenzi et al. (2018), conclude that the topic of commodity price risks is underexplored: Although these risks are mentioned frequently in general supply chain research, there is very little research that focuses on them. The existing research regarding these risks can be described as procurement focused (Arnold et al., 2009; Liu & Yang, 2015; Manikas & Kroes, 2016) and/or financial hedging focused (Bandaly et al., 2014; Buhl et al., 2011; Turcic et al., 2014).

18.3 Strategies to Increase Supply Chain Resilience

This article focuses on strategies to reduce a supply chain's dependency on commodity price changes or, in other words, to increase resilience to commodity price risks. So, in the three-staged process of "supply chain risk management," this article is located in the last step of "risk mitigation," which follows the steps of "risk identification" and "risk assessment" (Kern et al., 2012; Manuj & Mentzer, 2008; Tummala & Schoenherr, 2011).

A typical supply chain (comprising one or more companies) that purchases commodities produces a product and sells it to end customers, suffers a loss if the prices of the required commodities rise (Boyabatli et al., 2011; Hong et al., 2018; Pellegrino et al., 2019). Consequently, both a high positive price "trend" and a high price "volatility" are negative for the supply chain: While a positive price trend can be considered as forecasted (or expected) loss, high volatility increases the uncertainty of the material costs and thus also the uncertainty of the supply chain's success.

Besides these two purely exogenous factors, several other "factors" from across the whole supply chain can be found that can influence its commodity price risk situation:

In column 2 of Table 18.1, in total ten "factors," i.e., characteristics, situations, features, decisions, or parameters that can either positively or negatively influence commodity price risks in supply chains, are collected.

Any measures that aim at changing these factors in a way to reduce a company's commodity price risk, i.e., "strategies" to increase resilience to commodity price risks (Fischl et al., 2014; Pellegrino et al., 2019; Zsidisin & Hartley, 2012), can be found in the last column of Table 18.1. Embedded in the categories from Table 18.1, these 17 strategies are described in detail below:

Table 18.1 Commodity price risks: factors that influence the risk and strategies to increase resilience

Category	Factor that influences commodity price risk	Additional information	Derivable strategies to increase supply chain resilience
Procurement	Supplier portfolio	Supplier number, type, reliability, and relationships	I. Supplier diversification
	Procurement mode	Mainly quantities and timing: Set by strategy, planning, flexibility, etc.	II. Purchase timing
	Supply contracts and their details	Contract type and important details: Price (formulas), volumes, contract duration, quality, etc.	III. Forward contracting IV. Escalator clause V. Window clause
Warehousing and production	Material efficiency	Amount of material required per product	VI. Innovation VII. Recycling
	Warehousing and throughput time	Stock levels and throughput times on all steps of the production process	VIII. Strategic stocks
	Production flexibility	In terms of flexibility regarding, e.g., timing, capacity, input	IX. Vertical integration X. Commodity substitution
Sales	Product assortment	Influenced by setup, strategies, seasonality, etc.	XI. Product diversification
	Customer price sensitivity	Limits the possibility to pass material price increases to customers	XII. Strengthen customer relations XIII. Strengthen brand value
	Sales contracts and their details	Type and important details: Price (formulas), product specifications, volumes, contract duration, etc.	XIV. Price formulas XV. Pass through clauses XVI. Contract diversification
Financial market positions	Market positions and their details	Size and type (futures, options) of financial instruments held	XVII. Financial hedging

Sources: Aggarwal and Ganeshan (2007), Assefa et al. (2017), Arnold et al. (2009), Boyabatli et al. (2011), Chopra and Sodhi (2004), Dong and Liu (2007), Finley and Pettit (2011), Fisch and Ross (2013), Fischl et al. (2014), Fu et al. (2012), Gaudenzi et al. (2018), Hardt (2011), Hofmann (2011), Hong et al. (2018), Johnson et al. (2011), Kinlan and Roukema (2011), Kouvelis et al. (2013, 2018), Krishnamurthi and Raj (1991), Lapko et al. (2016), Li et al. (2009), Mahapatra et al. (2017), Manikas and Kroes (2016), Merzifonluoglu (2015), Pellegrino et al. (2019), Poitras (2013), Ni et al. (2012), Reiner et al. (2014), Xiaofeng et al. (2017), Zhang et al. (2014), and Zsidisin and Hartley (2012)

18.3.1 Category 1: Procurement

The influence of the quantities, the pricing, and the timing of raw material purchases on a supply chain's commodity price risk is evident. Therefore, it is not surprising that research regarding this risk is procurement focused (see paragraph 18.2).

18.3.1.1 Supplier Portfolio

The first factor from the procurement side that influences the commodity price risk is the "supplier portfolio": On the one hand, a low number of suppliers increases the order quantities at each of them and thus may lead to lower overall spending due to volume discounts ("economies of scales"), strong relationships, and stable quality (Chopra & Sodhi, 2004; Li et al., 2009; Mahapatra et al., 2017). On the other hand, a higher number of different suppliers reduces supply uncertainty and the dependency on single companies and can help to strengthen the (price) negotiation position (Dong & Liu, 2007: Finley & Pettit, 2011; Wiedenmann & Geldermann, 2015).

The directly derivable strategy to increase supply chain resilience to commodity price changes is called "I. Supplier Diversification "or "supplier switching": It aims at building up a portfolio of multiple suppliers to enable price comparison and to choose the best priced option whenever material is needed (Chopra & Sodhi, 2004; Gaudenzi et al., 2018; Hardt, 2011, pp. 290–291; Hong et al., 2018; Pellegrino et al., 2019).

18.3.1.2 Procurement Mode

The "procurement mode" or "ordering policy" determines the procurement quantities, sequences, batch sizes, and timing (Arnold et al., 2009; Kouvelis et al., 2013; Li et al., 2017). As commodity prices are constantly changing, it can play a very important role "when" and "what amount" of material is purchased. Especially with infrequent but large purchases, this is crucial: Single purchases can randomly happen at very high (or very low) prices, and thus the variance of the purchasing costs is smaller with many smaller orders, where random effects are balanced out faster.

Obviously, buying the material when prices are "low" (forward buying) and waiting when they are "high" (postponement) would be the optimal purchasing strategy (Gaudenzi et al., 2018; Hong et al., 2018; Inderfurth et al., 2018; Li & Kouvelis, 1999). Such active "II. Purchase Timing" requires not only a flexible procurement department to react to price changes but also a flexible warehousing and/or production system to absorb the resulting supply fluctuations (Boyabatli et al., 2017; Fischl et al., 2014; Lapko et al., 2016; Liu & Yang, 2015; Zhang et al., 2014). It must be noted that whether this strategy (frequently described in the literature) can work at all is highly controversial: It requires a prediction of the commodity price to make a differentiation between "low" and "high" that is also meaningful for the future (Li et al., 2017; Manikas & Kroes, 2016; Zsidisin & Hartley, 2012, pp. 9–54), and according to the so-called efficient market hypothesis, such a prediction of market prices is impossible (Dimson & Mussavian, 1998; Hillebrand, 2003, pp. 32–37; Malkiel, 2003).

18.3.1.3 Supply Contracts and Their Details

A manufacturer can short-term purchase commodities on "commodity markets" (or "spot markets") at the current market price ("spot price") (Chen et al., 2013; Fu et al., 2012; Mahapatra et al., 2017). This has the advantage of independence from specific suppliers, full volume flexibility, high liquidity, and full price transparency (Dong & Liu, 2007; Li et al., 2009; Merzifonluoglu, 2015; Xu et al., 2015). On the other hand, to increase planning security for both a manufacturing company and its supplier(s) and to strengthen their relationship, long-term "supply contracts" can be signed (Aggarwal & Ganeshan, 2007; Chopra & Sodhi, 2004; Kouvelis et al., 2018; Reiner et al., 2014). They determine (and guarantee) details like delivery mode or batch size; main parameters like volume, contract duration, and material quality; and also the most important parameter: the price.

Also in long-term supply contracts, the contractual partners can agree on the "spot price" (taken from a reference price source such as "London Metal Exchange" or "Independent Chemical Information Service") for the material (Boyabatli et al., 2017; Li & Kouvelis, 1999; Zhang et al., 2014). As commodity prices change daily, this is the option with the highest uncertainty and fluctuations of the purchasing costs (Aggarwal & Ganeshan, 2007; Inderfurth et al., 2018; Xu et al., 2015).

So, to improve the predictability of the costs, it can be beneficial for the manufacturer to fix the price for a certain period of time: One way to do so is to sign a "III. Forward Contract" with its supplier, which enables to secure a fixed price for a purchase of a defined volume, for example, 1 month ahead. This strategy both "smoothens" the price fluctuations and increases planning security for the company (Aggarwal & Ganeshan, 2007; Merzifonluoglu, 2015; Zhang et al., 2014).

Another often suggested option to improve supply chain resilience against price changes is the so-called "IV. Escalator Clause": Instead of fixing the price for a certain period of time, they fix the price in a specified range. So, the commodity price is in general fixed for the contract's period but gets automatically adapted if the market price exceeds a specific level ("threshold") (Gaudenzi et al., 2018; Johnson et al., 2011, pp. 274–275; Pellegrino et al., 2019; Wiedenmann & Geldermann, 2015; Zsidisin & Hartley, 2012, pp. 76–81). The opposite is the so-called "V. Window Clause": Here the price is in general equal to the current spot market price but has an upper and lower fixed limit for the contract duration (Boyabatli et al., 2011; Finley & Pettit, 2011; Li & Kouvelis, 1999; Singh et al., 2016).

18.3.2 Category 2: Warehousing and Production

Although the literature strongly focuses on the procurement side, there are also operational strategies from "warehousing and production" that can help to decrease a supply chain's commodity price risk:

18.3.2.1 Material Efficiency

First of all, the production process determines what type and what amount of raw material the procurement department has to purchase. So, the whole production process and especially all factors that affect its "material efficiency" and thus the amount of raw material required, like the production technology, the product design, or the amount of waste (e.g., process related or due to quality problems), can influence the commodity price risk (Assefa et al., 2017; Fischl et al., 2014; Lapko et al., 2016; Zsidisin & Hartley, 2012).

From this strongly influencing factor "material efficiency," the two strategies "VI. Recycling" and "VII. Innovation" can be derived: Collecting the waste of the production process, like excess material and chips but also defective products, and reusing it can increase a supply chain's material efficiency and so decrease its dependence on commodity prices to some extent (Fischl et al., 2014; Hardt, 2011, pp. 272–274; Lapko et al., 2016). In addition, the material efficiency of a supply chain can be increased by "innovations," like new machines, a new production method, or a new product design (Assefa et al., 2017; Gaudenzi et al., 2018; Lapko et al., 2016; Zsidisin & Hartley, 2012, pp. 87–88).

18.3.2.2 Warehousing and Throughput Time

Another very important factor is "warehousing and throughput time" (Chen et al., 2013; Kouvelis et al., 2013; Liu & Yang, 2015). Commodity stocks can be seen as a manufacturing company's assets, which fluctuate in value if market prices change. So, a company that has high stock levels profits from rising commodity prices (because inventory value increases) and on the other hand records a loss if the prices drop (Assefa et al., 2017; Moser et al., 2017; Reiner et al., 2014). In addition to this speculative character, high stock levels give the opportunity to react to price fluctuations and so to "buffer" them (Boyabatli et al., 2017; Hardt, 2011, pp. 280–282; Zsidisin & Hartley, 2012, pp. 66–67). This is true for warehousing in all production steps and also for material that is currently "in production" or "in transit" (Boyabatli et al., 2017; Inderfurth et al., 2018; Wu & Olson, 2010). However, especially if demand of different products is to be met continuously, high stock levels of raw material and/or semi-finished goods (which can be processed into different products) are to be preferred over warehousing of finished products (Chopra & Sodhi, 2004).

The resilience-increasing strategy of maintaining higher stock levels on a permanent basis can be called "VIII. Strategic Stocks": As described above, since inventory values increase if material prices increase, this strategy is especially suitable for manufactures that suffer (e.g., due to their contracting situation) from rising prices, to offset their risk (Bandaly et al., 2014; Chopra & Sodhi, 2004; Finley & Pettit, 2011; Kouvelis et al., 2013).

18.3.2.3 Production Flexibility

The third factor from "warehousing and production" that can be identified is "production flexibility": Similar to stock keeping, also higher flexibility regarding the required materials and regarding the capacity and timing of the production process can help to adequately react to commodity price changes (Fischl et al., 2014; Pellegrino et al., 2019; Zsidisin & Hartley, 2012, pp. 71–82).

The resilience-increasing strategy that can be derived from "production flexibility" is the possibility of "IX. Commodity Substitution" (Fisch & Ross, 2013; Fischl et al., 2014; Gaudenzi et al., 2018; Hardt, 2011; pp. 278–280; Lapko et al., 2016; Li & Kouvelis, 1999; Zsidisin & Hartley, 2012, pp. 71–75). Pellegrino et al. (2019) have shown that a production process that can switch between different raw materials as input (e.g., if one increased in price) can significantly decrease the commodity price risk. Typical examples are switching between platinum and palladium for catalytic converters, replacing steel structures with aluminum, or switching between different plastics for packaging.

Another strategy that requires "flexibility" is "X. Vertical Integration": This strategy aims at reducing the dependency on commodity price changes by having the possibility of producing the material also in-house (Buhl et al., 2011; Gaudenzi et al., 2018; Hardt, 2011, pp. 293–295).

18.3.3 Category 3: Sales

As can be seen in Table 18.1, also the sales side influences the commodity price risk situation of a supply chain. Changing factors like the product assortment or the sales contracts can significantly decrease commodity price risks.

18.3.3.1 Product Assortment

The sales side in general and the "product assortment" in particular determine what and how many products are produced and sold: In general, the more units that have high and volatile material costs are sold, the higher the commodity price risk (Lapko et al., 2016; Manikas & Kroes, 2016; Moheb-Alizadeh & Handfield, 2018). In contrast, having a wide assortment of different products which require different (non-correlating) raw materials helps to lower the dependency on single commodity prices due to diversification (Andren et al., 2005; Dong & Liu, 2007; Mishra et al., 2004). This strategy can be called "XI. Product Diversification."

18.3.3.2 Customer Price Sensitivity

Furthermore, "price-sensitive customers," which do not accept product price increases, enhance a manufacturer's commodity price risk: If demand is price sensitive, which is typical for nonessential goods, the manufacturer can either absorb material price increases himself and thus lose margin or pass the increase on to the customers and thus lose demand (and revenue) (Fu et al., 2012; Gaudenzi et al., 2018; Liu & Yang, 2015; Manikas & Kroes, 2016). The price sensitivity of customers can be reduced by increasing brand loyalty due to characteristics like high customer service, a unique product, high quality, or high customer satisfaction levels, which all can be part of the strategies "XII. Strengthen Brand Value" and "XIII. Strengthen Customer Relations." Both strategies and their damping effects on price sensitivity are well examined in marketing literature (Erdem et al., 2002; Kaul & Wittink, 1995; Krishnamurthi & Raj, 1991).

18.3.3.3 Sales Contracts and Their Details

Equivalent to its "supply contracts," a company can conclude long-term "sales contracts" with its customers (which are the "supply contracts" for them) to increase planning security for both and to strengthen their relationship (Assefa et al., 2017; Hofmann, 2011; Kouvelis et al., 2018).

In contrast to the procurement side of a manufacturing supply chain, where standardized "commodities" with transparent and fluctuating market prices are purchased, the sales side deals with more processed, more unique products, where in general no daily updated market prices exist (Feng et al., 2013; Kouvelis et al., 2013; Noble & Gruca, 1999). So, while the standard price for a commodity is a daily changing "spot price" (see page 3), the standard price for a supply chain's final product is in many industries a "fixed price" that is valid for a certain period of time (e.g., the duration of a contract): This combination of fluctuating purchasing and fixed sales prices is the main reason for the commodity price risk of manufacturers (see paragraph 18.1). So, from a price risk point of view, short-term sales contracts, which enable more frequent price negotiations to pass on increased material costs to customers, are beneficial for a manufacturing company (Assefa et al., 2017; Singh et al., 2016).

To achieve both the positive effects on customer relationships of long-term contracts as well as increased resilience to commodity price risks, manufacturers can negotiate for "XIV. Price Formulas" in their long-term sales contracts: In addition to a "fixed part" (or "value added part"), such price formulas consist of a variable "material part," which links the price of the product to the price development of the commodities that are required to produce it (Hardt, 2011, pp. 268–270; Hofmann, 2011; Kouvelis et al., 2018; Lapko et al., 2016; Turcic et al., 2014; Zhang et al., 2014). So, the product's price is calculated by multiplying the commodity amount that is required to produce one product with the commodities market price from a specified reference time. This reference time can also be the commodity's spot price, e.g., on the day of delivery, but, to reflect production time, it is more often a past period of time, like the previous quarter's average price, the last month's closing price, last December's price, etc. (Assefa et al., 2017; Johnson et al., 2011, pp. 273–275; Zsidisin & Hartley, 2012, pp. 76–81).

The extreme case of a price formula is a "XV. Pass Through" clause, which allows a manufacturing company to directly charge its customers its actual material costs and thus completely eliminates its price risk (Assefa et al., 2017; Kouvelis et al., 2018; Zsidisin & Hartley, 2012). Whether such strategies are possible mainly depends on the specific industry standards as well as the relationship and the "power" of the negotiating partners (Dong & Liu, 2007; Johnson et al., 2011, pp. 273–276; Moser et al., 2017; Zhang et al., 2014).

Also, "XVI. Contract Diversification" is a strategy to reduce a manufacturer's price risk: Having multiple long-term sales contracts with different price agreements can help to smoothen the variance of sales prices and thus dampen the dependence on price changes (Assefa et al., 2017; Feng et al., 2013; Kannegiesser et al., 2009).

18.3.4 Category 4: Financial Market Positions

The last category of "factors" which influence the commodity price risk situation is any "open positions" of the company on the financial market. Manufacturing companies almost exclusively purchase financial instruments for one reason: for the most described and explored strategy (e.g., by Bandaly et al. (2014), Dong and Liu (2007), Kouvelis et al. (2013), and Turcic et al. (2014)) to increase resilience to commodity price risks, the so-called "XVII. Financial Hedging". A hedge is in general an investment position that offsets another position. For a typical manufacturing company, which makes a loss if specific commodity prices rise, buying a financial instrument that profits from rising prices of that commodity would be a financial hedge that mitigates the company's dependence on changes in the commodity's price because losses in the core business would be offset with gains from financial markets and vice-versa (Finley & Pettit, 2011; Gaudenzi et al., 2018; Hofmann, 2011; Wiedenmann & Geldermann, 2015).

Financial instruments that enable such a compensation and that were initially developed exactly for this purpose are the so-called futures contracts: Their value linearly increases and decreases parallel to the commodity price development and thus eliminates the price risk but also eliminates possible benefits of "positive price developments" (Bandaly et al., 2014; Buhl et al., 2011; Kouvelis et al., 2013; Turcic et al., 2014).

Another financial instrument which is offered on futures exchanges is a so-called options contract or option: It gives the "right," but not the obligation, to purchase or sell an asset at an agreed price sometime in the future (Gardner, 1977; Poitras, 2013, pp. 158–160; Wolf, 1987). So, while increasing resilience against "negative price developments" (from the manufacturer's point of view usually commodity price increases), option holders still benefit from positive ones. The value of this "asymmetric return" has to be compensated with an "option price," which has to be paid at the time of conclusion of the contract (Chan et al., 2019, pp. 67–85; Kouvelis et al., 2013; Schofield, 2011).

The main disadvantage of financial hedging is that it requires specialized financial expertise, and the main benefit is that it neither influences operational processes nor supply chain partners (Adam-Müller & Panaretou, 2009; Pellegrino et al., 2019; Zsidisin & Hartley, 2012, pp. 82–86).

18.4 Classification of the Strategies

Many of the strategies presented in Table 18.1 can be categorized into two general approaches to increase supply chain resilience: "Diversification" and "flexibility" (Chopra & Sodhi 2004; Pettit et al., 2013; Sheffi & Rice, 2005; Talluri et al., 2013). The variance-reducing effect of diversification can, for example, be applied to the supplier portfolio ("I. Supplier Diversification"), to the types of the sales contracts ("XVI. Contract Diversification"), or to the purchased materials due to the product assortment ("XI. Product Diversification"). "Flexibility" on the other hand can help to reduce the risk by having "real options" if a material increases in price: Such options are to substitute it for another material ("IX. Commodity Substitution"), to purchase it from another supplier ("I. Supplier Diversification"), to produce it in-house ("X. Vertical Integration"), or to recycle it ("VI. Recycling").

Also, the approach of "securing" the current commodity price for a certain time in the future can be implemented with different strategies: Physical buying and warehousing the required amount of material ("VIII. Strategic Stocks"), signing a supply contract over a fixed price for later delivery of the material ("III. Forward Contracting"), and purchasing suitable future contracts of the same size ("XVII. Financial Hedging") all generate this effect (Kouvelis et al., 2013; Manikas & Kroes, 2016; Zhang et al., 2014).

All strategies from Table 18.1 have one characteristic in common: They all cause costs. For example, securing the current material price by physical stock keeping ("VIII. Strategic Stocks") causes storage costs, and securing it by a "III. Forward Contract" with a supplier will most likely only be possible if a premium is paid. Preserving different options in parallel to stay flexible (like "IX. Commodity Substitution" or "XVII. Financial Hedging" with options) obviously causes costs too (a so-called option premium). Also, strategies that increase diversification, like "I. Supplier Diversification" or "XVI. Contract Diversification," come at a price: They reduce economies of scales (for details, see page 2).

This trade-off between risk and cost, or in other words between resilience and profit maximization, is by no means a special characteristic of managing commodity price risks: It is the main challenge of any supply chain risk management approach (Aven, 2016; Chopra & Sodhi, 2004; Jüttner et al., 2003; Talluri et al., 2013).

18.5 Conclusion

The uncertainty of the future development of commodity prices is one of the main risk sources in manufacturing. Mainly due to their potential for very large financial damage, they are well known in both academia and practice. Therefore, it is astonishing that they are still underexplored in supply chain risk research.

This article provides an overview of "strategies" to increase supply chain's resilience to commodity price risks. They range from very specific measures like financial hedging or price formulas in sales contracts, which mainly influence the price risk situation, to more general measures like material efficiency or product diversification, which can change the whole supply chain's setup.

Managing commodity price risks with strategies from the two categories "procurement" and "finance" (for details, see Table 18.1) is mentioned frequently in supply chain literature. So, it is remarkable that only 6 of the 17 strategies found in this article originate in these areas, while the majority (11) comes from "warehousing and production" and "sales."

Thus, managing commodity price risks seems to be a cross-functional or even cross-organizational task that requires on the one hand very specific knowledge but on the other hand also broad information from a wide range of fields (Assefa et al., 2017; Finley & Pettit, 2011; Gaudenzi et al., 2018; Kouvelis et al., 2013; Zsidisin & Hartley, 2012, p. 55). This cross-functional character is also backed up by practice, where multiple different strategies are combined to increase resilience to commodity price risks: In a survey from Gaudenzi et al. (2018), 12 out of 12 "commodity managers" and "value chain risk managers" from different manufacturing industries around the globe stated to actively manage the operational setup in order to manage commodity price risks. At the same, 11 of them use contracting strategies, and 8 use financial hedging. Also, another survey in the German-speaking manufacturing industry concludes that at least 58% of the investigated companies time their purchasing, 59% use price clauses, and 48% use financial hedging (Debus et al., 2014).

References

Adam-Müller, A., & Panaretou, A. (2009). Risk management with option and futures under liquidity risk. *The Journal of Future Markets, 29*(4), 297–318.

Aggarwal, P., & Ganeshan, R. (2007). Using risk-management tools on B2Bs: An exploratory investigation. *International Journal Production Economics, 108*, 2–7.

Andren, N., Jankensgård, H., & Oxelheim, L. (2005). Exposure-based cash-flow-at-risk: An alternative to VaR for industrial companies. *Journal of Applied Corporate Finance, 17*(3), 76–86.

Arnold, J., Minner, S., & Eidam, B. (2009). Raw material procurement with fluctuating prices. *International Journal of Production Economics, 121*, 353–364.

Assefa, T., Meuwissen, M., & Lansink, A. (2017). Price risk perceptions and management strategies in selected European food supply chains: An exploratory approach. *NJAS - Wageningen Journal of Life Sciences, 80*, 15–26.

Aven, T. (2016). Risk assessment and risk management: Review of recent advances on their foundation. *European Journal of Operational Research, 253*, 1–13.

Babich, V., & Kouvelis, P. (2018). Introduction to the special issue on research at the Interface of finance, operations, and risk management (iFORM): Recent contributions and future directions. *Manufacturing & Service Operations Management, 20*(1), 1–18.

Bandaly, D., Satir, A., & Shanker, L. (2014). Integrated supply chain risk management via operational methods and financial instruments. *International Journal of Production Research, 52*(7), 2007–2025.

BDO USA LLP. (2016). *2016 BDO manufacturing RiskFactor report*. BDO USA LLP.

Boyabatli, O., Kleindorfer, P., & Koontz, S. (2011). Integrating long-term and short-term contracting in beef supply chains. *Management Science, 57*(10), 1771–1787.

Boyabatli, O., Nguyjen, J., & Wang, T. (2017). Capacity management in agricultural commodity processing and application in the palm industry. *Manufacturing and Service Operations Management, 12*, 1–39.

Buhl, H., Strauß, S., & Wiesent, J. (2011). The impact of commodity price risk management on the profits of a company. *Resources Policy, 36*, 346–353.

Chan, R., Guo, Y., Lee, S., & Li, X. (2019). *Financial mathematics, derivates and structured products*. Springer.

Chen, J., Sohal, A., & Prajogo, D. (2013). Supply chain operational risk mitigation: A collaborative approach. *International Journal of Production Research, 51*(7), 2186–2199.

Chopra, S., & Sodhi, M. (2004). Managing risk to avoid supply-chain breakdown. *MIT Sloan Management Review, 46*(1), 53–61.

Debus, C., Adam, T., Rettl, D., Nadjmabadi, B., Kramm, T., & Jaron, A. (2014). *Rohstoff- und Energierisikomanagement in Industrie und Handelsunternehmen. Ergebnisse einer Umfrage bei Unternehmen in Deutschland, Österreich und der Schweiz.* KPMG AG Wirtschaftsprüfungsgesellschaft.

Dimson, E., & Mussavian, M. (1998). A brief history of market efficiency. *European Financial Management, 4*(1), 91–103.

Dong, L., & Liu, H. (2007). Equilibrium forward contracts on nonstorable commodities in the presence of market power. *Operations Research, 55*(1), 128–145.

Erdem, T., Swait, J., & Louviere, J. (2002). The impact of brand credibility on consumer price sensitivity. *International Journal of Research in Marketing, 19*, 1–19.

Feng, Y., Martel, A., D'Amours, S., & Beauregard, R. (2013). Coordinated contract decisions in a make-to-order manufacturing supply chain: A stochastic programming approach. *Production and Operations Management, 22*(3), 642–660.

Finley, B., & Pettit, J. (2011). Creating value at the intersection of sourcing, hedging and trading. *Journal of Applied Corporate Finance, 23*(4), 83–89.

Fisch, J., & Ross, J. M. (2013). Timing the start of material substitution projects: Creating switching options under volatile material prices. *Journal of Product Innovation Management, 31*(3), 567–583.

Fischl, M., Scherrer-Rathje, M., & Friedli, F. (2014). Digging deeper into supply risk: A systematic literature review on price risks. *Supply Chain Management: An International Journal, 19*(5/6), 480–503.

Fu, Q., Zhou, S., Chao, X., & Lee, C. (2012). Combined pricing and portfolio option procurement. *Production and Operations Management, 21*(2), 361–377.

Gardner, B. (1977). Commodity options for agriculture. *American Journal of Agricultural Economics, 59*(5), 986–992.

Gaudenzi, B., Zsidisin, G., Janet, H., & Kaufmann, L. (2018). An exploration of factors influencing the choice of commodity price risk mitigation strategies. *Journal of Purchasing & Supply Management, 24*(1), 218–237.

Hardt, C. (2011). *Rohstoffpreisrisikomanagement in industriellen supply chains: dargestellt am Beispiel der Automobilindustrie*. Josef Eul Verlag.

Hillebrand, E. (2003). *Mean reversion models of financial markets*. Universität Bremen.

Hofmann, H. (2011). Natural hedging as a risk prophylaxis and supplier financing instrument in automotive supply chains. *Supply Chain Management: An International Journal, 16*(2), 128–141.

Hong, Z., Lee, C., & Zhang, L. (2018). Procurement risk management under uncertainty: A review. *Industrial Management & Data Systems, 118*(7), 1547–1574.

Inderfurth, K., Kelle, P., & Kleber, R. (2018). Inventory control in dual sourcing commodity procurement with price correlation. *Central European Journal of Operations Research, 26*, 93–119.

Johnson, F., Leenders, M., & Flynn, A. (2011). *Purchasing and supply management* (14th ed.). McGraw Hill.

Jüttner, U., Peck, H., & Christopher, M. (2003). Supply chain management: Outlining an agenda for future research. *International Journal of Logistics: Research & Applications, 6*(4), 197–210.

Kannegiesser, M., Günther, M., Van Beek, P., Grunow, M., & Habla, C. (2009). Value chain management for commodities: A case study from the chemical industry. *Operation Research Spectrum, 31*, 63–93.

Kaul, A., & Wittink, D. (1995). Empirical generalizations about the impact of advertising on price sensitivity and price. *Marketing Science, 14*(3), 151–160.

Kern, D., Moser, R., Hartmann, E., & Moder, M. (2012). Supply risk management: Model development and empirical analysis. *International Journal of Physical Distribution & Logistics Management, 42*(1), 60–82.

Kinlan, D., & Roukema, D. (2011). When is an escalation clause necessary? Dealing with Price fluctuations in dredging contracts. *Terra et Aqua, 125*(1), 3–9.

Kouvelis, P., Li, R., & Ding, Q. (2013). Managing storable commodity risks: The role of inventory and financial hedge. *Manufacturing & Service Operations Management, 15*(3), 507–521.

Kouvelis, P., Turcic, D., & Zhao, W. (2018). Supply chain contracting in environments with volatile input prices and frictions. *Manufacturing & Service Operations Management, 20*(1), 1–40.

KPMG International. (2007). *Energie- und Rohstoffpreise – Risiken und deren Absicherung*. KPMG International Cooperative.

Krishnamurthi, L., & Raj, S. (1991). An empirical analysis of the relationship between brand loyalty and consumer price elasticity. *Marketing Science, 10*(2), 172–183.

Lapko, Y., Trucco, P., & Nuur, C. (2016). The business perspective on materials criticality: Evidence from manufacturers. *Resources Policy, 50*, 93–107.

Li, C., & Kouvelis, P. (1999). Flexible and risk-sharing supply contracts under price uncertainty. *Management Science, 45*(10), 1378–1398.

Li, S., Murat, A., & Huang, W. (2009). Selection of contract suppliers under price and demand uncertainty in a dynamic market. *European Journal of Operational Research, 198*, 830–847.

Li, Q., Niu, B., & Chu, L. (2017). Forward sourcing or spot trading? Optimal commodity procurement policy with demand uncertainty risk and forecast update. *IEEE Systems Journal, 11*(3), 1526–1536.

Liu, Y., & Yang, J. (2015). Joint pricing-procurement control under fluctuating raw material costs. *International Journal of Production Economics, 168*, 91–104.

Mahapatra, S., Levental, S., & Narasimhan, R. (2017). Market price uncertainty, risk aversion and procurement: Combining contracts and open market sourcing alternatives. *International Journal of Production Economics, 185*, 34–51.

Malkiel, B. (2003). The efficient market hypothesis and its critics. *Journal of Economic Perspectives, 17*(1), 59–82.

Manikas, A., & Kroes, J. (2016). Improved forward buying of commodity materials. *International Journal of Production Research, 54*(15), 4568–4583.

Manuj, I., & Mentzer, J. (2008). Global supply chain risk management. *Journal of Business Logisctics, 29*(1), 133–155.

Merzifonluoglu, Y. (2015). Risk averse supply portfolio selection with supply, demand and spot market volatility. *Omega, 57*(1), 40–53.

Mishra, A., El-Osta, H., & Sandretto, C. (2004). Factors affecting farm enterprise diversification. *Agricultural Finance Review, 64*(2), 151–166.

Moheb-Alizadeh, H., & Handfield, R. (2018). The impact of raw materials price volatility on cost of goods sold (COGS) for product manufacturing. *IEEE Transactions on Engineering Management, 2018*, 1–14.

Moser, P., Isaksson, O., & Seifert, R. (2017). Inventory dynamics in process industries: An empirical investigation. *International Journal of Production Economics, 191*, 253–266.

Ni, J., Chu, L., Wu, F., Sculli, D., & Shi, Y. (2012). A multi-stage financial hedging approach for the procurement of manufacturing materials. *European Journal of Operational Research, 221*(1), 424–431.

Noble, P., & Gruca, T. (1999). Industrial pricing: Theory and managerial practice. *Marketing Science, 18*(3), 435–454.

Pellegrino, R., Costantino, N., & Tauro, D. (2019). Supply chain finance: A supply chain-oriented perspective to mitigate commodity risk and pricing volatility. *Journal of Purchasing and Supply Management, 25*(2), 118–133.

Pettit, T., Croxton, K., & Fiksel, J. (2013). Ensuring supply chain resilience: Development and implementation of an assessment tool. *Journal of Business Logistics, 34*(1), 46–76.

Poitras, G. (2013). *Commodity risk management*. Routledge.

Polanyi, K. (1968). *Primitive, archaic, and modern economics*. Anchor Books.

Reiner, G., Jammernegg, W., & Gold, S. (2014). Raw material procurement with fluctuating prices using speculative inventory under consideration of different contract types and transport modes. *International Journal of Production Research, 52*(22), 6557–6575.

Schofield, N. (2011). *Commodity derivatives: Markets and applications*. Wiley.

Sheffi, Y., & Rice, J. (2005). A supply chain view of the resilient enterprise. *MIT Sloan Management Review, 47*(1), 41–48.

Singh, R., Billa, R., & Arora, B. (2016). *Index based pricing: Managing risk and profitability* (pp. 1–4). Deloitte Touche Tohmatsu Limited.

Talluri, S., Kull, T., Yildiz, H., & Yoon, J. (2013). Assessing the efficiency of risk mitigation strategies in supply chains. *Journal of Business Logistics, 34*(4), 253–269.

Tummala, R., & Schoenherr, T. (2011). Assessing and managing risks using the supply chain risk management process (SCRMP). *Supply Chain Management: An International Journal, 16*(6), 474–483.

Turcic, D., Kouvelis, P., & Bolandifar, E. (2014). Hedging commodity procurement in a bilateral supply chain. *Manufacturing and Service Operations Management, 17*(2), 135–272.

Weber, E. (2008). *A short history of derivative security markets*. University of Western Australia Business School.

Wiedenmann, S., & Geldermann, J. (2015). Supply planning for processors of agricultural raw materials. *European Journal of Operational Research, 242*, 606–619.

Wolf, A. (1987). Optimal hedging with future options. *Journal of Economics and Business, 39*(2), 141–158.

Wu, D., & Olson, D. (2010). Enterprise risk management: A DEA VaR approach in vendor selection. *International Journal of Production Research, 48*(16), 4919–4932.

Xiaofeng, N., Boyaci, T., Gümüs, M., Ray, S., & Zhang, D. (2017). Joint procurement and demand-side bidding strategies under price volatility. *Annual Operations Research, 257*, 121–165.

Xu, J., Feng, G., Jiang, W., & Wang, S. (2015). Optimal procurement of long-term contracts in the presence of imperfect spot market. *Omega, 52*, 42–52.

Zhang, W., Zhou, D., & Liu, L. (2014). Contracts for changing times: Sourcing with raw material price volatility and information asymmetry. *Manufacturing & Service Operations Management, 16*(1), 133–148.

Zillner, M. (2020). *A simulation approach for quantifying commodity price risks in supply chains.* Vienna University of Economics and Business.

Zsidisin, G., & Hartley, J. (2012). *Managing commodity price risk: A supply chain perspective.* Business Expert Press.

Matthias Zillner is an entrepreneur in the fields of commodity trading and price risk management. He holds a master's degree in Mechanical Engineering and received his doctorate in Supply Chain Management under the supervision of Prof. Tina Wakolbinger in 2020.

Chapter 19
Achieving Supply Chain Resilience Through Additive Manufacturing

Matthias M. Meyer, Andreas H. Glas, and Michael Eßig

Abstract Disruptive events such as natural disasters become increasingly frequent, demonstrating the need for resilient supply systems. Additive manufacturing (AM) is an emerging technology which can help to solve supply bottlenecks as seen during SARS-CoV-2. AM was able to mitigate supply bottlenecks of medical spare parts, in times when globally arranged traditional supply sources failed. This chapter presents and discusses how AM can help to increase resilience. For this purpose, our contribution examines modern portfolio theory and the interplay of a hedged sourcing approach (traditional, formative with AM). This is assessed by using a single case study. The results indicate that using AM as a hedged source of supply to traditional supply sources increases the overall resilience of the supply system.

19.1 Introduction

Times of crisis have always intensified the call for new or enhanced approaches to adapt and overcome supply chain vulnerabilities. The global reach of supply chains, shorter product life cycles, and increasing customer demands, together with global awareness for and perception of earthquakes, hurricanes, fuel or water crisis, terrorism, or, recently, the COVID-19 pandemic, are making the vulnerabilities of today's supply chains obvious. Supply chain research has addressed the topic for around two decades. Foundational contributions from Christopher and Peck (2004) and Sheffi and Rice (2005) marked the beginning of a steady growth of contributions on supply chain resilience. Specifically, the term "resilience" is used in research to discuss how enterprises adapt and grow in the face of turbulent change (Fiksel et al., 2015).

Remarkably, resilience goes beyond risk mitigation. Fiksel et al. (2015) point out that it "enables a business to gain competitive advantage by learning how to deal with disruptions more effectively than its competitors and possibly shifting to a new

M. M. Meyer (✉) · A. H. Glas · M. Eßig
Procurement Research Group, Bundeswehr University München, Neubiberg, Germany
e-mail: ma.meyer@unibw.de

S. Kummer et al. (eds.), *Supply Chain Resilience*, Springer Series in Supply Chain Management 17, https://doi.org/10.1007/978-3-030-95401-7_19

equilibrium." Keeping this notion in mind, one must consider that resilience calls for the capability to deal with vulnerabilities. This capability, however, is necessary but not sufficient because resilience is also the ability to become stronger or more innovative through a crisis.

An innovative manufacturing technology that has received increased attention during the last decade is additive manufacturing (AM). In contrast to traditional manufacturing (TM) methods, such as cutting, milling, and drilling, AM builds a product from raw materials layer by layer in an automated way based on a digital model (Zijm et al., 2019). Today, quite a variety of AM technologies exists, and 3D printing is often used as a synonym for AM. The characteristics of AM are the anchor of this contribution, as we show that AM can be the right technology to achieve a new resilience equilibrium. Thus, this chapter investigates how AM can be used in supply chains to enforce resilience. Specifically, this chapter uses a combination (hedging) of AM and TM that goes beyond traditional risk-splitting and dual-sourcing approaches.

19.2 Problem Framing

The idea of supply chain resilience was established in 2003 after several disruptive events affecting supply chains (e.g., SARS, 9/11 terror attacks, and foot-and-mouth disease) and was based on the theory of resilient systems (Fiksel, 2004, 2006). It is strongly connected to business-continuity management and refers to an objective rather than being a holistic concept (Tandler & Essig, 2013). Vulnerabilities are a company's "susceptibility to a disruptive event in the supply chain" (Wagner & Bode, 2006) that threatens the short- and long-term continuity of supply organizations. Below, some of the vulnerability factors of supply chains are mentioned:

- Globalized supply chains (Wagner & Bode, 2006)
- Single sourcing (Wagner & Bode, 2006)
- Geographical concentration of suppliers (Wagner & Bode, 2006)
- Supplier dependency (Wagner & Bode, 2006)
- Product uniqueness (Blackhurst et al., 2008)
- Just-in-time delivery (Blackhurst et al., 2008)
- Specialized factories (Pettit et al., 2010)
- Centralized distribution (Pettit et al., 2010)
- Increased outsourcing (Pettit et al., 2010)
- Volatility of demands and disasters (Pettit et al., 2010)

Resilience aims to overcome these vulnerability factors and enable supply chains to adapt to disturbances (Fiksel et al., 2015). These goals are achieved through increasing levels of flexibility and agility within a supply chain (Tandler & Essig, 2013). Concerning the concept of resilience, such flexibility or agility factors pertain to the supply chain's ability to overcome potential disruptions (Pettit et al., 2010).

Some selected supply chain capabilities proposed by Pettit et al. (2010) are the following:

- Collaboration (i.e., the ability to work effectively with other entities)
- Capacity (which involves redundancies and reserve capacities
- Efficiency (which produces outputs with minimum resource requirements and involves product variability reduction, waste elimination, and asset utilization)
- Recovery (i.e., the ability to move back to normal operations quickly through the mobilization of resources)
- Dispersion (which features a distribution of assets, decentralized decision-making, and the use of decentralized production capacities)
- Adaptability (which involves the possibility of lead-time reduction and a fast adjustment of requirements)
- Anticipation (which involves continuity management strategies such as high preparedness and contingency plans)
- Flexibility in sourcing (which involves the usage of multiple supply sources that can be contracted and changed quickly)

The list of supply chain capabilities indicates that research is quite aware of what can be done to increase resilience. However, resilience must also balance effectiveness and efficiency. Too few capabilities would harm the survival of the firm due to disruptive events. The goal is to establish a supply chain that can react to external disruptions and establish a "new equilibrium" (Fiksel, 2004). Too many supply chain capabilities would shrink the rate of return within organizations in purchasing and supply management (PSM) on which the long-term competitive advantage of the firm would be treated as well. Pettit et al. (2010) provide a fit model that explains that the proper equilibrium of resilience (i.e., the zone of right resilience level) always needs to be found. Furthermore, Pettit et al.'s (2010) model shows that extreme supply chain events recently revealed a new quality of supply chain vulnerability. Thus, vulnerabilities increased due to root causes such as a volatility, uncertainty, complexity, and ambiguity (VUCA) environment. Because supply chains act in a VUCA environment, their vulnerability is increasing (see Fig. 19.1).

To underpin the assumption of increased vulnerability, we reflected on the last 30 years, when the number of people affected by disasters and catastrophic events has increased enormously. Within the past decade (2011–2021), several disruptive events have occurred that exemplify the further amplification of vulnerabilities: the Tohoku earthquake and tsunami leading to the Fukushima nuclear disaster (2011); the wars in Syria (2011), Iraq (2013), and the Donbas region in Ukraine (2014); hurricanes Sandy (2012), Harvey (2017), and Maria (2017); COVID-19 (2020); and the Suez Canal's marine traffic jam (2021). All of them have disrupted globally arranged supply chains and made vulnerabilities rise; hence, effectively safeguarding business continuity has become even more challenging. These low-probability, high-impact events move toward higher probability and are therefore also called "supply chain tsunamis" (Akkermans & van Wassenhove, 2017).

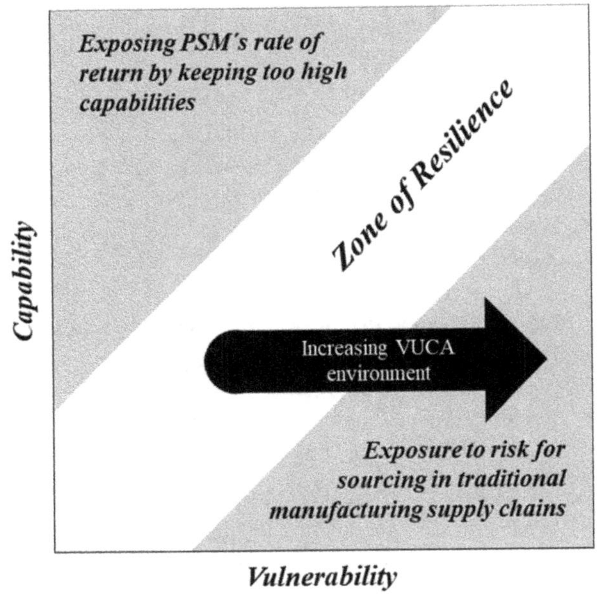

Fig. 19.1 Zone of resilience based on Pettit et al. (2010)

19.3 Solution: Beyond Dual Sourcing, Toward Supply Chain Hedging

19.3.1 Hedging Manufacturing Technology: Insights from Portfolio Theory

In the following section, we underpin our reasoning by means of portfolio theory, which is embedded into the larger theoretical framework of decision theory. The principle of hedging risks using the diversification effect for risk mitigation was first introduced within financial risk management (Markowitz, 1952) and later established into strategic management (e.g., Ansoff, 1957). Kraljic (1983) adopts this principle into his purchasing strategy portfolio and suggests implementing a diversification strategy if the company's relative strength in the supply market is low and the company is therefore highly exposed to supply risks (Kraljic, 1983). By considering the resilience portfolio (Fig. 19.1), Kraljic (1983) proposes a "right" strategy/procurement capability to cope with bottleneck, strategic, leverage, or noncritical demand items. Traditionally, procurement diversification addresses supplier dependency and single-sourcing rather than manufacturing technology.

Ansoff (1967) distinguishes potential diversification strategies by geographic region, customer demand, and technology. Even if sourcing the same demand within different geographic regions (local-/global sourcing) has become a key task for procurement, the sourcing of the same demand through different technologies (additively and traditionally) is a blind spot in current research (Meyer et al.,

2020b). The potential of hedging AM and TM and its consequences for resilience are briefly explained below.

The hedging mechanism explains the simple strategy "not to put all eggs in one basket" (Oehler & Unser, 2001). Ansoff (1967) already identified the possibility to hedge production technologies; however, it took until recent years, when a new production technology emerged with a significant hedging effect (AM) within the supply chain. The first analysis shows that hedging AM and TM seems promising from a supply risk perspective (Meyer et al., 2020a, 2021).

The target of diversification strategies is to optimize the rate of return or the mitigating of risks, which involves hedging against existential risks ("continuity management"), compensating fluctuations effects ("stabilizing function"), or increasing a company's flexibility ("creating options") (Löbler, 1988). Modern portfolio theory explains this mechanism mathematically and was first introduced by Markowitz (1952), whose work marked one of the crucial steps in risk-management literature.

Markowitz presumes a risk-averse, utility-maximizing, and rationally acting investor who wants to calculate the optimal combination in the trade-off between the return and the risk of their financial investments, which are arbitrarily separable. This combination is expressed through the efficiency ratio, in which there is no lower risk for the portfolio with the same expected return. The risk is operationalized as the statistical standard deviation (σ) from the expected return (μ) based on historical data. Using the portfolio approach, financial assets that are not fully correlated can be combined so that the unsystematic risk is minimized due to the diversification effect.

The correlation coefficient (p) of the investments i and j is calculated as follows:

$$p_{i,j} = \frac{cov_{i,j}}{\sigma_i * \sigma_j}.$$

The more negatively correlated the investments become, the lower the risk of the portfolio becomes, as seen in the following equation:

$$\sigma_p = \sqrt{\sum_{i=1}^{n} \sum_{j=1}^{n} \sigma_i * x_i * \sigma_j * x_j * p_{i,j}}.$$

Systematic risks to which both investments (or even the complete market) are sensitive in the same manner cannot be mitigated. This applies to risks on which two financial assets are completely positively correlated at $p = 1$. It becomes impossible to mitigate the risk position through hedging, as no diversification can take place. We might consider a dual sourcing situation where both suppliers are from the same geographical region and thus exposed to the same risks (from traffic jam, labor dispute, earthquakes, failure to export, or currency risks).

By creating a more offsetting risk position with a correlation <1, a mitigation of the risk position through hedging becomes possible and reaches its maximum at a correlation coefficient of -1. The target of reaching a position as negatively correlated to an existing investment as possible is referred to as a hedging strategy, which aims to minimize the spread risk from the expected value of financial assets.

The mathematical explanation by Markowitz (1952) reveals that the more negatively correlated supply sources can be arranged, the more risk can be mitigated. Risk diversification can also be completed without considering AM; however, this is challenging to establish by sourcing with TM because using suppliers from different industries becomes highly difficult, and suppliers would source their demands probably also from the same sub-suppliers (Blome & Henke, 2009). Thus, it will be shown that manufacturing technology is one major factor that allows a completely different supply chain design compared to a traditional manufacturing one.

However, opening a second source of supply comes at the cost of economies of scale. Furthermore, Markowitz (1952) presumes the nonexistence of transaction costs (as introduced by Coase, 1937), which is seen as one of the external grand theories of supply management (Spina et al., 2015). Transaction costs can be divided into information costs, agreement costs, execution costs, and control and adaption costs (Picot, 1991). As regards transaction costs in portfolio theory, the diversification effects are reduced (Pogue, 1970). As the market itself already diversifies supply sources at a low asset specificity, demands of higher asset specificity require high initiating costs. There is a long research tradition on how uncertainty and asset specificity influence transaction cost.

This reasoning guides us to two assumptions concerning AM in relation to portfolio theory: the first assumption is that when hedging a TM with an AM supply source, a more negative correlation coefficient can be reached compared to sourcing solely through TM supply sources.

$$p_{\mathrm{AM,TM}} < p_{\mathrm{TM_1,TM_2}} \rightarrow \sigma_{\mathrm{AM,TM}} < \sigma_{\mathrm{TM_1,TM_2}}.$$

The second assumption is that an additional AM supply source is less transaction costly than a second TM source. Both assumptions are well-grounded in previous AM research and briefly elaborated on in the next section.

19.3.2 Relative Characteristics of Additive Manufacturing Technology

AM strongly differs from TM, and important differences include the following four characteristics (Meyer et al., 2020a):

1. *Direct and immediate interaction of the virtual and physical world:* One synonym for AM is "direct digital manufacturing" (Berman, 2012), which incisively describes AM's merits in transitioning from the virtual to the physical world. Products can easily be modified by solely changing the computer-aided design (CAD) file so one can "press a button" to create the physical product with a 3D printer, which makes the postponement of supply possible.

2. *Decreased asset specificity:* In contrast to TM, AM is "tool-free". For example, it is possible to manufacture products with different geometries synchronously in just one print job, which minimizes lead times and therefore increases the recovery rate of a disrupted supply system. Flexible supply sources provide a hedging demand effect (Tomlin & Wang, 2005), increasing supply redundancy and enabling stabilization in case of fluctuations (Löbler, 1988). This decreased specificity promotes decentralized manufacturing close to the customer, providing increased robustness for a supply system. In addition, AM minimizes the clear separation of manufacturers and users of a product – for example, within the maker movement. Hence, product consumers become manufacturers. Additionally, AM allows sourcing flexibility (Eyers et al., 2018), which Pettit et al. (2010) mention as an important step toward reaching supply capabilities. Additionally, 3D printers can be shared among supply organizations (Hedenstierna et al., 2019), thereby serving as a backup supply source of short-term capacities.
3. *Changed cost structure:* AM has significantly different cost structures than TM: for example, an increase in a product's geometrical complexity does not lead to additional costs ("complexity for free"). On the other hand, the use of economies of scale is highly limited, such that AM is mostly used to produce small quantities (Baldinger, 2016). Hence, a complete switch to AM as regular supply source for large quantities comes at high opportunity costs of TM's economies of scale, especially in the case of a stable environment.
4. *Increased resource efficiency:* As material is only applied where required, higher material utilization can be guaranteed. It is also possible to directly print functional components without requiring sub-suppliers, thus reducing process steps such as assembly.

Altogether, the technical characteristics allow designing an AM supply chain that significantly differs from traditional ones. AM is often related to decentralized, local, on-demand, and low-lot-size production layouts, whereas TM can usually be linked to global supply chains in centralized mass-production plants (Braziotis et al., 2019). Thus, AM often requires less time for set-up and logistics, whereas TM can typically produce at lower unit costs in a mass-production setting. Then, "AM is faster but more costly." This can be illustrated with an ideal cost-value curve that compares TM and AM (Fig. 19.2, Meyer et al., 2020a).

The figure also shows that AM is, relative to TM, the other extreme. According to portfolio theory, AM can be a more negatively correlated supply source than TM, which confirms our first assumption. Furthermore, AM only depends on data and raw material. No specific tooling is required, which also confirms our second assumption, namely, that the establishment of an AM supply source requires less effort than the establishment of a second TM source.

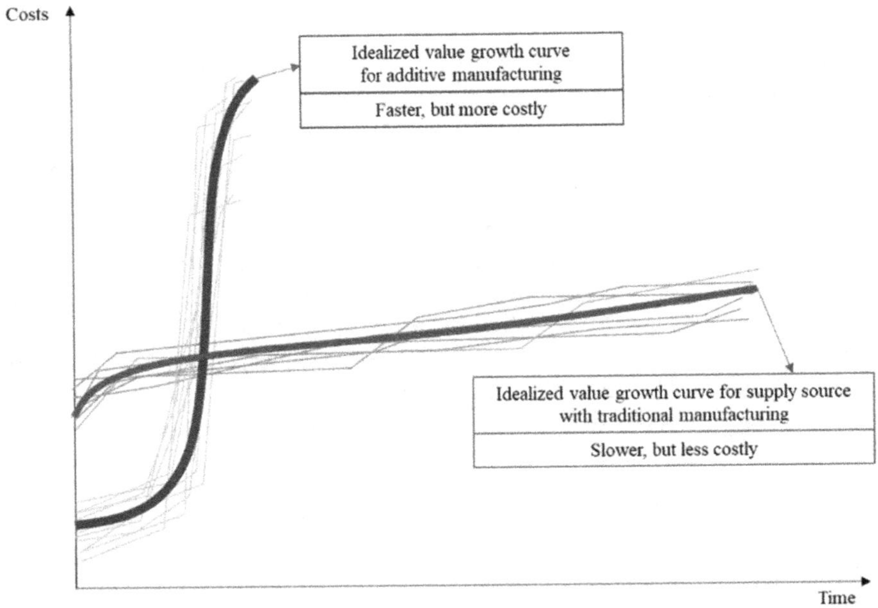

Fig. 19.2 Cost value curve

19.4 Relevance: Case Illustration of Resilience Effects by Hedging AM and TM

The introduced approach to achieve resilience in supply chains is further examined with regard to managerial practice. The relevance of the concept is discussed with regard to a proof of concept in recent practice. For this purpose, we provide some insights into cases of the COVID-19 pandemic and discuss the approach with regard to supply vulnerability factors. We conducted case study research to investigate a phenomenon in depth within a real-life context (Yin, 2014). Here, we focus on the vulnerability and turbulences caused by a global pandemic. From a methodological viewpoint, this kind of disruption is new for a globalized economy; hence, we implemented a qualitative research design.

The case is about a regional hospital in Brescia, Italy. That hospital was affected by bottlenecks of medical spare parts (ventilator valves) and decided to source these via an AM supply source from a local AM service provider.

For this case, we collected publicly available secondary data, which were consolidated after the first pandemic wave in July 2020, and stored within a case database (Yin, 2014). Inclusion criteria for secondary data were English or German as the language of the articles as well as sources with a high level of confidence, such as reports, press statements of companies involved, and the government. The study was cross-checked to ensure reliability (Yin, 2014). We drew on additional sources of evidence to increase the results' validity (Yin, 2014). Therefore, we collected primary data in the form of a semi-structured interview with the CEO of the AM service provider.

The case is partitioned into a sourcing situation before the supply disruption, the resilience approach within the pandemic bottleneck situation, and the post-disruption situation.

In the regional hospital in Brescia, valves are required for the artificial respiration of patients. Due to their geometry, the valves have a high product specificity and were therefore globally sourced before the pandemic by a single traditional supply source from the UK and held in stock in the hospital. COVID-19 led to an increased demand for valves. The globally increased demand in combination with limited capacities of the OEM led to a global shortage in the middle of March 2020.

> Because of the incredibly high demand of the component from all over the countries given by COVID-19 pandemic, the valve supply was very low, and the component was hard to find.

The hospital faced a potential stock-out situation, as it could already foresee that the remaining stock of ventilators would be entirely consumed in the short term without the prospect of receiving the products from the traditional supply source. The company contacted the local AM service provider Issinova spontaneously; the provider held decentralized AM production capacities.

> We had no contacts before the emergency. The hospital, which went out of the Venturi valve supply, contacted the local newspaper to make an appeal, and the newspaper decided to contact us, asking our help.

From the remaining valves, the virtual drawing data was created via re-engineering (3D scanning) and used to create a prototype by FDM [fused deposition modeling] within 24 h.

> The reason for the AM use was the rapidity of the 3D scanning and remaking of the component in a very short time without using an injection molding press.

The hospital tested this prototype to check if it fulfilled the requirements. Afterwards, the hospital used the AM service provider as a backup supply source. Potential risks of violating property rights were taken to keep administering life-support measures to the patients.

> The emergency created the possibility to use an emergency device. Of course, it was necessary for the product to be medical. In our case, we took the risk.

Additionally, another AM service provider was contacted and collaborated by quickly providing additional production capacities so that the number of received valves could be scaled and printing capacities further utilized:

> First, we used our own resin [Stereolithography, SLA] and filament [FDM] printers (2 or 3 printers) so that we were able to replicate one piece in a few hours. When we realized that the pieces were working, we decided to lean on one of our biggest partners, which was able to replicate a high number of valves using a large powder 3D printer [Powder Bed Fusion, PBF]. The Venturi valve is made of only one piece, but it is necessary to refine the piece manually to remove residues and refine geometries.

Hence, 100 valves per day were sourced from two AM suppliers (multiple sourcing). The cost per valve was €1.70–€2.55. Due to the possibility of copyright issues, the virtual drawing file was not shared on the Internet, even though it could have been used by other hospitals:

> The hospital uses the normal and standard equipment now. The supply arrived after some difficulty during the first months of the pandemic. The regular supplier was happy about our initiative. They thanked us for the help we were able to carry on with.

This case exemplifies the effect of AM on supply chain resilience. AM enabled the hospital in Brescia to quickly recover from its bottleneck situation. The collaboration of the hospital with the AM service provider was easily established, and a prototype was produced with short lead times, showing the adaptability of sourcing with AM. The supplies were created within a decentralized decision-making with decentralized production capacities, providing a high degree of dispersion. As capacities were at their limit, an additional service provider was contracted, and it shows an increased flexibility in sourcing. Thereby, the overall capacity was quickly increased, and further asset utilization of the 3D printers was provided, enhancing overall efficiency. As the CAD data could have been saved and used to anticipate upcoming supply bottlenecks, it was possible to learn from the crisis, and a higher degree of preparedness was achieved on how to organize future supplies within disruptions:

> With AM, a network to share knowledge and means can be created to guarantee a high production quantity in a short time.

The proposition derived from portfolio theory shows that the original supply chain was designed globally, whereas AM provided a local supply source. The valves were sourced from a single traditional supplier, whereas AM provided a scalable multiple-sourcing solution. Additionally, the medical industry sector of the TM supply source was diversified to the engineering and service sector. Hence, a higher degree of diversification was reached. Coming back to portfolio theory, the correlation coefficient of the alternative is lower (p), which reduces the risk (σ).

$$p_{\mathrm{AM,TM}} < p_{\mathrm{TM_1,TM_2}} \rightarrow \sigma_{\mathrm{AM,TM}} < \sigma_{\mathrm{TM_1,TM_2}}.$$

19.5 Conclusion

Finally, it is necessary to contextualize the main elements of this contribution, namely, resilience equilibrium, portfolio theory, and hospital case. To start with, the case study, in sum, has exemplified that an extreme event such as COVID-19 has uncovered supply chain vulnerabilities of a new and highly unexpected quality. The hospital was not prepared. Its traditional resilience strategy (keeping a sufficient number of valves in stock) was sufficient in the face of an expected event (e.g., a flu

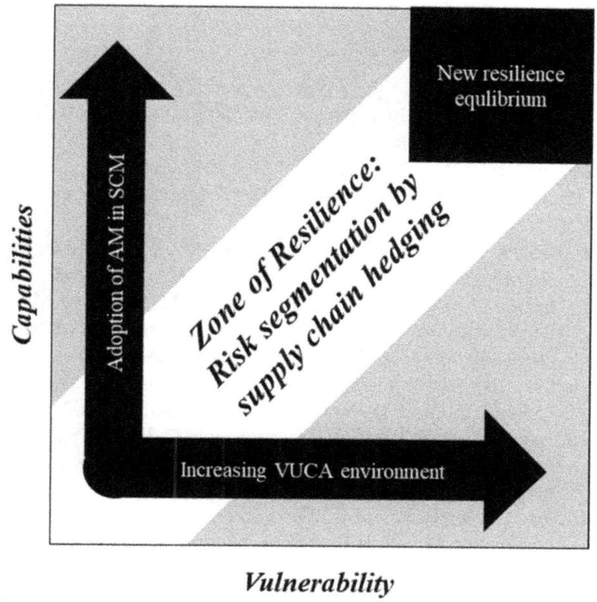

Fig. 19.3 Resilience equilibrium by supply chain hedging

epidemic). However, that strategy was ineffective in the case of the pandemic, which triggered the search for ways to foster supply chain capabilities. The establishment of a second AM source solves the current bottleneck of urgent demand and is the basis for a higher level of resilience in the future.

Linking this aspect to portfolio theory, AM can supplement TM, and its characteristics then lead to risk reduction. The build-up of an AM source increases supply chain capability. In the face of increased vulnerabilities due to VUCA environmental dynamics, the hedging of AM and TM achieves a new level of supply chain resilience (Fig. 19.3).

The potential of hedging AM and TM is high. Supply chains that are exposed to risks (e.g., military and humanitarian supply chains) have already adopted intensively (US Army, 2020; Romero-Torres & Vieira, 2016). Overall, AM bears the potential to increase resilience. However, switching a supply organization's full demand to AM only would increase costs dramatically while not bringing a strong competitive advantage. A symbiosis of AM and TM supply chains needs to be created based on portfolio theory to achieve a new resilience equilibrium. As Fiksel (2004) points out, the goal is not to build a resistant system but to use resilience to build a system with more than one equilibrium point.

References

Akkermans, H., & van Wassenhove, L. (2017). Supply chain tsunamis: Research on low-probability, high-impact disruptions. *Journal of Supply Chain Management, 54*. https://doi.org/10.1111/jscm.12162

Ansoff, H. I. (1957). Strategies for Diversification 1957.

Ansoff, H. I. (1967). *Corporate strategy. An analytic approach to business policy for growth and expansion* (15th ed.). McGraw-Hill.

Baldinger, M. (2016). *Supply chain management für additive manufacturing. Konzepte, Werkzeuge und Prozesse für die Zusammenarbeit mit Dienstleistern zur Reduktion der Risiken beim Einstieg in additve Manufacturing*. Unter Mitarbeit von Mirko Meboldt und Paul Schönsleben: ETH Zurich. Retrieved June 13, 2019, from https://www.research-collection.ethz.ch/bitstream/handle/20.500.11850/114551/eth-48847-02.pdf?sequence=2&isAllowed=y

Berman, B. (2012). 3-D printing: The new industrial revolution. *Business Horizons, 55*(2), 155–162. https://doi.org/10.1016/j.bushor.2011.11.003

Blackhurst, J. V., Scheibe, K. P., & Johnson, D. J. (2008). Supplier risk assessment and monitoring for the automotive industry. *International Journal of Physical Distribution & Logistics Management, 38*(2), 143–165. https://doi.org/10.1108/09600030810861215

Blome, C., & Henke, M. (2009). Single versus multiple sourcing: A supply risk management perspective. In F. S. Hillier, G. A. Zsidisin, & B. Ritchie (Eds.), *Supply chain risk* (Vol. 124, pp. 125–135). Springer.

Braziotis, C., Rogers, H., & Jimo, A. (2019). 3D printing strategic deployment: The supply chain perspective. *Supply Chain Management: An International Journal, 24*(3), 397–404. https://doi.org/10.1108/SCM-09-2017-0305

Christopher, M., & Peck, H. (2004). Building the resilient supply chain. *International Journal of Logistics Management, 15*, 1–13. https://doi.org/10.1108/09574090410700275

Coase, R. H. (1937). The nature of the firm. *Economica, 4*(16), 386–405. https://doi.org/10.2307/2626876

Eyers, D., Potter, A., Gosling, J., & Naim, M. (2018). The flexibility of industrial additive manufacturing systems. *International Journal of Operations & Production Management, 38*. https://doi.org/10.1108/IJOPM-04-2016-0200

Fiksel, J. (2004). Designing resilient, sustainable systems. *Environmental Science & Technology, 37*, 5330–5339. https://doi.org/10.1021/es0344819

Fiksel, J. (2006). Sustainability and resilience: Toward a systems approach. *Sustainability: Science, Practice and Policy, 2*(2), 14–21. https://doi.org/10.1080/15487733.2006.11907980

Fiksel, J., Polyviou, M., Croxton, K., & Pettit, T. (2015). from risk to resilience: Learning to deal with disruption. *MIT Sloan Management Review, 56*, 79–86.

Hedenstierna, C. P. T., Disney, S. M., Eyers, D. R., Holmström, J., Syntetos, A. A., & Wang, X. (2019). Economies of collaboration in build-to-model operations. *Journal of Operations Management, 65*(8), 753–773. https://doi.org/10.1002/joom.1014

Kraljic, P. (1983). Purchasing must become supply management. *Harvard Business Review, 1983*(61), 109–117.

Löbler, H. (1988). *Diversifikation und Unternehmenserfolg. Diversifikationserfolge und -risiken bei unterschiedlichen Marktstrukturen und Wettbewerb* (OIKOS Studien zur Ökonomie) (Vol. 21). Gabler Verlag.

Markowitz, H. (1952). Portfolio selection. *The Journal of Finance, 7*(1), 77–91. https://doi.org/10.1111/j.1540-6261.1952.tb01525.x

Meyer, M. M., Glas, A. H., & Eßig, M. (2020a). Der Einfluss additiver Fertigung auf operational performance. *Controlling, 32*(3), 14–21. https://doi.org/10.15358/0935-0381-2020-3-14

Meyer, M. M., Glas, A. H., & Eßig, M. (2020b). Systematic review of sourcing and 3D printing: Make-or-buy decisions in industrial buyer–supplier relationships. *Management Review Quarterly*. https://doi.org/10.1007/s11301-020-00198-2

Meyer, M. M., Glas, A. H., & Eßig, M. (2021). Learning from supply disruptions caused by SARS-CoV-2: Use of additive manufacturing as a resilient response for public procurement. *Journal of Public Procurement, ahead-of-print, 22*(2021), 17–42.

Oehler, A., & Unser, M. (2001). *Finanzwirtschaftliches Risikomanagement*. Springer.

Pettit, T., Fiksel, J., & Croxton, K. (2010). Ensuring supply chain resilience: Development of a conceptual framework. *Journal of Business Logistics, 31*, 1–21. https://doi.org/10.1002/j.2158-1592.2010.tb00125.x

Picot, A. (1991). Ein neuer Ansatz zur Gestaltung der Leistungstiefe. *Schmalenbachs Zeitschrift für betriebswirtschaftliche Forschung: ZfbF, 43*(4), 336–357.

Pogue, G. A. (1970). An extension of the markowitz portfolio selection model to include variable transaction costs. An extension of the Markowitz portfolio selection model to include variable transaction costs, short sales, leverage policies and taxes. *The Journal of Finance, 25*(5), 1005–1027. https://doi.org/10.1111/j.1540-6261.1970.tb00865.x

Romero-Torres, A., & Vieira, D. R. (2016). Is 3d-printing transforming the project management function in the aerospace industry? *Journal of Modern Project Management, 4*(1), 112–119. Retrieved from http://search.ebscohost.com/login.aspx?direct=true&db=buh&AN=115469131&site=ehost-live

Sheffi, Y., & Rice, J. (2005). A supply chain view of the resilient enterprise. *MIT Sloan Management Review, 47*.

Spina, G., Caniato, F., Luzzini, D., & Ronchi, S. (2015). Assessing the use of external grand theories in purchasing and supply management research. *Journal of Purchasing and Supply Management, 22*. https://doi.org/10.1016/j.pursup.2015.07.001

Tandler, S., & Essig, M. (2013). Conceptual framework of supply chain safety. In M. Essig, M. Hülsmann, K. Eva-Maria, & S. Klein-Schmeink (Eds.), *Supply chain safety management: Security and robustness in logistics* (pp. 3–40). Springer.

Tomlin, B., & Wang, Y. (2005). On the value of mix flexibility and dual sourcing in unreliable newsvendor networks. *Manufacturing & Service Operations Management, 7*(2005), 37–57.

US Army. (2020, February 10). *Army leverages new alliance for 3-D printing goals. Aberdeen proving ground.* Retrieved from https://www.army.mil/article/232428/army_leverages_new_alliance_for_3_d_printing_goals

Wagner, S., & Bode, C. (2006). An empirical investigation into supply chain vulnerability. *Journal of Purchasing and Supply Management, 12*, 301–312. https://doi.org/10.1016/j.pursup.2007.01.004

Yin, R. K. (2014). Case Study Research 2014.

Zijm, W. H. M., Knofius, N., & van der Heijden, M. (2019). Additive manufacturing and its impact on the supply chain. In *Operations, logistics and supply chain management* (pp. 521–543).

Matthias M. Meyer, M.Eng. is a Research Fellow and a Doctoral Candidate with research focus on additive manufacturing and supply risk management.

Andreas H. Glas, Ph.D., is an Assistant Professor, and a director of the Research Center for Defense Acquisition & Supply Management (DASM).

Michael Eßig, Ph.D., is a Full Professor and Director at the Procurement Research Group, including the Research Center for Law and Management of Public Procurement, the Audi Procurement Research Group, and the Research Center for Defense Acquisition & Supply Management (DASM).

Chapter 20
Resilience in Warehousing

Clemens Schuhmayer

Abstract Due to the fact that warehousing is one of the most critical functions in supply chains, resilience should be considered and planned in advance. This includes dimensioning of warehouses, required stock and buffer levels, all critical processes in warehouses, the geographical structure and the structure of different warehouse levels, collaboration between different partners vertically or along horizontal lines.

Outsourcing should also be considered from the perspective of resilience and should not only be evaluated based on economic figures. Also technology, automatization and warehouse equipment, IT-infrastructure and digitalization play major roles in this context. This contribution tries to give an overview of these topics and aims at discussing what has to be done to make warehousing more resilient.

20.1 Introduction

Warehousing is one of the most critical functions in supply chains. In times without massive cutbacks or crises, companies are constantly challenged to run their warehouses with low costs while meeting demand in their markets. In practice, this leads to different levels of efficiency and performance, which mean different competitive advantages or disadvantages for companies.

Less thought is given to unforeseeable events such as health crises or other unpredictable disasters. Many logistics managers do not want to impair efficiency in normal times with security solutions or reserves.

Nevertheless, management should be aware of how they can react in the event of an emergency in the area of warehousing and, above all, how they can prevent it in order to continue the warehouse function and supply their markets in unforeseen situations.

C. Schuhmayer (✉)
Institute for Transport and Logistics Management, WU (Vienna University of Economics and Business), Vienna, Austria
e-mail: clemens.schuhmayer@wu.ac.at

S. Kummer et al. (eds.), *Supply Chain Resilience*, Springer Series in Supply Chain Management 17, https://doi.org/10.1007/978-3-030-95401-7_20

The most essential areas for action in the area of storage and resilience are presented and discussed below.

20.2 Dimensioning of a Warehouse

The correct dimensioning of a warehouse as a whole and the individual functional areas such as incoming goods area, storage areas, outgoing goods area, outdoor storage, and traffic areas is one of the greatest challenges in logistics. Too big facilities lead to higher costs and competitive disadvantages. Too small facilities lead to bottlenecks, delays, and poor performance in the market. In any case, an appropriate system must be installed to fulfil their regular and extraordinary market requirements.

One of the most difficult topics in this context is to evaluate future developments like growth of markets or developments of products and assortments which lead to higher or smaller space requirements. A particular challenge is quantifying the impact of unpredictable events such as earthquakes, floods, or health issues on a warehouse. It may also be almost impossible to predict what the future will bring, so dealing with resilience means developing different options (Schulz, 2020, p. 16).

A solution for sudden additional requirements, for example, due to the failure of another site, could be a flexible expansion area. It is important that this is provided for in advance, and that it is well planned and can therefore be implemented quickly if necessary.

20.3 Higher Stock and Buffer

Generally, higher stock levels and buffers lead to more safety and can smoothen ups and down of demand especially when they are unexpected. Nevertheless, it is a goal for almost all companies to avoid higher inventories in order to avoid storage space costs and capital commitment costs as well as higher process costs, for example, due to longer distances in larger warehouses.

Of course, more extra inventory would only delay the critical effect of a material bottleneck (Van Hoek, 2020, p. 350).

There is also the question of whether higher inventory levels generally lead to more resilience or whether the focus should be on which goods should be placed more on inventory to achieve a disproportionate effect. This could mean that the total stock level could be kept within limits by well-considered measures and selective stock increases and that the creation of additional, expensive storage capacity could be prevented or kept within limits.

20.4 Warehouse Processes

Warehouse processes are always measured by their efficiency. Key figures for evaluating are, for instance, the picking performance, the number of ingoing units, or error rates. In terms of resilience, the focus is on the flexibility and adaptability of processes. Changing market needs lead to changing demand and thus to different order structure or time requirements. This can mean, for example, that picking processes or logics are changed or expanded. Since process changes should always be well considered and require organizational things such as software adaptations or additional hardware, suitable concepts should be prepared.

In the case of personnel, flexibility in the warehouse means that new employees or temporary forces such as temporary workers can be quickly integrated into the work process and perform efficiently and without errors. This means, for example, the avoidance of special cases or the requirement of knowledge of conditions by individual employees.

Companies are generally well advised to design their warehouse processes with this in mind, and in times of crisis this topic gains additional importance.

20.5 Warehouse Structure

The number of warehouse locations is an important issue for larger companies and should also be questioned from time to time. Especially from crises, logistics managers have learned to analyze production sites and warehouses (Norman & Wieland, 2020, p. 642).

The larger a warehouse, the more possibilities there are to automate processes and to save personnel costs due to lower unit costs. Typically, the size of a warehouse increases with the degree of centralization of the warehouse structure. Usually, costs of stock are lower in a central warehouse than in a decentralized warehouse structure due to the safety stock. On the other hand, the decentralized structure makes short lead times possible.

However, decentralized storage locations can also mean more security. If one location fails, other warehouse locations may be able to take over the function or market supply of the failed location. This option is not available, for example, with a single central warehouse. The challenge in this area is to balance the achievable service levels and the costs of the different structures during normal operations with the possibilities in the event of an unforeseen event.

Collaboration can also be an alternative to creating your own resilient site structures.

20.6 Collaboration

Collaboration is one of the most cited formative elements for supply chain resilience (Sawyerr & Harrison, 2020, p. 85). Especially in crises or when bottlenecks occur, the common use of resources or the transparency of stocks between the supply chain partners can help to supply goods and to provide markets with required goods. Concerning warehouses, collaboration can happen on the same warehouse level (horizontal collaboration) or on different levels along the supply chain (vertical collaboration).

20.6.1 Horizontal Collaboration

In some businesses, it is common to ask competitors for goods to fulfil customer orders in the case of stock-out situations. To create resilience, this would mean that competitors get stock information if required, or warehouses and stock levels are transparent between competitors as far as the legal situation allows. The advantage would be that in crises goods for the market are available in a well-planned and organized way. However, this requires proactive instead of reactive management of risks and measures (Norman & Wieland, 2020, p. 642). It also requires trust, which is regularly on a different level, depending on businesses and companies.

20.6.2 Vertical Cooperation

For different levels of warehouses (for raw materials, parts and components, semi-finished goods, or finished goods), replenishment and delivery times as well as complexity to get goods from suppliers or to produce them can differ widely. Usually, or often, in supply chains, there are some bottlenecks (e.g., concerning the capacity of a few raw materials or a specific production step) where other steps are easy to handle with minor quantitative limits, for instance, by getting material from additional suppliers or installing an additional shift.

Resilience in this context means to keep the whole supply chain, especially capacity of warehouses and stock levels in mind to prevent bottlenecks or shortages in advance. Partners should talk about scenarios and the utilization of their equipment. A consequence can be to increase stock levels for defined raw materials or products and to expand warehouses for this purpose.

Of course, this can lead to higher costs for one or some supply-chain partners, and the question is, especially in times without active troubles or crises, if additional costs will be shared between the partners or how they can get them from the market.

20.7 Outsourcing

Companies have to decide to operate their own warehouse or to engage suppliers of warehousing services. Outsourcing of warehousing services is often portrayed as a flexible resource that can be called upon or terminated at relatively short notice and at will.

From the point of view and experience of the author, this is only partly true. On the one hand, outsourcing partners have to utilize their warehouse capacities as fully as possible in order to achieve competitive cost rates. This means that free capacities are sometimes or often scarce, especially at short notice. On the other hand, land and real estate for warehouses are scarce, especially in urban areas. Extension of capacities takes time and also capital resources. Additionally, the economic growth of recent years and decades has led to a shortage in warehouse capacities.

Consequently, the use of outsourcing partners must be considered in advance. The market and the capacity situation of potential partners should always be monitored. This applies in particular to goods with special requirements, such as temperature or hygiene requirements in the warehouse.

20.8 Storage Technology

Storage technology in general is always planned and dimensioned for a specific demand. This means that the type of racks or the forklift trucks are designed to make good use of the space and enable efficient processes.

Resilience in this context means above all flexibility. Rapid retooling and adaptation of technical systems and equipment to meet all requirements in changing situations is the key to success here. Concrete examples could be the conversion by retracting compartments and levels from pallet locations to small parts locations to make possible picking for a larger number of smaller orders from private customers instead of big orders from shops or wholesalers.

Standardization of warehouse technology is also important in this context. For example, common pallet racks can be easily procured, and products from different manufacturers can be used side by side.

20.9 Automatization

The degree of automatization is regularly driven by the quantity of ingoing, stored, and outgoing articles and as a consequence of the investment calculation, which compares manual processes and a higher level of personnel costs with costs of automated systems which lead to a lower rate of process costs.

Unplanned events can lead to different consequences. On the one hand, staff could become unavailable due to a virus as in the COVID-19 pandemic or due to other effects. In this case, completely manual warehouses could be operated by other staff as far as they are available. Automated warehouses systems can have advantages or disadvantages compared with manual warehouses:

Mini-load or automated storage of pallets with retrieval machines: in case of a technical breakdown, access to the storage locations is no longer possible, for instance, due to missing electricity or service staff. There is also no alternative to get to the goods. Particularly, sensitive products could additionally be stored outside such systems in order to remain deliverable at short notice in the event of failures.

Shuttle systems for small parts or pallets: There is access through service ways in the different aisles. This makes ingoings and pickings possible, especially of smaller quantities under low performance. Thus, an emergency operation is possible. However, alternative processes must be worked out in advance for this, for example, to transport the goods from the individual work levels downwards.

In some areas, the pandemic has led to more interest in automation, specifically in the warehouse equipment space (Hodges, 2021, p. 31). Automated warehouses can be designed today so that only a few processes, such as unpacking full pallets from plastic foils, cannot be automated. The advantage is that fully automated warehouses can be operated with only a couple of employees when the technology including the warehouse management system remains functional.

20.10 IT and Digitalization

Managing the corporate IT system and equipment might contribute to managing risks, especially in the case of increasing vulnerability of modern supply chains (Fischer-Preßler et al., 2020, p. 234).

Larger and especially automated warehouses cannot be operated without a functioning warehouse management system or material flow computers. Just think of a chaotic storage, where only the warehouse management system has the information about the storage locations of products.

Usually, the issue of risk is solved by means of security systems. This can be, for example, an IT system running in parallel, which can be switched to in the event of an emergency. Within a company, achieving resilience is still relatively easy.

It becomes more difficult with regard to the connection of partner companies. Today, electronic data interchange is a common technology that connects the IT systems of many companies. Resilience in this context would mean that alternatives for different scenarios are developed and tested in advance so that, in the event of an emergency, a tried-and-tested IT infrastructure could be accessed quickly and flexibly. The question now is whether, after the experience of the COVID-19 pandemic, appropriate cross-company scenarios will be developed and concepts implemented.

20.11 Redundancies and Buffer Capacities

Building in redundancies, which means similarities in equipment like sorters, can be a strategy to prevent breakdowns (Trebilcock, 2021, p. 24). Redundancies are a common topic in automized warehouses. Breakdowns of the IT system, especially the warehouse management systems, conveyors, sorters, or storage, can lead to a stop of all or some activities in a warehouse.

Generally, companies have emergency generators, a second IT infrastructure which operates in parallel, maintenance staff for fast repairs or more retrieval machines than necessary in use. However, how can breakdowns be prevented where the root cause is more than a typical and localized technical problem?

One solution could be to operate more warehouses than required and/or to keep free capacities. This sounds logical and realistic in special situations like pandemics. However, without such conditions, logistics and supply chain managers have to minimize their costs and to increase performance. Typical performance indicators for a warehouse are inventory accuracy, capacity utilization, product damage rate, order cycle time, maintenance costs, or labor productivity and utilization (Laosirhongthong et al., 2018, p. 1709). Arguing to carry higher costs for possible or undefined risks can then be hard.

Ericsson, for instance, operates three manufacturing sites as a way to hedge risks although one site would be sufficient from an operational perspective (Norman & Wieland, 2020, p. 643).

20.12 Site Evaluation

Scoring risks within sites or a whole system can be a strategy to reduce risks and increase resilience (Norman & Wieland, 2020, p. 655).

Such a scoring model could be implemented, for example, by evaluating categories such as risk susceptibility, flexibility of storage systems, flexibility of processes, flexibility of capacity modification, as well as feasibility, effort, and reaction speed for such measures and weighting them accordingly.

What is important in this context, of course, is that in order to build resilience, such assessments are conducted proactively. Only in this way can measures and activities be adequately planned and, if necessary, quickly implemented.

20.13 E-Commerce

The COVID-19 pandemic has accelerated growth in e-commerce and technology, and the results are changing the way many companies think about their supply chains—in ways that will transform logistics (Zimmermann, 2020, p. 9).

The switch to e-commerce is a very big challenge for warehouses. Basically, they are defined and designed for defined market requirements. A rather slow steady adjustment is generally expected today. Processes can be adapted successively, and extensions or automations can be implemented step by step.

Immediate reactions to extraordinary situations make exceptionally fast implementations of warehouses necessary. Therefore, they should be very well thought out in advance. Furthermore, activities like reshoring manufacturing operations to the home country, transforming physical stores into full-blown delivery hubs, and investing in more technology and automation can be realized (McCrea, 2021, p. 55).

20.14 Conclusion

Most companies in the field of warehouse management avoid efforts and accept higher costs for possible risks and exceptional situations. There is also a lack of awareness. Nevertheless, the topic of resilience should be taken very seriously in the area of bearings, as the COVID-19 crisis has taught us.

In general, a higher degree of flexibility and alternative scenarios developed in advance at the site or in the interaction of several warehouse sites can help to respond quickly to crises. This can be done in-house or together with supply chain partners or outsourcing partners.

The topic of resilience should be dealt with proactively by companies, as measures in the area of warehouses are often associated with comprehensive process changes, including the adaptation of IT systems, structural changes, or construction projects.

References

Fischer-Preßler, D., Eismann, K., Pietrowski, R., Fischbach, K., & Schoder, D. (2020). Information technology and risk management in supply chains. *International Journal of Physical Distribution & Logistics Management, 50*(2), 233–254.

Hodges, S. L. (2021). *Strenght & resilience: Equipment leasing & finance magazine* (Vol. 2021, pp. 28–32). Equipment Leasing and Finance Association.

Laosirhongthong, T., Adabanjo, D., Smarananyake, P., Subramanin, N., & Boon-itt, S. (2018). Prioritizing warehouse performance measures in contemporary supply chains. *International Journal of Productivity and Performance Management, 67*(9), 1703–1726.

McCrea, B. (2021). Supply chain redesign – Expecting the unexpected. The top trends driving supply chain design decision for the coming year – and beyond. *Supply Chain Management Review, 2021*, 54–57.

Norman, A., & Wieland, A. (2020). The development of supply chain risk management over time: Revisiting Ericsson. *International Journal of Physical Distribution & Logistics Management, 50*(6), 641–666.

Sawyerr, E., & Harrison, C. (2020). Developing resilient supply chains: Lessons from high reliability organisations. *Supply Chain Managément: An International Journal, 25*, 77–100.
Schulz, J. D. (2020). Resilience put to the test. *Logistics Management, 2020*, 16–19.
Trebilcock, B. (2021). Making resilience a core competence. *Modern Materials Handling, 2021*, 18–26.
Van Hoek, R. (2020). Research opportunities for more resilient post-COVID-19 supply chain – closing the gap between research findings and industry practice. *International Journal of Operations & Production Management, 40*(4), 341–355.
Zimmermann, M. (2020). The year in logistics 2020: Resilience tested. *Supply Chain Management Review, 2020*, 4–9.

Dr. Clemens Schuhmayer is a self-employed logistics consultant with a focus on planning and optimizing warehouses and production sites for leading companies in different areas including production and retailing in Austria as well as abroad. Besides this, he is a Senior Lecturer at WU (Vienna University of Economics and Business) where he teaches Logistics Management.

Chapter 21
How to Successfully Master a Pandemic in a Global Distribution Network?

Roeland Baaijens and Jan Busch

Abstract The supply chain impact of COVID-19 led to varying levels of uncertainty in every country. For Hilti, a global manufacturing company supplying the construction industry, with a vertically integrated supply chain, the following specific risks arose: closures of suppliers, production plants, or country borders could lead to production stops or import stops limiting the replenishment capabilities from the supply side.

To illustrate how the company copes with these challenges this business case focuses on the warehousing function as it represents the "moment of truth," the final delivery to the customer. During the COVID pandemic Hilti benefited from the existing structure and could bring the different resilience elements—visibility, flexibility, collaboration, and control—into play. The combination of ad-hoc actions and at the same time strengthening supply chain resilience within its global logistics strategy was the key to successfully manage the delivery challenges and to keep operations up and running with limited customer impact.

While business environments become more complex and uncertain, previous methods of risk mitigation reach their limits and a resilient supply chain becomes a critical key factor for future business success.

21.1 Introduction

Hilti is a global manufacturing company supplying the construction industry with a wide portfolio range. With headquarters based in Schaan, Liechtenstein, Hilti employs approx. 30,000 people in more than 120 countries and has a yearly turnover of around CHF 6 billion. The main product groups in the portfolio are anchoring systems, fire protection products, electric tools for drilling and cutting, direct fastening and diamond drilling—complemented with system solutions, software, and services. For many areas, Hilti covers the entire value chain from product

---

R. Baaijens (✉) · J. Busch
Global Logistics, Hilti Corporation, Schaan, Liechtenstein
e-mail: Roeland.Baaijens@hilti.com

S. Kummer et al. (eds.), *Supply Chain Resilience*, Springer Series in Supply Chain Management 17, https://doi.org/10.1007/978-3-030-95401-7_21

Fig. 21.1 Hilti Global Distribution Center in Liechtenstein

development, manufacturing, and distribution to sales and after-market services including repair. This vertically integrated supply chain network with a direct sales approach comprises 19 global production facilities, about 650 suppliers, roughly 13,000 different items and a global logistics network to support the business model. This translates into more than 250,000 customer contacts and over 150,000 customer order lines per day in the logistics network comprising demand and supply planning, warehousing, and transport management.

21.2 Problem Framing

The supply chain impact of COVID-19 started out as a supply crisis, transitioned into a global demand crisis, and finally led to varying levels of uncertainty in every country. In this business case, the focus is on the warehousing function as this represents the "moment of truth," the final delivery to the customer. It is essential for the revenue stream of Hilti: You can only invoice what has been delivered (Fig. 21.1).

The pandemic confronted the business with three main challenges:

Unpredictable virus spread patterns: Each country with its population was affected in a different way and at a different moment.

Unpredictable and varying government reactions, especially in the beginning, are more emotional than rational. Restrictions, directives, and even full lockdowns came into effect often without early warnings.

Unpredictable influence on people's reactions: This was a "non-transferable experience" and affected private and professional life alike. People could not imagine that the pandemic would hit their personal life and that they also would be subject to a lockdown—many countries lived in denial for a very long period—which could change from one moment to the other in a crisis situation which restricted people's personal lives significantly.

Out of the above challenges, the following specific supply chain risks arose for Hilti regarding supply, demand, and delivery. Closures of suppliers, production plants, or country borders could lead to production stops or import stops limiting the replenishment capabilities from the supply side.

Governmental lockdowns of the construction industry or customers closing their business could lead to steep drops in demand.

Shutdowns of local Hilti warehouses or Hilti stores due to regional restrictions could strongly limit the ability to fulfill customer demand.

Whereas production or import delays can be partially mitigated by inventory, closures of warehouses directly negatively impact customer availability, inventory turnover, and revenue. Therefore, managing the global warehouse and Hilti Store network is crucial for business success.

21.3 Solution

To be ready to cope with these challenges, Hilti Global Logistics (GL) is relying on ad hoc actions and at the same time strengthening supply chain resilience within its strategy GL2020+; based on four pillars – visibility, flexibility, collaboration, and control – embedded in a governance framework building on people, processes, and digitalization.

Tracking and monitoring supply chain events and patterns and gaining insights (visibility) links with the ability to deduct actions and adapt to disruptions accordingly without high operational cost impact (flexibility). Both are facilitated by the development of long-term trust-based relationships across departments as well as strategic supply chain partners (collaboration) and the capability to implement and follow guiding principles and processes that avert disruptions.

During the COVID-19 pandemic, Hilti benefited from the existing structure and could bring the different resilience elements into play to successfully manage the delivery challenges:

Visibility is about creating real-time transparency end-to-end, on one hand of the inventory and production capacity along the supply chain and on the other hand of the expected demand. In Hilti, all sales and operations planning activities are executed in one global ERP system. There is one global source for key master data for customers and products. On top all containers at sea have been real-time tracked with Wakeo, and so system ETA (estimated time of arrival) is always up to date. Flexibility adds the component of being able in a cost-effective way to adjust supply to the volatility in demand. At Hilti, the S&OP frequency has been increased from monthly to weekly, which leads to a more accurate steering of the material flow adjusted to the abrupt changes in demand during the beginning of the pandemic. As a result, the inventories in the warehouses around the world are further optimized to serve the Hilti customers. Hilti has a decentralized distribution network to enable next-day customer delivery. For example, in Europe alone, there are 15 warehouses (globally more than 80), which means that, in case of a lockdown of one warehouse, the customers can be supplied from a different location within two days. Also, the network of more than 480 Hilti stores worldwide plays an important role to continue to deliver to customers. During the pandemic, a number of the stores were selected to stock more mainstream products, just in case the warehouse in that country would be locked down. To be really effective in creating visibility and flexibility, the collaboration between the different functions within the company is essential. Hilti invested in fostering collaboration and building strong relationships over many years. There are institutionalized ways like "Glomex[1]," "Culture Journey[2]," S&OP meetings, and cross-functional shop floor management. There are also many opportunities for informal moments like in trainings and personal exchanges. To extend the visibility and flexibility beyond the supply chain controlled by a company, collaboration with suppliers is crucial. At Hilti, there are long-standing relationships with the main 3PLs, meetings on executive level and ongoing initiatives together to improve the performance.

When the crisis struck, the company could directly leverage the established structures and the environment of mutual trust and eagerness to control the supply chain to the best extent possible.

First and foremost, Hilti set three overall priorities for the company which were guiding all decisions and activities (in order of importance):

1. Protect team members and business partners
2. Go the extra mile for customers
3. Act in a financially viable way

Within this framework, global and regional core teams and task forces (clear roles and responsibilities) have been created to start working on how to master the delivery challenges in a structured way.

As COVID-19 was a nontransferable experience, central guidance was essential to facilitate decentral decision-making as well as actions and escalation steps. For Hilti, the main part has been "Operation Hard Brake." It aligned the whole company to work with the hypothesis that demand in March, April, and May would be reduced by 30%. This was steering corrective actions in the entire supply chain.

At the same time, the decision power remained with the local market organizations and teams, so all were still accountable and could decide what exact measures to take given their local circumstances.

[1]GLOMEX = Global Logistics Meeting Experts: a bi-annual meeting over several days to share best practices, work on ongoing topics, and celebrate successfully closed projects.

[2]Culture Journey – The Hilti way – All employees participate on a regular basis to retreats focusing on strategy and company core values (integrity, courage, teamwork, and commitment).

The interplay of existing supply chain structures and engaged teams enabled Hilti to keep operations up and running with limited customer impact. Warehouses could continue operations (meeting all governmental requirements) and were not "flooded" with unnecessary inventory. Consequently, the ambitious 2020 inventory target was reached, and customer availability was at a satisfactory level of 97%, though slightly below target. With all company efforts, Hilti managed to remain highly profitable in 2020 and had no recorded case of COVID-19 infection passed between employees, which was the first priority: To protect all team members.

21.4 Relevance

Sailing through these stormy times successfully confirms that Hilti's company culture and global logistics strategy (GL2020+) sets the right direction for the ongoing supply chain resilience journey. Based on experiences and learnings combined with external research, strategy and step changers have been critically reviewed. All principles and key elements are valid, but the review process identified two potential areas for acceleration: digitalization and sustainability. Both have already been part of the strategy yet need to be further prioritized. For example, Hilti decided to accelerate the implementation of a new TMS (transportation management system) and to streamline the EWM (extended warehouse management) globally. By extending visibility and flexibility in distribution, transparency and agility along the entire chain are further strengthened. This also prepares the way toward more distribution control, intelligent routings, carrier changes, and overall a better utilization of transport capacity leading to reduced CO2 emissions.

Hilti's way of handling COVID-19 in distribution is exemplary for all supply chain functions. The different Glomex and regional communities worked smoothly together with regional task forces, sharing essential information, experiences, and best practices.

Similarly to internal collaboration, long-term relationships with suppliers are also important to align supply chain priorities and achieve successful outcomes. Even when full integration is not possible, trustworthy relationships and good judgment often result in a win/win for both sides.

21.5 Conclusion

While business environments become more complex and uncertain, previous methods of risk mitigation reach their limits, and a resilient supply chain becomes one of the critical key factors for future business success. The COVID-19 pandemic certainly boosted awareness and advancements. However, resilience is not a rigid one-time initiative but a continuous process of assessment, learning, and adaption.

For Hilti, this litmus test proved that the supply chain is already quite resilient, the applied strategic framework could be confirmed, and improvement areas were identified: collaboration was one major success factor, whereas strategic elements of digitalization and sustainability need to be further accelerated.

Talking about good collaboration is easy, but in practice it is hard work associated with time and costs to build and maintain relationships and foster mutual cooperation. It is an element which plays a role in every supply chain function and continues to be in Hilti's focus.

The company's digitalization journey with implementations of systems and associated trainings (e.g., TMS, EWM) will be, together with sustainability, Hilti's priority areas to accelerate. Sustainability is not only "the right thing to do" but also improves supply chain resilience and customer engagement. Being ahead of governmental laws and restrictions and anticipating customer expectations keep the operation radius wide open and allow to focus on customer satisfaction.

This way Hilti logistics continues to adapt and ensures a resilient supply chain as a key factor for future business success.

Roeland Baaijens Executive Vice President, Global Logistics, Hilti. Roeland is a member of the Executive Management Team of the Hilti Group since January 2010. He has the global responsibility for all the logistics activities including transport, warehousing, materials management, and customs.

Before Roeland joined Hilti he worked 13 years for Nestlé in the Netherlands and in the HQ in Switzerland. In the Netherlands, he was responsible for the procurement, planning, warehousing, and transport activities including agricultural services. In Switzerland, he was leading the global support function for warehousing and transport. Later on, he became the Lean program manager.

Roeland started his career at FrieslandCampina as a management trainee and worked later on as a production and planning manager.

Roeland holds a master's degree in industrial engineering from the Eindhoven Technical University. He is also a graduate of the Program Executive Development (PED) from IMD.

Jan Busch holds a master's degree in Industrial Engineering from the Karlsruhe Institute of Technology. He joined the global Hilti team in November 2019 as a Global Process Manager Planning. Within his responsibility for demand planning and planning systems area, he partners with other key functions to drive operational improvements and lead S&OP projects to continue Hilti's planning excellence journey. Before transitioning to his global role Jan worked 4 years in Hilti's Central Europe region hub as a Materials Manager and later as a Sales & Operations Planning Manager focusing on regional forecasting, inventory management, and large customer project coordination.

Chapter 22
Resilience Strategies for Freight Transportation: An Overview of the Different Transport Modes Responses

Eveline Beer, Jasmin Mikl, Hans-Joachim Schramm, and David M. Herold

Abstract For the transport and logistics industry, the COVID-19 pandemic can be regarded as one of the most difficult challenges since the beginning of the globalization. Studies showed that transport and logistics sector suffered more than the average economy and had to deal with both high supply and demand fluctuations, leading to major personnel, operational, and strategic changes. In this chapter, we present the (re)actions of the different transport modes, namely maritime shipping, airfreight, rail, road, and infrastructure. In particular, this chapter will not only provide an overview about the resilience strategies of transport and logistics companies as a response to the COVID-19 pandemic but will also present the impacts on the different transport modes and discuss specific initiatives and actions taken by transport and logistics companies. These discussions and the actions presented will provide academics as well as managers with a crucial understanding of the impact of the COVID-19 pandemic on the different transport modes and thus provide a theoretical and practical foundation to further spark discussions about the role of resilience in the transport and logistics sector.

22.1 Introduction

The transport and logistics industry was one of the most severely hit sectors during the beginning of the COVID-19 pandemic. For transport and logistic managers, who experienced the emergence of globalization, the evolution of the just-in-time supply chain and the rise of e-commerce, the pandemic can be considered as a crucial challenge. Birshan et al. (2020) found that the transport and logistics sector suffered more than the average economy. However, it also seems that the transport and logistics sector was able to cope with these changes—and the companies' and their managers reacted quickly and found ways to adapt to these situations.

E. Beer (✉) · J. Mikl · H.-J. Schramm · D. M. Herold
Institute for Transport and Logistics Management, WU (Vienna University of Economics and Business), Vienna, Austria
e-mail: eveline.beer@wu.ac.at

S. Kummer et al. (eds.), *Supply Chain Resilience*, Springer Series in Supply Chain Management 17, https://doi.org/10.1007/978-3-030-95401-7_22

In the following subsections, we will present the (re)actions of the different transport modes, namely, maritime shipping, airfreight, rail, road, and infrastructure. In particular, the subsections will provide a brief discussion of what companies have done to adapt to the COVID-19 pandemic and thus build more resilient supply chains and operations.

22.2 Transport Mode Resilience Strategies

22.2.1 Maritime Shipping

Traditionally, maritime shipping was and is always subject to more or less predictable market cycles, where a steady increase (decrease) in demand for transport capacity triggers an increase (decrease) in supply in the form of new buildings (demolitions) of vessels in the mid- to long run (Goulielmos, 2020). Due to the nature of maritime shipping operations characterized by rather long planning horizons in general, carriers have limited options to adapt to rapidly changing market conditions, and the deployment of certain supply side flexibility tactics is key (Mason & Nair, 2013). In a downturn market, slow steaming, rerouting on longer voyages, blanking of sailings, mothballing or decommissioning for maintenance, and scrapping or conversion for other future purposes help to fine-tune fleet size and so actual transport capacity offered to the market. Accordingly, in an upturn market, overall speeding up of operations, minimizing idle time caused by maintenance, keeping old vessels longer in use, chartering additional ones, and purchasing secondhand tonnage whenever there is an opportunity to do so are corresponding short-term actions of carriers to keep pace with an increasing demand for transport capacity.

In 2020, however, maritime shipping experienced an unprecedented rollercoaster ride, starting with an overall slowdown of seaborne trade in the first half year driven by lockdowns in China, shortly after the Chinese New Year, followed by Europe and North America, resulted in deeply depressed freight markets in both bulk and liner shipping (UNCTAD, 2020). Many vessels were laid up, and shipping schedules were cut down to a minimum with a myriad of blanked sailings. Then, in the second half, changes in consumption and shopping patterns of consumers during lockdowns, in connection with stimulus packages to alleviate the economic effect of the pandemic crisis, led to a heavy surge in import demand especially for manufactured consumer goods and office equipment commonly sourced in China or other Southeast Asian countries (Dynamar, 2021). This coincided with an overall slowdown of seaport operations forced by necessary pandemic measures, including the occasional shutdowns of seaports to counter local COVID-19 outbreaks, and a sudden blockade of the Suez Canal for six days in March 2021 by the ultra large container vessel Ever Given exacerbated the situation even further. Subsequently, port-handling capacities were overstretched, so that vessels are queued for days to enter ports, resulting in a heavily deteriorated schedule reliability in both bulk and liner shipping. In addition to this, these seaport congestions crippled further transport operations from/to the hinterland to a high extent so that, in the end, freight rates skyrocketed by the end of 2020 to all-time highs in liner shipping.

By mid-2021, there was little hope for a quick recovery, with virtually all vessels able to load containers employed and container equipment rarely available, as it takes about 20% more containers to transport the same amount of goods than normal under the present circumstances (Baker, 2021). The same is valid (albeit to a lower extent) for bulk shipping struggling with up-ticking demand and port congestions, too. However, there is an emerging consensus that here the usual mechanism of the shipping cycle will not just be new construction, as order books of ship yards are already filled up with container vessels for a long period (Miller, 2021).

22.2.2 *Airfreight*

Due to the sharp reduction in passenger flights during the COVID-19 crisis, the airfreight industry was down in May 2020 to 10–15% of 2019 levels (IATA, 2021). The connection between passenger flights and transported cargo results from the fact that the so-called belly cargo is transported in the lower section of passenger aircraft, and this type of cargo makes up 50% of the world's air cargo. This unprecedented decline has affected all elements of the air transport value chain: aircraft manufacturers, airlines, airports, and related sectors such as hospitality and retail. However, as important goods were transported by air during the crisis and the e-commerce sector has increased significantly, despite expectations, freight rates increased. Some freight forwarders even reported increasing congestion at airports due to delays (Remko, 2020). Although volumes were still down in comparison to 2019, in April 2020, there was an increase in capacity and volume goods handled. As the overall capacity expansion was greater than the net decline, air freight rates further increased (Twin et al., 2020).

To overcome this problem and close capacity gaps, airlines immediately started to work closely with airports, and many companies have used creative alternatives to their usual means of transportation. As described earlier, the reduction in passenger flights has also reduced the airplane belly cargo capacity, meaning that contrary to earlier crisis situations, there has been a shortage of supply and too much demand. For this reason, DHL, e.g., has used charter flights to facilitate shipments to and from China. In addition, airlines have also used passenger aircraft for cargo transport and transported the goods in the passenger cabins without major adjustments (Twin et al., 2020). During the crisis, shipment visibility and connectivity were more important than ever. To maintain resilience and strengthen long-term competitiveness, the Changi Air Cargo Community System (ACCS) was introduced at the Singapore air cargo hub. This open ecosystem is a collaborative community-based application based on an information-sharing platform. It brings together all data from all cargo handling processes of the parties involved. The main purpose of this is to help optimize or increase operational efficiency and enable end-to-end digitalization of air cargo supply chains (Changi-Airport, 2020). Furthermore, as a resilience measure, even outside the pandemic, switching to another mode of transport or cooperation between airlines and operators of other modes of transport can be a solution. Due to the expansion of the Silk-Belt-Road, air traffic between China and Europe can be handled by rail easily. Experts are even predicting a boom in the rail route between China and Europe, as 60% of the air freight capacity on this route has been lost to date (Rooley, 2021). Observing long-term strategies for building resilience, the airline industry should relocate their fleets partly to exclusively serve air cargo demand. According to IATA, states have the greatest role to play in developing their own air transport system, which should be resilient to future crises. This system should be supported by regulatory oversight and capacity (ICAO, 2021).

To sum up, the aviation industry was one of the sectors most affected by the crisis. Although some measures were taken by airlines, airports, and companies to maintain capacity, it is important to develop a resilient solution for such crises in the future. In addition to the development of separate air freight capacities (independent of passenger transports), the development of an end-to-end digital information chain as well as the cooperation with other modes of transport is recommended.

22.2.3 Rail

As rail transport is predominantly used to transport bulk goods, this mode of transport also faced major challenges during the COVID-19 crisis, particularly in connection with the slowdown in industrial production. However, rail freight has come through the crisis better than other modes of transport and has even managed to improve on some routes. In times of crisis, rail freight has proven its resilience, e.g., it proved that it can operate even in sectors where it is not yet so strongly represented. For example, the rail industry has quickly managed to adapt its transport to types of goods that were previously not part of its core business. For example, the Scandinavian-Mediterranean rail corridor has been instrumental in making rail a fast means of transporting bulk goods (Bešinović, 2020). Furthermore, rail transport has made it possible for important foodstuffs such as pasta to be transported from Italy to Germany. In comparison to other modes of transport, the railroad has also offered retailers the ability to respond flexibly to supply shortages, and it allows consumers to maintain their shopping. Moreover, if we look, for example, at freight traffic between the EU and China via trans-Eurasian rail lines, we can see that it has remained largely unaffected by the negative consequences of the COVID-19 crisis. Unlike other modes of transport, trans-Eurasian rail transport is even experiencing a period of growth. Before the health crisis, its services were eight times cheaper than air freight at three times the time required (DSV, 2020). At the same time, rail transport was twice as expensive as sea freight, but the transit time was half as long from China to Europe. The crisis has not only led to higher air freight prices, as discussed above, but also to longer transit times for air and ocean freight, which has increased the competitiveness of rail. As a result of the lack of viable modes of transportation between the EU and China due to the crisis, trans-Eurasian rail lines became a reliable and economical option for companies that needed to receive and ship goods (Shepard, 2020; Tardivo et al., 2021). However, in order to make European rail freight even more resilient to pandemics or similar threats in the future, measures need to be taken. In the long term, for example, a higher degree of automation and digitalization (Dobrovnik et al., 2018) of operations could create a different system that is less vulnerable to disruption (Tardivo et al., 2021).

Overall, the advantages of the rail freight industry throughout 2020 were rooted in their capacity and cost efficiency especially for the e-commerce business. Experts say and data shows that rail freight responded very well to rapid demand shifts during the crisis and had the ability to transport goods outside their normal range.

22.2.4 Road

The pressure for the road/trucking sector stemming from COVID-19 can be considered as one of the greatest among all transportation modes (maybe except for the parcel express industry) (Ivanov & Das, 2020; Kim, 2021). In particular, service breakdowns and delays were the most critical aspects along the trucking supply chain as most of the trucking companies rely on hub-and-spoke terminal networks which involve load/unload issues at each terminal, in particular for LTL shipments (Paul & Chowdhury, 2020; Queiroz et al., 2020). As such, usually at least three drivers are involved in a complete shipment; thus if one driver is delayed or missing, the entire shipment is delayed. Moreover, trucking companies laid off workers during the beginning of the pandemic (when demand was dropping) and had problems to rehire them when volumes began to increase. Because of the additional volatility of demand, transit times were stretched, leading to extensive delays both for shippers and consumers (JOC, 2020).

In order to address these delays and problems stemming from COVID-19, trucking companies implemented strategic and tactical measures. One of the first initiatives was the protection of the workforce, not only because of safety reasons but also to maintain operations through availability of the workforce (Birshan et al., 2020; Kramer & Kramer, 2020; Ritter & Pedersen, 2020). As a consequence, trucking companies limited truck driver access to the respective facilities and told drivers to stay in their truck cabins, while others prohibited indoor pick-up and deliveries. However, the limited access also led to a loss of capacity and longer unloading and loading times, which trucking companies addressed by higher staffing levels and increased working hours as well as limiting the paperwork (JOC, 2020).

In addition, trucking companies enforced electronic bills of landing to reduce the risk of transferring the COVID-19 virus via the paperwork or hand-to-hand handovers (Yang, 2019). As a consequence, most trucking companies and shippers waived the requirement to sign the delivery receipt (or POD = Proof of delivery) and implemented digital documents instead, thereby increasing paperless processes throughout the organization (Hribernik et al., 2020; Mikl et al., 2020). To build further resilient processes, trucking companies strived to enhance their operational flexibility by hiring more subcontractors but also increased communication with the sales force to pinpoint potential problems and plan ahead for strategic customers (Herold et al., 2021). Hattrup-Silberberg et al. (2020), in a McKinsey report, found also that companies adjusted their strategies to reimagine the future of mobility through autonomous driving, connected cars, electrified vehicles, and shared mobility.

Overall, the trucking industry can be regarded as one of most severely hit industries during the pandemic. The main thing to consider is that the trucking industry can often not be separated from other industries, as most physical goods are transported by truck and the industry thus represents a crucial ink in today's local and global supply chains. However, we can see that trucking companies have reacted quickly to address the problems stemming from the COVID-19 pandemic and have implemented initiatives not only to enhance operational flexibility and enforce digitalization and data management but also to optimize logistics, infrastructure capacity, and personnel capacity.

22.2.5 Infrastructure

The companies operating infrastructure assets were facing the COVID-19 crisis from a twofold perspective. As mentioned in the chapters above, changes in goods transported and people employed led to changes in the volumes and response times across the transportation sector. In addition, COVID-19 increased the risk of compromising the response abilities of critical infrastructures against catastrophies resulting from climate change (Clark-Ginsberg et al., 2020). Looking at transportation assets, highway operators in particular took a strong hit caused not only by the challenges to provide operational and maintenance services but also because of the strong impact of COVID-19 on traffic levels (Cruz & Sarmento, 2021).

In order to provide a response to the challenges and respond to disruptions, highway operators started to focus on the safety of their employees and clients first. Levels of traffic though are still under investigation given the remaining uncertainty around transport levels going forward (Cruz & Sarmento, 2021). At seaports that suffered from disruptions in the maritime supply chains, responses to the crisis were dependent on the type of terminal and its place within the supply chain. Measures included the usage of long-term storage yards, the increase of volumes for goods with high demand, or the increase in stored goods at low prices independent of current demand. Even goods that pre-crisis had been sold only on the domestic markets were prepared to be shipped internationally through maritime supply chains (Mańkowska et al., 2021). For railway carriers, charges to gain infrastructure access are major. The European Parliament established measures by Regulation 2020/1429 of 7 October 2020 recommending to reduce, defer, or waive the respective (e.g., track access or reservation) charges for using railway infrastructure for railway carriers (Pomykała, 2021). Some airport operators were forced to fully shut down operations, leading to major organizational changes for reopening. Airports in particular, not only for passengers but also for freight, faced major challenges given the volume of people working and passing through them. Increasing safety levels in line with governmental guidelines and collecting and processing health data led to new standards likely to stay (Blišťanová et al., 2021).

Overall, the operators of transportation infrastructure assets faced major challenges in responding to the COVID-19 pandemic. As discussed above, infrastructure operators can find appropriate reactions to the current and future crises in various, often not directly linked, fields of business. It has been shown that a holistic view including all stakeholders and their areas of business is a key factor in addressing the current pandemic. An integrated approach including not only the infrastructure operation, but also human resources, the entire transport supply chain, technology, and health of personnel and customers, is integral. Furthermore, it is noted that some of the measures implemented will likely stay with us for the time being, resulting in improved resilience, increasing safety standards, and an increased flexibility in organizational and managerial decisions. However, it is recommended to view the responses to the current pandemic in light of the overall circumstances of climate change and its impact on transportation infrastructure.

22.3 Conclusion

In this chapter, we set out to provide an overview of the (re)actions and resilience strategies of transport and logistics companies as a response to the COVID-19 pandemic. We presented brief overviews of the impact on the different transport modes and discussed initiatives and actions taken by organizations. Of course, our discussions and the actions presented here are not exhaustive, but we hope that the comprehensive presentation of the main aspects per transportation mode, maritime shipping, airfreight, rail, road and infrastructure will inform the reader and thus provide a theoretical foundation to further spark discussions about resilience in the transport and logistics sector.

References

Baker. (2021). Container capacity shortage set to last until fourth quarter. *Lloyd's List*. Retrieved May 21, 2021, from https://lloydslist.maritimeintelligence.informa.com/LL1136867/Container-capacity-shortage-set-to-last-until-fourth-quarter

Bešinović, N. (2020). Resilience in railway transport systems: A literature review and research agenda. *Transport Reviews, 40*(4), 457–478.

Birshan, M., Lund, S., Alicke, K., Smit, S., Bariball, E., Woetzel, J., et al. (2020). *Risk, resilience, and rebalancing in global value chains*. Retrieved from https://www.mckinsey.com/~/media/McKinsey/Business%20Functions/Operations/Our%20Insights/Risk%20resilience%20and%

20rebalancing%20in%20global%20value%20chains/Risk-resilience-and-rebalancing-in-global-value-chains-full-report-vH.pdf
Blišťanová, M., Tirpáková, M., & Brůnová, Ľ. (2021). Overview of safety measures at selected airports during the COVID-19 pandemic. *Sustainability, 13*(15), 8499.
Changi-Airport. (2020). *How does Changi Airport manage air cargo during the pandemic?* Retrieved from https://www.changiairport.com/corporate/media-centre/changijourneys/faces-of-changi/CargoInterview.html
Clark-Ginsberg, A., Rueda, I. A., Monken, J., Liu, J., & Chen, H. (2020). Maintaining critical infrastructure resilience to natural hazards during the COVID-19 pandemic: Hurricane preparations by US energy companies. *Journal of Infrastructure Preservation and Resilience, 1*(1), 10.
Cruz, C. O., & Sarmento, J. M. (2021). The impact of COVID-19 on highway traffic and management: The case study of an operator perspective. *Sustainability, 13*(9), 5320.
Dobrovnik, M., Herold, D. M., Fürst, E., & Kummer, S. (2018). Blockchain for and in logistics: What to adopt and where to start. *Logistics, 2*(3), 18.
DSV. (2020). *Rail freight transport between China and Europe*. Retrieved from https://www.dsv.com/en/insights/expert-opinions/rail-freight-between-europe-and-china
Dynamar. (2021). *DynaLiners Trades Review 2021*. Dynamar.
Goulielmos, A. M. (2020). An anatomy of cycles in shipping industry, 1946-2020. *Modern Economy, 11*, 1671–1695. https://doi.org/10.4236/me.2020.1110116
Hattrup-Silberberg, M., Hausler, S., Heineke, K., Laverty, N., Möller, T., Schwedhelm, D., & Wu, T. (2020). *Five COVID-19 aftershocks reshaping mobility's future. McKinsey & Company.*
Herold, D. M., Nowicka, K., Pluta-Zaremba, A., & Kummer, S. (2021). COVID-19 and the pursuit of supply chain resilience: Reactions and "lessons learned" from logistics service providers (LSPs). *Supply Chain Management: An International Journal, 26*(6), 702–714.
Hribernik, M., Zero, K., Kummer, S., & Herold, D. M. (2020). City logistics: Towards a blockchain decision framework for collaborative parcel deliveries in micro-hubs. *Transportation Research Interdisciplinary Perspectives, 8*, 100274.
IATA. (2021). *Annual review of the air industry*. Retrieved from https://www.iata.org/
ICAO. (2021). *Building resilience*. Retrieved from https://www.icao.int/covid/cart/Pages/CART-Report%2D%2D-Building-Resistance.aspx
Ivanov, D., & Das, A. (2020). Coronavirus (COVID-19/SARS-CoV-2) and supply chain resilience: A research note. *International Journal of Integrated Supply Management, 13*(1), 90–102.
JOC. (2020). *JOC Insights: COVID-19 Impacts Freight Transit Times*. Retrieved from https://www.joc.com/sites/default/files/u45421/Whitepapers/JOC-LTL-COVID-19%20Impacts-WP-81404-v5.pdf
Kim, K. (2021). Impacts of COVID-19 on transportation: Summary and synthesis of interdisciplinary research. *Transportation Research Interdisciplinary Perspectives, 9*, 100305.
Kramer, A., & Kramer, K. Z. (2020). The potential impact of the Covid-19 pandemic on occupational status, work from home, and occupational mobility. *Journal of Vocational Behavior, 119*, 103442.
Mańkowska, M., Pluciński, M., Kotowska, I., & Filina-Dawidowicz, L. (2021). Seaports during the COVID-19 pandemic: The terminal operators' tactical responses to disruptions in maritime supply chains. *Energies, 14*(14), 4339.
Mason, R., & Nair, R. (2013). Supply-side strategic flexibility capabilities in container liner shipping. *International Journal of Logistics Management, 24*(1), 22–48. https://doi.org/10.1108/IJLM-05-2013-0053
Mikl, J., Herold, D. M., Ćwiklicki, M., & Kummer, S. (2020). The impact of digital logistics start-ups on incumbent firms: A business model perspective. *The International Journal of Logistics Management, 32*(4), 1461–1480.
Miller, G. (2021). *Shipping bulls are back: First container stocks, now dry bulk*. American Shipper. Retrieved April 4, 2021, from https://www.freightwaves.com/news/shipping-bulls-are-back-first-containers-now-dry-bulk

Paul, S. K., & Chowdhury, P. (2020). A production recovery plan in manufacturing supply chains for a high-demand item during COVID-19. *International Journal of Physical Distribution & Logistics Management, 51*(2), 104–125.

Pomykała, A. (2021). Railway infrastructure access rates in the context of the COVID-19 pandemic. In *Problemy Kolejnictwa* (Issue 190, pp. 105–112). Railway Reports.

Queiroz, M. M., Ivanov, D., Dolgui, A., & Wamba, S. F. (2020). Impacts of epidemic outbreaks on supply chains: Mapping a research agenda amid the COVID-19 pandemic through a structured literature review. *Annals of Operations Research*, 1–38.

Remko, V. H. (2020). Research opportunities for a more resilient post-COVID-19 supply chain–closing the gap between research findings and industry practice. *International Journal of Operations Production Management, 40*(4), 341–355.

Ritter, T., & Pedersen, C. L. (2020). Digitization capability and the digitalization of business models in business-to-business firms: Past, present, and future. *Industrial Marketing Management, 86*, 180–190.

Rooley, J. (2021), *COVID-19 impact on the air cargo industry*. Retrieved from https://www.willistowerswatson.com/en-US/Insights/2021/01/covid-19-impact-on-the-air-cargo-industry

Shepard, W. (2020). *China-Europe Rail is set to boom COVID-19 chokes*. Retrieved from https://www.forbes.com/sites/wadeshepard/2020/03/31/china-europe-rail-is-set-to-boom-as-covid-19-chokes-air-sea-and-road-transport/

Tardivo, A., Carrillo Zanuy, A., & Sánchez Martín, C. (2021). COVID-19 impact on transport: A Paper from the Railways' systems research perspective. *Transportation Research Record*, p. 0361198121990674.

Twin, I., Qureshi, N., Conde, M. L., Guinea, C. G., & Rojas, D. P. (2020). *The impact of Covid-19 on Logistics*. Retrieved from

UNCTAD. (2020). *Review of Maritime Transport 2020*. United Nations Conference on Trade and Development.

Yang, C.-S. (2019). Maritime shipping digitalization: Blockchain-based technology applications, future improvements, and intention to use. *Transportation Research Part E: Logistics and Transportation Review, 131*, 108–117.

Eveline Beer is a research and teaching associate at the Institute for Transport and Logistics Management at WU (Vienna University of Economics and Business). Her research focuses on infrastructure financing and investments and in particular on the impact of emerging technologies on transport infrastructure. In addition, she works on consulting and research projects in the same field. Eveline holds a degree in International Business Administration from WU (Vienna University of Economics and Business) as well as the CEMS Master in International Management. Eveline has more than ten years of private sector experience in working on infrastructure projects for international investment banks and asset managers.

Jasmin Mikl is a university assistant at the Institute for Transport and Logistics Management at WU (Vienna University of Economics and Business). Her research focuses on digitalization in logistics and in particular on the digitalization of freight forwarders and digital startups. She also works on numerous different management consulting and research projects. Jasmin holds a B.A. and M.A. in Business Administration from WU (Vienna University of Economics and Business).

Hans-Joachim Schramm is a Senior Lecturer at WU (Vienna University of Economics and Business) and an External Lecturer at Copenhagen Business School (CBS). He holds a diploma degree in economics from Humboldt-University at Berlin and a doctoral degree from the Dresden University of Technology. Being a forwarding agent by profession and a secretary general of Internationaler Verband der Tarifeure (IVT)—Organisation of Tariff and Transport Experts (http://www.int-int.org), the main focus of his research and teaching activity is about international transport and logistics management as well as digitalization, economics, and policy issues in sea, air, rail, and road transport markets. So far, he authored quite a few papers and monographs in this domain, contributed to peer-review processes to several journals, and is an Editorial Advisory Board member at the International Journal of Logistics Management (IJLM).

David M. Herold is a postdoctoral researcher at WU (Vienna University of Economics and Business) with a focus on sustainable supply chains. He completed his doctorate degree from Griffith University, Australia and also holds B.A. in Business Administration, a MBA degree, and a M.A. in International Relations and has held several visiting and teaching positions across Asia-Pacific and Europe. Prior to his academic career, David worked for more than ten years in a Fortune 500 Global Logistics company and has extensive industry and management experience in strategic operations planning and business development.

Chapter 23
Thoughts About Individual Resilience Impact to Team and Organization

Anna Sparty

Abstract Resilience is not anymore fancy word but necessity in the world disrupted by COVID-19 pandemic and its after waves in supply chains, companies work, and private lives.

In the article, the author uses own experiences and insights from different sources like podcasts, Ted talks, books with key inspiration from New York bestselling author Brene Brown. She presents importance of individual soft skills, leadership, and company culture in building resilience.

The world is changing faster than we can become more resilient. However, if we stay curious, open for development, and build change into our daily habits we may be able to keep pace with some of the changes and uncertainty of the world.

23.1 Introduction

"In the past, jobs were about muscles, now they're about brain, but in the future, they'll be about heart."—Minouche Shafik, director of London School of Economics. 2020, greatly affected everyone's lives, forcing us to reflect on what we knew as stable and unchangeable. We all observed significant differences in reactions and speed of actions. This raises key questions of what is behind resilience in individuals and groups of people, who are the decision makers in organizations, countries, and individual lives.

To start, let me share a personal story as reference for my thoughts on people resilience traits and behaviors. I started my senior leadership journey working in Bangkok taking responsibility for the South East Asian region. It was my first big role in a complex region while I was a total greenhorn to Asian culture. My first month's discoveries were not only spicy food and hot weather (as all my colleagues in Europe thought) but first symptoms of serious supply chain crisis. Months later at a business dinner with CEO, he inquired as to how I was able to manage the crisis so well. I boasted back, "Managing crises is in my blood as I constantly needed to deal

A. Sparty (✉)
Supply Chain Management, Vienna, Austria

S. Kummer et al. (eds.), *Supply Chain Resilience*, Springer Series in Supply Chain Management 17, https://doi.org/10.1007/978-3-030-95401-7_23

with them while growing up during collapse of communism in Poland. . . ." This was just small part of the answer.

Many years later after collecting more experience leading teams through various difficulties, reorganizations, bottlenecks, and crises, I began reflecting on the types of people I worked with. This made me acknowledge the personality traits and behaviors that make some people more resilient than others and some quicker to bounce back than others.

Why is resilience becoming the area of focus for so many people today? This has much to do with the speed of changes that we experience every day with digitalization and constantly evolving technologies that make it close to impossible for most to keep up with. We feel further out of the loop, as with technological advancement we no longer have the capacity to manage our most basic information. How do you feel about algorithms being always at hand, observing, listening to your shopping behaviors, and supplying you with what you need before you notice it? Cool? Scary? Not in control? We feel less in control, no longer able to manage our own data or even understand how it's distributed. While we may be accustomed to this, it nonetheless creates a tension that can accumulate stress.

This speed of changes, complexity, and lack of full control are daily professional and personal challenges that are managed better or worse depending on one's resilience skill set. In the business environment, the speed of reactions and the ability to quickly find opportunities in challenges defines who the frontrunner is. Therefore, we can observe companies focus on building soft skills of their employees to foster resilience and agility.

23.2 Company Culture as a Key to Resilience in Organizations

What are the key elements to develop resilience in organization? First, and most important, is the company culture. Long-term company DNA is what attracts, develops, and promotes right fitting people. How can we know that we have people with the right resilience capabilities? One of the answers which are on the top priorities now for many companies is diversity across genders, age, cultures, experience, and personalities. This is great focus acknowledging that a team's diversity enriches organization by driving better performance with innovative ideas. Diversity provides different perspectives that allow one to develop solutions that could not be found in homogenous environments.

Importantly, building culture is much more than PowerPoint presentations or posters with set values covering the firm's walls. Culture is an experience; it is lived by the people whose experience depends on leaders being role models for each team. As the saying goes, example comes from the top. Inspirational role models are the most important to encourage people on experimenting, risk-taking, and innovating. And the essential emotion for unlocking courage and resilience is building trust, the secret of all successful leaders. You can hear it in a very powerful Ted talk by Simon Sinek "*Why good leaders make you feel safe*."

Another podcast (which I think will subsidize reading) from the series *Unlocking us*—Brene with Oprah Winfrey and Dr. Bruce D. Perry on Trauma, Resilience, and Healing—was very interesting as it underlines how important our past is in shaping how we behave. It discusses how past traumas impact our resilience and how people may be privileged with safe upbringing. Understanding people's life stories may help us comprehend the behavior and different reactions to stress and crisis.

This discussion brought me to the concept I was also influenced by in another book "*Care to Dare*" by George Kohlrieser, Susan Goldworthy, and Duncan Coombe. There, the concept of Secure Base Leadership is described as "a person, place, goal or object that provides a sense of protection, safety and caring and offers a source of inspiration and energy for daring, exploration, risk taking and seeking challenge." In the book, we can find out a lot about how trust is the essential base for secure base leadership which unleashes astonishing potential of individuals and teams. Authors name some practices of safe base leadership which to me very much link to resilient people behavior. Just to name a few: staying calm, accepting the individual, focusing on the positive, and encouraging risk-taking.

23.3 Role Model Leaders as a Key to Resilience in Organizations

Once we have culture base and some inspirational role model leaders, then one needs to focus on teams and individuals and building more resilient behaviors within these. We know that trainings are just a small start as the real learning happens in practice and in daily actions. Therefore, companies move from classroom or team call trainings to on-the-job development, coaching, and mentoring programs. This year my company introduces the concept of learning agility which helps us identify people's potential and development areas via reflecting on mental agility, people agility, change agility, and results agility. You can find more details on this in book "*Becoming an Agile Leader*" by Victoria V. Swisher. I am personally just starting to put this concept into practice for myself and my team. To me it's very exciting as it requires self-reflection and underlines skills that are not easy to name but are essential to "Know what to do… when you don't know what to do."

Staying at home during the lockdowns allowed me among many others to rediscover home-based activities. Namely, having begun reading more, I found accidentally in the top of New York bestsellers a book that attracted me with its title and with which I changed how I labeled leadership skills—"*Dare to lead*" by Brene Brown.

Do you also sometimes have this moment of "wow … this is exactly what I think and now somebody put it in words and structure and finally all this makes more sense"? This is how I felt reading the book. It truly inspired me to reflect on the growing importance of soft skills managing human emotions and leadership authenticity. Brene Brown is a recognized research professor at the University of Houston, studying for 20 years topics such as courage, vulnerability, shame, and empathy. In the last chapter of "*Dare to Lead*," she focuses on teaching resilience. Seeing resilience as "learning to rise," she argues that courage and resilience are not limited to some talented individuals, but we all can learn how to become more courageous and resilient. "We have to teach people how to land before they jump. When you go skydiving, you spend a lot of upfront time jumping off a ladder and learning how to hit the ground without hurting yourself (. . .). The same is true in leadership—we can't expect people to be brave and risk failure if they're not prepped for hard landings. (. . .) If we don't have the skills to get back up, we may not risk failing."

Brene Brown's three-step approach of building more resilience with learning to rise include: the reckoning, the rumble, and the revolution. The reckoning is especially an aspect that I have linked to my experiences. It is the ability to realize what emotions we feel and how they impact our behavior. To me it is a crucial differentiator in the speed of resilient behavior and leading the team and organization. Let's take two examples, one person in a stressful, unexpected situation who bursts out in emotions, blames, and finger points to all others, while the second person in the same situation analyzes the facts, asks for opinions, and then leads the team to action. Comparing the two, can you see which behavior leads to faster and more solid team response?

The secret of risers (highly resilient people) is they realize fast when they are emotionally hooked, and they become curious about their own response. Curiosity is a very important aspect of emotional awareness, which helps us gain perspective and calm down. ". . . the skill that the most resilient among us share. Slow down, take deep breath and get curious about what's happening." I love Brene's summary: "Get curious or get crazy." The choice is ours and if you are interested in different techniques and strategies on how to be more curious rather than crazy, see the last chapter of the book.

When I entered a crisis in Thailand, I followed my belief that I need to behave the way I would like my boss to behave when I am in trouble:-). I tried not to freak out when I got the call on Friday late afternoon with information that a factory does not know what to produce on Monday as the only knowledgeable production planner resigned. You need to know that in Thai culture telling bad news to the boss (especially new foreign boss) is the very last thing you do, only when there is no other way possible:-). So after a crisis meeting on Monday early morning, I knew that the scale of the problem was greater than one planner resignation. We needed to start crisis management and get experts support immediately. I can share lots of crazy stories out of this crisis, but the bottom line is that I have learned the importance of detailed fact analysis done by experts, urgency of acting and aligning with top stakeholders, taking fast decisions, and steady, consequent realization of the improvement plan. On the soft skills part, what allowed me to deal with this crisis and sit at the dinner table with CEO was being calm and fact based while presenting a simple message (which I personally find very important when presenting to executives who are not necessary production experts). However, the most important success ingredient was to ask for help and involve all experts while getting support from the team, peers, and top management. Also, in the competitive organization, the skill of asking for help and support is not so obvious anymore. Therefore, when I explained to the CEO how I managed this crisis, I concluded that the great support allowed for a fast and effective solution to the crisis.

Going back to Brene Brown's reckoning step in learning to rise path, I have recently listened to the podcast she did with Dr. Angela Duckworth on grit and importance of trying new things (*Dare to Lead* podcasts on Spotify). What intrigued me in it was the linkage of grit, which she defines as passion with perseverance, to the resilience skills set. She illustrates how important trying new things is to build our experiences in risk-taking, failures, and successes, which then improve our resilient responses. I am also a strong believer that especially negative experiences and crises help us get "thicker skin" and that allow us to go through new challenges more prepared and with more confidence. Therefore, whenever I experience with my team problems or mistakes, a part of me is happy to get new lessons that will allow us to find new solutions and approaches for the future.

Thinking about the importance of grit in overcoming difficulties, there is a very interesting paradox used by Brene Brown and described in Jim Collins's bestseller "Good to Great." It is called (. . .) "the Stockdale Paradox" named after Admiral Jim Stockdale, who spent eight years as prisoner of war in Vietnam. He was tortured more than twenty times during his imprisonment. In addition to fighting to stay alive, he worked every day to help the other prisoners survive. When Jim Collins interviewed him, he asked, "Who didn't make it out?" Stockdale replied, "oh, that's easy. The optimists." Stockdale explained that the optimists would believe they'd be out by Christmas and Christmas would come and go. Then, they would believe they'd be out by Easter, and the date would come and go, and the years would tick by like that. He explained to Collins, "they died of broken hearts."

Stockdale told Collins, "This is a very important lesson. You must never confuse faith that you will prevail in the end – which you can never afford to lose with the discipline to confront the most brutal facts of your current reality, whatever they might be."

Brene Brown uses this example in her book and names this as gritty faith and gritty facts. She highlights the importance of taking responsibility for both hope and reality checking of hope with facts.

I love this example as for me it condenses and summarizes resilience power – it is having faith, passion, or vision, being perseverant in actions while having a strong sense of reality and facts.

As the last point, let me share with you a summary of key thoughts on resilience, condensed to 26 minutes in a podcast "*Resilience in a post-pandemic world*" (by Head spring executive development on channel Learning Rewired). You will hear that nowadays resilience is about development and becoming better as bouncing back to original position is not enough anymore.

The world is changing faster than we can become more resilient. However, if we stay curious, open for development, and build change into our daily habits, we may be able to keep pace with some of the changes and uncertainty of the world.

Anna Sparty is a supply chain professional with 20 years of experience in supply chain managerial roles at Nestle and Beiersdorf.

She worked in Europe and Asia in four different countries and currently is responsible for complex supply chain in Eastern Europe.

Part VI
Supply Chain Resilience in Different Industries

Chapter 24
Resilient Supply Chains in the Parcel Shipping Sector

Peter Umundum and Constantin Wittek-Saltzberg

Abstract The Austrian Post is Austria's leading player in the parcel shipping sector, an industry that has been hit hard by the COVID-19 pandemic. Unlike other parts of the economy, CEP was confronted with sudden growth rates—especially during times of lockdown where classic retail was forced to stay closed.

The key factors to master this challenging time were high investments into the logistics infrastructure and ongoing efforts into innovations and digitalization. This chapter provides a deeper look into the measures that have been taken before and during the pandemic and gives insights into emerging technologies that will enable parcel shipping companies to handle not only the fast growing, e-commerce driven parcel volume but also future, unforeseeable disruptions.

24.1 Introduction

The Austrian Post as Austria's leading parcel shipping company has just recently been awarded the prize as the second-best postal company in the world by the Universal Postal Union (Universal Postal Union, 2020). This yearly rating is built on four major pillars, which are reliability, reach, relevance, and resilience. The latter is a measurement that has become increasingly important in the parcel shipping sector, and recent disruptions like the COVID-19 pandemic have shown that constant investments in infrastructure and innovations are key for minimizing negative effects on the supply chain.

P. Umundum
Parcel and Logistics, Austrian Post, Vienna, Austria

C. Wittek-Saltzberg (✉)
Digital Supply Chain/Parcel and Logistics, Austrian Post, Vienna, Austria
e-mail: Constantin.Wittek-Saltzberg@post.at

S. Kummer et al. (eds.), *Supply Chain Resilience*, Springer Series in Supply Chain Management 17, https://doi.org/10.1007/978-3-030-95401-7_24

24.2 The Pandemic and Its Consequences for Austrian Post

COVID-19 has revealed how sensitive and vulnerable modern, highly optimized supply chains are. Unlike other parts of the economy, the parcel shipping sector was confronted with sudden growth rates—especially during times of lockdown where classic retail was forced to stay closed. This different kind of disruption was not less challenging—especially in a time of high uncertainty for customers, employees, and the company itself.

The parcel shipping business in normal times is relatively well predictable with higher volumes during the high season between October and mid-January. Annual growth rates of more than 10% in recent years are reflecting the global trend of an upcoming e-commerce business where the major part still seems to be ahead of us (Dragendorf et al., 2019, p. 8).

When the COVID-19 pandemic hit Central Europe in March 2020 relatively unprepared, governments decided to reduce public life to a minimum to stop the spread of the virus. Among the few reasons one was allowed to leave the house, post offices remained open during the entire pandemic as part of the critical infrastructure. However, to keep up the provision of the population, a huge supply network had to perform constantly while being confronted with unplannable high volume and further interferences due to COVID-19. The following measures that were taken before and during the pandemic were key to mastering this disruption.

24.3 Investments and Innovations in Logistics and Its Infrastructure

Austrian Post invested about half a billion euros in the last three years in its logistics infrastructure to handle the rising volume with the expected quality. These investments help to absorb planned and unplanned peaks, bring certainty, and thus garner trust of our customers, which is one of the most important values in uncertain times.

In addition to the investments in sorting centers and delivery bases, Austrian Post was a pioneer in developing 24/7 solutions at multiple touchpoints of the customer journey. With these inventions, it is not only possible to post a package in one of the self-service drop-offs, but also the receiving process is supported by pickup stations in post offices. To further improve the experience, medium-size boxes are being mounted in the stairways of residential buildings where customers can receive and soon also post their packages without having to leave the house.

Besides the obvious competitive advantage in the 2C business, these 24/7 self-service solutions have turned out to be a huge enabler during the pandemic as people tried to avoid personal contacts as well as crowded places during opening hours.

Testing new last mile concepts is important to have various options available in times of disruption. While more and more approaches and ideas are growing how to reinvent inner city logistics, Austrian Post has already been testing different concepts

Fig. 24.1 Austria's first electric driven parcel delivery cars in Graz, where the last mile will be CO2-free by the end of 2021 (Source: Austrian Post)

in major cities for more than two years. With these close to production test runs, it was not only possible to boost productivity but also to prove how sustainable and eco-friendly city logistics can be. This is a further step to reduce traffic in densely populated areas, even if a recent study of WU's Institute for Transport and Logistics Management showed that CEP services only add up to 0.8% of inner-city traffic (Kummer et al., 2019, p. 17).

Another step toward strengthening the supply chain is to adapt to new, more reliable and less service-intensive technologies like LNG/hydrogen-driven trucks and battery-powered delivery vehicles. With more than 2000 vehicles, Austrian Post already today operates Austria's biggest battery-powered fleet, and Graz has become Austria's first major city where even all high-volume parcel delivery cars are being equipped with battery-powered drives (see Fig. 24.1). This was a huge step toward reaching the long-term goal to become CO2-free on the last mile in 2030.

The solar panels that are mounted on all big facility roofs produce enough power to charge the entire e-fleet (see Fig. 24.2). That brings flexibility and helps become more independent from external disruptions.

Fig. 24.2 In the sorting center Hagenbrunn, next to Vienna, solar panels help produce electric power to run the facility (Source: Austrian Post)

24.4 Regionality

The longer and more complex supply chains tend to be, the higher is the risk of failure. That is one of the reasons why, especially in times of uncertainty and global supply shortages, we can observe a trend toward more regional products. Early in the pandemic, Austrian Post started a campaign to support small to medium-sized regional producers. One of the measures was to simplify and drastically speed up the onboarding process at the Austrian Post's online shopping portal called "shöpping." By using shöpping, regional producers were able to start offering their products online within days, keep their expenditures low by not hosting their own shopping portal, and benefit from the reach of one of Austria's biggest marketplaces.

24.5 Digital Supply Chain

For decades, operating high-performing supply chains would have been unthinkable without IT systems. Forecasting demand, sorting parcels, and tracking are just some of the basic features in the CEP industry that are mainly supported by computer systems. With rapidly growing volume and increasing customer demands, these systems help to keep the business up and running.

As the pace of IT developments has been increasing for decades, adopting emerging technologies to strengthen the supply chain was one of the key factors to overcome the COVID-19 pandemic well from a logistical point of view.

For Austrian Post, key drivers for digitalization are increasing transparency, productivity, and resilience. A perfect example of development in this field is the IoT-Hub. Here, data from multiple sources are combined to increase transparency as a first step. After that, further steps are control, optimization, and finally automation in different parts of the business logic.

The latest successful project here has been to mount active asset trackers on roll cages and swap bodies. Here, too, transparency is the first objective of this asset tracking project. Nevertheless, the ultimate aim will be to achieve automation—like an automatically controlled order management for these empties.

Another very promising trend is to create a digital copy—a digital twin—of supply chain processes. These simulations not only become handy for long-term planned adaption of the logistical infrastructure and its procedures but also to quickly adapt the supply chain after unforeseeable disruptions.

24.6 Conclusion

Since the COVID-19 pandemic has shown us the trade-off between speed, efficiency, and resilience, the future challenge will be to find the right balance in this competitive market. Even quicker than the speed of the technical evolution is the development of the customer's needs and requirements. Only those competitors will be successful in the long run who constantly evolve and prepare for possible disruptions.

References

Dragendorf, J., Mohr, D., Ecker, T., Neuhaus, F., Briest, P., Beretzky, E. & Zimmermann, T. (2019). *The endgame for postal networks. How to win in the age of e-commerce*. Retrieved June 28, 2021, from https://www.mckinsey.com/industries/travel-logistics-and-infrastructure/our-insights/the-endgame-for-postal-networks-how-to-win-in-the-age-of-e-commerce

Kummer, S., Dobrovnik, M., Herold, D., Hribernik, M. & Mikl, J. (2019). Endbericht der Studie Citylogistik Wien: Der Einfluss von Paketdienstleistern auf den Gesamtverkehr.

Universal Postal Union. (2020). *Postal Development Report 2020Achieving higher performance amid a major crisis*. Retrieved August 25, 2021, from https://www.upu.int/UPU/media/upu/publications/2020-Postal-Development-Report.pdf

Peter Umundum earned a degree in informatics and technical mathematics and started his professional career in 1988 at Steirerbrau AG. In 1994, he joined Styria Medien AG, where he became the managing director of its subsidiary Media Consult Austria GmbH after only two years. In 1999, he co-founded redmail and became its managing director. In 2001, Peter Umundum was entrusted with the position of a managing director of the newspaper "Die Presse." Three years later, he was appointed a managing director of the daily "Kleine Zeitung." In 2005, he joined Austrian Post as an executive in the letter mail division, the company's largest division. On 1st April 2011, Peter Umundum has been appointed a Member of the Board, responsible for Parcel & Logistics. In addition, Peter Umundum took over the chairmanship of the Supervisory Board of the European transport network EURODIS and is additionally a president of the Vienna Economic Forum since early 2020.

Constantin Wittek-Saltzberg studied business law at WU (Vienna University of Economics and Business) and is currently finishing an Executive MBA program at CEU in Budapest and Vienna. After specializing in logistics during his studies, he was working in this field for an Austrian construction equipment manufacturer, followed by 5 years working for a route optimization software company in Germany. Returning to Vienna in 2018, he started working for Austrian Post where he is currently—as a head of Digital Supply Chain—deep diving into IoT use cases, new parcel locker technologies, and tour-optimization tasks.

Chapter 25
Deep Dive on Resilience in the Aviation Industry: Between Resilience for Short-Term Disruptions and Focus on Long-Term Preparedness

Mario Danner and Alexander M. Geske

Abstract Volatility and disruptions have always been two main characteristics of aviation, even though the causes for short-term disruptive events and long-term uncertainty shocks have changed as the industry became more mature over the years.

Surprisingly, disruption planning has mainly focused on short-term events. Uncertainty shocks were neglected, although those rare occurrences hit with a high impact and far-reaching consequences on a supra-regional level, taking the aviation industry a significant period to return to the original state.

But even without a proper preparation, the aviation industry was able to recover from those shocks in the past through flexibility, fast adaption to the new reality, and by relying on the lessons learned from previous crises.

Accordingly, initially the aviation industry tried to resort to proven actions and learnings from past crises to mitigate the impact of COVID-19. But it soon became apparent that this was an unprecedented event and only relying on earlier shocks is insufficient.

The major impact of COVID-19 resulted in a reprioritization of resources, both on the industry's side and in the research community. It enabled the necessary shift of focus on long-term resilience measures to become economically more sustainable.

25.1 Vulnerabilities and Resilience Characteristics in the Aviation Industry

Volatility and disruption have always been two main characteristics of the aviation industry. As a man-made socio-technical system and a variable environment (Chialastri & Pozzi, 2008, p. 6), all stakeholders have to be constantly prepared

M. Danner (✉) · A. M. Geske
Institute for Transport and Logistics Management, WU (Vienna University of Economics and Business), Vienna, Austria
e-mail: mario.danner@s.wu.ac.at

S. Kummer et al. (eds.), *Supply Chain Resilience*, Springer Series in Supply Chain Management 17, https://doi.org/10.1007/978-3-030-95401-7_25

for unexpected events (Hirsh & Kamleh, 2020). Fiksel et al. (2015) identified six fundamental vulnerabilities that make a supply chain enterprise susceptible to disruptions, which are applicable for the aviation industry as well:

- **Turbulence**: There are frequent changes in the environment, which cannot be controlled by a company. In aviation, these are, for example, weather, exchange rates and inflation risks, aircraft groundings, COVID-19, or fuel prices.
- **Deliberate threats**: Attacks, which are intended, lead to disrupted operations or cause human or financial harm. Such threats may be terrorist attacks, wars, labor actions, or ransomware attacks.
- **External pressures**: These are generated by influences, which do not target the company but still constrain business or create barriers. Examples in aviation may be emission trading schemes, noise restrictions, short haul flight bans, or flight shaming.
- **Resource limits**: Output is constraint by the availability of input factors of production. This could be lack of staff, spare part shortages, or slot restrictions.
- **Sensitivity**: This stresses the importance of having controlled conditions to ensure integrity for processes and products. In the context of aviation, this might be safety and quality concerns, air quality discussions on board, or handling stops due to technical or personal errors (Fiksel et al., 2015).

Over the years, the causes for disruptions have changed. While poor technical reliability, which led to plane crashes and bankruptcies due to little confidence and trust, characterized the early stages of aviation, the aviation industry became more mature and resilient over the course of the twentieth century (Hirsh & Kamleh, 2020).

A resilient supply chain must be adaptable to be able to recover to its original state or even a more desirable state after being disrupted (Ponomarov & Holcomb, 2009). The faster this original or more desirable state can be reached again, the lower the negative financial impact is. In this context, Wang et al. (2019) describe resilience as "the ability of a system to withstand and stay operational in the face of an unexpected disturbance or unpredicted changes" (p. 2694). For Evler et al. (2021), "resilience is the capacity of a system not only to absorb, but to use existing flexibility and reserves for adapting and recovering from a loss in system performance" (p. 2). According to Chialastri and Pozzi (2008), "[aviation] resilience engineering focuses on the capabilities on all levels of a system to respond to regular and irregular threats in a robust yet flexible manner, and to anticipate the consequences of disruptions" (p. 2).

Wang et al. (2019) refer to four main properties of resilience of Caverzan and Solomos (2014), which were suggested by Bruneau et al. (2003):

- **Robustness** is the strength or capability of systems (and elements) to maintain functionality in the event of disruption.
- **Redundancy** deals with the substitutability of elements, parts, or systems in case of damage or malfunction of certain elements in the system.
- **Resourcefulness** means "the capacity to identify problems, establish priorities, and mobilize resources when conditions exist that threaten to disrupt" (Bruneau

et al., 2003, pp. 737–738). Furthermore, it means having the ability to apply material and human resources to meet established priorities and achieve goals.

- **Rapidity** targets the speed to recover in order to meet goals, restrain losses, and avoid disruption (Bruneau et al., 2003).

Hirsh and Kamleh (2020, 2021) identified four pillars of airport resilience, which are not only valid for airports but for the aviation industry overall.

- **Operational resilience**: This ensures a smooth operation in case of unexpected or unforeseen events and can be found in the three training levels: avoid, detect, and mitigate. It should focus on possible outcomes instead of anticipating different causes of disruption.
- **Financial resilience:** This ensures generating income during disruptions and having cash reserves to survive external shocks or macroeconomic stresses. Non-passenger related revenues, for example, from cargo or real estate, could play a major role.
- **Workforce resilience**: Cross-training employees is one way to achieve operational flexibility, as airports are able to deploy their workforce in different functions. Besides this, advanced in-house training also improves workforce resilience. Furthermore, digitalization becomes more and more important.
- **Network resilience:** This deals with the professional and institutional ecosystem of an airport, which involves key partners of the private and public sector such as airlines, regulators, ground handlers, customs, health, immigration authorities, and many more.

Nowadays, disruptions mainly fall into two categories: short-term disruptive events and uncertainty shocks.

Air transport systems regularly face short-term disruptive events due to:

- Convective weather conditions (e.g. fog, heavy rain, snow)
- Unexpected mechanical failures (e.g. aircraft component breakdown or runway system failures and approach light outages)
- Human-intended interruptions (e.g. air traffic controller strikes or pilot strikes)
- Accidents (Wandelt et al., 2015; Wang et al., 2019).

These kinds of events usually have a locally or regionally limited impact, reduce the airport's capacity briefly, and let the system return to the original state soon after the disruption has been resolved (Wang et al., 2019).

Second are uncertainty shocks, which can be clustered into four groups (Air Transport Bureau, 2020; Dube et al., 2021; Hirsh & Kamleh, 2020; Sobieralski, 2020):

- Financial crises (e.g. Oil Crisis 1973, Iran-Iraq War in the early 1980s, Gulf Crisis in the early 1990s, Asian Financial Crisis 1997, financial crises of 1998/1999 or 2007/2008)
- Natural disasters
- Terror-related events (e.g. 9/11 terrorist attacks)

- Disease outbreaks (e.g. severe acute respiratory syndrome (SARS) outbreak in 2003, Avian influenza H5N1 in 2006, Swine influenza H1N1 pandemic in 2009).

They tend to occur rarely, but with a high impact and far-reaching consequences on a supra-regional or even global level. After such events, it takes the aviation industry a significant period to return to the original state.

Despite these downturns, global air traffic has shown stable long-term growth over the last 50 years and grew in line with the long-term trend (Oxley & Jain, 2015). On average, it takes 5 years for the industry to recover; around 72% of the impact of the initial shock persists one year after the event and around 50% still after 2 years. After 5 years, the effect is below 20% (Oxley & Jain, 2015).

25.2 Reactions to Disruptions

Actions in aviation are often based on the 4-P approach, which ensures possessing the appropriate resources in the right situations:

- Philosophy: Every decision in an airline should follow the principle "safety first".
- Policies: Set up by management to achieve operational targets.
- Procedures: These determine how to do tasks and are developed by manufacturer's recommendation, regulators, and management to ensure a safe and smooth operation.
- Practices: Closes the gap between procedures and reality (Chialastri & Pozzi, 2008).

Due to the chronic lack of cash flow in the aviation sector, especially on the airlines' side, financial and personnel resources are more than limited (IATA, 2020). Therefore, based on the 4-P approach, most of the resources in preparation for disruptions, which may include, but are not limited to, (contingency) planning and process adaption were shifted to short-term disruptive events and neglected uncertainty shocks. First, due to their regular occurrence, short-term disruptions have a regular effect on the financial results of aviation stakeholders. Second, the extensive reach of uncertainty shocks leads in most cases to a wide range of third parties involved and more uncertainty about duration and extent, which limits planning capabilities. Third, the industry was still not able to build up the necessary financial resilience needed to cope with the ever-recurring costs imposed by uncertainty shocks. Last, they can be better analyzed due to a larger number of comparable events in the past, while each uncertainty shock differs significantly from previous events (Dube et al., 2021).

Comparing the events with a major impact on aviation:

- The 1979 oil shock saw a shallow, but longlasting downturn.
- The global recession of the early 1980s accounted for a negative passenger gap until 1987.

- The combined 2000–2001 shock of the dotcom bust and 9/11, and the 2008 shock of the global financial crisis resulted in deep drops in passenger traffic—but in both cases, traffic had returned to its trend level within 4 years (Oxley & Jain, 2015).

Figure 25.1. provides an overview of the impact of various events since the oil crisis including COVID-19 until 2021 on passenger numbers. Even before COVID-19 hit, publications emphasized the lack of disruption planning and processes as well as of research for uncertainty shocks and resilience. Instead, low profitability led to a reduction of slack in the aviation system to increase the utilization of costly resources, which reduced the ability to absorb external shocks and disruptions even further (AhmadBeygi et al., 2010; International Air Transport Association, 2011). In response to this development, new models of "slack re-allocation" have been suggested. "[...] namely, aircraft re-routing (Borndörfer et al., 2010; Lan et al., 2006), flight schedule re-timing (AhmadBeygi et al., 2010; Lan et al., 2006), and block time adjustment (Sohoni et al., 2011) have been proposed in the literature" (Chiraphadhanakul & Barnhart, 2013, p. 278).

According to Wang et al. (2019), only selected aspects like scheduled block time reliability (Hao & Hansen, 2014), weather or natural disasters leading to the closure of airports (Cook et al., 2016; Janić, 2015), or the cost of achieving resilience by the means of an air traffic management system (Cook et al., 2016) have been studied. Evler et al. (2021) conclude that they are the first to analyze the inherent resilience potential available to airlines during ground times.

A further focus was laid on the robustness of airport networks in which airports represent the nodes and direct flights the edges (Wang et al., 2019). Gao et al. (2016) found three factors that impact the resilience of a network: network density, heterogeneity, and symmetry (Gao et al., 2016).

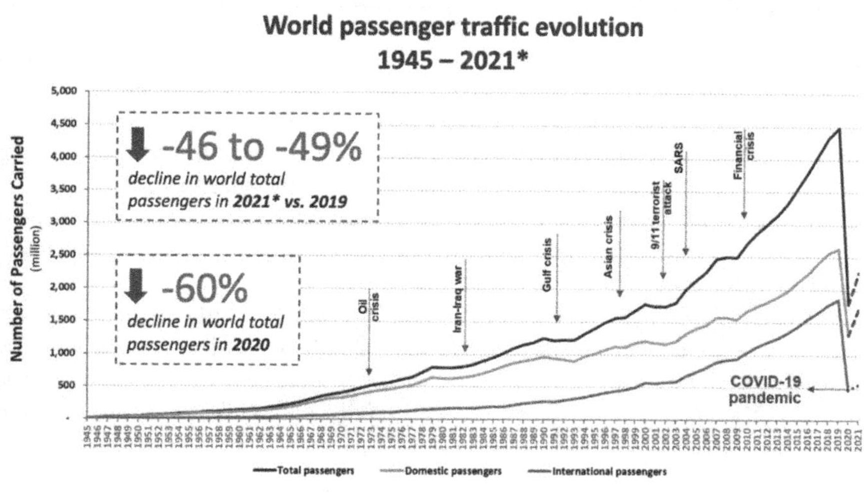

Fig. 25.1 The impact of different disruptive events on world passenger traffic evolution (Source: Air Transport Bureau (2021), ICAO Economic Analysis of COVID-19 on Civil Aviation https://www.icao.int/sustainability/Pages/Economic-Impacts-of-COVID-19.aspx)

As there is no common way, apart from delay and punctuality, to measure resilience in transport systems, Wang et al. (2019) suggest the following four measures:

- Airport departure delay as the difference between scheduled and actual time of departure.
- System-wide delay (SWD) represents demand and supply.
- Punctuality as a fraction of on-time departures (with less than 15 min departure delay) of scheduled flights.
- General resilience index (GRI) following Nan and Sansavini (2017), who suggested to consider absorptive, adaptive, and restorative capabilities and their impact on the system's performance. Wang et al. (2019) developed a function of the capability of resisting disruption (minimum performance during disruption), the performance decline during disruption, the rate of recovery of the system, the time average performance loss, and the recovery ability (Wang et al., 2019).

A study of more than 200 global airlines by Sun and Wandelt (2018) shows that only two to four airports need to fail to reduce the size of the network's giant component[1] to 20%. Some full-service carriers with a multi-hub operation and a considerable share of point-to-point connections (e.g. Hainan Airlines or China Southern) along with the low-cost carrier Ryanair show a higher degree of robustness compared to others. Nevertheless, there are lower levels of betweenness centrality[2] in point-to-point networks compared to hub-and-spoke networks. Disruptions of nodes with a high betweenness have a greater impact and quickly lead to a breakdown of the entire network. As a result, point-to-point networks of low-cost carriers (LCC) do not have a single point of failure and are therefore more robust to airport disruptions by targeted attacks and random failures (Sun & Wandelt, 2018). Moreover, disconnecting the hub airport of a full-service carrier has a greater impact than the interruption of an LCC's base airport (Lordan et al., 2016).

Chung (2015) focuses on the lack of an effective and efficient pandemic control approach for the aviation industry, referring to the estimated at least 320,000 unknown zoonotic viruses circulating in mammals, the recurrence of pandemics every 10–50 years, and the special role of air travel for disease propagation patterns. "This means that without effective containment systems, previously localized outbreak of diseases would rapidly spread worldwide via the aviation network resulting in global pandemic" (Chung, 2015, p. 50). Furthermore, Chung (2015) cites the unpreparedness for a pandemic threat of such a scale as the SARS epidemic when it happened in 2003 and the shortcomings in pandemic control exposed during the following swine influenza H1N1 pandemic in 2009.

As a result, COVID-19 hit the aviation industry not only hard but without proper preparation or contingency plans. Dube et al. (2021) re-emphasized the low capacity and resilience of the aviation sector to deal with disasters and other internal as well as external shocks in general and COVID-19 especially, despite the vulnerability of the

[1] In the giant component, a significant share of nodes is connected together.

[2] "Betweenness centrality quantifies the number of times a node acts as a bridge along the shortest path between two other nodes" (Du, n.d., p. 17).

aviation industry to uncertainty shocks. Although IT preparations such as computer models and simulations were improved over time, they see the lack of adequate financial resilience to cope with disasters as well as other internal and external shocks as the main issue.

The COVID-19 impact on world scheduled passenger traffic for the year 2020 (estimated actual results), compared to 2019 levels shows:

- Overall a reduction of 50% of seats offered by airlines,
- Overall a reduction of 2.699 million passengers (−60%) and
- Approx. USD 371 billion loss of gross passenger operating revenues of airlines (Air Transport Bureau, 2021).

The COVID-19 impact on world scheduled passenger traffic for the year 2021 (preliminary estimates), compared to 2019 levels display:

- Overall a reduction of 38% to 40% of seats offered by airlines,
- Overall a reduction of 2.057 to 2.199 million passengers (−46% to −49%) and
- Approx. USD 303 to 323 billion loss of gross passenger operating revenues of airlines (Air Transport Bureau, 2021) (Fig. 25.1).

25.3 Mitigation Actions Applied During the COVID-19 Pandemic

The aviation industry was able to recover from past major disruptions even without properly preparing for them. Such preparation included (contingency) planning and process adaption set-up through flexibility, a fast adaption to the new reality, and by relying on the lessons learned from previous crises. Airport and airline emergency response manuals are living documents, with a regular revision cycle to incorporate actual events and recommendations. For example, during the Avian influenza (H5N1) in 2006 and Swine flu (H1N1) in 2009, the control measures implemented were largely based on those deployed during the SARS epidemic in 2003 and enabled a fast first response (Chung, 2015).

In case of safety and health-related disruptions, the recovery afterwards depends on how fast (potential) travelers can be persuaded that travel on board and that the stay at their respective destinations are safe again. Therefore, the aviation and tourism industries are dependent on a coordinated, harmonized, and consistent supra-national or even global approach. Not only in crises, airport and airline operations are affected by the lack of harmonization in terms of regulations, processes, and requirements (Taba et al., 2020).

Accordingly, at first, the aviation industry tried to resort to proven actions and learnings from past crises to mitigate the impact of COVID-19, mainly COVID-2003 and 9/11 as other sectors did as well. Although the situation in 2003 had similarities, due to a relatively low transmissibility, the epidemic could be contained to Asia, limiting the impact to the region without major effects on the Americas and Europe. In addition, the virus died out only eight months after the detection of the first case. Furthermore, in strong contrast to the actions of the US authorities after 9/11, the Asian authorities acted quickly to declare air travel safe again, further reducing the long-time impact (Lange (2020) in Garrow and Lurkin (2021)). Concerning 9/11, the industry mostly tried to avoid the mistakes made when imposing many new processes in an uncoordinated way. Alexandre de Juniac, then Director General and CEO of the International Air Transport Association (IATA), described it as "we ended up with a mess of measures piled on top of measures. And nearly 20 years later we are still trying to sort it out" (International Air Transport Association (IATA), 2020).

As de Juniac put it in April 2021, the aviation industry has never been shuttered on this scale before. "Consequently, we have no experience in starting it up" (International Air Transport Association (IATA), 2020). To prevent the collapse of the aviation system and the exit of many stakeholders, governments worldwide initiated support programs for airports, airlines, and other system partners (Christiansen, 2021). As there is no single event that provides a roadmap for recovery from this pandemic, the aviation industry could only rely on a combined understanding of lessons learned from earlier shock events to chart a way forward.

It became more and more apparent that COVID-19 is an unprecedented event and only relying on learnings from earlier shocks proved insufficient. In line with the 4-P approach, the aviation industry and research community shifted a large part of their resources to COVID-19. The International Civil Aviation Organization (n.d.) came to the conclusion that a flexible approach is required to achieve a sustainable recovery in air transport. In order to achieve the required level of resilience, along with a clear, transparent, and ongoing communication, a strong commitment and engagement is required from all stakeholders. This includes governmental and non-governmental organizations on international and regional level (such as aviation and health authorities), the entire aviation value chain, and air passengers. A focus on managing risks and preparation for crisis situations is essential to be able to deal with unexpected situations. Measures, plans, policies, etc. should be harmonized among stakeholders. As the preparedness depends on the ability of countries to improve and reinforce their national emergency plans, the International Civil Aviation Organization (n.d.) suggests expanding the State Safety Programmes (SSP) in Annex 19 to the Chicago Convention—Safety Management—to facilitate an integrated management of risks for countries and service providers (International Civil Aviation Organization, n.d.).

The COVID-19 pandemic has led to the need of unprecedented flexibility along with the need of quick decision-making. Rohit (2020) splits the actions in response to the COVID-19 pandemic along three time horizons. In the time period between three and 6 months, the focus must be laid on the direct consequences as well as on the "protection of our staff, travel and events, our supply chains, operating locations, demand for our products and services, cash flow, pricing, marketing, and brand reputation" (Rohit, 2020). During the next twelve months, processes, aspects, and operating models of the business need to be critically reviewed in case the impacts on the economic situation persist, including the above-mentioned aspects. In the midterm (up to 3 years), actions are required that deal with "the shape of our business, location footprint, sourcing, routes to market, product and service offerings, staffing models, and use of technology if the knock-on effects have a more dramatic impact on our markets and the economy more widely" (Rohit, 2020).

The need for flexible and quick decision-making under uncertainty and limited availability of historic data poses a big challenge to several functional areas such as long-term fleet planning, network planning as well as scheduling, crew planning, operations, and revenue management (Garrow & Lurkin, 2021). Due to the dynamically changing environment of countries opening up and closing down, airlines are required to develop multiple network scenarios, which are jointly developed by scheduling and revenue management to leverage opportunities for demand (Stomph (2020) & Reynolds (2020) in Garrow and Lurkin (2021)). In the early stages of the recovery process, airlines publish more flights than are actually going to fly. Over time, they reduce the number, which presents another challenge to revenue management as they have to deal with more capacity being offered than actually produced (Ruhlin (2020) in Garrow and Lurkin (2021)).

On a more strategic level, responses to crises based on Wenzel et al. (2020) are the following:

- **Retrenchment** aims at "reductions in costs, assets, products, product lines, and overhead (Pearce and Robbins (1993, p. 614) in Wenzel et al. (2020)).
- **Persevering** considers measures to maintain business activities and keeping the status quo while focusing on the mitigation of crisis impacts (Wenzel, 2015; Wenzel et al., 2020).
- **Innovating** relates to measures to strategically renew in the organization to cope with the crisis (Wenzel et al., 2020).
- "**Exit** refers to the discontinuation of an organization's activities. It can be either a forced outcome of an unviable business setting or a strategic response to crisis" (Albers & Rundshagen, 2020).

Albers and Rundshagen (2020) used those strategies by Wenzel et al. (2020) (see above) to categorize airlines' responses to COVID-19. The authors split the retrenchment category into short- and long-term measures. While the short-term focus includes partial or complete groundings, job cuts, or worktime reductions in accordance with national short-term work policies, long-term measures include fleet reductions and order cancellations, accelerated phase-out of certain aircraft types, restructuring networks (especially domestic), and stopping growth strategies. Persevering measures included state aid, loans, or guarantees for most airlines, while some were relaunched or committed themselves to push/force price competition. In the innovating category, the authors also differentiate between crisis-specific measures like reconfiguration to transport cargo, using passenger aircrafts for cargo flights, and longer-term measures like opening new transfers, destinations, entering new markets, or focusing more on joint ventures. Exit was also split into the subcategories failure, where airlines ceased operations or filed for bankruptcy, and withdrawals, which means closing bases or subsidiaries or withdrawing from takeovers. Lastly, Albers and Rundshagen (2020) added "resume" as a fifth category (Albers & Rundshagen, 2020).

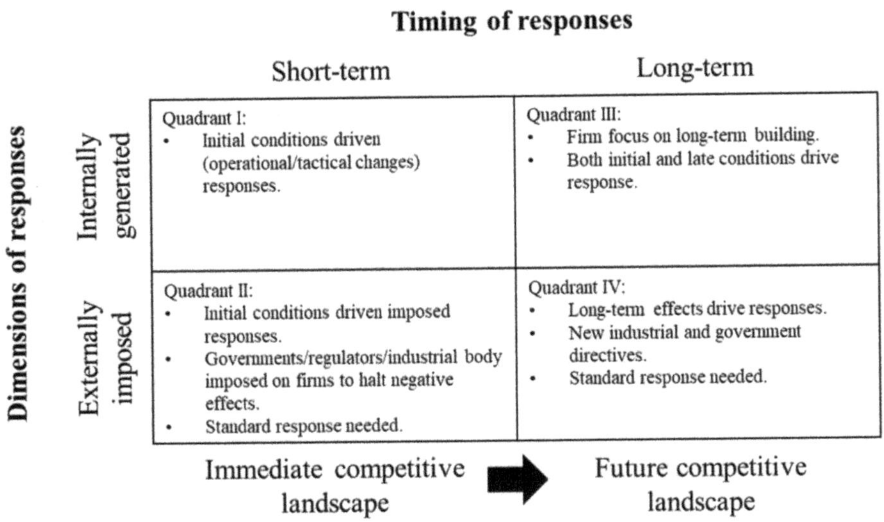

Fig. 25.2 A unified organizing framework of firm responses (Adapted from Amankwah-Amoah (2020))

Amankwah-Amoah (2020) developed a two-dimensional framework of firms' responses to crises. The author distinguishes between short- and long-term responses as well as between internally generated or externally imposed responses. Short-term measures introduced by companies or regulatory bodies mainly focus on operational and tactical levels, including deep-cleaning and disinfection of aircraft cabins, additional safety measures such as inflight social distancing, service reductions, etc. Internally generated long-term measures target strategic and operational activities to prepare for recovery and the post-crisis period. Apart from lobbying for state aid (Amankwah-Amoah, 2020), great efforts focused on cost reductions, which include renegotiations of supplier contracts, re-dimensioning of firms, and reduction of salary spending. While many airlines laid-off people, others focused on a salary reduction in order to keep workers and be able to quickly respond to increasing demand (Cornwell, 2020; Klar, 2020). Long-term externally imposed regulations involve industrial and governmental directives (Amankwah-Amoah, 2020) (Fig. 25.2).

25.4 Summary and Outlook

As in the past, the aviation industry will face challenges from uncertainty shocks in the future. The practiced go-to approach of only copying the actions from previous crises became more and more inadequate. The major impact of COVID-19 resulted in a reprioritization of resources, both on the industry's side and in the research community. For sure, the derived information and guidelines will help the aviation industry to master future crises better.

Nevertheless, it should not be taken for granted that the aviation industry recovers after an uncertainty shock, as many influencing factors are beyond control. Especially in the regulatory environment, an uncoordinated or patchwork approach with diverging regulations on regional or even per-country level impedes the industry's ability to respond to such crises and must therefore be avoided at all costs. To increase the resilience of aviation, a better visibility and closer collaboration between all relevant stakeholders must be the cornerstones of future development to cope with the given environment and uncertainties.

Still, it is questionable whether any individual and detached preparation or pre-cautions by the aviation industry would have been able to cushion the impact without the corresponding supra-national or global coordinated action by authorities and other stakeholders. Gössling (2020) suggests using COVID-19 as a starting point to reconsider the aviation system. While this industry creates opportunities for businesses and individuals, society carries the risks (Gössling, 2020). In the assessment of the economic performance and the sector's societal importance, climate change and vectoring pathogen distribution are being ignored. He says that aviation has only a limited financial resilience often due to small profit margins (Aviation Environment Federation, 2020; Gössling, 2020). Dube et al. (2021) support the argument of a lack of financial resilience in aviation. The reduction of real cost of air travel has led to some negative side effects. It generates traffic and changes transport flows. Deregulation and productivity increases have led to capacity growth (Gössling et al., 2017). This increase capacity has caused a 60 percent decline in air rates over the course of the last two decades (IATA, 2019). In order to create a resilient aviation system, Gössling (2020) raises the question of how much air transport is required. Besides this, risk must be accounted for in parts of the costs and therefore must be reflected in prices for air transportation. "[...] risks and vulnerabilities have to be weighed against short-term benefits, if the sector's future resilience is to improve" (Gössling, 2020, p. 4).

Whatever measures will be taken and lessons learned from the current crisis (Lange (2020) in Garrow and Lurkin (2021)), Terry (2020, p. 1) suggest five guiding principles to steer successfully through a crisis. First, decisive and courageous action is more important than getting it perfect ("speed over elegance"). Second, ensuring the continued existence of the organization represents the highest priority and the base to emerge stronger from the crisis ("mission first"). Third, the strategic orientation and implemented solutions must be aligned with the core values of the organization ("design from the heart"). Fourth, the narrative must be consistent with the core values of the organization ("own your narrative"). Last, a proper preparation for disruptions including (contingency) planning and process adaption set-up is essential to weather any crisis ("embrace the long view") (Terry, 2020, p. 1).

The aviation industry has always focused on short-term measures to cover disruptions of the system. However, COVID-19 has shown that the industry must focus on long-term resilience measures to become economically more sustainable. It is uncertain whether the COVID-19 crisis has changed the industry's mindset toward long-term thinking and increased collaboration or if financial pressure will lead to a relapse into old patterns.

References

AhmadBeygi, S., Cohn, A., & Lapp, M. (2010). Decreasing airline delay propagation by re-allocating scheduled slack. *IIE Transactions, 42*(7), 478–489. https://doi.org/10.1080/07408170903468605

Air Transport Bureau. (2020). *Effects of Novel Coronavirus (COVID-19) on Civil Aviation: Economic Impact Analysis*. Retrieved July 04, 2021, from https://www.aaco.org/Library/Files/Uploaded%20Files/Economics/Corona%20studies/3dec%20ICAO_Coronavirus_Econ_Impact.pdf

Air Transport Bureau. (2021). *Effects of Novel Coronavirus (COVID-19) on Civil Aviation: Economic Impact Analysis*. Retrieved August 25, 2021 from https://www.icao.int/sustainability/Documents/Covid-19/ICAO_coronavirus_Econ_Impact.pdf

Albers, S., & Rundshagen, V. (2020). European airlines' strategic responses to the COVID-19 pandemic (January-May, 2020). *Journal of Air Transport Management, 87*, 101863. https://doi.org/10.1016/j.jairtraman.2020.101863

Amankwah-Amoah, J. (2020). Note: Mayday, Mayday, Mayday! Responding to environmental shocks: Insights on global airlines' responses to COVID-19. *Transportation Research Part E: Logistics and Transportation Review, 143*, 102098. https://doi.org/10.1016/j.tre.2020.102098

Aviation Environment Federation. (2020). *Risks, resilience and the future of aviation*. Retrieved May 30, 2021, from https://www.aef.org.uk/2020/09/18/risks-resilience-and-the-future-of-aviation/

Borndörfer, R., Dovica, I., Nowak, I., & Schickinger, T. (2010). Robust Tail Assignment.

Bruneau, M., Chang, S. E., Eguchi, R. T., Lee, G. C., O'Rourke, T. D., Reinhorn, A. M., Shinozuka, M., Tierney, K., Wallace, W. A., & von Winterfeldt, D. (2003). A framework to quantitatively assess and enhance the seismic resilience of communities. *Earthquake Spectra, 19*(4), 733–752. https://doi.org/10.1193/1.1623497

Caverzan, A., & Solomos, G. (2014). JRC SCIENE AND POLICY REPORT. Review on resilience in literature and standards for critical built - infrastructure. Retrieved July 04, 2021, from https://core.ac.uk/download/pdf/38629354.pdf

Chialastri, A., & Pozzi, S. (2008). *Resilience in the Aviation System.* Paper presented at the Computer Safety, Reliability, and Security, Berlin, Heidelberg.

Chiraphadhanakul, V., & Barnhart, C. (2013). Robust flight schedules through slack re-allocation. *EURO Journal on Transportation and Logistics, 2*(4), 277–306. https://doi.org/10.1007/s13676-013-0028-y

Christiansen, H. (2021). *State Support to the Air Transport Sector: Monitoring developments related to the Covid-19 crisis*. Retrieved September 08, 2021, from https://www.oecd.org/corporate/State-Support-to-the-Air-Transport-Sector-Monitoring-Developments-Related-to-the-COVID-19-Crisis.pdf

Chung, L. H. (2015). Impact of pandemic control over airport economics: Reconciling public health with airport business through a streamlined approach in pandemic control. *Journal of Air Transport Management, 44-45*, 42–53. https://doi.org/10.1016/j.jairtraman.2015.02.003

Cook, A., Delgado, L., Tanner, G., & Cristóbal, S. (2016). Measuring the cost of resilience. *Journal of Air Transport Management, 56*, 38–47. https://doi.org/10.1016/j.jairtraman.2016.02.007

Cornwell, A. (2020). *Emirates To Suspend All Passenger Operations Starting March 25. The airline will stop nearly all passenger flights this week and cut staff wages because of the coronavirus impact on travel demand.* Retrieved July 13, 2021, from https://www.huffpost.com/entry/emirates-to-suspend-passenger-operations_l_5e777bc8c5b63c3b64924504

Du, D. (n.d.). *Social Network Analysis: Centrality Measures.* Retrieved September 16, 2021, from https://www2.unb.ca/~ddu/6634/Lecture_notes/Lecture_4_centrality_measure.pdf

Dube, K., Nhamo, G., & Chikodzi, D. (2021). COVID-19 pandemic and prospects for recovery of the global aviation industry. *Journal of Air Transport Management, 92*, 102022. https://doi.org/10.1016/j.jairtraman.2021.102022

Evler, J., Asadi, E., Preis, H., & Fricke, H. (2021). Airline ground operations: Schedule recovery optimization approach with constrained resources. *Transportation Research Part C: Emerging Technologies, 128*, 103129. https://doi.org/10.1016/j.trc.2021.103129

Fiksel, J., Polyviou, M., Croxton, K., & Pettit, T. (2015). From risk to resilience: Learning to deal with disruption. *MIT Sloan Management Review, 56*, 78–86.

Gao, J., Barzel, B., & Barabási, A.-L. (2016). Universal resilience patterns in complex networks. *Nature, 530*(7590), 307–312. https://doi.org/10.1038/nature16948

Garrow, L., & Lurkin, V. (2021). How COVID-19 is impacting and reshaping the airline industry. *Journal of Revenue and Pricing Management, 20*(1), 3–9. https://doi.org/10.1057/s41272-020-00271-1

Gössling, S. (2020). Risks, resilience, and pathways to sustainable aviation: A COVID-19 perspective. *Journal of Air Transport Management, 89*, 101933. https://doi.org/10.1016/j.jairtraman.2020.101933

Gössling, S., Fichert, F., & Forsyth, P. (2017). Subsidies in aviation. *Sustainability, 9*(8). https://doi.org/10.3390/su9081295

Hao, L., & Hansen, M. (2014). Block time reliability and scheduled block time setting. *Transportation Research Part B: Methodological, 69*, 98–111. https://doi.org/10.1016/j.trb.2014.08.008

Hirsh, M., & Kamleh, M. (2020). *What is a Resilient Airport?* Retrieved May 30, 2021, from https://airporturbanism.com/articles/what-is-a-resilient-airport

Hirsh, M., & Kamleh, M. (2021). *Airport resilience: the human factor.* Retrieved May 30, 2021, from https://airporturbanism.com/articles/airport-resilience-the-human-factor

IATA. (2019). *Economic Performance of the Airline Industry.* Retrieved July 13, 2021, from https://www.iata.org/en/iata-repository/publications/economic-reports/airline-industry-economic-performance%2D%2D-december-2019%2D%2D-report/

IATA. (2020). *COVID-19 Airlines' Liquidity Crisis.* Retrieved September 19, 2021, from https://www.iata.org/en/iata-repository/publications/economic-reports/covid-19-airlines-liquidity-crisis/

International Air Transport Association. (2011). *Vision 2050. Report.* Retrieved September 08, 2021, from https://www.iata.org/contentassets/bccae1c5a24e43759607a5fd8f44770b/vision-2050.pdf

International Air Transport Association (IATA). (2020). *Press Release No: 28. 25 Million Jobs at Risk with Airline Shutdown.* Retrieved August 27, 2021, from https://www.iata.org/en/pressroom/pr/2020-04-07-02/

International Civil Aviation Organization. (n.d.). *CART Report - Building Resilience.* Retrieved July 11, 2021, from https://www.icao.int/covid/cart/Pages/CART-Report%2D%2D-Building-Resistance.aspx

Janić, M. (2015). Reprint of "Modelling the resilience, friability and costs of an air transport network affected by a large-scale disruptive event". *Transportation Research Part A: Policy and Practice, 81*, 77–92. https://doi.org/10.1016/j.tra.2015.07.012

Klar, R. (2020). *Emirates cuts almost all passenger flights.* Retrieved July 13, 2021, from https://thehill.com/policy/transportation/488902-emirates-cuts-almost-all-passenger-flights

Lan, S., Clarke, J.-P., & Barnhart, C. (2006). Planning for robust airline operations: Optimizing aircraft routings and flight departure times to minimize passenger disruptions. *Transportation Science, 40*(1), 15–28. https://doi.org/10.1287/trsc.1050.0134

Lange, R. (2020, October 20–23). *Senior Vice President at Airbus. Keynote speaker. AGIFORS 60th Annual Symposium.*

Lordan, O., Sallan, J. M., Escorihuela, N., & Gonzalez-Prieto, D. (2016). Robustness of airline route networks. *Physica A: Statistical Mechanics and its Applications, 445*, 18–26. https://doi.org/10.1016/j.physa.2015.10.053

Nan, C., & Sansavini, G. (2017). A quantitative method for assessing resilience of interdependent infrastructures. *Reliability Engineering & System Safety, 157*, 35–53. https://doi.org/10.1016/j.ress.2016.08.013

Oxley, D., & Jain, C. (2015). The Travel & Tourism Competitiveness Report 2015. Chapter 1.4: Global Air Passenger Markets: Riding Out Periods of Turbulence. In R. Crotti & T. Misrahi (Eds.), *The Travel & Tourism Competitiveness Report 2015. Growth through Shocks* (pp. 59–61).

Pearce, J. A., & Robbins, K. (1993). Toward improved theory and research on business turnaround. *Journal of Management, 19*(3), 613–636. https://doi.org/10.1016/0149-2063(93)90007-A

Ponomarov, S. Y., & Holcomb, M. C. (2009). Understanding the concept of supply chain resilience. *The International Journal of Logistics Management, 20*(1), 124–143. https://doi.org/10.1108/09574090910954873

Reynolds, P. (2020, October 20–23). *Manager Network Ops Systems and Logistics at Emirates. Panelist in the Crew Panel: COVID-19: In search of gems amongst the lumps of coal. AGIFORS 60th Annual Symposium.*

Rohit, T. (2020). *Help navigating Covid-19 impacts on your business*. Retrieved May 29, 2021, from https://troymedia.com/business/help-navigating-covid-19-impacts-on-your-business/#.YLIq8OdCTb0

Ruhlin, E. (2020, October 20–23). *Managing Director Revenue Decision Support at United Airlines. Panelist in the Revenue Management Panel: COVID-19: A chance to reset revenue management practices? AGIFORS 60th Annual Symposium.*

Sobieralski, J. B. (2020). COVID-19 and airline employment: Insights from historical uncertainty shocks to the industry. *Transportation Research Interdisciplinary Perspectives, 5*, 100123. https://doi.org/10.1016/j.trip.2020.100123

Sohoni, M., Lee, Y.-C., & Klabjan, D. (2011). Robust airline scheduling under block-time uncertainty. *Transportation Science, 45*(4), 451–464. https://doi.org/10.1287/trsc.1100.0361

Stomph, S. (2020, October 20–23). *Vice President at KLM Royal Dutch Airlines. Keynote speaker. AGIFORS 60th Annual Symposium.*

Sun, X., & Wandelt, S. (2018). Complementary strengths of airlines under network disruptions. *Safety Science, 103*, 76–87. https://doi.org/10.1016/j.ssci.2017.11.010

Taba, I., Westwater, B., & Reyes, P. (2020). *Up in the air: Resilience amidst uncertainty in the aviation sector*. Retrieved May 30, 2021, from https://www.wsp.com/en-NZ/insights/ca-up-in-the-air

Terry, B. (2020). *COVID-19: Rising to the challenge with resilience*. Airline Sector. Retrieved May 30, 2021, from https://www2.deloitte.com/content/dam/Deloitte/global/Documents/About-Deloitte/COVID-19/gx-understand-sector-impact-airlines.pdf

Wandelt, S., Sun, X., & Cao, X. (2015). Computationally efficient attack design for robustness analysis of air transportation networks. *Transportmetrica A: Transport Science, 11*(10), 939–966. https://doi.org/10.1080/23249935.2015.1089953

Wang, Y., Zhan, J., Xu, X., Li, L., Chen, P., & Hansen, M. (2019). Measuring the resilience of an airport network. *Chinese Journal of Aeronautics, 32*(12), 2694–2705. https://doi.org/10.1016/j.cja.2019.08.023

Wenzel, M. (2015). Path dependence and the stabilization of strategic premises: How the funeral industry buries itself. *Business Research, 8*(2), 265–299. https://doi.org/10.1007/s40685-015-0021-4

Wenzel, M., Stanske, S., & Lieberman, M. B. (2020). Strategic responses to crisis. *Strategic Management Journal, 41*(2), V7–V18. https://doi.org/10.1002/smj.3161

Mario Danner is an external lecturer for Aviation Management at the Institute for Transport and Logistics Management at WU (Vienna University of Economics and Business). He has earned a master's degree in International Business Administration and is currently completing his doctoral studies in Social and Economic Sciences focusing on Aviation Efficiency. After more than 18 years at Lufthansa Group in commercial affairs, political affairs, flight operations, and as a Senior Director Applications Operation Center and IT-Governance he joined biztribution, a deep tech aviation startup as COO.

Alexander M. Geske is Research Associate at the Institute for Transport and Logistics Management at WU (Vienna University of Economics and Business). He has earned a bachelor's degree in International Business Administration and a master's degree in Supply Chain Management. With a professional career in the transportation industry, Alexander combines the practical and academic perspective.

Chapter 26
Semiconductor Supply Chain: A 360-Degree View of Supply Chain Risk and Network Resilience Based on GIS and AI

Sucharita Gopal, Petra Staufer-Steinnocher, Yingqiang Xu, and Joshua Pitts

Abstract The semiconductor industry is essential to modern global economies, as chips and other components are crucial in consumer and industrial goods. In the past decade, the explosion of new technologies, such as the Internet of Things (IoT), Big Data, Artificial Intelligence (AI), and 5G telecommunication infrastructure has created a sustained demand for semiconductors that is reshaping every industry on its path to digitization and automation. We first characterize the supply chain of semiconductors, which over time have been honed to deliver maximum efficiency and speed, and we examine the drivers of past disruptions, especially due to the COVID-19 pandemic, natural hazards, and increasing geopolitical tensions between China and the West. Second, we present the rationale for resiliency management in this critical sector by probing what countries and companies plan to do given these disruptions. Finally, we are examining the role of Geographic Information Systems (GIS), spatial analysis, and AI in semiconductors supply chain management. While the specific tools and analytics for supply chain analysis remain an open question for researchers and managers, in order to model, predict, and plan for larger scale disruptions, such as pandemics, they definitely will rely heavily on data-driven approaches.

S. Gopal
Department of Earth and Environment and Center for Remote Sensing, Boston University, Boston, MA, USA

P. Staufer-Steinnocher (✉)
Department of Socioeconomics, Institute for Economic Geography and GIScience, WU (Vienna University of Economics and Business), Vienna, Austria
e-mail: Petra.Staufer-Steinnocher@wu.ac.at

Y. Xu
Department of Civil Engineering, Vanderbilt University, Nashville, TN, USA

J. Pitts
Global Development Policy Center, Boston University, Boston, MA, USA

S. Kummer et al. (eds.), *Supply Chain Resilience*, Springer Series in Supply Chain Management 17, https://doi.org/10.1007/978-3-030-95401-7_26

26.1 Introduction

The semiconductor industry is essential to modern global economies, as chips and other components are crucial in consumer and industrial goods, enabling multitudes of products spanning everything from consumer electronics to household appliances, and even cars. In the lead up to the twenty-first century, consumer demand led to increased consumption in electronics fueling semiconductor demand, continuing to today. Now, in the past decade, the explosion of new technologies, such as the Internet of Things (IoT), Big Data, artificial intelligence (AI), and 5G telecommunication infrastructure, has created a sustained demand for semiconductors that is reshaping every industry on its path to digitization and automation. A decade ago, it may have been unheard of, but today, industries such as agriculture, insurance, and even home sales are adopting new semiconductor-based technologies such as drones that are quickly becoming essential to their respective industries.

Global semiconductor sales in 2020 exceeded 466 billion US dollars, representing an increase of 10% from 2019 (Alsop, 2021). Memory semiconductors, graphics processing units (GPUs), and 5G chips led semiconductor market growth in 2020. On top of growth and increased demand in current semiconductor applications, new and emerging technologies are further driving demand. For example, smartphone manufacturer Qualcomm is now targeting virtual reality/augmented reality in the manufacturing of next-generation phones (Zafar, 2020), and Tesla is planning "4D" sensing in its driverless car technology (Lambert, 2020). Indeed, other new technologies such as blockchain/cryptocurrency mining, 5G deployments, and autonomous drones are also taking hold globally to drive demand. The low cost and availability of some of these technologies are further driving growth in (and demand from) new and emerging markets.

The paper has three objectives. The first objective is to characterize the supply chain of semiconductors and examine the drivers of past disruptions. The second objective is to present the rationale for resiliency management in this critical sector by probing what countries and companies plan to do given these disruptions. Finally, we will be examining the role of Geographic Information Systems (GIS), spatial analysis, and AI in semiconductors supply chain management.

26.2 Background

The semiconductor supply chain consists of many segments—from research and development (R&D) to design, manufacture, assembly, and testing—even before it reaches the end consumer. Global demand for consumer electronics and other semiconductor applications continues to increase and is expected to further increase through the year 2024 and beyond. Figure 26.1 highlights the significant market size increase projected from 2019 to 2024, with smartphones leading the growth. With the prices of smartphones and other handheld electronics declining, this opens up

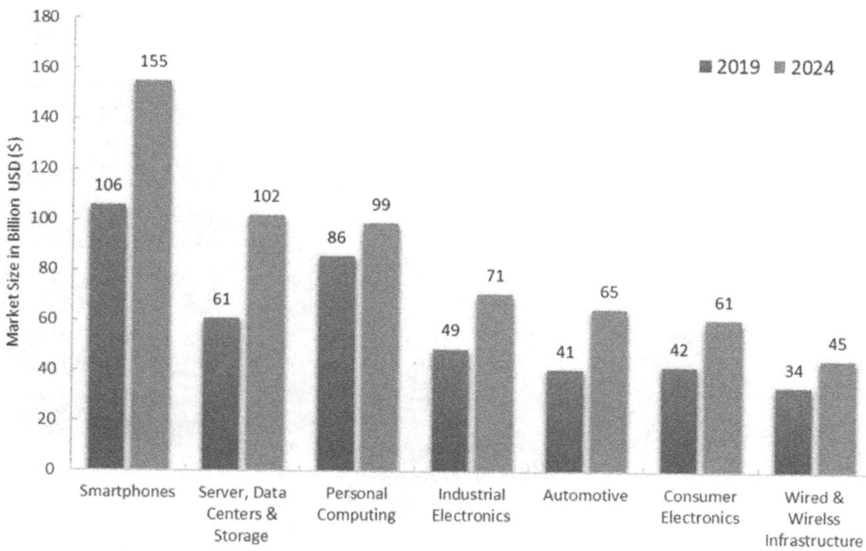

Fig. 26.1 Global semiconductor market size in 2019 and estimated 2024 (Data: Alsop, 2021)

market access in new and emerging economies. In addition, Internet access availability continues to increase in rural and remote communities, further driving device demand in many areas that have not had access before. Increasing business digitization, IoT, blockchain, and emerging technologies further accelerate the demand.

The Semiconductor and Other Electronic Component Manufacturing (listed under codes NAICS 33441) comprise companies manufacturing semiconductors and other related electronic components. These companies' products include capacitors, resistors, microprocessors, bare and loaded printed circuit boards, electron tubes, electronic connectors, and computer modems, among others. A single computer (DRAM) chip production may require more than 1000 steps, passing through international borders many times before reaching the end customer and in some cases may pass through over 70 countries (Ezel, 2021). This complexity often renders any analysis around the supply chain, such as risk/threat analysis and logistics planning, a difficult task.

There are five to seven steps in the supply chain, as shown in Fig. 26.2. R&D advances all supply chain steps and includes exploratory research on foundational technologies and advancing the leading edge of semiconductor technology. Several recent reports found that due to challenging market conditions, R&D and innovation rank first in strategic priority (see e.g., Zanni et al., 2019). US chip companies spent about 20% of their annual revenue on R&D in 2019 (Semiconductor Industry Association, 2020). Companies such as Inphi Corporation, Marvell Technology, Silicon Labs, and Xilinx have spent more than 23% on R&D in terms of share of their sales. Notably, R&D spending is the highest in semiconductors compared with all other industries.

The United States is a global leader in the R&D-intensive activities of the semiconductor industry. This R&D encompasses electronic design automation

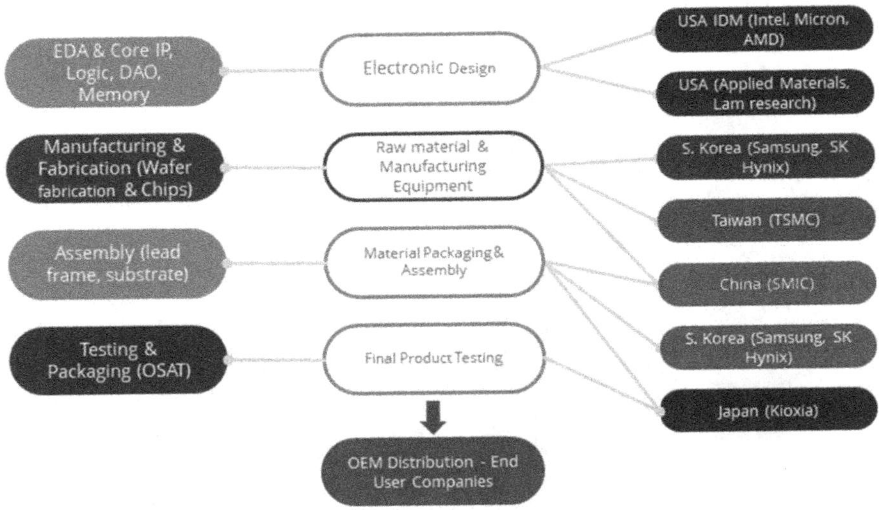

Fig. 26.2 The semiconductor supply chain, examples, and steps (discrete, analog, and other (DAO), electronic design automation (EDA), integrated device manufacturer (IDM), outsourced semiconductor assembly and test (OSAT), original equipment manufacturer (OEM))

(EDA), core intellectual property (IP), chip design, and advanced manufacturing equipment. Taiwan (Taiwan Semiconductor), South Korea (Samsung), and Japan (Kioxia) are leaders in wafer fabrication. This part of the semiconductor supply chain requires government subsidies and incentives, a robust infrastructure and energy (Gopalakrishnan et al., 2010), and a skilled workforce. All three countries have spent decades specializing in this segment of the supply chain. China, on the other hand, is a leader in assembly, packaging, and testing, which require less skilled labor and capital investments, but China wants to aggressively expand throughout the semiconductor value chain. This type of geographical specialization of the supply chain worked when semiconductors were required for high-end electronics and computers. However, the increasing demand from smartphones, electric cars, AI automation, robotics, and IoT necessitates a rethinking of the semiconductor supply chain given risks and geopolitical tensions. Many countries, including the United States, have proposals to increase their domestic production of chips to address vulnerabilities and enhance resiliency in their semiconductor supply chains.

26.3 COVID-19, Geopolitics, and Extreme Weather Events

Each segment of the semiconductor manufacture has a different NAICS (North American Industry Classification System) code. For example, semiconductor companies that are part of NAICS 33441 are primarily based in the United States, Taiwan, South Korea, Japan, and Western Europe. Figure 26.3 shows the global

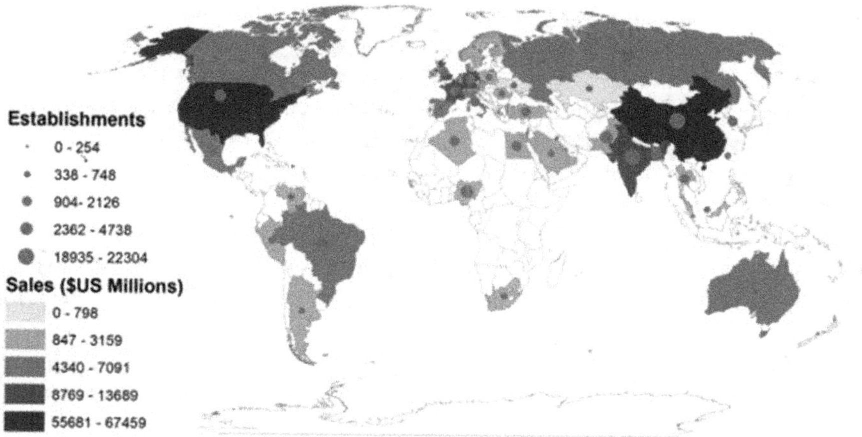

Fig. 26.3 Semiconductor and Other Electronic Component Manufacturing in various countries in terms of sales and establishments (Data: Barnes, 2021, pp. 11–12)

distribution of NAICS 33441: Semiconductor and Other Electronic Component Manufacturing. This code shows the establishments making capacitors, resistors, microprocessors, bare and loaded printed circuit boards, electron tubes, electronic connectors, and computer modems (Barnes, 2021). A disruption in a company in any of these key countries can cause a ripple effect across the entire supply chain impacting the end-user companies. During the first quarter, 2020, this problem was seen when China, among other Asian countries, had a COVID-19 lockdown, restricting many imports, exports, as well as labor for many weeks and even months.

As semiconductor supply chains are critical to the functioning of a country, supply chain vulnerabilities and resilience questions are now being raised in the light of recent events such as the global COVID-19 pandemic. COVID-19 pandemic has increased demand in specific industries like smartphones and PCs, which are heavy users of semiconductors. Broadcom's (chip manufacturer) lead times, the duration between when an order for a chip is placed and when it actually gets filled, stretched from 12.2 weeks in February 2020 to 22.2 weeks in March 2021 (King et al., 2021).

The semiconductor shortages and geopolitics have led to recent trade tensions between China and the West (Farrell & Newman, 2020). The United States is a leading chipmaker with a rich history in manufacturing chips that spurred the technology boom in Silicon Valley. Chips are considered a vital strategic asset. China's global market share and competitiveness in semiconductors, especially concerning Chinese-headquartered firms, are smaller than its global peers (Grimes & Du, 2020). Thus, China sees chips as crucial to its future growth and one of the key targets of "Made in China 2025," an initiative set to boost high-tech industries and increase domestic production.

Another contributing factor in the global chip wars is the fast-changing chip technology. Moore's law notes that the doubling every two years in the number of transistors in a microchip roughly corresponds to the computational power, measured in terms of speed and capability of the computer. As of 2021, Moore's law does not hold as strongly, as it is now more expensive and more logistically challenging to double the number of components in electronic circuits (DeBenedictis, 2017; Lambrechts et al., 2018; Li et al., 2019). In addition, there is an increasing threat of counterfeit electronics in the semiconductors supply chain (Guin et al., 2014).

Extreme weather events such as droughts also impact the semiconductor industry, which requires large quantities of water to produce chips. Unprecedented drought in Taiwan has affected its semiconductor wafer-fabrication factories, which account for more than 60% of the global revenue, further straining an acute global chip shortage. Taiwan Semiconductor Manufacturing Co. TSM, the world's biggest contract chipmaker, is impacted, leading to a shortage of chips for General Motors and other car companies that use semiconductors in engines, braking systems, and other vehicle components. The Japanese Tsunami and earthquake in 2011 caused severe damages in large-scale inland and coastal areas of Honshu. It disrupted and damaged many industrial supply chains, including semiconductor manufacturing; for example, damage caused to Renesas Electronics translated into Toyota manufacturing disruption (Matsuo, 2015). The global pandemic led to the shutdown of the manufacturing and assembly of semiconductors in several critical vehicle components that has halted the assembly of cars at General Motors (Wayland, 2021).

The global distribution of supply chains and associated specialization across countries have significant implications for future technological competition and international security. For example, China and its contentious relationship with the West around Taiwan may jeopardize the semiconductor supply chain. Recently, the Biden administration met with chip companies to address the global semiconductor shortage. One plan was to do more manufacturing in the United States by providing funds (Shepardson, 2021). Thus, the semiconductor industry is impacted by geopolitics, rapid demand for new chips, natural disasters, and other events across the global stage.

26.4 Supply Chain Security and Resiliency Management

The complexities of the semiconductor supply chain make long-term analysis, risk assessment, and planning difficult. The rapidly changing global dynamics also mean that models and analyses used in 2020 have limited applicability to 2021, only a year later. COVID-19 has highlighted vulnerabilities in supply chains globally, showing the need for better analytics, risk measurement, and planning. However, can a pandemic be planned for, and if, how?

Typical risk analyses, such as SWOT analyses, work well in identifying broad supply chain vulnerabilities and risk. These can be applied to each individual supply chain step or to suppliers and partners to provide a detailed look at how to approach the management at each step.

However, as more data becomes available globally, better analytics must be adopted to model supply chain resilience. More data includes drone and IoT data for real-time monitoring of logistics operations, GIS data for siting analysis and country- or region-specific considerations, as well as point of sale (POS) and customer data from suppliers and partners to provide demand-side metrics.

26.5 AI/Machine Learning and Big Data Analytics in Supply Chain Management

With increasing digitization, companies have access to "Big Data" characterized by volume, velocity, variety, veracity, and value (see e.g., Addo-Tenkorang & Helo, 2016). AI and machine learning (ML) are used in multiple ways to identify risks as well as demand forecasting that could mitigate the effect and enhance resiliency in the supply chain (Feizabadi, 2020; Sanders et al., 2019), real-time monitoring and sustainable design to eliminate waste (Dash et al., 2019), predicting in uncertain and dynamic environments (Modgil et al., 2021), and real-time monitoring (Calatayud et al., 2019). Thus, AI/ML is helping companies find insights, opportunities, and risks to enhance the resiliency of their supply chains.

26.6 GIS and Geospatial Technologies: Supply Chain Visualization and Optimization and Location Siting

GIS and geospatial technologies can be used to design, model, and visualize resiliency in the supply chains. GIS can help visualize the entire supply chain and identify real-time threats (natural disasters, shipping delays, labor strikes, terrorists/cyberattacks, and other issues) posed on the supply chain. GIS can then assist in locating backup facilities for storage of any business-critical systems or materials subject to different spatial hazard exposure (Ivanov et al., 2019; Ratick et al., 2008) and manufacture in case of extreme emergencies. Frost and Hua (2019), for example, quantify spatiotemporal impacts of the interaction of water scarcity and water use by the global semiconductor manufacturing industry. Deng et al. (2019) discuss the role of GIS in construction supply chain management including supplier selection and tracking a number of material deliveries, where distance and time matter. The increasing emphasis on sustainability and green buildings also requires GIS for siting and tracking green resources and energy (Yang et al., 2020). GIS can provide support in assessing sustainability metrics in the semiconductor manufacturing industry (Frost & Hua, 2019), such as the quantification of the spatiotemporal impacts of the interaction of water scarcity and water use.

GIS can also aid in rerouting a critical supply chain under threat if there is some advanced warning. Supply chains often utilize optimization, which maximizes or minimizes an objective function—cost or time or distance. Frequently, optimization methods in this context are solutions to the traveling salesman (TSP) and vehicle routing (VRP) problems as well as location allocation (Gopal, 2016). Simply put, solutions for the TSP aim to find the least-cost possible tour starting from a depot with a given list of destinations and their pairwise distances, under the constraint that the TSP visits each destination exactly once and, finally, returns to the depot.

GIS has been combined with linear and mixed-integer programming models to make strategic, tactical, and operational decisions (Balaman, 2019; Gopal, 2018; Jeong et al., 2019). For example, using GIS and a modeling/optimization technique, such as mathematical modeling or simulation, enables us to parametrize the decision models reliably. The mixed-integer program (MIP) has resulted in a model of the semiconductor supply chains to model discrete aspects of decision-making (Denton et al., 2006). GIS can be used for siting facilities (Church & Murray, 2009). Zokaee et al. (2021), for example, propose the development of a resilience location-routing model for post-disaster reconstruction supply chain endeavors. Their model implemented in GAMS utilizes GIS capabilities where necessary for, e.g., optimizing the allotment of restricted reconstruction resources to damaged areas or minimizing the costs of location, routing, and disruption in the post-disaster reconstruction circumstances.

GIS can be further utilized for semiconductor sustainability and ESG (environmental sustainability goals) materiality mapping. Thus, GIS can be used to strengthen and build resiliency in the semiconductor supply chain by spotting risk and vulnerabilities, rerouting or creating emergencies, or siting in new locations.

While GIS has emphasized visualization and analysis related to proximity, demographics, and path planning, AI workflows can add more dynamic real-time data on consumer mobility and purchase patterns. Thus, AI/machine learning provides advanced analytics, often in real time, to assist in market analysis, linking patterns to location (Cross, 2020; ESRI, 2018, 2019). Deep learning and AI can assist in monitoring and tracking assets and material based on real-time analysis of imagery, satellite, or drone. AI can also enable using "Big Data" to generate different scenarios of business risks. This AI helps "hedge against the risk of uncertainty" (Goldfarb et al., 2019).

26.7 Conclusion

Semiconductor supply chains facilitate the production of everything from computers and cars and consist of thousands of parts sourced from diverse geographies worldwide. Over time, these supply chains have been honed to deliver maximum efficiency and speed. Nevertheless, there are disruptions in the supply chains due to the COVID-19 pandemic, natural hazards, and increasing geopolitical tensions between China and the West.

As data availability and computational power increase, the analysis and models around the semiconductor and other supply chains will continue to improve. While today's analysis around supply chains can be accomplished by business analysts using traditional business analysis processes, such as SWOT, these approaches are becoming outdated and are slowly being replaced with more sophisticated analytics using data-driven approaches. While the specific tools and analytics for supply chain analysis remain an open question for researchers and managers, in order to model, predict, and plan for larger-scale disruptions, such as pandemics, they definitely will rely heavily on data-driven approaches.

These considerations should be brought to bear by academic institutions as well as corporations supply chain teams who will need to seek candidates with greater technical expertise and stronger proficiencies in data science and analytics approaches.

References

Addo-Tenkorang, R., & Helo, P. T. (2016). Big data applications in operations/supply-chain management: A literature review. *Computers & Industrial Engineering, 101*, 528–543.

Alsop, T. (2021). *Semiconductor market size worldwide 2019 & 2024, by application*. Retrieved June 15, 2021, from https://www.statista.com/statistics/498265/cagr-main-semiconductor-target-markets/

Balaman, S. Y. (2019). Decision-making for biomass-based production chains. In *The basic concepts and methodologies* (pp. 46–47). Academic Press.

Barnes. (2021). *2021 Worldwide Semi-Conductor & Electronic Components Mfg. Industry*. Industry & Market Report. Barnes Reports, C. Barnes & Co

Calatayud, A., Lechmacher, W., Betti, F., & Katz, R. (2019). *Supply Chain 4.0 global practices and lessons learned for latin*. America and the Caribbean. World economic forum.

Church, R. L., & Murray, A. T. (2009). *Business site selection, location analysis, and GIS* (pp. 259–280). Wiley.

Cross, B. (2020). Four ways AI and Location Intelligence are guiding the future of Business. *Forbes Magazine*, June 9, 2020 Retrieved August 12, 2021, from https://www.forbes.com/sites/esri/2020/06/09/four-ways-ai-and-location-intelligence-are-guiding-the-future-of-business/?sh=6505ca33b416

Dash, R., McMurtrey, M., Rebman, C., & Kar, U. K. (2019). Application of artificial intelligence in automation of supply chain management. *Journal of Strategic Innovation and Sustainability, 14*(3), 43–53.

DeBenedictis, E. P. (2017). It's time to redefine Moore's law again. *Computer, 50*(2), 72–75.

Deng, Y., Gan, V. J., Das, M., Cheng, J. C., & Anumba, C. (2019). Integrating 4D BIM and GIS for construction supply chain management. *Journal of construction engineering and management, 145*(4), 04019016.

Denton, B. T., Forrest, J., & Milne, R. J. (2006). IBM solves a mixed-integer program to optimize its semiconductor supply chain. *Interfaces, 36*(5), 386–399.

ESRI. (2018). *The Science of Where: Putting AI and Location Intelligence to Work*. ESRI. Retrieved August 17, 2021, from https://www.esri.com/content/dam/esrisites/en-us/media/ebooks/artificial-intelligence-ebook.pdf

ESRI. (2019). *The Science of Where: Discover the Value of Location Intelligence Technology*. ESRI. Retrieved August 17, 2021, from https://www.esri.com/content/dam/esrisites/en-us/media/pdf/private/g237565-Brand-Location-Intelligence-eBook-dl-FNL.pdf

Ezel, S. (2021). *Moore's Law under attack: The impact of China's policies on global semiconductor innovation*. ITIF Information Technology & Innovation Foundation Retrieved May

29, 2021, from https://itif.org/publications/2021/02/18/moores-law-under-attack-impact-chinas-policies-global-semiconductor
Farrell, H., & Newman, A. L. (2020). Chained to globalization: Why it's too late to decouple. *Foreign Affairs, 99*, 70.
Feizabadi, J. (2020). Machine learning demand forecasting and supply chain performance. *International Journal of Logistics Research and Applications*, 1–24.
Frost, K., & Hua, I. (2019). Quantifying spatiotemporal impacts of the interaction of water scarcity and water use by the global semiconductor manufacturing industry. *Water Resources and Industry*, 22, 100115. https://doi.org/10.1016/j.wri.2019.100115.
Goldfarb, A., Gans, J., & Agrawal, A. (2019). *The economics of artificial intelligence: An Agenda.* University of Chicago Press.
Gopal, S. (2016). Artificial neural networks in geospatial analysis. *International Encyclopedia of Geography: People, the Earth, Environment and Technology*, 1–7.
Gopal, S. (2018). *The internet of things (IoT) for GIS in transportation. US department of Transportation, GIS in Transportation Newsletter, Guest Editorial.* US Department of Transportation Newsletter. Retrieved from https://www.gis.fhwa.dot.gov/documents/Newsletter_November2018.asp
Gopalakrishnan, B., Mardikar, Y., & Korakakis, D. (2010). 'Energy analysis in semiconductor manufacturing', Energy Engineering Journal of the Association of Energy Engineering. *Taylor & Francis Group, 107*(2), 6–40. https://doi.org/10.1080/01998591009709867
Grimes, S., & Du, D. (2020). China's emerging role in the global semiconductor value chain. *Telecommunications Policy*, 101959. https://doi.org/10.1016/j.telpol.2020.101959
Guin, U., Huang, K., DiMase, D., Carulli, J. M., Tehranipoor, M., & Makris, Y. (2014). Counterfeit integrated circuits: A rising threat in the global semiconductor supply chain. *Proceedings of the IEEE, 102*(8), 1207–1228.
Ivanov, D., Dolgui, A., Das, A., & Sokolov, B. (2019). Digital supply chain twins: Managing the ripple effect, resilience, and disruption risks by data-driven optimization, simulation, and visibility. In D. Ivanov, A. Dolgui, & B. Sokolov (Eds.), *Handbook of ripple effects in the supply chain, International Series in Operations Research & Management Science* (Vol. 276, pp. 309–332). Springer.
Jeong, H., Sieverding, H. L., & Stone, J. J. (2019). Biodiesel supply chain optimization modeled with geographical information system (GIS) and Mixed-Integer Linear Programming (MILP) for the northern great plains region. *Bioenergy Research, 12*(1), 229–240.
King, I., Wu, D., & Pogkas, D. (2021). *How a chip shortage snarled everything from phones to cars* Retrieved June 12, 2021, from https://www.bloomberg.com/graphics/2021-semiconductors-chips-shortage/
Lambert, F. (2020). *Tesla is adding a new '4D' radar with twice the range for self-driving* Retrieved May 29, 2021, from https://electrek.co/2020/10/22/tesla-4d-radar-twice-range-self-driving/
Lambrechts, W., Sinha, S., Abdallah, J. A., & Prinsloo, J. (2018). *Extending Moore's law through advanced semiconductor design and processing techniques*. CRC Press.
Li, M. Y., Su, S. K., Wong, H. S. P., & Li, L. J. (2019). How 2D semiconductors could extend Moore's law. *Nature*, 169–170.
Matsuo, H. (2015). Implications of the Tohoku earthquake for Toyota's coordination mechanism: Supply chain disruption of automotive semiconductors. *International Journal of Production Economics, 161*(C), 217–227.
Modgil, S., Gupta, S., Stekelorum, R., & Laguir, I. (2021). AI technologies and their impact on supply chain resilience during COVID-19. *International Journal of Physical Distribution & Logistics Management.*
Ratick, S., Meacham, B., & Aoyama, Y. (2008). Locating backup facilities to enhance supply chain disaster resilience. *Growth and Change, 39*(4), 642–666.

Sanders, N. R., Boone, T., Ganeshan, R., & Wood, J. D. (2019). Sustainable supply chains in the age of AI and digitization: Research challenges and opportunities. *Journal of Business Logistics, 40*(3), 229–240.

Semiconductor Industry Association. (2020). *State of the U.S. semiconductor industry*. Retrieved June 12, 2021, from https://www.semiconductors.org/wp-content/uploads/2020/06/2020-SIA-State-of-the-Industry-Report.pdf

Shepardson, D. (2021). *Commerce chief says U.S. could help boost chips transparency* Retrieved May 22, 2021, from https://www.reuters.com/business/autos-transportation/us-commerce-chief-holding-meetings-chips-shortage-sources-2021-05-20/

Wayland, M. (2021). *GM and Ford cutting production at several North American plants due to chip shortage*. CNBC. https://www.cnbc.com/2021/04/08/gm-cutting-production-at-several-plants-due-to-chip-shortage.html

Yang, Z., Sun, J., Zhang, Y., & Wang, Y. (2020). Synergy between green supply chain management and green information systems on corporate sustainability: An informal alignment perspective. *Environment, Development and Sustainability, 22*(2), 1165–1186.

Zafar, R. (2020). *Qualcomm expands 5G Extended Reality (XR) collaboration to include operators*. Retrieved June 12, 2021, from https://wccftech.com/qualcomm-expands-5g-extended-reality-xr-collaboration-to-include-operators/

Zanni, T., Clark, L., Gentle, C., Jones, S., & Lohokare, S. (2019). *Semiconductors: As the backbone of the connected world, the industry's future is bright*. KPMG's 14th Semiconductor Outlook Report. Retrieved April 29, 2021, from https://assets.kpmg/content/dam/kpmg/us/pdf/2019/03/kpmg-semiconductor.pdf

Zokaee, M., Tavakkoli-Moghaddam, R., & Rahimi, Y. (2021). Post-disaster reconstruction supply chain: Empirical optimization study. *Automation in Construction, 129*, 103811. https://doi.org/10.1016/j.autcon.2021.103811

Sucharita (Suchi) Gopal Ph.D., is a Professor at the Department of Earth and Environment & Center for Remote Sensing, a Research Professor at the Pardee Center for the Study of the Longer-Range Future as well as with the Boston University Marine Program (BUMP). Her research is multidisciplinary dealing with spatial analysis and modeling, GIS, data mining and information visualization and artificial neural networks to address a variety of problems in biology, environmental science, public health, and business. She is a Chief Executive Officer and Co-Founder of Chatmine Technologies and has a long-lasting collaboration with WU (Vienna University of Economics and Business) also teaching in the SCM Master program.

Petra Staufer-Steinnocher is an Associate Professor and Deputy Head of the Institute for Economic Geography and GIScience at WU (Vienna University of Economics and Business). Her research areas are: GIScience and Technology, Location/Allocation Modeling, and Spatial Supply Chain Analytics.

Yingqiang Xu is a Master student at the Department of Earth and Environment & Center for Remote Sensing, Boston University.

Joshua Pitts Ph.D., is a Chief Technical Officer and Data Architect at Chatmine Technologies also working with the Global Development Policy Center, Boston University on the Global China Initiative (GCI) interactive public databases.

Chapter 27
Ways to Build Resilient Inbound Transportation Logistics in the Automotive Industry

Mirko Hoppe and Werner Podkowik

Abstract The chapter illustrates that supply chain resilience has recently become a critical strategic task to counter sustainably reduced car production worldwide due to the inherent semiconductor shortages and COVID-19-effects. The authors suggest a three-stage approach to improve supply chain resilience in the automotive industry holistically. An operative task force set-up mitigates adverse short-term effects to a minimum. Risk-management activities identify and address weaknesses on a mid-term horizon. A long-term strategic path will support achieving the key strategic goal for more supply chain resilience in the future. This approach will be discussed in detail on inbound transportation logistics with examples from practice. As a result, inbound transportation logistics resilience implies long-term development. This development will follow the suggested approach and focus intensely on more collaborative partnerships in the automotive industry, based on improved information transparency in the supply chain.

27.1 Problem Framing and Definition

Supply chain risks have become more and more of a challenge for manufacturing companies. Just consider the number of natural disasters in recent years: earthquakes in Japan or yearly hurricanes in the US Southern states causing massive damage, flooding, and devastation. Otherwise, think about the current global crisis in the automotive industry. The semiconductor supply shortages are interrupting and slowing down automobile production on a worldwide level. Among other examples like power outages in Texas, the blocking of the Suez Channel, and the ongoing pandemic coronavirus disease (COVID-19), there is an accumulation of those events simultaneously. The return of a growing global economy in 2021 intensifies the

M. Hoppe (✉)
Spartanburg, SC, USA

W. Podkowik
Lippstadt, Germany

S. Kummer et al. (eds.), *Supply Chain Resilience*, Springer Series in Supply Chain Management 17, https://doi.org/10.1007/978-3-030-95401-7_27

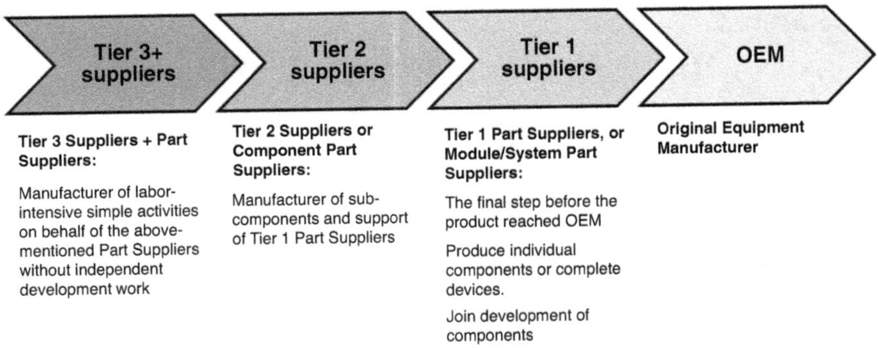

Fig. 27.1 Supply chain structure for the automotive industry

pressure on existing production and transportation capacities. It translates into how to operate robustly and think about ways to build resilient inbound transportation logistics.

The article is aimed at anyone interested in building a more resilient inbound transportation logistics as one part of a supply chain. Inbound transportation includes the pickup of material at part suppliers' different tiers and the transportation to the final destination at the original equipment manufacturer (OEM) (Fig. 27.1).

Christopher and Peck (2004) approach the definition of resilience, first distinguishing the terms "robustness" and "resilience." Robustness in IT is defined as *"the ability of a computer system to cope with errors during execution."* The robustness of a process can be measured by key performance indicators (KPIs). One example in transportation logistics is a KPI, such as "on-time pickup" in percentage: the proportion of all pickups compared to late pickups at the part supplier. Furthermore, it influences a subsequent process: "on-time delivery" at the final destination. The KPIs as robustness measurement can be the first indicator for a resilient supply chain.

According to the results of Christopher and Peck (2004), a robust process may be desirable but does not equate to a resilient supply chain. The authors define "resilience" as *"the ability of a system to return to its original state or move to a new, more desirable state after being disturbed."* The definition is similar to Wieland and Durach (2021). They suggested that resilience does not just relate to the ability of a system to "bounce back" after an upcoming event but also to the capacity to adapt and transform.

27.2 Solution

Managing exceptions and developing a resilient supply chain at the same time – three stages have to be considered:

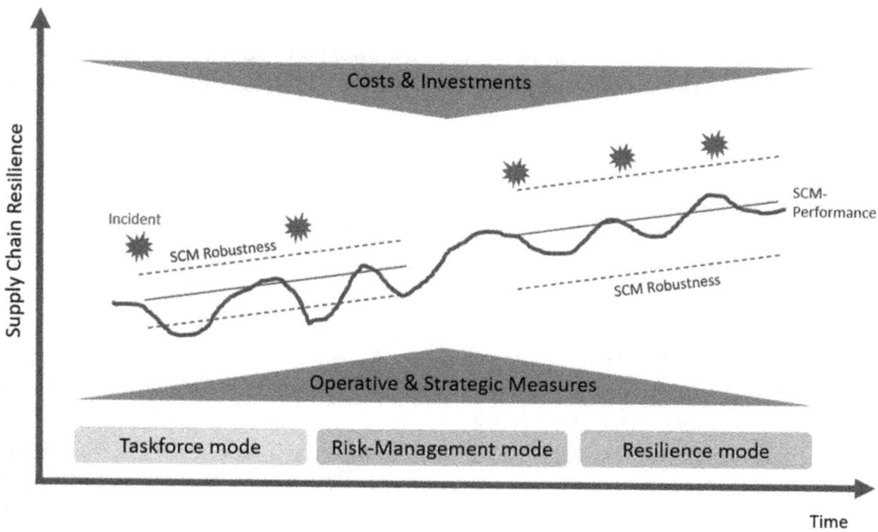

Fig. 27.2 Development of resilient supply chains

- Short term – Taskforce mode
- Midterm – Risk management mode
- Long term – Resilience mode

Figure 27.2 illustrates the effects of operative and strategic measures to improve supply chain performance and adaption. Resilience-building measures are restricted by the applied costs and investment. Although only selected cost-feasible measures will be implemented, the systematic approach will increase supply chain resilience.

Let's assume that one or more critical events co-occur. The production is at risk due to several shortages of multiple materials, such as semiconductors with low available transportation capacities due to the COVID-19 situation. Therefore, several production line stops are possible on a short-term horizon.

27.2.1 Short Term: Taskforce Mode

React directly; it is advisable to set up a taskforce. It can be an interdisciplinary team with internal and external process partners. The team operates daily. Build a taskforce team; three key success factors are decisive: team organization, responsiveness, and transparency.

Several core teams are required in addition to project management:

- *Direct Purchasing* to support the part supplier communication to critical partners and evaluate the current/future risks. In parallel alternative sources have to be checked (e.g., electronics brokers)

- *Plant Logistics*, including material steering departments to evaluate the existing days-on-hand at the production location to simulate potential customer effects
- *Development* and *Product Management* to evaluate possible material, software, and process alternatives
- *Sales* to lead the communication to the end customer

The main focus of the taskforce is to identify the upcoming operative risks in supply and respond to them immediately. This comprises the entire inbound material portfolio on a material number base as well to execute immediate short-term counter actions to mitigate supply risks. Additional tasks are exchanging materials within the production network or checking availability with electronic brokers to avoid line stoppages. In a limited manner, alternative materials can be identified and applied, which could consume more time until a countermeasure is applicable in the case of the OEM customer qualification process.

When alternatives are defined, the missing material must be transported faster than the standard transportation lead times. Here, management of the "expedite transportation network" will become a decisive factor. Expedites include dedicated ground transportation (e.g., team drivers, loading to sprinter vans, or parcel services). Airfreight, including hand-carry, helps to avoid a critical supply situation. Furthermore, a professional trade compliance team for customs clearance is needed.

The taskforce mode already provides valuable information about internal and external vulnerabilities/risks of supply chain processes. They need to be collected systematically to use for further measures in risk mode and resilience mode.

27.2.2 *Midterm: Risk management Mode*

Midterm, supply chain risk management must initiate.

27.2.2.1 Transparency on Master Data and Scenario Simulations

The taskforce has to identify potential risks in the supply chain. The accurate and consolidated reports, such as stock, days-on-hand information, or bill-of-material (BOM) breakdowns depend on the IT capability. Different enterprise resource planning (ERP) systems limit the accuracy of profound statements. Incorrect, outdated, or missing data in the ERP systems impact the correctness of results. This leads to a failure-prone manual process with several data sources, which takes crucial time.

In other words, the data capability of the entire supply chain is crucial to achieving full transparency and demands correct responsive actions. The more harmonized the ERP systems are, the more accurately the database can be set up, the better can the foundation be built for a robust and resilient supply chain.

27.2.2.2 Supply Chain Mapping, Risk Categorization, and Costs Effects

An additional step to building a resilient supply chain is to create transparency about the existing inbound transportation relations. The SC mapping provides a better understanding of the freight movements. Strategic risks can be identified and categorized on their impact. Interdisciplinary teams should create a risk categorization matrix design involving purchasing, operations, logistics, legal, HR, and controlling as stakeholders. As a result, the supply chain can evaluate its impact on potential risk categories, such as financial or performance effects. These categories need to be operationalized with KPIs. With these activities, strategic decisions for improvements can be derived. Guidelines can be developed to adapt and transform to a resilient supply chain set-up in the future.

Identified improving measures can lead to higher costs. Additionally, alternative material qualification, multiple sourcing, or higher stocks of critical materials can include additional costs. Therefore, all measures must be evaluated on their positive resilience effect, their profit, and investment expenditures. As a result, a selected bundle of a resilience program with feasible measures must decide.

What does this mean for inbound transportation? Let's assume the supply chain risk evaluation results reveal that various part suppliers in a specific geographical region are critical for major disruptions. Therefore, it needs to analyze the existing transportation network for its robustness and resilience. That could lead to the following questions regarding the mapping of the specific inbound transportation set-up for this region:

- Which ground transportation carriers operate in their local region? Do the carriers already operate in the existing transportation network indirectly or directly? What is the operational experience and reputation of the carrier?
- Where is the next airport close to the critical part supplier located? What are the operating hours? What size of aircraft can the airport handle?
- How capable are the available customs brokers to handle airfreight on weekends? Which licenses and EDI system does the customs broker provide?
- Continuing this thought process, aspects of border-crossing activities have to be investigated. Which border-crossing points can be used for hazmat freight? What are the operation hours of the crossing points on the border?

To summarize, the current transportation network can be mapped out based on collected data stored in a standardized database, and risks can be identified and categorized. On this basis, improvement measures can be derived, evaluated for feasibility, and implemented to establish a more robust supply chain.

27.2.3 *Long Term : Resilience Mode*

Some of the above-identified risks will lead to strategic programs to improve the resilience on the company level and as a part of inbound transportation. These strategic programs include a bundle of measures. The measures are related to inbound transportation and support supply chain performance and flexibility, countering disruptions or unforeseen events. Some examples:

27.2.3.1 Supply Chain Collaboration in Material Forecasting

In the long-term material planning process, it is crucial to ensure material availability on a long-term horizon. All partners in the supply chain need to focus on the early set-up and maintenance of relevant and correct ordering data within the supply chain. That includes a risk evaluation of certain material groups, which will lead to safety material buffers at different stages. This approach should be checked during an SCM audit at an early stage of the pre-start-of-production phase to prove the correct data set-up and risk mitigation maturity. This also applies to actual series production projects, where engineering change management events might occur. Changes need to be monitored from a material forecasting point of view with high accuracy and strict monitoring.

27.2.3.2 Supply Chain Visibility and Integration

Based on the abovementioned proactive set-up, part suppliers can be integrated faster and with better transparency. Part supplier integration enables visibility from the material pickup to the transport to the final destination at OEM.

Investing in open and integrated systems for all involved partners is advantageous to enable a suitable end-to-end tracking of freight movements and transportation expectations. Established systems require contracts between the partners, where roles, responsibilities, tasks, and consequences will be fixed and monitored during operative operations.

However, integration remains a challenge. The presence of "silo thinking," trust issues, and changes within the partner network could lead to SC performance issues and cause trouble during the crisis mode. Therefore, long-term relationships must be established to build trust between the partners. A recommendation is "relationship talks" with suppliers, different tiers, and carriers as specific subprojects of a strategic program to reach supply chain resilience.

27.2.3.3 Standardized Components for Multiuse Products and Intensifying Flexible Sourcing

As a precondition to counter material bottlenecks, the product development teams need to explore strategies to develop products which are not dependent on unique and customized parts. The focus is on critical products, which cannot be replaced short term in a material bottleneck crisis. The identified products need to be designed with standardized components, which can be used in various applications and variants to avoid exclusivity. With that, multiple sources can be contracted to share the risks of a potential shortage. Part supplier contracts need to be negotiated on a higher range of volume flexibility to counter their potential capacity shortfall.

This approach also applies to inbound transportation. Flexible sourcing requires a proactive planning integration of transportation planning into the sourcing process. All sources need to be evaluated and integrated into the transportation network. In crisis mode, the network should adapt all selected sources for emergency transportation as a standard without reduced SC performance.

27.2.3.4 Emergency Transportation Network Design

Focusing on the network design of emergency transportation, two strategies are conceivable:

- Strategy 1—dedicated emergency transportation network—to build a separate expedite network in addition to a standard transportation network.
- Strategy 2—standard transportation network—can require the carrier to run both standard transportation and emergency transportation as expedites for all origin-destination transportation relations.

From a commercial point of view, strategy 1 may be advantageous. Expedite operation (EO) providers (e.g., UPS, FedEx, Panther) specialize in specific EO transportation. Their standardization and specialization advantages could be passed on to the customer regarding lower transportation costs with long-term agreed rate sheets. On the other hand, customization—customer-orientated solutions—is challenging due to the high standardization.

From an operational point of view, strategy 2 can preferably be operated by the same carrier, responsible for the standard and expedites transportation, including the liability. Expectations and responsibilities must be clearly defined and communicated. Streamline transportation networks have fewer links to break. For example, when freight is already in transit, interfaces between different carriers can lead to time and communication risks.

From our point of view, the possible commercial advantages of strategy 1 are outweighed by the operational requirements. A dedicated network should be established only for specific commodities in high-risk areas where the standard service provider cannot operate.

To avoid production line stops, airfreight operations are crucial to achieve the goal. Even in noncrisis mode, it could be advantageous to secure airfreight capacities in advance. This is hardly possible due to market conditions and missing forecast. One strategy is to build a close business relationship with airlines and airline brokers. Furthermore, it is crucial to bring together and mediate between airlines and airports. The flexibility of the infrastructure operator in terms of landing options and ground handling can gain critical hours to avoid production line stops.

27.2.3.5 Review Capacity Footprint and Update of Crisis Contingency Plans

Prepared for upcoming challenges, there is a need to review the current capacity footprint of production lines to check for potential capacity reserves. This is relevant for opportunities to change production in case of a shortfall inside the company and recover back orders after a certain period of minimum supply. It also requires reviewing the current crisis contingency plans. From the OEM perspective, audits regarding the crisis management capability on all supplier tiers will become a decisive aspect.

Also, on this aspect, inbound transportation needs to proactively plan the strategic increase of volumes and update contingency plans with carriers in the network. Carriers are required to set up short-term scaling of capacities in both directions. Furthermore, their crisis contingency plans need to be enhanced by specific measures to counter identified strategic risks. These measures must be capable of ensuring full operation in crisis mode.

27.3 Conclusion

How can a resilient supply chain with a focus on inbound transportation logistics be built? What are the necessary steps?

It has become apparent that supply chain resilience is no longer understood in terms of stability but in terms of adaptation and transformation.

Therefore, an evolutionary three-stage path to building a more resilient supply chain is recommended. Inbound transportation logistics is used as an example. The three-stage path starts with the company's ability to respond to short-term disruptions in the supply chain:

- In taskforce mode, an interdisciplinary team of experts focuses on production stops avoiding material steering and the management of expedite transportation networks to return to the original state quickly.
- Midterm—risk management mode deals with a systematic analysis of company and transportation network risks. With risk mapping, risks can be identified and

categorized within the transportation network. Measures will be derived, evaluated, and implemented to establish a more robust supply chain.
- Long-term, certain features engineered into the supply chain can improve its resilience. The resilience stage focuses on improvements on the company and strategic levels. Here, changes will need a longer time horizon for implementation and effect various company functions. Some selected examples like collaboration in material forecasting, multiple sourcing, or emergency transportation network design need to be highly collaborative.

This approach requires a more comprehensive capability and set-up of the IT infrastructure and data management. The decisions on all stages need accurate data from a quality and timing point of view. Building resilient inbound transportation cannot be done isolated. An isolated improvement of one partner in the supply chain will only lead to suboptimal results. All partners need to be integrated to build a more resilient supply chain.

Despite building a resilient supply chain, the costs and investments involved need to be highlighted, which might restrict all those resilience-building measures. However, a focus solely on costs without considering the negative risk implications will lead to limited success in risk avoidance.

Resilience implies long-term development of inbound transportation logistics, which goes beyond short-term process redesign and focuses on collaborative supply chain relationships based on greater information transparency.

References

Christopher, M., & Peck, H. (2004). Building the resilient Supply Chain. *International Journal of Logistics Management, 15*(2), 1–13.

Wieland, A., & Durach, Ch. (2021). *Two perspectives on supply chain resilience, Journal of Business Logistics*, Vol. 42, Online Version.

Mirko Hoppe studied Transport and Traffic Sciences and earned his doctorate at the Technical University of Dresden, Germany. He has held various positions in the airline and automotive industry in China and USA. He is an author of numerous publications on transport and logistics topics with lectures in Vienna, Dresden, and Leipzig.

Werner Podkowik studied Business Administration at the University of Applied Science in Koblenz and earned a Master of Business Administration (MBA) with a major in Logistics Management. He worked for PricewaterhouseCoopers as a consultant and held several Management positions in Logistics and Supply Chain Management at an Automotive supplier in Germany, China, and the Czech Republic. He is responsible for the European Logistics of a business division there.

Chapter 28
Overview of the Enablers of Humanitarian Supply Chain Resilience

Ioanna Falagara Sigala and Amin Maghsoudi

Abstract Disasters have an effect not only on individuals but also on the local infrastructure and the supply chains that are highly detrimental to aid delivery. The most effective way of delivering aid to disaster-affected areas is by reestablishing pre-disaster supply chains to enable disrupted supply chains to get back to normal conditions. Consequently, developing a resilient supply chain is one approach to improve the effectiveness and efficiency of aid delivery. In this chapter, we review and discuss the enablers of humanitarian supply chain resilience.

28.1 Problem Framing

Disasters have an effect not only on individuals but also on the local infrastructure, markets, and the supply chains which are highly detrimental to aid delivery. Humanitarian supply chains are characterized by extreme uncertainty, unpredictability of demand, lack of resources, poor infrastructure, and high dependency on donor funding (Kovács & Spens, 2007). The most effective way of delivering aid to the disaster-affected areas is by reestablishing pre-disaster supply chains and building resilience. Supply chain resilience is built on capabilities (i.e., enablers) to cope with the consequences of unavoidable events to return to the original operations or move to a new, more desirable state (Christopher & Peck, 2004; Ponomarov & Holcomb, 2009). In the humanitarian context, the term resilience is used mainly for disaster and community resilience and covers all phases of a disaster, from preparedness to response, recovery, and development (Altay et al., 2018).

Building on the dynamic capability, view enablers help policy makers to utilize the scarce resources effectively in an event of a disruption to obtain an improved performance and competitive advantage (Ponomarov & Holcomb, 2009). According to the literature on commercial supply chains, there are multiple enablers for supply chain resilience. They relate to collaboration, agility, and risk awareness

I. Falagara Sigala (✉) · A. Maghsoudi
Department of Marketing, HUMLOG Institute, Hanken School of Economics, Helsinki, Finland
e-mail: ioanna.falagarasigala@hanken.fi

S. Kummer et al. (eds.), *Supply Chain Resilience*, Springer Series in Supply Chain Management 17, https://doi.org/10.1007/978-3-030-95401-7_28

(Christopher & Peck, 2004); to collaboration, flexibility, visibility, and velocity (Jüttner & Maklan, 2011); to structural, relational, and cognitive factors (Johnson et al., 2013); and to knowledge management (Scholten et al., 2014), effective procurement (Pereira et al., 2014), and information sharing (Scholten & Schilder, 2015).

The literature on commercial supply chain resilience is rich, mainly because of the significant negative impact on business continuity of major disruptive events, such as the COVID-19 pandemic (Christopher & Peck, 2004; Jüttner & Maklan, 2011). Yet the literature on humanitarian supply chain resilience is scant (e.g., Altay et al., 2018). This chapter contributes to the humanitarian supply chain literature by reviewing the key enablers of resilience in humanitarian settings. Addressing the key enablers helps humanitarian practitioners and academics to have a better understanding of enablers of supply chain resilience to be adaptable to the humanitarian context. The focus of this chapter is on humanitarian supply chain resilience at the organizational level. We discuss enablers of supply chain resilience of humanitarian organizations that provide aid to disaster-affected populations across all phases of disasters.

The structure of the chapter is as follows. In section two, we discuss the various enablers of supply chain resilience in the humanitarian context. In particular, we focus on the concepts of agility, visibility, modularity and standardization, flexibility, redundancy, collaboration, market sensitiveness, localization, and supply chain security. In Sect. 28.3, we present the conclusions.

28.2 Enablers of Humanitarian Supply Chain Resilience

An enabler is considered as a capability that facilitates the supply chain processes using the scarce resources to improve performance outcomes (Santos et al., 2016). Existing literature in commercial settings focuses mainly on the key enablers of supply chain resilience according to the phase of a disruption (preparedness, response, and recovery). However, this categorization is flawed in humanitarian settings, given that a humanitarian organization might need the same enablers across different phases of a disaster.

We discuss enablers of humanitarian supply chain resilience which are identified from the extant literature and practical insights from the humanitarian sector. The enablers are based on the dynamic capability view, which argues that a focal organization needs to focus on its capabilities (i.e., enablers) and try to improve them using the available resources to cope with the extremely disrupted and changing environment. Below, we present the main enablers of resilience adapted from both the commercial and humanitarian supply chain literature. Table 28.1 summarizes the different enablers.

Table 28.1 Enablers of humanitarian supply chain resilience

Enablers	Dimensions	Literature
Agility	• Reconfiguring scarce physical resources • Human capital resources • External resources • Coordination and alignment between the supply chain networks • Interoperability of information systems • Adaptability in the local conditions and infrastructure	Falagara Sigala et al. (2020), Lee (2004), Scholten et al. (2010), Kovács and Tatham (2009).
Visibility	Enhancing the visibility along the humanitarian supply chains in terms of: • Goods • Cash and voucher assistance • Data and information	Barrat and Oke (2007), Ahimbisibwe et al. (2016), Jüttner and Maklan (2011).
Modularity	• Modularity of product design • Modularity of service design • Standardization of relief items • Standardization of relief services	Jahre and Fabbe-Costes (2015), Voss et al. (2009), Kabra and Ramesh (2015), Chandes and Paché (2010)
Flexibility	• Flexible supply contracts and framework agreements • Flexible transportation and distribution network • Postponement • Flexible supply base • Sourcing strategies • Labor arrangements • Order fulfilment flexibility	Day (2014), Balcik and Ak (2013), Besiou et al. (2014), Tang (2006)
Redundancy	• Pre-positioning of relief items • Having contingency plans with respect to the supply chain network • Developing a pool of trained employees to be implemented when a disaster occurs • Protecting suppliers against disruptions by increasing redundancy in their operations • Decentralized distributions sites • Extending the capacity (increased safety stock, skilled staff, funding, mobile cash distribution sites)	Christopher and Peck (2004), Stewart and Ivanov (2019), Toyasaki et al. (2017), Kovács and Falagara Sigala (2021), Sawik (2013)
Collaboration	• Public-private partnership • Collaboration in sharing of resources • Other complementary skills necessary for recovery from a disruption	Carland et al. (2018), Kovács and Spens (2007), Scholten et al. (2014)
Market sensitiveness	• Ensuring the markets are functioning and could be physically accessible for affected populations • The local market is sufficiently stable and competitive to cope with the increased inflow of cash or commodities • The current levels of inflation on commodities allow local procurement and production	Christopher (2000), Castillo (2021), Vogel et al. (2021)

(continued)

Table 28.1 (continued)

Enablers	Dimensions	Literature
Localization	• The transfer of knowledge from international supply chain actors to local actors on how to prepare their supply chain to respond to a disaster • Assessments of the potential needs and gaps relying on data obtained by local actors	Frennesson et al. (2021), Jahre et al. (2016)
Enhanced security	• Interlinking with the current policies, rules, and procedures on cross-border supply movements • Using the available technology to protect, monitor, and trace securely supply chain assets including data, information, and supplies • Protecting the life of humanitarian staff in danger-zone areas • Adding a safety and security plan and integrating it in logistics preparedness	Voss et al. (2009), Guidero (2020)

28.2.1 Agility

Lee (2004, p. 105) describes agility as the ability to "respond quickly to short-term changes in demand or supply and handle external disruptions smoothly." Humanitarian organizations typically operate in environments characterized by unpredictability, uncertainty, and ad hoc-based supply chains. Agility is considered as a key pillar in humanitarian preparedness and responses. Agility requires the coordination and alignment between the supply chain networks, interoperability of information systems between stakeholders, and adaptability to the local conditions and infrastructure (Falagara Sigala et al., 2020).

Kovács and Tatham (2009) argued that humanitarian organizations need to increase their agility in responses by quickly reconfiguring the scarce physical resources (e.g., prepositioned inventory), human capital resources, and organizational external resources (e.g., relationship with donors for funding). Resilience necessitates agility to respond rapidly to random events and sustain benefit in a disaster environment. However, being agile is costly especially for humanitarian organizations whose existence is largely dependent on donors' support. In addition, the size of the humanitarian organization affects its ability to adopt and integrate fully the elements of agility, using, for example, digital technologies (Scholten et al., 2010). The lack of agility in responses may lead to the late delivery of aid. For example, during the hurricane Maria response in 2017, while the church community provided their rapid deployment of pre-positioned resources delivering to affected populations in Puerto Rico, the US government was criticized for moving the supplies with delays (Lauren, 2018).

28.2.2 Visibility

Supply chain visibility is defined as the extent to which actors within a supply chain have access to their operations or can share useful information with them (Barrat & Oke, 2007). Humanitarian organizations need to respond quickly to changing environments and quickly mobilize resources. Thus, they must have proper supply chain visibility regarding the flow of materials, cash, and information to inform decision-making and respond to humanitarian needs (Maghsoudi & Pazirandeh, 2016). A high supply chain visibility contributes to shorter lead times, lower inventories, increased fill rates, and ultimately more velocity in humanitarian responses (Ahimbisibwe et al., 2016). Implementation of information systems to increase visibility should be considered by actors, including humanitarian organizations and donors. Donors should not only fund disaster responses but also be prepared to increase the resilience of humanitarian supply chains.

The lack of visibility could be exacerbated by the lack of coordination and collaboration among humanitarian organizations, as this was the case in the aftermath of the 2015 Nepal earthquake. That said, the increasing data privacy concerns between implementing partners and beneficiaries prevented information sharing and thus hampered the visibility of information flows along humanitarian supply chains (Baharmand et al., 2017).

28.2.3 Modularity and Standardization

Modularity and standards both in product and services as well as in processes are viewed as enablers of responsiveness in humanitarian supply chains (Jahre & Fabbe-Costes, 2015) and ultimately enablers of resilience. Modularity in product design or service design (Voss et al., 2009) makes it possible to decompose products or services sourced from different suppliers and to facilitate the assembling of the components. This capability is very important in the humanitarian sector that manages relief items to respond to beneficiaries' needs.

Creating standards for relief items will facilitate the production and transportation as well as the distribution of aid to beneficiaries. Furthermore, it improves compatibility, coordination (Kabra & Ramesh, 2015), collaboration, and flexibility (Chandes & Paché, 2010). Standardization of the humanitarian relief items and process helps organizations to be more agile and resilient when responding to a disaster.

28.2.4 Flexibility

The extant research denotes the importance of flexibility along the humanitarian supply chains, for instance, in terms of sourcing and adaptative capacity (Day, 2014), flexible supply contracts and framework agreements (Balcik & Ak, 2013), and flexible transportation (Besiou et al., 2014). In addition to that, sub-dimensions of the flexibility in terms of postponement, flexible supply base, labor arrangements, and flexible order fulfilment (Tang, 2006) have the potential to enhance the resilience in supply chains.

In addition, flexibility in distribution networks is also important in humanitarian settings. For example, due to the COVID-19 pandemic, UNHCR had to flexibly deliver its humanitarian assistance via various delivery mechanisms. In fact, due to the restrictions on supply chain movements during the pandemic, UNHCR adapted and postponed its aid program through a phased approach using three steps of cash distribution in refugee camps, cash distribution to internally displaced people in camps, and door-to-door cash distribution to beneficiaries residing in non-camp areas.

Being flexible for the last mile delivery helps to avoid mass gatherings at distribution sites. In some other instances, due to the suspension of all ATM cards by private banks in Syria, UNHCR temporarily blocked all active ATM cards and began delivering cash through counter distribution (UNHCR, 2020). Such efforts reveal the fact that humanitarian organizations should be capable of handling and managing aid distribution flexibly by using multiple delivery mechanisms at the last mile and contribute to strengthening their supply chain resilience.

28.2.5 Redundancy

Redundancy involves the strategic use of capacity and inventory that can be used during a disruption (Christopher & Peck, 2004). Increasing redundancy in the supply chain is a key factor for improving resilience (Stewart & Ivanov, 2019). In humanitarian settings, redundancy can be applied in terms of having reserved inventory as well as building capacities and relationships with the suppliers. There are several approaches to build redundancy:

- Pre-positioning of relief items (i.e., reaching the maximum level of safety stock) in different facilities (Toyasaki et al., 2017)
- Having contingency plans with respect to the supply chain network (e.g., if there is no option to import items from the main ports/borders, the focal organization needs to have a plan B for another location (Stewart & Ivanov, 2019))
- Developing a pool of trained employees to be implemented when a disaster occurs (Kovács & Falagara Sigala, 2021)
- Protecting suppliers against disruptions by increasing redundancy in their operations (Sawik, 2013)

- Preparing for safety stocks, multiple suppliers and sourcing, multiple distribution sites, backup sites, and transportation capacity (Dolgui et al., 2020)

Overall, redundancy as a mean of having buffer stock through decentralized prepositioning of necessary items improves the responsiveness and resilience of operations (Maghsoudi et al., 2018). Strategic prepositioning occurs long before the disaster. It involves the expansion of resources for increasing capacity and establishes contractual agreements with suppliers and financial service providers. Operational prepositioning refers to the inventory levels and distributions sites. We argue that both operational and strategic preparedness are required in advance, to reduce the risk of shortage, stockout, or denial of financial service providers to collaborate in emergencies, as was the case in the Syrian conflict. Therefore, if there is a precontract framework and negotiation with multiple potential suppliers, based in multiple locations, the responsiveness and resilience can be improved. The redundancy needs to be extended in responses, for instance, in terms of funding, aid supplies, skilled staff, transportation, allocation of extra distributions sites, and mobile cash distribution.

28.2.6 Collaboration

Supply chain resilience depends on a network of organizations that must coordinate and collaborate, to manage the consequences of disasters and produce outcomes that sustain life and revitalize communities. Therefore, partnerships and collaboration between the different sectors in humanitarian settings need to be established, to effectively respond to a disaster. Collaboration facilitates sharing of resources and other complementary skills necessary for recovery (Scholten et al., 2014).

Partnerships between the private and public sectors can play an important role in building supply chain resilience in disaster-affected areas (Carland et al., 2018). Public-private partnership is increasingly considered as an innovative tool for bringing services and products to disaster areas. They are expected to improve service delivery, supporting humanitarian organizations to learn from commercial supply chains (Kovács & Spens, 2007), and contributing to improve supply chain resilience. Public-private partnerships are conceived as a set of activities that involve collaboration among local governmental disaster agencies and private companies. Indeed, the role of the private sector is crucial, being one of the main suppliers (of water, food, fuel, healthcare and medical products, power, and telecommunications) and logistics service providers (offering storage, transportation, and personnel). Thus, for the humanitarian supply chain to be resilient, public-private partnerships could and should play a prominent role. Building public-private partnerships is a long-term process and needs a lot of investment in terms of time and resources. For example, UN agencies have established long-term partnerships with logistics service providers such as Kuehne and Nagel and UPS. In addition, in the response to the COVID-19 pandemic, governments asked private companies from different sectors to adjust their production lines and to produce medical equipment and respiratory devices. UNICEF is also collaborating with governments and the private sector to achieve the innovative and equitable access to COVID-19 diagnostics tools, treatments, and vaccines in developing countries (COVAX, 2020).

28.2.7 Market Sensitiveness

Market sensitiveness is considered as the key pillar of supply chain resilience after a major disruption. Market sensitiveness refers to the supply chain capability to react to the actual need during the disruption (Christopher, 2000). This could be very vital in humanitarian settings, as there is a market failure or collapse during the early stage of disasters. Commonly, the local market is not functioning, or the suppliers are not reachable in the early phase of a response. Often, due to the road disruption, beneficiaries have difficulties getting access to the markets. Therefore, humanitarian organizations should conduct a rapid market assessment to determine whether:

- The markets are functioning and could be physically accessible by the affected populations.
- The local market is sufficiently stable and competitive to cope with the increased inflow of cash or commodities.
- The current levels of inflation on commodities allow local procurement (WFP, 2017).

Humanitarian organizations need also to ensure the market is favorable for beneficiaries. If it is, then they will be able to select an appropriate mode of assistance to deliver safely. Certain criteria exist to assess the market in terms of, for instance, risks of inflation, potential market distortions, and secondary impacts of markets (Castillo, 2021).

Finally, there is evidence that the delivery of humanitarian assistance in terms of cash and vouchers positively contributes to market growth and the local economy, although they need to ensure the commodities sold in the market are not dominated or controlled by a few main suppliers as was the case of the Lebanese market in response to the Syrian refugee crisis (Vogel et al., 2021).

28.2.8 Localization of Humanitarian Preparedness and Response

Localization of the humanitarian response is an important topic in humanitarian supply chain research. It refers to the involvement of regional, national, and local actors in the delivery of humanitarian aid (Frennesson et al., 2021). By localizing the supply chain and logistics preparedness, local supply chain actors can enhance their capacity and be more prepared and resilient for the next disaster. Logistics preparedness is defined as the implementation of processes, structures, and systems connecting the local community and national and international actors by designing, planning, and training for efficient, effective, and responsive mobilization of material, financial, human, and informational resources when and where needed. This encompasses a range of activities, including needs assessment, procurement, warehousing, transporting, distributing, waste management, and performance measurement for the purpose of alleviating the suffering of vulnerable people (Jahre et al., 2016, p. 383).

Thus, we refer to the enhanced capacity to effectively respond to and recover from the impacts of disasters by building the capacity of local suppliers and making markets more resilient. Such capacities and capabilities include (Frennesson et al., 2021):

- The transfer of knowledge from international supply chain actors to local actors on how to prepare their supply chain to respond to a disaster
- Assessments of the potential needs and gaps
- Sourcing strategies and framework agreements
- Information systems to increase visibility of the supply chains
- Pre-positioning

Localization of the humanitarian response could bring more sustainable, effective, rapid, accountable, and context-adapted response and thus more resilient supply chains (Frennesson et al., 2021).

28.2.9 Supply Chain Security

Supply chain security refers to the application of policies, procedures, and technology to protect supply chain assets (i.e., people, supplies, facilities, information, data, and equipment) from theft, damage, cyberattack, crime, and terrorism and to prevent the introduction of unauthorized contraband, people, or weapons into the supply chain (Voss et al., 2009). Working in humanitarian environments poses a great number of risks and security issues for the supply chain and humanitarian employees (Guidero, 2020). The safety and security of humanitarian staff, commodities, and assets have always been a key principle of humanitarian organizations. Ensuring the humanitarian supply chain security can enable resilience across all phases of disaster; the commodities can be delivered safely to affected populations, cash can be transferred in a secure supply chain, and information can be shared through a secure platform among multiple actors.

28.3 Conclusion

The aim of this chapter was to review the main enablers of humanitarian supply chains relying on insights from the extant literature.

In this chapter, we argued that humanitarian supply chain resilience could be enabled by more agile, visible, modular, flexible, redundant, collaborative, and secure supply chains as well as the localization of humanitarian response. All those capabilities are highly linked, and each of them depends on the others to be effective.

Humanitarian organizations operate under extreme uncertainty with limited resources. They can address supply chain vulnerabilities effectively when all supply chain members and stakeholders share information and collaborate with each other. Humanitarian organizations responding to the disaster globally are part of complex supply chains and have not only logistical and infrastructural constraints but also political, cultural, and funding constraints. To achieve more resilient supply chains, humanitarian organizations as well as donors and the private sector need to invest in building relationships and innovative solutions. Greater information access and security between actors would increase humanitarian organizations' capability to respond and adapt quickly to changes in their uncertain environment and strengthen the resilience of the supply chain.

Further research is suggested to operationalize the enablers identified and determine their impact on resilience and performance outcomes.

References

Ahimbisibwe, A., Ssebulime, R., Tumuhairwe, R., & Tusiime, W. (2016). Supply chain visibility, supply chain velocity, supply chain alignment and humanitarian supply chain relief agility. *European Journal of Logistics, Purchasing and Supply Chain Management, 4*(2), 34–64.

Altay, N., Gunasekaran, A., Rameshwar Dubey, R., & Childe, S. J. (2018). Agility and resilience as antecedents of supply chain performance under moderating effects of organizational culture within the humanitarian setting: A dynamic capability view. *Production Planning & Control, 29*(14), 1158–1174.

Baharmand, H., Comes, T., & Lauras, M. (2017). Managing in-country transportation risks in humanitarian supply chains by logistics service providers: Insights from the 2015 Nepal earthquake. *International Journal of Disaster Risk Reduction, 24*, 549–559.

Balcik, B., & Ak, D. (2013). Supplier selection for framework agreements in humanitarian relief. *Production and Operations Management, 23*(6), 1028–1041.

Barrat, M., & Oke, A. (2007). Antecedents of supply chain visibility in retail supply chain: A resource - based theory perspective. *Journal of Operations Management, 25*(6), 1217–1233.

Besiou, M., Pedraza-Martinez, A. J., & Van Wassenhove, L. (2014). Vehicle supply chains in humanitarian operations: Decentralization, operational mix, and earmarked funding. *Production and Operations Management, 23*(11), 1950–1965.

Carland, C., Goentzel, J., & Montibeller, G. (2018). Modeling the values of private sector agents in multi-echelon humanitarian supply chains. *European Journal of Operational Research, 269*(2), 532–543.

Castillo, G. J. (2021). Deciding between cash-based and in-kind distributions during humanitarian emergencies. *Journal of Humanitarian Logistics and Supply Chain Management, 11*(2), 272–295.

Chandes, J., & Paché, G. (2010). Investigating humanitarian logistics issues: From operations management to strategic action. *Journal of Manufacturing Technology Management, 21*(3), 320–340.

Christopher, M. (2000). The agile supply chain: competing in volatile markets. *Industrial Marketing Management, 29*(1), 37–44.

Christopher, M., & Peck, H. (2004). Building the resilient supply chain. *International Journal of Logistics Management., 15*(2), 1–13.

COVAX. (2020). *COVAX explained*. https://www.gavi.org/vaccineswork/covax-explained

Day, J. M. (2014). Fostering emergent resilience: The complex adaptive supply network of disaster relief. *International Journal of Production Research, 52*(7), 1970–1988.

Dolgui, A., Ivanov, D., & Rozhkov, M. (2020). Does the ripple effect influence the Bullwhip effect? An integrated analysis of structural and operational dynamics in the supply chain. *International Journal of Production Research, 58*(5), 1285–1301.

Falagara Sigala, I., Kettinger, W. J., & Wakolbinger, T. (2020). Digitizing the field: designing ERP systems for Triple-A humanitarian supply chains. *Journal of Humanitarian Logistics and Supply Chain Management, 10*(2), 231–260.

Frennesson, L., Kembro, J., de Vries, H., Van Wassenhove, L., & Jahre, M. (2021). Localisation of logistics preparedness in international humanitarian organisations. *Journal of Humanitarian Logistics and Supply Chain Management, 11*(1), 81–106.

Guidero, A. (2020). Humanitarian (in)security: Risk management in complex environments. *Disasters*.

Jahre, M., & Fabbe-Costes, N. (2015). How standards and modularity can improve humanitarian supply chain responsiveness: The case of emergency response units. *Journal of Humanitarian Logistics and Supply Chain Management., 5*(3), 348–386.

Jahre, M., Pazirandeh, A., & Van Wassenhove, L. (2016). Defining logistics preparedness: A framework and research agenda. *Journal of Humanitarian Logistics and Supply Chain Management, 6*(3), 372–398.

Johnson, N., Elliott, D., & Drake, P. (2013). Exploring the role of social capital in facilitating supply chain resilience. *Supply Chain Management, 18*(3), 324–336. https://doi.org/10.1108/SCM-06-2012-0203

Jüttner, U., & Maklan, S. (2011). Supply chain resilience in the global financial crisis: An empirical study. *Supply Chain Management: An International Journal, 12*, 246–259.

Kabra, G., & Ramesh, A. (2015). Analyzing drivers and barriers of coordination in humanitarian supply chain management under fuzzy environment. *Benchmarking: An International Journal, 22*(4), 559–558.

Kovács, G., & Falagara Sigala, I. (2021). Lessons from humanitarian logistics to manage supply chain disruptions. *Journal of Supply Chain Management., 57*(1), 41–49.

Kovács, G., & Spens, K. M. (2007). Humanitarian logistics in disaster relief operations. *International Journal of Physical Distribution and Logistics Management, 37*(2), 99–114.

Kovács, G., & Tatham, P. H. (2009). Responding to disruptions in the supply network - from dormant to action. *Journal of Business Logistics, 30*(2), 215–229.

Lauren, G. (2018). Donald Trump attacked for calling Hurricane Maria response an 'incredible success. *The Guardian*. Archived from the original on September 17, 2018.

Lee, H. L. (2004). The triple-A supply chain. *Harvard Business Review, 82*(10), 102–113.

Maghsoudi, A., & Pazirandeh, A. (2016). Visibility, resource sharing and performance in supply chain relationships: Insights from humanitarian practitioners. *Supply Chain Management, 21*(1), 125–139.

Maghsoudi, A., Zailani, S., Ramayah, T., & Pazirandeh, A. (2018). Coordination of efforts in disaster relief supply chains: the moderating role of resource scarcity and redundancy. *International Journal of Logistics Research and Applications, 21*(4), 407–430.

Pereira, R., Christopher, M., & Da Silva, A. L. (2014). Achieving supply chain resilience: The role of procurement. *Supply Chain Management, 19*(5/6), 626–642. https://doi.org/10.1108/SCM-09-2013-0346

Ponomarov, S. Y., & Holcomb, M. (2009). Understanding the concept of supply chain resilience. *The International Journal of Logistics Management, 20*(1), 124–143.

Santos, A. L. R., Wauben, L. S., Goossens, R., & Brezet, H. (2016). Systemic barriers and enablers in humanitarian technology transfer. *Journal of Humanitarian Logistics and Supply Chain Management, 6*(1), 46–71.

Sawik, T. (2013). Selection of resilient supply portfolio under disruption risks. *Omega, 41*(2), 259–269.

Scholten, K., Sharkey, S. P., & Fynes, B. (2010). (Le)agility in humanitarian aid (NGO) supply chains. *International Journal of Physical Distribution & Logistics Management, 40*(8/9), 623–635.

Scholten, K., Sharkey Scott, P., & Fynes, B. (2014). Mitigation processes – antecedents for building supply chain resilience. *Supply Chain Management: An International Journal, 19*(2), 211–228.

Scholten, K., & Schilder, S. (2015). The role of collaboration in supply chain resilience. *Supply Chain Management, 20*(4), 471–484. https://doi.org/10.1108/SCM-11-2014-0386

Stewart, M., & Ivanov, D. (2019). *Design redundancy in agile and resilient humanitarian supply chains*. Annuals of Operations Research.

Tang, C. (2006). Robust strategies for mitigating supply chain disruptions. *International Journal of Logistics., 9*(1), 33–45.

Toyasaki, F., Arikan, E., Silbermayr, L., & Falagara Sigala, I. (2017). Disaster relief inventory management: horizontal cooperation between humanitarian organizations, the case of UNHRD. *Production and Operations Management, 26*(6), 1221–1237.

UNHCR. (2020). *Multi Purpose Cash Assistance: 2020 Mid-Year Post Distribution Monitoring Report - Jordan | ReliefWeb*. Retrieved from https://reliefweb.int/report/jordan/multi-purpose-cash-assistance-2020-mid-year-post-distribution-monitoring-report (AccRelevance)

Vogel, B., Tschunkert, K., & Schlaepfer, I. (2021). The social meaning of money: Multidimensional implications of humanitarian cash and voucher assistance. *Disasters*.

Voss, M. D., Closs, D. J., Calantone, R. J., Helferich, O. K., & Speier, C. (2009). The role of security in the food supplier selection decision. *Journal of Business Logistics: Council of Supply Chain Management Professionals*.

WFP. (2017). *Contextual Analysis in Support of a Cash Based Intervention, World Food Program, Angola*. Retrieved from https://docs.wfp.org/api/documents/WFP 0000019280/download/

Ioanna Falagara Sigala is a Project Researcher at Humanitarian Logistics and Supply Chain Research Institute (HUMLOG Institute)—Hanken School of Economics. She holds a Ph.D. in Economics and Social Science from WU (Vienna University of Economics and Business). Her primary research interests include and not limited to the disruptions of health care supply chains caused by COVID-19, the digitalization of humanitarian supply chain, the outsourcing of humanitarian logistics, and the role of public–private partnerships in building supply chain resilience. Ioanna is also worked as a consultant for humanitarian organizations in project related to the digitalization of humanitarian supply chains.

Amin Maghsoudi is a Postdoctoral Researcher at the Humanitarian Logistics and Supply Chain Research Institute (HUMLOG Institute)—Hanken School of Economics in Finland. He holds a Ph. D. in Operations Management. His research interest is mainly related to supply chain areas with a special focus on humanitarian logistics, risk and resilience, coordination, financing, and the use of technology. Some of Amin's research work have been published in the established journals such as International Journal of Operations & Production Management.

Chapter 29
Resilience and Military Supply Chain Management

Gerhard Gürtlich and Stefan Lampl

Abstract Military supply chain management (MSC) represents a crucial role in the military sector to ensure operation sustainability. A MSC is concerned with focused logistics, precision and velocity, coordinated delivery schedules, fast and flexible distribution, resilience planning, and good infrastructure and equipment at distribution centers. Starting from the challenges of military organizations in the future, the article aims to give an overview about essential parts of a military supply chain for a military operation in missions abroad, the military definition of resilience, the integration of risk and resilience planning, and in the military operational planning. In summary, a military supply chain network must adapt to any change in requirements and recover quickly and stainability from a disruption, and is influenced by properties and activities that must be established and well though through in advanced of the creation of a military network.

G. Gürtlich
Military Expert at the Federal Ministry of Defence of Austria, Vienna, Austria

Institute for Transportation and Logistics Management, WU (Vienna University of Economics and Business), Vienna, Austria

S. Lampl (✉)
Institute for Transportation and Logistics Management, WU (Vienna University of Economics and Business), Vienna, Austria

Austrian Forces Logistics School at the Federal Ministry of Defence of Austria, Vienna, Austria
e-mail: stefan.lampl.4@bmlv.gv.at

S. Kummer et al. (eds.), *Supply Chain Resilience*, Springer Series in Supply Chain Management 17, https://doi.org/10.1007/978-3-030-95401-7_29

29.1 Introduction

A closer look at many events of the last few decades reveals that, in addition to what may be referred to as the classic causes of conflict,[1] tensions triggered by economic[2] and ecological changes[3] are also increasing in significance. Such tensions can lead to hostilities in the military sense, as actors resort to arms to resolve conflicts on their terms. Such developments lead to conflicts both within a state and between communities of states; in some cases, the historically evolved ethnic and moral structures are decisively influenced or even eliminated by new actors.

Apart from their willingness to resort to violence and their negation of the state's monopoly on the use of force, non-state actors are gaining more and more influence over states, for example, through their superior knowledge, their networks, or their moral reputation.[4] The policy of finger wagging, with exaggerated objectives as the point of departure, is not easily opposed.

The use of armed force by non-state actors seems to have become acceptable. Non-state actors include both armed and non-armed groups and alliances. "What they have in common is that they are not part of the state monopoly on the use of force and can therefore act largely independently. In some cases, they are politically and economically dependent on the war or profit from it. A differentiation between victim and perpetrator groups is difficult or impossible to make, especially in this context."[5]

The core competence of a state's armed forces—and this is a nonnegotiable aspect—still is the ability to fight. In addition, however, capabilities in cyber warfare, digitization on and off the battlefield, and intelligence are becoming increasingly important. Failed states, destabilization, a lack of prospects for large population groups, and the vulnerability of states resulting from digital networking

[1] cf., e.g., Anna Geis, *Den Krieg überdenken. Kriegsbegriffe und Kriegstheorien in der Kontroverse*, https://www.pw.ovgu.de/ipw_media/Downloads/Geis/Geis__Einleitung_Den_Krieg_berdenken_9_43-p-90.pdf [23 March 2021] Die "... Kriegsursachen- und Konfliktforschung, die den Wandel des Krieges ... untersucht, verweist darauf, dass sich weniger die Realität verändert habe als vielmehr die Wahrnehmung, die viel zu lange von der Logik des Kalten Krieges verzerrt worden sei." [ibid. p. 16]

[The ... research on the causes of war and conflict, which examines the changes war has undergone ... points out that it is not so much the reality that has changed as its perception, which has been distorted for far too long by the logic of the Cold War.]

[2] cf., e.g., Petersen (2020), pp. 259–268.

[3] cf., e.g., Dröge (2019), pp. 405–416.

[4] cf. https://www.osa.fu-berlin.de/politikwissenschaft/beispielaufgaben/internationale_beziehungen/index.html [20 March 2021].

[5] http://www.whywar.at/akteure/nicht-staatliche-akteure/[10 March 2021] [Gemeinsam ist ihnen, dass sie nicht Teil des staatlichen Gewaltmonopols sind und deshalb weitgehend unabhängig agieren können. In manchen Fällen sind ... sie politisch und ökonomisch vom Krieg abhängig oder profitieren davon. Die Trennung zwischen Opfer- und Tätergruppen ist gerade in diesem Kontext schwer oder unmöglich zu ziehen.]

will lead to increased security threats.[6] Hybrid threats[7] call for increased readiness on the part of armed forces, awareness of the dangers, and a competent response.

A high level of readiness is also necessary to protect a state's critical infrastructure from degradation. Critical infrastructure and emergency supply facilities are particularly vulnerable aspects of a society; infrastructure failures and significant supply shortfalls must be expected after just a few hours. This threat calls for heightened resilience.[8] "In addition to geopolitics, the risk of resilience-threatening events such as serious blackouts, cyberattacks which endanger sovereignty, pandemics and uncontrolled mass migration remains undiminished. The greatest risk for a next systemic crisis in Austria would certainly be a nationwide power, infrastructure and supply failure (blackout)."[9]

In future, the operational-level command of the armed forces will be characterized by the need for antifragility, self-sufficiency, agility, mobility, and resilience, as well as by military self-protection in all areas. The responsibility of command will no longer be defined in terms of areas of operation but will be determined by "effect-based action."[10] Modern armed forces have the capability to deliver an impact which is both far-reaching and concentrated in time and space. Long-range weapon systems in conjunction with a "transparent battlefield" are gaining in importance; the degree of autonomy and the need for digitization will increase,[11] as will the demands on the resilience of armed forces.

---

[6]cf. Bundesheer (2017), p. 1.

[7]Meaning the simultaneous and adaptive use of conventional and unconventional approaches and methods to achieve goals and to produce at least a destabilizing effect.

cf: Gürtlich and Lampl (2017), pp. 549–551.

[8]cf. Bundesheer (2017), p. 11.

[9]Frank (2021), p. 35.

[Neben der Geopolitik bleibt das Risiko resilienzgefährdender Ereignisse wie gravierende Blackouts, souveränitätsgefährdende Cyber-Angriffe, Pandemien und unkontrollierter Massenmigration unvermindert hoch. Das größte Risiko für eine nächste Systemkrise in Österreich bringt sicherlich ein flächendeckender Strom-, Infrastruktur- und Versorgungsausfall (Blackout).]

[10]cf., e.g., Landesverteidigungsakademie Institut für Höhere Militärische Führung, ed., *Effektbasiertes Handeln – Lehrskriptum*, Vienna, 2016, esp. pp. 26 ff

[11]In short: "Militärische Auseinandersetzungen werden zunehmend zeitgleich in mehreren Dimensionen (Land, Luft, See, Weltraum, Cyber) bestritten. Besonders die Bedeutung des Cyber- und Informationsraums steigt stark an. Als Reaktion darauf, kommen vermehrt neue Technologien zum Einsatz, die große Mengen an (teil-)autonom und automatisiert gesteuerte Systeme beinhalten. Daher gewinnen auch im militärischen Umfeld Themen, wie Künstliche Intelligenz, IoT, Cloud-Anwendungen, Automation und Autonomie an Bedeutung." https://www.computerwoche.de/a/mit-der-ueberlegenheit-von-cyberinformationen-zum-erfolg,3550765 [23 March 2021]

[Military conflicts are increasingly being contested simultaneously in several dimensions (land, air, sea, space, cyber). The importance of the cyber and information space in particular is increasing sharply. In response to this, new technologies are increasingly being used which involve large numbers of (partially) autonomously and automatically controlled systems. Therefore, topics such as artificial intelligence, IoT, cloud applications, automation, and autonomy are also gaining importance in the military environment.]

"Resilience research developed from developmental psychology, which examined the influences of risk on childhood development, especially in the 1970s. The focus was more or less on children who developed very well despite the most difficult conditions ... Instead of combating risks and pathogenic influences, resources should be strengthened to make people resistant to risks."[12] At their core, resilience and response capability are two sides of the same coin.

Despite all the new developments, one thing has not changed and is not likely to change in the foreseeable future: logistic capabilities and military supply chains are critical to battlefield sustainability and therefore a valuable target for state and non-state actors.

29.2 Requirements of a Military Supply Network

Military logistics has broken with the Cold War paradigm in which supply requirements were met by accumulating massive supplies and large reserves at successive points along supply lines extending from the depot to the soldier in the combat position, and embraced the just-in-case concept,[13] in which the rapid movement of supplies and equipment reduces the need for huge inventories and large reserves[14] and which builds on detailed knowledge and the predictability of supply and demand.[15]

In today's threat scenarios, military logisticians are faced with the task of providing the necessary resources by means of real-time information about the supply requirements of the soldier in the field. A prerequisite here is the ability to respond quickly to the needs communicated. This approach is based on principles of industrial supply chain management[16] applied to the requirements of a military supply network. In military operations, soldiers are the customers who depend on

[12] Fröhlich-Gildhoff and Rönnau-Böse (2019), p. 14.

[Die Resilienzforschung entwickelte sich aus der Entwicklungspsychologie, die vor allem in den 1970er Jahren die Risikoeinflüsse auf die Entwicklung von Kindern untersuchte. Dabei wurde der Blick mehr oder weniger auf die Kinder gerichtet, die sich trotz schwierigster Bedingungen sehr gut entwickelten ... Anstatt Risiken und krankmachende Einflüsse zu bekämpfen, sollen Ressourcen gestärkt werden, um den Menschen gegen Risiken widerstandsfähig zu machen.]

[13] Understood as demand-synchronized supply, in which materials are produced only in the quantity required and delivered only as needed for the fulfilment of an assignment (order). cf: https://de.wikipedia.org/wiki/Just-in-time-Produktion [31 March 201].

[14] Although "full stores" have the advantage of masking planning errors and compensating for information deficits.

[15] With the exception of inventories for strategic purposes, e.g., to cope with blackouts or pandemics.

[16] "Eine Supply Chain ... umfasst alle an der Entwicklung, Erstellung, Lieferung und Entsorgung eines Produkts Beteiligten vom Rohstofflieferanten bis zum Endkunden." Kummer/Grün/Jammernegg, *Grundzüge der Beschaffung, Produktion und Logistik*, fourth edition, Vienna, 2019, p. 82.

the products, namely, weapons, ammunition, food, water, energy, medicine, hygiene, clothing and equipment, vehicles, fuels, as well as information and information tools, in order to accomplish their mission (Fig. 29.1).[17]

The military supply network can basically be divided into three sectors, each with specific requirements:

- The first sector—urgent requirements, low volume—relates to goods that do not need maintenance or repair (e.g., food, medical supplies, clothing and equipment, spare parts, ammunition).
- The second sector—major items, high volume—comprises weapons systems requiring maintenance and repair over long periods of time (e.g., tanks, armored vehicles, anti-aircraft systems, etc.).
- The third sector—operational-level—relates to troops, which must be quickly transported and continuously supplied under difficult conditions (terrain, climate, infrastructure, threat, etc.).

One circumstance that increases the demands made on a military supply chain network is the fact that there is not only forward movement—as in most supply operations in the civilian sector—but also reverse and lateral movements of forces plus the possibility of many small forces dispersed in multiple and perhaps inaccessible locations.

A military supply network must make it possible to establish a "town" with a population of 50,000 in a hostile environment following a short planning phase, guarantee supply and disposal for the people living there, maintain marching capability at an average speed of 10 km/h in different directions, and produce a resilient response to extraneous conditions, unpredictable fluctuations in demand, and disruptions to supply channels.

The response to changing (framework) conditions and disasters (disaster management[18]) are linked by a common approach: "In recent years ... resilience has gained prominence as a topic in the field of disaster research, supplanting the concept of disaster resistance.

- Disaster resistance emphasizes the importance of pre-disaster mitigation measures that enhance the performance of structures, infrastructure elements, and institutions in reducing losses from a disaster.
- Resilience reflects a concern for improving the capacity of physical and human systems to respond to and recover from extreme events.

[A supply chain ... includes all those involved in the development, production, delivery and disposal of a product, from the raw material supplier to the end customer.]

[17] In commercial language, his "production goal".

[18] Disaster management is defined as the totality of all coordinated measures in the areas of disaster prevention, disaster preparedness, disaster response, and post-disaster recovery, including continuous evaluation of the measures taken in these areas. https://www.bmi.gv.at/204/Katastrophenmanagement/start.aspx [01 April 2021].

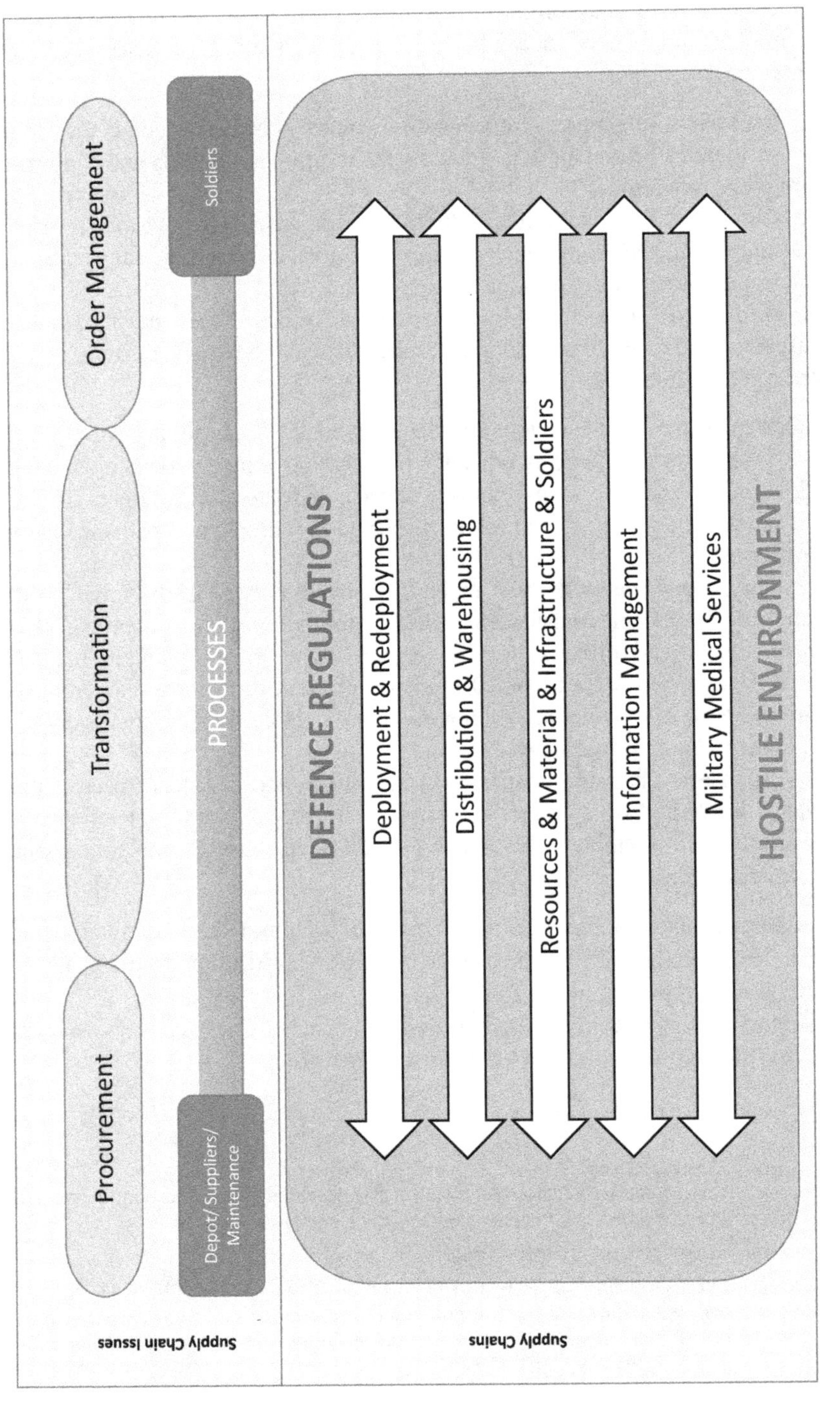

Fig. 29.1 Military supply processes. Source: the authors

- Resilient systems reduce the probabilities of failure and the consequences of failure—such as deaths and injuries, physical damage, and negative economic and social effects and the time for recovery."[19]

29.3 Possible Disruptions to the Military Supply Network

The ideal state of a resilient military supply network can basically be defined in terms of four attributes:

- Robustness—the ability of systems to withstand disaster forces without significant degradation or loss of performance
- Redundancy—the extent to which systems are capable of satisfying functional requirements if significant degradation or loss of functionality occurs
- Resourcefulness—the ability to diagnose and prioritize problems and to initiate solutions
- Rapidity—the capacity for timely restoration of functionality[20]

It can be stated that "Without functioning supplies, chaos quickly threatens, as could be observed with the supply of important protective equipment during the Corona crisis. And yet the logistics still worked, even if there were short-term gaps in the supply of individual goods ... The Corona crisis revealed ... [that modern] societies are hardly prepared for far-reaching networked crises and supply interruptions."[21]

A functioning military supply network must include four elements:[22]

- A logistics system designed for war, which is adapted for peace. – The goal is the provision of effective support during the whole spectrum of a military operation.
- A lean and flexible logistics organisation. – The military logistics network should be able to support military operations with its own resources in a high-intensive operation but should also not waste resources in peacetime or humanitarian operations.

---

[19] Kathleen Tierney and Michel Bruneau, *Conceptualizing and Measuring Resilience. A Key to Disaster Loss Reduction*, https://onlinepubs.trb.org/onlinepubs/trnews/trnews250_p14-17.pdf [22 March 2021].

[20] cf. Kathleen Tierney and Michel Bruneau, https://www.coursehero.com/file/p2eokhfb/and-Redundancy-Resiliency-Triangle-Source-Tierney-and-Bruneau-2009/ [23 March 2021].

[21] Saurugg (2021), p. 316.

[Ohne funktionierende Versorgung droht rasch ein Chaos, wie das auch bei der Versorgung mit wichtigen Schutzausrüstungsgütern während der Coronakrise zu beobachten war. Dabei hat die Logistik noch funktioniert, auch wenn bei einzelnen Gütern kurzfristige Versorgungslücken aufgetreten sind ... Die Coronakrise hat offengelegt ... [dass die moderne] Gesellschaft kaum auf weitreichende vernetzte Krisen und Versorgungsunterbrechungen vorbereitet ist.]

[22] Sheikh et al. (2016), pp. 6ff.

- Effective information management. – Transparency concerning the status of military assets and platforms is necessary. A logistics information system which gathers and synthesizes data and then securely presents it to the decision makers is crucial.
- A flexible and skilled workforce. – Through the right training and proper manpower planning the soldiers and contractors are able to run and adapt the necessary processes.
- When planning a military supply network, consideration must therefore be given to where, when, and what extent stressors (disruptions) could occur which would impede or prevent the deployment or transportation of forces, equipment, weapons systems, and other resources.

External disruptions to a military supply network can be divided into three categories, which are political, physical, and market disruptions:[23, 24]

Political Disruption: Political disruptions are far more common within the military supply chain than within its civilian equivalents, because military operations are based on political decisions. Export controls (embargoes, etc.) by foreign governments, political and social unrest in the homelands of the troop-contributing nations, industrial action and strikes at home and abroad, epidemics, and governmental bans on the use of specific weapons systems are only some examples which can disrupt a military supply chain directly or indirectly and can have a degrading or immediate impact on the performance and sustainability of the system.

Physical Disruption: It seems that physical disruptions have more direct impact on supply chain performance, but they can also generate political and market disruptions through public and political demand for mitigating actions. Direct military attacks on the military supply and transportation network, military conflicts involving attacks on production sites and infrastructure, maritime conflicts and attacks on sea lanes and ports, terrorist attacks and sabotage with conventional and non-conventional weapons, and also natural disasters (earthquakes, floods, etc.) require immediate action to stabilize the supply chain.

Market Disruption: Market disruptions are often the most difficult to identify, predict, or account for within the military supply chain. Changes can occur very slowly, but the magnitude of the impact on the supply chain can be high. Higher prices and longer delivery times due to increased demand and reduced supply of military equipment and resources, monopolistic control over resources and/or the necessary means of transport, and industrial restructuring leading to a possible reliance on a single resource provider are some examples which can have an impact on the military supply chain.

In addition to these external factors, a military supply network may also be affected by internal sources of disruption, including human error, lack of preparation or training, inadequate coordination, insufficient provision of mission-critical

[23] cf. https://www.dla.mil/Portals/104/Documents/Headquarters/StrategicPlan/SupplyChainSecurityStrategy.pdf [06 April 2021].

[24] cf. Summers (2018), pp. 99 ff.

supplies, inflexibility, or lack of resilience. "In engineering, resilience describes ... how a structure can return to its initial state after a disruption. In psychology, it is the ability of an individual to cope with a traumatic experience. In general, resilience describes the ability of an object or system to adapt to change while maintaining functionality." [25]

Modern military supply chains are highly complex entities, encompassing a vast number of individual components and subsystems with different national restrictions and demands that require sourcing and sometimes complex supporting activities to ensure a sustainable support to military operations. For an international military operation with a large number of troop-contributing nations, such as the former NATO operation in Afghanistan, a global military supply chain is necessary to meet all resource needs in order to guarantee mission success and an uninterrupted military operation. While such a global military supply chain provides many benefits to military logisticians and suppliers, it also increases the level of exposure to uncertainty and risk. This is because the system has an increased geographical footprint, higher numbers of nodes and links, a multifaceted information management system, a complex multimodal transport management system, and a volatile global environment within which the supply chain is expected to exist and operate. the greatest challenges in a global military supply chain are the management and synchronization of the different troop-contributing nations' national supply chain goals.

The overall military logistics mission for a multinational operation is to provide globally responsive, operationally precise, and cost-effective joint logistics support to the military troops in the operation. The military supply system must effectively respond to battlefield needs under the constrains of force capabilities, the combat environment, enemy capabilities, threats, and doctrine. In general, for the land component of a military system, the system creates buffer stocks at different levels to adapt to the volatile, uncertain, complex, and ambiguous environment and uses tools and procedures to prevent a so-called bullwhip effect.

In order to make a military supply network both adaptive and responsive, use can be made of the following tools and procedures derived from the civilian sector:[26, 27]

---

[25] Rummel (2019), p. 2.

[Im Ingenieurwesen beschreibt Resilienz ... wie eine Struktur nach einer Störung wieder zum Ausgangszustand zurückkehren kann. In der Psychologie ist es die Fähigkeit eines Individuums ein Trauma zu verarbeiten. Allgemein beschreibt Resilienz die Fähigkeit eines Objektes oder eines Systems, sich Änderungen anzupassen und dabei die Funktionsfähigkeit zu wahren.]

[26] https://www.brookings.edu/techstream/how-to-build-more-secure-resilient-next-gen-u-s-supply-chains [06 April 2021].

[27] cf. file:///tmp/mozilla_vm0/RAND_RRA425-1.pdf [06 April 2021].

- Establishment of a transparent and uniform inventory management system in the area of operations, including a safety (emergency) inventory, if necessary with the aim of minimizing the inventory ("Optimizing the logistic footprint"[28])
- Dual sourcing of day-to-day resources in the area of operations, with requirements split on an 80/20 basis with the provision that the second or third supplier be able to meet 100 percent of requirements in a crisis situation
- Alternative procurement of goods outside the area of operations
- Establishment of a multinational situation picture of supply security in the area of operations across all levels of command
- Creation of a database on the supplies available in the area of operations by the host nation or by another nation participating in the operation.
- Tracking of supplies so that shipments can be monitored from source to destination, even in longer supply chains.
- Preparation of alternative plans to model the impact of major disruptions on the military logistics supply network and determine the options for action (use of operational research models[29]).
- Collaboration with all stakeholders in the military supply network (e.g., collaboration with government agencies for host nation support, contacts in troop-contributing states, and civilian service providers).[30]

The objective is to maintain inventories in the area of operations in balance (in a force parallelogram) between mobility of the force, security of supply in the event of disruptions, and loss of resources due to the non-transportability of goods.

[28] "The use of multinational logistic options can optimize the overall deployment of logistic resources and reduce infrastructure requirements." https://assets.publishing.service.gov.uk/government/uploads/system/uploads/attachment_data/file/907825/doctrine_nato_logistics_ajp_4.pdf [06 April 2021].

[29] An abstract model is developed for a segment of reality so that analyses can be performed in order to create a basis for decision-making. Areas of application include production planning, supply chain management, distribution, location planning, inventory management, and personnel planning and scheduling. https://www.enzyklopaedie-der-wirtschaftsinformatik.de/lexikon/technologien-methoden/Operations-Research [02 April 2021].

[30] https://www.brookings.edu/techstream/how-to-build-more-secure-resilient-next-gen-u-s-supply-chains [06 April 2021].

29.4 Resilience of a Military Supply Network

At the Warsaw Summit held on July 8–9, 2016, the heads of state and government of the NATO member countries made a commitment to fundamentally improve the resilience of the alliance[31] by targeting seven basic requirements for civilian supply:[32]

- Assured continuity of government and critical government services
- Resilient and secure energy supplies
- Ability to deal effectively with uncontrolled movements of people
- Resilient food and water resources
- Ability to deal with mass casualties
- Resilient civil communications systems
- Resilient civil transportation systems

These commitments are based on the realization that the strategic environment can change rapidly and continuously and that the resilience of civil structures, resources, and services is both a vital basis for the modern societies of today and a key prerequisite for the conduct of military operations.

A US Air Force definition directly references the resilience of a military system: "The capability of an installation to sustain the projection of combat power by protecting against, responding to, and recovering from deliberate, accidental, or naturally occurring events that impede air, space, or cyberspace operations."[33] "Military installation" implies not only the physical infrastructure but also human activity and the support systems required for its operation.

The post-disruption process in Fig. 29.2 shows that all military commanders at all levels of command (i.e., the entire organization) must contribute to resilience planning, which is needed to support the preparation of risk assessments and studies that help inform decision-making for the adoption of countermeasures (point 1), and implement policies and strategies that help reduce risk (point 2). When all measures have been implemented and coordinated, a reduction in the implementation area can also be assumed (point 3).

The International Standard ISO 22316:2017(en)[34] defines organizational resilience as follows: "... the ability of an organization to absorb and adapt in a changing environment to enable it to deliver its objectives and to survive and prosper. More resilient organizations can anticipate and respond to threats and opportunities, arising from sudden or gradual changes in their internal and external context.

[31] Discussions focused on stability in the east and south, and also on Afghanistan. https://www.consilium.europa.eu/de/meetings/international-summit/2016/07/08-09/ [02 April 2021].

[32] https://www.nato.int/docu/review/articles/2016/03/30/resilience-a-core-element-of-collective-defence/index.html [23 March 2021].

[33] https://www.everycrsreport.com/reports/IN11566.html [29 March 2021].

[34] ISO 22316:2017(en) – Security and resilience, organizational resilience, principles and attributes (principles providing the foundation for enhancing an organization's resilience).

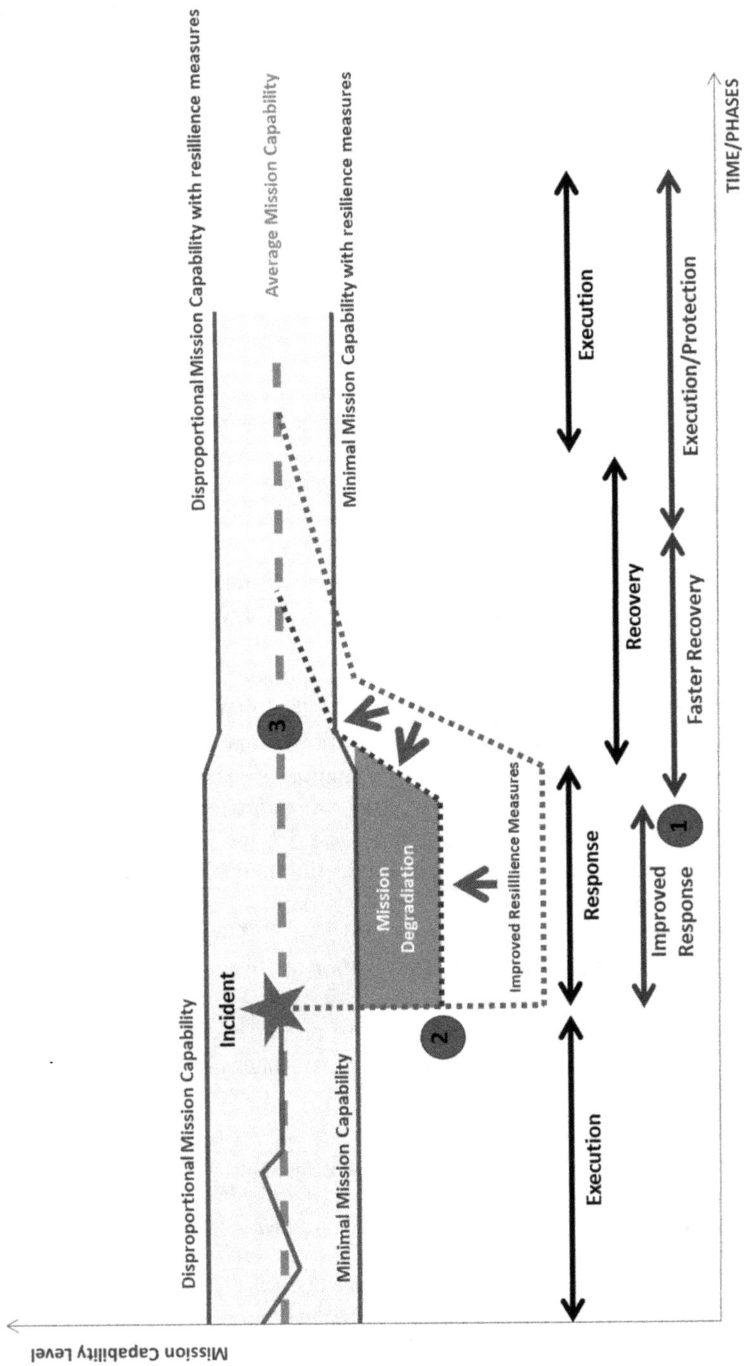

Fig. 29.2 Phases of the resilience process. Source: the authors

Enhancing resilience can be a strategic organizational goal, and is the outcome of good business practice and effectively managing risk."

In addition, the ISO standard lists the attributes conducive to resilience,[35] which can be fostered through targeted activities:

- Shared vision and clarity of purpose
- Comprehensive understanding of the organization's internal and external environments
- Effective and empowered leadership
- Shared beliefs and values
- Shared information and knowledge
- Shared communication system
- Availability of resources
- Transparent and coordinated planning and management process
- Support for continual improvement
- Ability to anticipate and manage change

The strength of a military logistics supply network at the operational command level is its responsiveness to changing conditions. Responsiveness in military logistics is a comprehensive term that encompasses all logistic factors which can have a positive impact on the combat effectiveness[36] and operational readiness[37] of armed forces: in general, being able to react quickly and appropriately to external events.

Individual, cumulative shortfalls in the military logistic supply network generate a logistic gap between the resources required and the resources actually available. Over a period of time, this logistic gap may reach a point (especially if the response capability of the logistic system is permanently inadequate) at which the missions of the tactical units can no longer be accomplished due to a lack of supplies. This condition of the military logistic supply network at this point in time is called the logistic culmination point. The goal of a military logistic supply network and associated planning is to avoid reaching the logistic culmination point.

In summary, it can be said that a resilient military supply chain network:

- must adapt to any change in requirements
- recover quickly and sustainably from a disruption

---

[35] At a relatively high level of abstraction.

[36] "Ist das Leistungsvermögen einer Truppe, das vor allem durch die personelle und materielle Stärke, durch taktische Leistungsparameter und durch Kräftemultiplikatoren bestimmt wird." *Militärlexikon ÖBH* [30 March 2021].

[Is the capacity of a unit, which is primarily determined by personnel and material strength, tactical performance parameters, and force multipliers.]

[37] "Ist die dem personellen und materiellen SOLL-Zustand des Bundesheeres oder dessen Teilen entsprechende Fähigkeit, jeweils zugeordnete Einsatzaufgaben zu erfüllen." *Militärlexikon ÖBH* [30 March 2021]

[Is the capability, corresponding to the personnel and material TARGET condition of the Austrian Armed Forces or elements thereof, to fulfil assigned operational tasks].

- is influenced by properties and activities that must be established well in advance of the creation of the network

It can therefore be concluded: "Resilient systems are able to bend under external pressure rather than break, thrive despite adverse conditions."[38]

29.5 Summary: Logistic Resilience, All Present and Correct?

Logistics in both military and commercial fields continues to be an art and a science. Civilian and military logisticians are hardworking and important contributors to organizational success. Both entities have consistently proven that an organization which understands the operating environment and adapts to change will be successful in mission conduct.

Risk management or resilient planning is necessary for successful military supply chain operations given globalization and greater supply chain interdependencies. To prevent the impact of disruption on future military supply chains, risk management must be incorporated into organizational culture, planning, and operations. This will mitigate vulnerabilities through increased supply chain security, flexibility, and resilience. The goal is a resilient military supply chain that minimizes the impact of disruption.

Despite all the knowledge available and progress made in the microcosm of military logistic resilience,[39] the downright frivolous treatment of resilience at the macrologistic level is astonishing.[40] The dependence of global trade on the challenges of steering large vessels along a waterway 195 meters wide,[41] for example, is an astonishing situation, which has more to do with negligence than resilience.

The press responded with incredulity:

> An artery of world trade is blocked . . . A damaged . . . container ship brings the Suez Canal to a standstill. This also causes disruptions to world trade . . . According to the operator of the Suez Canal, the cargo ship was unable to navigate due to high wind speeds and a sandstorm and ran aground. Since then, it has been lying athwartships, making the passage of the canal

---

[38] Welter-Enderlin (2015), p. 16
[Resiliente Systeme sind in der Lage sich bei äußerem Druck zu verbiegen anstatt dran zu zerbrechen; zu gedeihen trotz widriger Umstände.]

[39] Micrologistics includes the logistics systems of corporations as well as the supply systems of households, military installations, and other institutions (e.g., hospitals) which depend on supplies of material goods. cf. https://www.n-tu.de/logistik-lexikon/mikrologistik/ [02 April 2021].

[40] That is, at the level of international trade.

[41] The Suez Canal is 24 meters deep. In the north, it is 345 meters wide at water line and 215 meters wide at bottom. In the south, the corresponding dimensions are 280 m and 195 m. https://www.google.com/search?client=firefox-b-d&q=suezkanal+breite [03 April 2021].

impossible ... The canal ... carries about 12 % of the world's trade volume transported by ship. The share of global container traffic is even greater, at just under a third.[42]

This incident was a game changer for the commercial supply chain. Game changing scenarios with a massive impact on the entire system are also possible in military supply chains.

"The plume of ash from Iceland's Eyjafjallajokull volcano eruptions in 2010 has been a nightmare for commercial airlines, forcing massive flight cancellations and stranding thousands of travellers. But it also appears to have had a quiet impact on military operations in Iraq and Afghanistan as well."[43]

The military supply chain in Europe had to be adapted. "... aircraft, crews, and maintenance personnel from bases in Germany has to move to more southern staging locations in Spain. Medical evacuation missions into and out of the Middle East and Central Asia have also been re-routed ... Military aircraft may also have been damaged by the cloud of volcanic ash."[44] It took several weeks to adjust the military supply chain and return to normal operations. Some planned military operations in the areas of operation in Central Asia also had to be postponed.

The situation on the Suez Canal and the 2010 volcanic eruption can hardly serve as a textbook example of strategic resilience.

There is, however, hope for improvement in the long term at least to the logistics of global trade: "Two projects are intended to reduce dependence on this bottleneck in the future. In future, the United Arab Emirates want to pump up to 17 percent of the oil that is still transported westwards through the Suez Canal through the expanded pipeline from Eilat on the Red Sea to Ashkelon on the Mediterranean."[45]

In 2010, the military supply chain for the operations in Iraq and especially for the NATO operation in Afghanistan had been evaluated and adapted with alternative supply routes.

---

[42] https://www.nzz.ch/wirtschaft/eine-arterie-des-welthandels-ist-verstopft-welche-auswirkungen-hat-die-blockade-des-suezkanals-ld.1608299?utm_source=pocket-newtab-global-de-DE [25 March 2021]

[Eine Arterie des Welthandels ist verstopft ... Ein havariertes ... Containerschiff bringt die Durchfahrt des Suezkanals zum Erliegen. Dadurch kommt es auch zu Störungen des Welthandels ... Laut dem Betreiber des Suezkanals konnte das Frachtschiff wegen hoher Windgeschwindigkeiten und eines Sandsturms nicht mehr navigieren und ist auf Grund gelaufen. Seitdem liegt es quer und macht die Durchfahrt des Kanals unmöglich ... Über den Kanal ... wird rund 12 % des über den Schiffsweg transportierten Welthandelsvolumens abgewickelt. Der Anteil am weltweiten Containerverkehr ist mit knapp einem Drittel noch größer.]

[43] https://www.wired.com/2010/04/volcanic-cloud-disrupts-military-operations [11 July 2021].

[44] https://www.wired.com/2010/04/volcanic-cloud-disrupts-military-operations [11 July 2021].

[45] https://www.faz.net/aktuell/politik/ausland/suezkanal-israel-und-emirate-planen-projekte-fuer-neue-route-17265576.html?utm_source=pocket-newtab-global-de-DE [02 March 2021].

[Zwei Projekte sollen die Abhängigkeit von diesem Nadelöhr künftig verringern. So wollen die Vereinigten Arabischen Emirate künftig bis zu 17 Prozent des Erdöls, das heute noch durch den Suezkanal nach Westen transportiert wird, durch die ausgebaute Pipeline von Eilat am Roten Meer nach Aschkelon am Mittelmeer pumpen.]

Given that there is no such thing as a permanent fix, as the environment for military operations is in a constant state of flux, it is not enough simply to monitor daily supply chain performance, but small-scale, deliberate changes must be continuously integrated so as to reduce the long-term risk of a loss of operational capability and supply chain disruption. Such an approach increases the probability of greater effectiveness.

Resilience in logistics rules, OK?

References

Bundesheer, Ö. (Ed.). (2017) *Militärisches Konzept 2017* (p. 1). Vienna.

Dröge, S. (2019). Die Folgen des Klimawandels als sicherheitspolitische Herausforderung. *Zeitschrift für Außen- und Sicherheitspolitik, 12*, 405–416.

Frank, J. (2021). Risikobild Österreich 2021. In Bundesministerium für Landesverteidigung (Ed.), *Sicherheitspolitische Jahresvorschau 2021* (p. 35). Vienna.

Fröhlich-Gildhoff, K., & Rönnau-Böse, M. (2019). *Resilienz* (5th ed., p. 14). Munich.

Gürtlich, G., & Lampl, S. (2017). Logistik in Streitkräften und Einsatzorganisationen. In G. Gürtlich & S. Lampl (Eds.), *Grundfragen der Militärlogistik und der Logistik von Einsatzorganisationen* (2nd ed., pp. 549–551).

Petersen, T. (2020). Fünf Thesen zu den zukünftigen Herausforderungen für die Wirtschaftspolitik. *List Forum für Wirtschafts- und Finanzpolitik, 46*, 259–268.

Rummel, M. (2019). *Elektromobilität. Resilienz in der deutschen Automobilindustrie* (p. 2). Munich.

Saurugg, H. (2021). Herausforderung Blackout. In *Bundesministerium für Landesverteidigung* (Ed.), *Sicherheitspolitische Jahresvorschau 2021* (p. 316). Vienna.

Sheikh, H., Mark, B., & Dagher, S. (2016). *Making logistics a combat multiplier for GCC armed forces* (p. 6ff). Dubai.

Summers, M. (2018). Resilience in defence supply chains. In J. C. D. Smith (Ed.), *Defence Logistics – Enabling and sustaining successful military operations* (p. 99 ff). Kogan Page.

Welter-Enderlin, R. (2015). *Resilienz und Krisenkompetenz* (2nd ed., p. 16). Heidelberg.

Gerhard Gürtlich lecturer at the Institute for Transport and Logistics Management at WU (Vienna University of Economics and Business) and a visiting lecturer at the National Defence Academy, Vienna.

Stefan Lampl is the Commander of the Austrian Forces Logistics School in Vienna. He attended the general staff course of the Austrian Armed Forces at the National Defence Academy. During his career, he served in various command and staff assignments as military logistician in Austria and in missions abroad like Iraq, Kosovo, and Turkey. He is an author of various publications in military and civil journals with special focus on military logistics.

Chapter 30
Concluding Remarks

Tina Wakolbinger, Sebastian Kummer, Alexander M. Geske, and Lydia Novoszel

Abstract Supply chains have to deal with challenging environments caused by rare events with high impacts, climate change, limitations of natural resources, skilled labor shortage, geopolitical conflicts, and changing customer behavior and preferences. This book elaborates the topic of supply chain resilience and provides main insights from a theoretical and practical perspective. Supply chain-wide priorities, sustainability and resilience, alongside with the development of relevant technologies and processes to cope with an inherently volatile business environment are addressed.

While 2020 and 2021 have certainly been exceptional years with respect to supply chain disruptions, the future is expected to be no less challenging. Some of the reasons are the following:

Climate change and its associated effects will provide challenges for stakeholders along the supply chains. This includes natural disasters that will increase in frequency and magnitude. Novel legislation to reduce the environmental and social impact of company activities brings additional uncertainties for companies.

Natural resources are limited and not evenly distributed across the world. Competition for these resources is likely to intensify in the future. Striving for circular supply chains reduces the dependencies on natural resources but introduces new uncertainties with respect to timing and quality of product returns.

Shortages of skilled labor in many sectors, like transport and logistics, create strong bottlenecks to global supply chains. Competition for this skilled labor force will take place between companies, industries, and countries.

Geopolitical conflicts might worsen and bring back barriers to international trade. The COVID-19 crisis has shown that in times of crisis even within the EU, free trade

T. Wakolbinger (✉) · S. Kummer · A. M. Geske · L. Novoszel
Institute for Transport and Logistics Management, WU (Vienna University of Economics and Business), Vienna, Austria
e-mail: tina.wakolbinger@wu.ac.at; sebastian.kummer@wu.ac.at; alexander.maximilian.geske@wu.ac.at; lydia.novoszel@wu.ac.at

S. Kummer et al. (eds.), *Supply Chain Resilience*, Springer Series in Supply Chain Management 17, https://doi.org/10.1007/978-3-030-95401-7_30

was not guaranteed. Increasing competition for natural and human resources between countries could potentially worsen the situation.

Digitalization will provide multiple options to better manage supply chain disruptions. However, it creates its own vulnerabilities. Cyberattacks and blackouts are just two possible scenarios that will be especially detrimental to companies that are strongly reliant on technologies.

Quickly changing consumer behavior and increasing demands with respect to product availability and delivery times make demand forecasting more important but also more challenging. Current demographic developments lead to new population structures with novel demands.

All these challenges—if successfully addressed—provide the potential for innovative new business solutions and competitive advantage. In the future, it will be even more important for companies not only to focus on short-term gains but on developing business models that are sustainable in the long run. This includes the capability to deal with uncertain events. Hence, business resilience will be one of the decisive capabilities of companies that determine their survival.

In this book, we provide an overview of the topic of business resilience from a theoretical and practical view. From our perspective, the five main insights are the following:

The future is uncertain and things will happen that no one could foresee. Hence, rather than developing detailed plans how to react to specific disaster scenarios, strengthening companies' capabilities to respond to uncertain events is preferable. This is not an effort for a single function within a company but a comprehensive approach that covers all functions within a company as well as its partners along the supply chain.

Technology can support the development of resilient supply chains in the areas of sensing and responding to possible disruptions. Technology can facilitate information exchange within and between companies as well as improved decision-making that allows all stakeholders to react faster to disruptions. However, technology alone is not the solution and needs to be supported by skilled workers and appropriate processes.

Driven by consumer, investor, and employee demands as well as legislation, sustainability will play an ever-increasing role in the future. Leveraging sustainability initiatives to also create more resilient supply chains will be an urgent demand of the future.

Resilience has been a core competence in areas such as humanitarian logistics and the military. Hence, when looking at best practices, companies should go beyond their peers and look at other sectors that successfully mastered supply chain disruptions in the past.

Supply chain resilience is less and less a topic solely of individual companies and more an issue of national concern. Hence, countries will increasingly focus on identifying critical industries and infrastructure and how they can support their long-term survival and success. In this quest for national success, global collaboration should not be left out of sight.

Tina Wakolbinger Ph.D., is Professor of Supply Chain Services and Networks. She serves as Head of the Research Institute for Supply Chain Management and Deputy Head of the Institute for Transport and Logistics Management at WU (Vienna University of Economics and Business). Her research interests lie in the modeling and analysis of complex decision-making on network systems with a focus on global issues. She serves in editorial positions in Production and Operations Management and Central European Journal of Operations Research. Her work on supply chain management and humanitarian logistics is published in renown journals.

Sebastian Kummer is Head of the Institute for Transport and Logistics Management at WU (Vienna University of Economics and Business) as well as an Endowed Chair Professor at the Jilin University in Changchun, China. Previously he was Professor at the TU Dresden and worked at the WHU, Vallendar, where he received his Ph.D. Prof. Kummer is responsible for program development and teaching in the fields of transportation, logistics, and supply chain management. He carries out numerous successful research and practice projects for industrial and commercial companies and for transport and logistics service providers. He supports numerous transport and logistic tenders. His publication list includes more than 180 publications, including leading textbooks.

Alexander M. Geske is Research Associate at the Institute for Transport and Logistics Management at WU (Vienna University of Economics and Business). He has earned a bachelor's degree in International Business Administration and a master's degree in Supply Chain Management. With a professional career in the transportation industry, Alexander combines the practical and academic perspective.

Lydia Novoszel is Research Associate at the Institute for Transport and Logistics Management at WU (Vienna University of Economics and Business). With an international professional career in supply chain management, she incorporates practical relevance and perspectives in supply chain disruption research. Lydia has earned a master's degree in Mechanical Engineering and a master's degree in Business Administration.

www.ingramcontent.com/pod-product-compliance
Lightning Source LLC
Chambersburg PA
CBHW070122140425
25077CB00003B/28

* 9 7 8 3 0 3 0 9 5 4 0 0 0 *